CLASSICAL
COMPOSERS

Concert champêtre Raoul D

CLASSICAL COMPOSERS

Consultant and Principal Author
PETER GAMMOND

CRESCENT BOOKS
NEW YORK • AVENEL, NEW JERSEY

Credits

Editor
Philip de Ste. Croix

Original design concept
Roger Hyde

Designers
Jill Coote
Nigel Duffield

Production
Ruth Arthur
Sally Connolly
Neil Randles
Karen Staff
Jonathan Tickner

Director of production
Gerald Hughes

Typesetting
SX Composing Ltd, Essex

Color reproduction
HBM Print PTE Ltd,
Singapore

Printed and bound in
Hong Kong

CLB 4010

© 1994 CLB Publishing,
Godalming,
Surrey GU7 1XW,
United Kingdom

This 1994 edition published by
Crescent Books, distributed by
Random House Value
Publishing, Inc.,
40 Engelhard Avenue,
Avenel, New Jersey 07001.

Random House
New York · Toronto · London
· Sydney · Auckland

ISBN 0-517-10234-X

All rights reserved

8 7 6 5 4 3 2 1

A CIP catalog record for this
book is available from the
Library of Congress.

RIGHT: 'An Evening with
Liszt' painted by Josef
Danhauser (1804-45)
around 1840. The
admiring audience
surrounding Liszt at the
piano comprise (left to
right) Alexandre Dumas
(or possibly Alfred de
Musset), Victor Hugo,
George Sand, Niccolò
Paganini, Gioachino
Rossini and, at Liszt's feet,
his lover Marie d'Agoult.

Contributors

Consultant and Principal Author:
PETER GAMMOND

Peter Gammond is the author of over forty books on all types of music including, in the classical field, Music on Record (4 Vols); The Magic
Flute; Schubert; The Illustrated Encyclopaedia of Opera; Offenbach: His Life and Times; and was editor of The Encyclopaedia of
Classical Music. In a lighter vein he has written Bluffer's Guides to
Music, Opera, Jazz, British Class and Golf. In the field of popular
music he has written Duke Ellington; Scott Joplin and the Ragtime
Era; five volumes on the subject of Music Hall; Jazz on Record; and
edited The Decca Book of Jazz. His most considerable achievement is his
authorship of The Oxford Companion to Popular Music which went
into paperback in 1993.

PETER JONES

An entertaining and popular lecturer on musical subjects, teacher of
English and Latin, pianist and entertainer, he has been Chairman of the
long-established Sunbury Music Club for over twenty years. His wide-
ranging musical knowledge made him winner of the BBC Radio 4 music
quiz 'Counterpoint' in 1991.

PETER LYMBERY

Since becoming involved in the Torbay Musical Weekend and vice-
chairman of The Friends of Torbay, he has become increasingly in
demand as a knowledgeable and controversial speaker to music and
gramophone societies all over the United Kingdom. He is currently working on a comprehensive musical reference project.

ROBERT HARDCASTLE

Robert Hardcastle founded Discourses Ltd, a company whose recordings
have included educational and classical language issues, and an 'All
About Music' series which first recorded Julian Lloyd Webber. After an
earlier career on radio, he is now an author and editor of books on his two
main interests, music and military history – his published titles include the
recent Heroes for Victoria. He was a contributor to The Encyclopaedia of Classical Music, and is a popular Chairman of the Friends of Torbay, and an amusing talker on music and the spoken word.

CHRISTOPHER HEADINGTON

Christopher Headington is a composer and pianist, as well as a writer on
music, a teacher and broadcaster. His compositions include concertos for
violin and piano (the ASV recording of his Violin Concerto was widely
praised), song-cycles, string quartets, piano sonatas and other instrumental music. He has recorded as a pianist and regularly reviews for The
Gramophone. He has written eight books, including The Bodley Head
History of Western Music; Opera: a History, and a biography of the
singer Peter Pears which went into paperback in 1993.

PETER HERRING

A freelance musical journalist, with a second-string interest in railways,
Peter Herring is also a successful photographer, who worked in collaboration with David Redfern. He was Editor of Hi-Fi Sound for ten years
and Contributing Editor to Which Compact Disc? He was the author of
the book, Classical Music on Compact Disc and has written for many
record and hi-fi journals, in both serious and lighter vein. He contributed
sections on the Orchestra to The Encyclopaedia of Classical Music.

Contents

NOTE: **Bold** type indicates major entries

There are probably more people interested today in the world of classical music than ever before. It may begin only as a marginal interest or it may develop into a growing obsession that could lead to a really deep and rewarding experience of music; but at all stages, such an interest needs supporting and nurturing with easily available and approachably presented information, such as this book sets out to provide. A measure of the popularity of classic music is provided by the proliferation of recorded music from the days of the 78 vinyl record to the neatly presented CD, and has been given a broad-minded boost by the highly successful emergence of radio stations – such as Classic FM in the United Kingdom – devoted, in a like-minded way, to presenting music in approachable snippets accompanied by friendly information.

The book has an additional element to offer. It provides a pictorial setting for the music, including portraits of composers at key moments in their lives, their backgrounds and, above all, examples of the art that flourished at the time that they were composing and which often proved to be a valuable source of inspiration. Even if your interest in music is as marginal as it could be, this book, we believe, may still give you a lot of visual pleasure.

Creators of books that involve the compilation of information are liable to get letters mainly on the lines of 'How could you possibly have left out X?' or 'How did Y get in, when Z has been omitted?'. These avid letter-writers will certainly spot that we have given most space to a chosen twelve composers, most of whom will not have their worthiness debated – the likes of Bach, Beethoven, Mozart and Wagner. Others may be challenged, as will the choice of those who deserve a two-page spread or a briefer entry in the collective pages. It is those that were left out altogether that will cause most ink to flow; and for these omissions the only excuse is the one of space available and the necessity of having to make what is often a reluctant choice. We hope that what is included will prove a satisfying repast and may even offer an introduction to someone whose music the reader has not encountered before.

This is a very large book, a genuine coffee-table book. You have only to buy four attachable legs and you will have a coffee-table of quite practical dimensions! It was planned this way to ensure that it is not consigned to some dusty shelf but will hopefully remain on view somewhere near the radio, ready to be referred to when interest has been aroused by the brief information imparted in the hustle-bustle of a daily radio programme. We hope that you, the reader, will stay and browse, and then listen some more.

I am much indebted to a very knowledgeable team of writers, all of whom share my view that musicology should be lively and amusing and not too technical; and all of whom have willingly worked to the editor's specific requirements. I am equally indebted to a very demanding but indulgent editor who has a knowledge and love of music beyond the normal bounds of his calling.

We finally agreed that, because the book may prove a source of inspiration and encourage you to sample new music, a brief discography should be added. This has been done with an eye to including items that might be expected to have a reasonably long shelf-life; though there has never been any accounting for the whims of recording companies. Let us remain thankful for the rich offerings around and hope that our continued support may eventually reduce the prices.

Here's to continued enjoyment of the rich and wonderful world of music and to a growing appreciation of those who compose it and those who perform it; perhaps even of those who write about it.

Peter Gammond, Shepperton 1994

ISAAC **ALBÉNIZ**

(b. Camprodón, Lérida, 29 May 1860; d. Cambô-les-Bains, 18 May 1909)

This Spanish pianist-composer first appeared on the concert platform at the age of four, so astounding a Barcelona audience that trickery was suspected. Five years later he entered the Madrid Conservatory, but after some months he ran away and at the age of ten was already giving recitals. In 1872 he stowed away on a ship bound for South America and for five years led a precarious travelling existence that led him to places as different as Liverpool and Leipzig. Returning to Spain in 1877, he soon gained a scholarship to study at the Brussels Conservatory, and managed to fit in a further trip to America before winning a first prize in 1879. He then travelled to other European cities, including Vienna and Budapest, and became a pupil of Liszt in order to perfect his already remarkable technique. In 1883 he married, moving with his family to Madrid two years later and continuing his performing career, but around 1890 he ceased to perform publicly so as to be able to compose. He took lessons in Paris from Dukas and d'Indy, and knew and was influenced by Debussy. From 1890-3, Albéniz lived in London, where a wealthy banker and amateur man of letters commissioned him to set his librettos to music as operas, but of three resulting works only the lyric comedy Pepita Jiménez (1896) had success. The composer's talent lay rather in writing for his own instrument: his piano music (such as the Cantos de España, often heard on guitar, and Suite Española) is highly elaborate, rich in Spanish atmosphere and dauntingly difficult to play. Of his many piano works, it is the suite of twelve pieces called Iberia, begun in 1906 and occupying him for the rest of his life, which is recognized as a masterpiece.   C.H.

TOMASO GIOVANNI **ALBINONI**
(b. Venice, 8 June 1671; d. Venice, 17 January 1751)

*F*or many years Albinoni was merely regarded as a minor violinist-composer, who had written some 50 forgotten operas, a few of whose themes Bach chose to use as variation subjects. Latterly, while the operas still remain unregarded, his orchestral writings have become more highly rated. He was born in Venice of rich parents and, although he was academically trained, he chose to describe himself as a 'dilettante Venete', and was fortunate in having no need to earn a living as a composer. His style lay somewhere between Corelli and Vivaldi, light in nature, with many of his operas in the opera buffa category. The easy charm of his orchestral music can be enjoyed by anyone with the modern taste for the elegance of baroque. The various groups of Concerti a cinque, the Op. 5 set for strings, the Op. 7 for oboe and strings, the Op. 12 for violin and strings (12 in each set) are now frequently played and recorded. Curiously the work by which he is best known, the Adagio in G minor for organ and strings, is not exactly typical of him or his period, having been somewhat romantically arranged by its rediscoverer, Remo Giazotto (b. 1910). It is none the less pleasing, even moving in its calm serenity, and deserves its popular rating.   P.G.

THOMAS AUGUSTINE **ARNE**
(b. London, 28 May 1710; d. London, 5 March 1778)

*A*rne is usually described as the most distinguished English composer between Purcell and Elgar, but this somewhat limited compliment is further qualified by the competition he received during his lifetime from Handel and then from J.C. Bach (and, among Englishmen, from Boyce). Born to an upholsterer in Covent Garden, Arne was largely self-taught, but quickly became involved in attempts to develop an English opera tradition. Competition from Handel's Italian operas meant that he was more successful with the obsolescent masque form, as in Comus (1738) and Alfred (1740) (which contains 'Rule, Britannia'). One of his operas, Artaxerxes (1762), just survives, with ballad operas such as Thomas and Sally (1760) and Love in a Village (1762), but he is best known today for the charming songs he wrote for productions of Shakespeare at Drury Lane, where he was in charge of music from 1740 to 1775. In similar tuneful vein were many songs which he wrote for Vauxhall Gardens until he became less fashionable in the 1760s. Arne appears to have been a somewhat feckless man, always short of money (as was his son Michael Arne [1740 – 1786], composer of 'The lass with the delicate air'). His uncomplicated music is characteristic of the undemanding tastes of the English musical public of the time. P.L.

MALCOLM **ARNOLD**
(b. Northampton, 21 October 1921)

*O*nce a trumpet-player with the LPO, Malcolm Arnold is very much an individualist in the British music scene, a composer of abundant melodic inspiration, working in traditional forms with a spicing of the jazz age, and naturally writing interestingly and well for the wind sections. Most of his music is of the highest grade and he has hit the jackpot often enough to have secured his place in musical history. His two sets of four English Dances (later successfully used for the ballet Solitaire, 1956) are regular favourites, exhibiting his orchestral skill as well as his tunefulness, closely rivalled by such lively pieces as Beckus the Dandiprat and Tam o'Shanter. His symphonies are rich in humour and melody, if sometimes bombastic. Best of all is probably his finely wrought Guitar Concerto which compares well with the famous works of Rodrigo in this genre. The popular touch has also given Arnold a high standing in the specialist world of film music where he has provided many outstanding and effectively memorable background scores, the best-remembered probably those for Hobson's Choice (1954), The Bridge on the River Kwai (1957) and The Inn of the Sixth Happiness (1958).   P.G.

ABOVE: Isaac Albéniz photographed in 1900. One of Spain's most important and influential composers, he is probably best known for his piano music, most particularly the Iberia suite.

ABOVE: A portrait of the flautist Ferdinand Joseph Lamberger painted in Vienna in 1710 by Johann Kupetsky. The painting recalls the easy charm of much of Albinoni's orchestral music of this period.

JOHANN SEBASTIAN

Bach (b. Eisenach, 21 March 1685; d. Leipzig, 28 July 1750)

The Bach family history shows a line of musical talent stretching back for some 400 years and musical Bachs were abundant in Upper and Lower Saxony when Johann Sebastian was born, the youngest son of Johann Ambrosius Bach (1645-95), official town musician of Eisenach. It was naturally assumed that he would be a musician and he was taught the violin by his father. His mother died when he was nine and his father a year later and thereafter he was taken care of by his elder brother Johann Christoph (1671-1721) who was organist in a nearby town and had been a pupil of Johann Pachelbel (1653-1706). Outstripping his local music teachers, the young Sebastian was sent, in 1700, to a choir school run by Benedictine monks, where he won a scholarship. Although his voice broke soon after, he was kept on for his skill as an organist. By the age of 18 he had written many keyboard works and church chorales and his reputation was already spreading, so that he was summoned to Weimar to become court musician, playing violin in the court band. He was also appointed organist in Arnstadt and, for two happy years, was able to try out his choral works with a small choir at his disposal. He then asked for a month's leave so that he could visit the famous organist and composer Dietrich Buxtehude (1637-1707) who made him welcome and would have liked Bach to succeed him as organist at the Marienkirche in Lübeck.

RIGHT: *The best likeness of Johann Sebastian Bach was probably this one painted in 1746 by Elias Gottlob Haussmann (1695-1774). Bach was then living the turbulent years he spent as Kantor at St. Thomas's in Leipzig, and enjoying a growing national reputation.*

BELOW: *St. Thomas's Church and School in Leipzig where Bach was Kantor from 1723 to 1750. This colour engraving by Johann Gottfried Krügner (1684-1769) was made in 1723.*

Having overstayed his month's leave, Bach fell out with his Arnstadt employers and by 1708 he had found a post in Weimar. Having married his cousin, Maria Barbara Bach, in 1707 and come into a small legacy, he now settled in Weimar for the next nine years, becoming Konzertmeister to the Duke in 1714. Here he wrote many of his fine cantatas and became famous as an organist. In 1716 the post of Kapellmeister became vacant, but it was not offered to Bach and he decided to take a similar post in Anhalt-Cöthen. The Duke of Weimar proved difficult at this stage and had him imprisoned for a month, but eventually he was released. In Cöthen there was no organ and his main duties were as conductor of the court orchestra. It was for them that he wrote the Brandenburg Concertos, dedicated in 1721 to Duke Christian Ludwig of Brandenburg, in addition to his French and English Suites for the clavier and a large number of oratorios, passions, masses and cantatas. The only unhappy event of the years at Cöthen was the death of his wife, the mother of his first four children. But within a year he was married again to Anna Magdalena Wilcke, the daughter of a court musician, and for her he wrote some light pieces and songs of great charm which were preserved in personal notebooks and later revealed to the world. Bach now wished to move on, and, desiring better educational opportunities for his children, he applied for a vacant post as Kantor at St. Thomas's in Leipzig.

1. Die St. Thomas Kirche, 2. Die Thomas Schule. 3. Der Steinerne Wasser-Kasten.

The authorities there had wanted Telemann to take the post but he turned it down and the committee reluctantly took on Bach, feeling that he was very much a second-best choice.

The Church and the Music School at Leipzig were to be the centre of Bach's life from 1723 to 1750, although he kept his Kapellmeister appointment at Cöthen until the Duke died in 1728. It was never easy in Leipzig as he had to deal with three different and awkward authorities – the university, the church and the town council – and had to take on much non-musical teaching which he did not enjoy. In his first seven years there he wrote some 200 cantatas, only to have one set of officials complain that he was neglecting his teaching. He was not allowed to employ professional singers for the first performance of his St. Matthew Passion. The old rector had been a close friend but when he died, a young man was appointed and there were many clashes of temperament. Bach bore all these tribulations while he enjoyed his growing reputation in the country at large. His son, Carl Philipp Emanuel Bach, was employed by Frederick the Great and when Bach visited him at Court, he was received with great honour and praise. Still his fame was mainly as an organist and his music not greatly known outside Leipzig. Although he now wrote such masterpieces as the Goldberg Variations, the Musical Offering and the Art of Fugue, he only had a mere handful of his works actually published during his lifetime. In his last years his sight grew increasingly poor and, after an operation in 1749, he became totally blind. In 1750 his sight briefly returned, but soon after he suffered a stroke and died ten days later. Like Mozart, he was buried in an unmarked grave. His remains were rediscovered in 1894.

ABOVE: Bach's father, Johann Ambrosius Bach (1645-95), was the official town musician of Eisenach. He gave his son his early musical education and taught him the violin.

LEFT: The market place in Dresden, painted in 1751 by Bernardo Bellotto (better known as Canaletto the Younger) (1720-80). In the 1730's Bach sought closer ties with the royal court based in Dresden.

Below: *Part of the original manuscript score of the* St. Matthew Passion, *BWV244 (1727-9), showing the chorale 'Wenn ich einmal soll scheiden'. It was first performed in 1729 in the Thomaskirche in Leipzig.*

Above: *Johannes Remy and his family in Bendorf, near Koblenz, in 1766, painted by Januarius Zick (1730-97). Music-making was an integral part of life in cultured society at this time, as also was taking coffee, evidently.*

Although Bach wrote music without pause all his life, he did it with no wish for fame, his one desire being to serve the Church. Thus, at the heart of his creative output lie the 295 cantatas, now revered by the world and containing much of his very best music, but then simply written as a weekly chore to provide music for church services. Two hundred and sixty-five of these were written for St. Thomas's in Leipzig. Embedded in these shapely works, which might be described as sacred concerts, whose usage in church is now rare, are some of his now most popular melodies such as 'Sheep may safely graze', 'Jesu, joy of man's desiring' and the soaring chorale from Cantata 140 'Wachet auf' – 'Sleepers awake!'. Better known, however, for their size and grandeur, are the full-scale works that include the mighty *St. Matthew Passion*, which stands beside Handel's *Messiah* as an essential musical experience for devotees of church music, and which is subject to endless interpretations, distinguished and otherwise. Less reflective and more baldly, yet not less evocatively, stated is the *St. John Passion*; and less perfect but equally majestic is the great *Mass in B minor*, much of which he adapted from other works. The *Christmas Oratorio* (not really an oratorio but a set of six cantatas not intended to be performed at one sitting), the lesser-known *Easter Oratorio* and the joyful *Magnificat* all add to an impressive output of constantly inspired choral writing unequalled elsewhere.

LEFT: Altar-piece by Jan van Eyck (1390-1441) and Hubert van Eyck (?1370-1426), portraying (top) Mary, God the Father and John the Baptist, and (below) the Adoration of the Easter Lamb. Bach's sacred music shares the spirit of Christian devotion expressed by this painting.

1722 Writes Clavierbüchlein for Anna Magdalena. Applies for post as Kantor at St. Thomas's in Leipzig

1723 After a trial performance of his St. John Passion is elected Kantor of St. Thomas's, but is also able to retain Cöthen post until the death of the Duke. Magnificat performed in December

1725 Writes Notenbuch for Anna Magdalena. Large output of cantatas continues

1727 Begins to write St. Matthew Passion; some of it is performed at the funeral of Prince Leopold, with a full performance in 1729

1729 One of many quarrels with the council of St. Thomas's

1730 Achieves some improvements at St. Thomas's with the appointment of new rector

1731 Visits Dresden. Clavierübung Part 1 published

1732 Birth of son Johann Christoph Friedrich

1734 First performance of Christmas Oratorio

1735 Birth of son Johann Christian. For the next few years continues his troubled employment and writes prolifically

1740 His son C.P.E. Bach enters the service of Frederick the Great. Eyesight begins to fail

1747 Visits the court of Frederick to see his son. Is warmly welcomed at court and afterwards composes the Musikalisches Opfer (Musical Offering) for the king

1750 After an eye operation he loses his sight. It returns briefly but he then suffers a stroke. Dies 28 July

Nevertheless the world probably thinks of Bach firstly as the composer of the immortal *Brandenburg Concertos*, the Suites, the splendid concertos for violin, harpsichord and various combinations of instruments. It was these, particularly in their strangely emotive slow movements that often seem to anticipate a future world of romanticism, that had such an influence on later composers like Haydn and Mozart, who used them as models for their own compositions. The musical world has never ceased to be inspired by Bach and his reputation ever increases. And beside all this, we must recognise his organ works which are a perpetual delight and challenge to succeeding generations of organists, music where his exalted spirit and technical genius arose from years of experience as a practical musician. This repertoire outshines anything that any other composer for the instrument has achieved. Beyond this are the wide stretches of his writing for the clavier, equally effective when performed on harpsichord or piano, in spite of much controversy as to the correct choice. The *Art of Fugue* and the *Goldberg Variations* are prominent among them. Nor will finer writing for the violin be found than in the six Violin Sonatas; or for the cello than in the amazingly full-sounding suites for the solo instrument. There is still no more revered name in the whole of music than that of Johann Sebastian Bach.   P.G.

ABOVE: 'Lola of Valence', a painting by Edouard Manet (1832-83) which reflects something of the spirit of Arriaga's charming music.

ABOVE: Johann Christian Bach, a painting of the composer by Thomas Gainsborough (1727-88) completed in 1776.

JUAN CRISÓSTOMO **ARRIAGA**

(b. Bilbao, 27 January 1806; d. Paris, 17 January 1826)

*I*n spite of his tragically short life – he died just 10 days before his 20th birthday – Arriaga's musical achievement, though small in quantity, is now appreciated as being of a remarkably high quality. At the age of 11 he wrote an Octet for horn, strings, guitar and piano; and at 13 an opera, Los esclavos felices (1820), whose sturdy overture is still worthy of regular performance. It was on the strength of these that he was admitted to the Paris Conservatoire where he also showed promise as a violinist. While in Paris he wrote his attractive and well-shaped Symphony in D, somewhat in the vein of Hummel, which has been rediscovered by many conductors and well deserves a place in the standard orchestral repertoire. His three String Quartets are also substantial and likeable works which have been regularly performed since the full rediscovery of his potential genius in 1933, when his opera, symphony and octet were published. He also wrote two sacred works, part of another opera, and a number of piano pieces and songs. While his short life and consequent modest output have not left his name firmly imprinted in musical history, the discovery of his works, now quite generously recorded, could be an unexpected pleasure for anyone who has not yet had a chance to assess the worth of Arriaga.   P.G.

CARL PHILIPP EMANUEL **BACH**

(b. Weimar, 8 March 1714; d. Hamburg, 14 December 1788)

*T*he second son of the great Johann Sebastian Bach enjoyed a high reputation during his lifetime, a reputation which faded, however, as the greater talents of Haydn and Mozart came upon the scene. He was a very logical and forthright composer and is now recognized once more as a minor master of the period, even though greatly overshadowed by his father whose influence shows in his work, as does that of Handel and Scarlatti. His music has a gently emotional content, still restrained by the classical conventions, and can be seen as a step towards the growing romanticism of the great Viennese tradition. Among his orchestral works are a fine group of symphonies and, even more rewarding, a number of concertos, the Double Concerto for Harpsichord and Fortepiano in E flat being particularly interesting. It shows a composer moving well ahead of his time. Bach was educated, under his father, at St. Thomas's, and then went on to study law at Frankfurt University. Showing special talent as a musician, he became harpsichordist at the Court of Frederick the Great in Berlin, where he was to remain for 28 years, mainly called upon to accompany his flute-playing employer. He wrote a long-lasting book on keyboard playing. In 1768 he moved to Hamburg as successor to Telemann as Kantor, where he continued to lead a quietly affluent existence with his many friends in the musical world.   P.G.

JOHANN CHRISTIAN **BACH**

(b. Leipzig, 5 September 1735; d. London, 1 January 1782)

*T*he youngest of J. S. Bach's numerous sons turned out to be the most famous in his own right. He first studied with his elder stepbrother C. P. E. Bach, then went to Italy to study, to become a Roman Catholic, and organist at Milan Cathedral, all things that might not have been approved of by his strictly Protestant and Germanic father, had he still been alive. Johann Christian was especially interested in opera in the early part of his composing career and this led him to London where he became composer to the King's Theatre, Haymarket. He was a very popular and well-rewarded figure in England and has since become known as the 'London' Bach. He was music teacher to Queen Charlotte and moved in high social circles, later relinquishing his operatic traditions to write numerous fine symphonies, concertos and chamber works. When Mozart came to London as a child prodigy in 1764, Bach took him under his wing and guided his first steps as a composer, influencing his early works to a noticeable degree. His own music was pleasantly melodious and he is credited with being the first to introduce the clarinet into the modern opera orchestra. Moving into concert promotion he ran into debt, had a nervous breakdown in 1781, and died owing £4,000. His funeral was paid for by the Queen.   P.G.

MILY **BALAKIREV**

(b. Gorky, 2 January 1837; d. St. Petersburg, 29 May 1910)

*I*t is Balakirev's fate to be best remembered as the driving force behind Russian music in the late 19th century rather than as a composer. This should not obscure his own music, even though by his concern for other composers he limited his own output. Balakirev was associated from an early age with Russian musical scholars and composers, most notably Glinka, who inspired in him a mission to promote a distinctively Russian musical style. By 1860 he was fortunate enough to know Borodin, Rimsky-Korsakov, Mussorgsky and Cesar Cui (1835-1918), with whom he formed the famous 'mighty handful' and whose mentor he became. A complicated and difficult man, Balakirev seems to have been as much dictator as inspirer, but there is no doubt that his work as critic and taskmaster was invaluable, especially for such composers as Borodin and Mussorgsky. Later he performed much the same role for Tchaikovsky (though with more equivocal results) and others. The music he did have the time to write was distinguished, combining the authentically Russian qualities of Glinka and Borodin with a more Western European structure, as in his tone poem Tamara and the two symphonies he finally completed after his 'retirement' in 1895. He was a brilliant pianist: his best known piece is the formidable Islamey of 1869 , while his Piano Sonata in B flat is now becoming better known.   P.L.

SAMUEL **BARBER**

(b. West Chester, PA, 9 March 1910; d. New York, 23 January 1981)

*F*ew composers can have begun with more advantages than Barber. Born to a prosperous and musical family (his aunt was the famous contralto Louise Homer) and precociously gifted as pianist, cellist and singer, he entered the Curtis Institute in Philadelphia at the age of 14. His graduation piece was the brilliant overture The School for Scandal, soon followed by the sharply contrasted, reflective Dover Beach for baritone and string quartet, which he sang himself. This promise was fulfilled in the First Symphony (taken up by Bruno Walter) and the famous Adagio for Strings (from his String Quartet). All this early music is in the European romantic tradition, with little American character. Its undoubted melodic resource and feeling cannot disguise some lack of individuality. The Symphony won him the Prix de Rome, but his stay in that city did not widen his horizons beyond a few atonal experiments in his piano music. Perhaps his best work came in the 1940s with the Violin Concerto, Essays for Orchestra and the lovely soprano scena Knoxville: Summer of 1915, where a real American atmosphere does appear. His operas, Vanessa (1958) and Antony and Cleopatra (1966), were not well regarded, and the latter failure discouraged him from much more composing. His many successful songs and choral works, such as the Prayers of Kierkegaard, show his sensitivity to words. His later music generally lacks the youthful inspiration which concealed the lack of a distinctive style in his earlier works.   P.L.

ARNOLD **BAX**

(b. Streatham, 8 November 1883; d. Cork, 3 October 1953)

*D*espite his family's Quaker background, Bax can be described as a romantic in every sense, and he remained one throughout his life. In his youth he was converted by Yeats's poems to an identification with Ireland which led him to learn Gaelic, and even to write it under a pseudonym. He was also much affected by the Russian ballet and impetuous visits to Russia itself. His later life was punctuated by passionate affairs and long stays on the Atlantic coasts of Ireland and Scotland. His music was exactly what might be expected from this background: emotional, colourful, self-indulgent, with German romanticism overlaid by Russian colour and spiced with Irish melodic character and atmosphere. Bax's first successes were his tone poems from the period 1910-16, The Garden of Fand, Tintagel and November Woods, and these remain his most popular and arguably most satisfying works. After 1920 his range expanded with a series of seven symphonies: although these have much beauty of sound and exciting and moving passages, there is a steady loss of spontaneity and an increasing feeling of material being extended too far. His neglected chamber music is unexpectedly concise and some of his other orchestral music such as the Violin Concerto and Mediterranean has much charm. Bax was knighted in 1937 and made Master of the King's Musick in 1942.   P.L.

LENNOX **BERKELEY**

(b. Oxford, 12 May 1903; d. London, 26 December 1989)

*A*fter studying music at Oxford, he had lessons, in Paris 1927-33, as so many of his generation did, with Nadia Boulanger (1887-1979). This immediately tinged his music with the international strain that can be found in such composers as Poulenc, Copland and Stravinsky, and the elegance and love of clarity that they all share to some degree. He worked for the BBC 1942-5 and taught music at the Royal Academy 1946-68. He was knighted in 1974. With his French affiliations, he remained an isolated figure on the English musical scene, producing music that had none of the folky influences of the Vaughan Williams school, none of the weighty traditionalism of Elgar. It is perhaps best sampled in the pleasantly light and melodious Serenade for Strings written in 1939. The Four Poems of St. Teresa for contralto and strings (1947), memorably performed by Kathleen Ferrier, showed an exquisite beauty that was always present somewhere in his work, while the extra influence of his Roman Catholic faith appears in the Missa Brevis of 1959. A deeper strain is to be heard in his symphonies. His vocal works included three one-act operas, notably Nelson (1954), but none of these has stayed in the regular repertoire.   P.G.

ABOVE: Mily Balakirev photographed around 1900, by which time he was living in retirement.

ABOVE: Samuel Barber photographed at the time of the production of Antony and Cleopatra at the new Metropolitan Opera House in 1966.

LEFT: 'Le Concert Champêtre' by Jean Baptiste Pater (1695-1736), a scene of music-making contemporary with the Bachs.

BELÁ
Bartók <small>(b. Nagyszentmiklós, Hungary, 25 March 1881; d. New York City, 26 September 1945)</small>

The Hungary of Bartók's childhood was part of the Habsburg empire and the country town of his birth now belongs to Romania. His rural upbringing was to play a vital role in Bartók's later development as a composer, for it first introduced him to folk music. The young Bartók's musical gifts were nurtured by his widowed mother and, when the family moved to the larger town of Pressburg, he was able to begin a formal musical education and attend concerts for the first time.

At eighteen, Bartók entered the Budapest Conservatoire, initially concentrating on developing his talent for the piano. Soon after leaving the Conservatoire in 1903, he completed his first worthwhile composition, the symphonic poem, Kossuth. This was followed by the Liszt-inspired Rhapsody for Piano and Orchestra, but neither work suggested a composer who had found his own voice. Bartók remained best-known as a concert pianist specializing in Bach and Liszt.

Then, in the early years of this century, his interest in folk music enlarged to become a fully-fledged research project. Frequently accompanied by his friend and fellow-composer, Zoltán Kodály, Bartók made pilgrimages to the remotest corners of eastern Europe to collect folk melodies. It was a quest which also took him as far as north Africa, but his paramount discovery came from isolated Hungarian communities living among the foothills of the Carpathian Mountains. Here, Bartók first encountered authentic, untainted Magyar music, as opposed to the diluted, and sanitized version pedalled by 'gypsy' violinists in Budapest.

For Bartók, the collecting, editing and cataloguing of this music became second only in importance to composing his own (upon which it became the significant influence). By 1934, the collection had grown so much that Bartók took a part-time post with the Hungarian Academy of Sciences to organize it into publishable form.

Between the two World Wars, Bartók enjoyed success as a concert pianist – he toured the United States, Britain and the former Soviet Union – and a notoriety as a composer. Many loudly disapproved of his music. Given someone so convinced of the value of multi-ethnic influences on a culture, it is unsurprising that the notions of 'racial purity' espoused by the Nazis met with Bartók's disapproval. Following the death of his mother in 1939, he went into exile in the United States. There, his composing style mellowed, probably to find favour with American concert promoters and audiences. One result was his most popular work, the Concerto for Orchestra; sadly, another concerto, for viola, was left unfinished at the time of his death in 1945.

Bartók synthesized the folk music of eastern Europe with formal classical disciplines to produce a style of composition that was both individual and influential. His impact on the development of 20th century music was matched only by Stravinsky and Schoenberg, yet the forms he so successfully adapted were centuries old. Bartók was not the first composer to find inspiration in folk music but he differed from his predecessors in making no attempt to 'civilize' it. There was no softening of the spiky, percussive rhythms; no refining of the irregular melodic patterns or of the traditional scales that sounded so strange to western ears. The familiar chords and cadences were replaced by percussive, repeated notes, or by piano accompaniments derived from the bagpipe drones used in much folk music.

These were the elements of Bartók's radical harmonic language. His innate musicianship, however, ensured there was nothing primitive about its application. He could weave counterpoint as complex as Bach's, and deploy orchestral colours as skilfully as Mahler or Richard Strauss. Bartók was also adept at introducing an impressionistic evocation of the sounds of nature into his compositions, be it as evocative 'night music' or what he described as 'insect music' (collecting moths was one of his hobbies).

Bartók's contribution to 20th century music was immense. He composed in all musical genres although, with the notable exception of his solitary opera, Duke Bluebeard's Castle (1918), his towering masterpieces are to be found in the fields of orchestral, chamber and instrumental music. His six string quartets, considered by many commentators to be the finest composed for the medium since those of

ABOVE: A stage design for Duke Bluebeard's Castle (written in 1911 and first performed in Budapest in 1918) created by Wilhelm Matenaar for a 1984 production in Berlin. In the event, it was not used.

Beethoven, provide landmarks throughout the most creative phase of his life and chart Bartók's changing compositional style. His appreciation of the expressive potential of percussion instruments (largely under-estimated at the time) can be heard in the first two piano concertos and in the masterpiece of Music for Strings, Percussion and Celesta of 1936, a work which also makes striking use of antiphonal effects.

Bartók's sound-world remained unique, even in his more lyrical and conventional works such as the Concerto for Orchestra and the beguiling Third Piano Concerto with its atmospheric slow movement. He also composed two concertos for violin, of which the second is by far the finest, but failed to complete one for viola before his death. Another major work of his later years was the Sonata for Two Pianos and Percussion, Bartók at his most pungent. Yet in contrast to the acerbity of works such as the Solo Violin Sonata in 1944, Bartók could engage the ear with colourful pieces like the Divertimento and the rumbustious Romanian Folk Dances. He also composed two ballets, The Wooden Prince and The Miraculous Mandarin and made an important contribution to music tuition with his six books of teaching pieces entitled Mikrokosmos. There is no requirement to be a pupil of the piano to enjoy these delightful miniatures.　　P.H.

LUDWIG VAN *Beethoven*

(b. Bonn, Germany, 16 December 1770; d. Vienna, 26 March 1827)

The van Beethoven family was Flemish by descent, its origins in the farming area embraced by Brussels, Louvain and Mechelen in what is now Belgium. The fine bass voice of the composer's grandfather had so impressed the Elector-Archbishop of Cologne (who also held the Bishopric of Liège), that he engineered the singer's transfer to the Court Chapel at Bonn in 1733. That same year, he married Maria-Josepha Poll and they had a son, Johann, who also displayed the musical leanings of his father. He, too, became a singer at the Court and, in 1767, married a young widow, Maria Magdalena Keverich. She bore Johann van Beethoven 'seven children. The first died in infancy and his name, Ludwig, was passed on to his next brother, who was born on 16 December 1770.

It has been suggested that Beethoven's father was by then an alcoholic, but evidence suggests that he only began to show a fondness for the bottle after the deaths of both his wife and a daughter in the same year, 1787. However, the family was not especially well-off and, when his son began to show signs of exceptional musical talent, Johann van Beethoven sought to exploit it in the way Mozart's father had done so successfully twenty years earlier.

Theory and technique were bullied into the young Beethoven, probably explaining why later, more conducive tuition often remained anathema to him. The experience may also have contributed to his well-documented irascibility and intolerance.

Like his father and grandfather, Ludwig van Beethoven was employed by the Elector of Cologne. His teaching was now taken over by others and he so excelled at the piano that, at seven, he gave his first recital, on 26 May 1778. An important influence during this period was Christian Gottlob Neefe (1748-98) who took over as court organist in 1779 and organized Beethoven's tuition along more systematic lines. The benefits were such that, at eleven, Beethoven was able to deputize for his teacher as assistant organist and, in 1783, publish his first composition, a set of variations. Importantly, Neefe introduced Beethoven to the music of the progressive Mannheim and Leipzig schools and to the compositions of Johann Sebastian Bach and his son, Carl Philipp Emanuel.

In 1787, Beethoven went to Vienna for the first time, where he received some lessons from Mozart, but news of what proved to be his mother's fatal illness sent him hurrying back to Bonn after just three months. Notwithstanding their brief acquaintance, Mozart was in no doubt about Beethoven's potential, having heard him improvise at the piano: 'Watch him,' he remarked. 'Some day the world will talk about him.'

It was not until 1792 that Beethoven was able to return to Vienna to continue his studies. His principal tutor was the venerable Haydn but there was little rapport between the two and the lessons were unproductive, so much so that Beethoven took advantage of one of Haydn's visits to London early in 1794 to obtain tuition elsewhere.

RIGHT: This portrait of Beethoven, painted in 1815 by Willibrod Joseph Mähler (1778-1860), is said to be one of the best likenesses of the composer.

ABOVE: Portrait of Beethoven's grandfather, also named Ludwig van Beethoven (1712-73), a Kapellmeister in Bonn. It was painted in 1773 by Leopold Radoux.

ABOVE: *Beethoven's ear-trumpet and the manuscript of his Symphony No.3, Op.55 Eroica which are kept in the Gesellschaft der Musikfreunde in Vienna.*

The glowing recommendations which Beethoven had brought from Bonn gained him access to the highest circles of Viennese society. With a reputation for temperamental, as well as pianistic, fireworks, he played his first public concert in March 1795. That same year, discarding all his compositions from the Bonn years, he published his Opus 1, a set of piano trios.

It was while playing at a concert in Prague in 1796 that Beethoven first noticed a buzzing in his ears. Two years later came the first signs of deafness and, by 1802, he was despairing enough of his condition to contemplate suicide. The depression was overcome, but there was a significant change of character. He became increasingly difficult to deal with but, more importantly, his whole concept of music changed as he resolved to accept fate's challenge. The years 1802-9 saw an explosion of creativity.

In his personal relationships, however, Beethoven was less successful. Despite romantic links with several women, he never married, the bitterest disappointment coming in 1810 with the ending of his engagement to Thérèse von Malfatti.

Financially, Beethoven's position was unlike that of any of the great composers who preceded him. He was in the direct employ of no one; instead he relied upon patronage, principally from leading aristocrats. After 1808, his deafness forced him to give up public performance and concentrate upon composition. Further personal troubles awaited him after the death of his brother, Karl, when Beethoven was forced to contest the guardianship of his nephew.

By 1818, such was his deafness that ear trumpets and similar devices were no longer of any help and Beethoven was forced to communicate through what he called 'conversation books'. The isolation he felt saw him enter a phase where much of his music became more a kind of inner communion than a public statement. After completing the Missa Solemnis in 1823 and the Ninth Symphony the following year, he withdrew into the intimate realm of chamber music, distilling his final thoughts into a series of profound and intense string quartets.

On 24 March 1827, Beethoven signed the score of the String Quartet Op.131, asked for the last sacrament and died two days later, in his 56th year. Perhaps mirroring the impact he had made, and would continue to make, at that moment a mighty thunderstorm raged over Vienna.

An estimated 50,000 attended his funeral and the city's leading musicians acted as pallbearers. He was buried in the Währinger cemetery but his remains were subsequently reinterred in Vienna's central cemetery, which is where they lie to this day.

I t was with Beethoven that music became unpredictable. While the works of Bach, Haydn and Mozart contain their surprises, there is an inevitability in their music – an inevitability, it must be added, dictated by formal conventions rather than by any lack of originality or imagination. What Beethoven wanted to express could no longer be contained within these conventions. He became the first of music's revolutionaries in what, significantly, became an age of revolution. Through music, Beethoven sought to illuminate the essence of the human spirit, in a way that had not been attempted before. He soon found the prevailing musical idioms inadequate and, with an intellectual courage allied to artistic confidence, began to explore new and – for the period – radical forms of expression.

Beethoven's music bestrides two centuries and two eras. It developed out of C.P.E. Bach, Haydn and Mozart to establish the stage upon which Berlioz, Liszt, Wagner and others

Chronology

1770 Born in the ancient Rhineland town of Bonn, 16 December

1778 First public recital, 26 March

1783-4 First published compositions, all for piano

1785 Composes three string quartets

1787 Visits Vienna and receives tuition from Mozart; returns to Bonn to be with his ailing mother. She dies on 17 July

1789 Enrols at the University of Bonn

1790 Composes two cantatas and a ballet

1792 Leaves Bonn for Vienna, arriving on 10 November. Death of his father

1793 Studies with Haydn

1794 Composes his Opus 1, a set of piano trios; studies counterpoint with Albrechtsberger and vocal composition with Salieri

1795 First public concert at the Burgtheater, 29 March

1796 Visits Prague, Dresden and Berlin for concerts; first symptoms of deafness become apparent

1797-9 Composes a host of piano works, both sonatas and sets of variations, together with sonatas for violin and cello, songs, chamber music and two piano concertos

1800 Première of the First Symphony; composes the Op.18 String Quartets

1801 Music for The Creatures of Prometheus, Moonlight and Funeral March sonatas

1802 Writes the 'Heiligenstadt Testament', effectively a suicide note to his brothers as he struggles to come to terms with deafness. Completes the Second Symphony, the Violin Sonatas Op.30 and the Piano Sonatas Op.31

LEFT: 'The Creation of Adam', one of the frescoes on the vault of the Sistine Chapel in Rome, by Michelangelo Buonarroti (1475-1564). These paintings are one of the pinnacles of human artistic achievement, as is the music of Beethoven.

ABOVE: *Franz, Count von Brunsvik (1779-1849), friend and patron of Beethoven, to whom the composer dedicated his* Appassionata *sonata. Beethoven fell deeply in love with his sister, Josephine. The portrait is by Heinrich Thugut.*

1803 *First performance of the Piano Concerto No.3, 5 April; completes the* Kreutzer *sonata and the oratorio,* Christ on the Mount of Olives

1804 Waldstein *and* Appassionata *sonatas*

1805 *First public performances of Symphony No.3 (Eroica), 7 April, and of the opera, Leonore (Fidelio), 20 November. The opera is withdrawn by Beethoven for revision and not heard again for nine years*

1806 *Overture No.3 for Leonore; Symphony No. 4; Violin Concerto; Rasumovsky Quartets*

1807 *First performances of the Fourth Symphony, the Piano Concerto No.4*

1808 *At a concert on 22 December the Fifth and Sixth Symphonies and the Choral Fantasy Op.80 are performed for the first time*

1809 *Vienna bombarded and occupied by the French; completes the Piano Concerto No.5, Piano Sonatas Op.78, Op.79 and Op.81a, and the String Quartet Op.74*

1810 *Sets Goethe's Egmont to music; String Quartet Op.95; première of the Emperor Concerto in Leipzig*

1812 *Completes the Seventh and Eighth Symphonies and his last Violin Sonata, No.10 Op.96; meets Goethe at a spa in Bohemia, Teplitz*

could perform during the 19th century. Beginning with Beethoven, the emotional and spiritual content of music was no longer sublimated to a 'classical' objectivity or restraint. After him, anything was possible, yet even this hard-won freedom was to prove barely sufficient in many of his later compositions.

There are four cornerstones to Beethoven's achievement: his nine symphonies, sixteen string quartets, thirty-two piano sonatas and his concertos. Piano sonatas numbered among his first published works, compositions of assured craftsmanship but with no startling originality, although the *Pathétique* sonata of 1799 remains one of his best-loved pieces. It was only after weathering the personal crisis of 1802, that a new kind of energy and intensity became apparent. The three Piano Sonatas Op.31 clearly mark the transition and the *Waldstein* Sonata Op.53, with its agitated prestissimo introduction, and the fiery *Appassionata* Op.57 are both deeply personal statements. The next five piano sonatas, including the magical Op.81a *Les Adieux*, are in lighter vein, but with the Op.101 of 1816, Beethoven's piano music enters a new world of experience and of sonority. Two years later, he completed the mighty *Hammerklavier* Sonata Op.106, a composition said to be inspired by the gift of a new Broadwood piano from England. Beethoven's last three piano sonatas, the transcendental Op.109, Op.110 and Op.111 were composed in 1822 but his final masterpiece for the instrument was an extraordinary set of variations on a simple waltz theme, the *Diabelli Variations* of 1823.

The nine symphonies of Beethoven constitute one of the pillars of western art. In the first two, the composer seems to be flexing his creative muscles. The music is genial and exuberant, in the manner of Haydn, with more than a pinch of humour and a few touches of originality. Neither, however, prepares the listener for the impact of the Third Symphony, the *Eroica* of 1802. Here was a snapping of musical chains, embodied in the leaping chord which opens the work. Something remarkable had been unleashed.

The heroism of the subtitle is now idealized and depersonalized but Beethoven, an avowed republican, originally dedicated the work to Napoleon Bonaparte whom he saw as embodying his ideals of equality and freedom. He was bitterly disappointed when Napoleon took the title of Emperor and all the trappings that accompanied it, thus showing himself to be every bit as bent on self-aggrandisement as the autocratic aristocracy he had supplanted. Beethoven reacted by scratching out the dedication on the title page of the score with such force that he tore a hole in the paper.

The elation of the first movement of the *Eroica* is followed by a funeral march that seems hewn out of granite, at its apex undergoing a fugal development of awesome intensity and grandeur. Out of this sombre utterance emerges an impudent scherzo and the symphony concludes with a set of variations on a theme from the music Beethoven wrote for a ballet based on the Prometheus legend.

Robert Schumann described the Fourth Symphony as 'a slender Grecian maiden between two Nordic giants', the giants being the Third and Fifth Symphonies and it is music of a sunny, even romantic disposition, but the work is no light-weight and there are dark threads woven into its bright fabric. While writing the Fourth, Beethoven put aside sketches for another symphony which had occupied him since completing the *Eroica*. Its tautly-constructed first movement was noteworthy for being derived from one succinct four-note

ABOVE: *'The Traveller above the Mist' by Caspar David Friedrich (1774-1840) painted c. 1818. This romantic view of the solitary artist finds parallel expression in Beethoven's music.*

LEFT: *The occasion of the crowning as Emperor of Napoleon Bonaparte in Notre-Dame in 1804 by Pope Pius VII, painted by Jacques-Louis David (1748-1825). Beethoven had long been an admirer of Napoleon and dedicated his* Eroica *symphony to him, but later, furious at this act of self-aggrandisement, he scratched the dedication from the score.*

motif, arguably the most famous four notes in all music: the opening of Beethoven's Fifth Symphony.

The concert which saw Beethoven conduct the first performance of the Fifth was one of the most notable in history. Rarely can a musical form have 'broken the mould' twice in the same evening for, in the second half of the concert, the Sixth Symphony was first played. This was first 'programmatic' symphony, the forerunner of everything from Berlioz's *Symphonie fantastique* to Mahler's *Resurrection* Symphony. However, Beethoven was anxious to play down the descriptive side of his *Pastoral* Symphony: 'It is more an expression of feeling rather than painting,' he explained.

The Seventh Symphony, which was composed in 1811-12, was aptly described by Richard Wagner as 'the apotheosis of the dance' and the underlying pulse of each movement bears this out, especially the whirlwind vitality of the third and fourth. 'Could only have been written when drunk,' was the verdict of one contemporary critic!

After the relaxed charm of the short Eighth Symphony, Beethoven turned aside from the genre for three years. In 1817 he made the first sketches for a Ninth Symphony but the work remained stillborn until 1822 and was completed in 1823. He had wanted to set Schiller's poem *Ode to Joy* since his days in Bonn and it now formed the basis of the choral finale of the symphony, another musical 'first'.

The Ninth Symphony was Beethoven's final statement, at least on a public scale, of his highest hopes and ideals. The man whose life was so full of problems could nevertheless set with conviction the words, 'All men will be brothers'. And, hearing the Ninth, it is still possible to believe it.

Originality was not something Beethoven especially aspired to in his piano concertos, which were written to display his own virtuosity. Of the five, the last three nevertheless have the stamp of greatness on them, especially the lyrical Fourth Op.58 and the magisterial Fifth Op.73, the *Emperor*. Beethoven's solitary Violin Concerto, with its prominent and unexpectedly poetic role for the kettledrums, also has its qualities, although the finale teeters on the brink of banality.

Beethoven explored most of the forms available to him in the field of chamber music. He wrote ten violin sonatas, of which the *Spring* and the *Kreutzer* are the most famous; several piano trios (the *Archduke* and *Ghost* stand out); five cello sonatas; a genial septet and a solitary quintet.

His major contribution, however, was in the field of the string quartet, beginning with the ambitious Op.18 set of 1800, continuing with the trenchancy of the Op.59 *Rasumovsky* Quartets, and the engaging charm of Op.74. Austere and sober, the F minor Quartet Op.95 anticipates the six quartets Beethoven composed in his last years. This is Beethoven at his most profound and, in the sublime Cavatina of Op.130, the Adagio of Op.132, the finale of Op.127 and the Lento of Op.135, his most spiritual. Not all of the music is of such heavenly beauty; the Scherzo of Op.135 is harsh, even ugly, the result some have speculated of the deaf Beethoven being unable to hear the reality of what his head dictated. Given his experience of quartet writing, it is surely more likely that these uncomfortable, disturbing sonorities are exactly what he intended. The late quartets are not laments; valedictory, yes, but as vital as anything he had ever written.

Beethoven wrote little sacred music: a solitary oratorio, *Christ on the Mount of Olives*; a Mass setting in C. His mightiest contribution was the *Missa Solemnis* of 1822, where the choral writing is on a par with that of Bach. Yet, despite its grandeur and splendour, it remains an intensely personal testament of faith. The same can be said of his only opera, *Fidelio* (or as he wished it titled, *Leonore*), an uneven work but one which again broke new ground with its expression of political and human idealism. P.H.

VINCENZO Bellini
(b. Catania, 3 November 1801; d. Puteaux, nr. Paris, 23 September 1835)

Bellini was born into a family which had produced professional musicians for several generations. Unlike the popular image of a Sicilian, he grew into a tall, fair, blue-eyed young man, so that his unsatisfactory love affairs and failure to marry seem rather surprising. One suspects that he was totally absorbed in his work, and that his energies were sapped by the constant travelling, often in poor health, which took up a large part of his brief adult life.

As a young man, his music for church functions won the approval of the Catania authorities, who raised enough money to send him to the Royal College of Music in Naples, where he stayed for eight years. During this time he scored his first success, albeit only in a student production: his first opera Adelson e Salvini (1825) was widely praised, and the management of the famed San Carlo Opera in Naples commissioned a work from Bellini. This, too, was enthusiastically received (Bianca e Fernando) and a lucrative offer from La Scala quickly persuaded the twenty-four year old composer to make the long journey north to Milan.

Operatic history is full of instances where the work of the composer has been negated by silly libretti, so it was a major good fortune when Bellini was introduced to the dramatist Felice Romani, who in the course of a long life wrote the libretti for over a hundred operas by many of the leading composers of the day. Their collaboration resulted in an immediate success, Il Pirata (1827), which also launched the careers of two of the century's most illustrious singers, Rubini and Tamburini. Bellini was impatient of his fellow-composers, especially Donizetti, who could complete an opera in a few months; he laboured slowly and anxiously over each new work. His second opera for La Scala, La Straniera (1829), confirmed his success there, but when he and Romani had to rush to complete their next work, Zaira, for Parma, they experienced their first failure. At this time, Bellini became involved with the wife of a rich businessman, Giuditta Turina, and their affair proceeded erratically for the next five years, with increasing gossip when the offended husband denounced them publicly. Eventually, Bellini abandoned the unfortunate woman; he seemed to fear a lasting relationship, for every love affair from his college days to his final year seemed to cool before it was legalized.

1830 saw renewed success with Romani's free version of the Romeo and Juliet story I Capuleti ed I Montecchi, produced in Venice, and the following year saw two more triumphs at La Scala: La Sonnambula and Norma. Bellini embarked on a tour of Italian cities, acclaimed everywhere, but especially in his native Catania, which even to this day preserves his memory in a hundred ways. But the strain of travel, the growing bitterness of his affair with Giuditta, and the onset of dysentery took their toll. He quarrelled with Romani when Beatrice di Tenda failed in Venice in 1833, and after a summer in London, decided to settle in Paris. Here he enjoyed one final major success, I Puritani (1835), a story set in Plymouth during Cromwell's rule; with the four greatest singers of the day in the cast, its first performance became a legend in operatic history. That autumn, cholera was rife in Paris. A wealthy English Jew allowed Bellini the use of his home outside the city, and it was here that the body of the exhausted composer was discovered by a visitor seeking refuge from a storm.

RIGHT: Vincenzo Bellini, a portrait by an unknown artist now in the Museo Bibliografico Musicale in Bologna. He appears to be in his twenties, around the age when his first operas were being performed.

BELOW: The front of the Teatro alla Scala, Milan, a scene painted in 1852 by Angelo Inganni (1807-80). This was the venue for Bellini's main operatic triumphs.

The operas of Bellini have always been associated with the names of great singers. In the composer's lifetime, he trained a group of artists in the vocal style he demanded for his works, and so brought to fame names that were revered through the century: sopranos Pasta and Grisi, tenor Rubini, baritone Tamburini, and bass Lablache. In our own age, the revival of interest in Bellini which began in the 1950s is linked to the careers of Maria Callas and Joan Sutherland, and it seems possible that the decline in popularity that the composer has suffered from time to time reflects the absence of a prima donna who can worthily interpret his great soprano roles.

Bellini's greatest contribution to Italian opera was his wonderfully serene vocal line, elegant and moving: 'linked sweetness long drawn out'. Almost invariably, the protagonists in his operas are women and Bellini included in each work at least one extended soprano aria which, well performed, would provide the emotional highlight of the evening. Famous examples are 'Come per me sereno' (*La Sonnambula*), 'Qui la voce' (*I Puritani*) and above all the ethereal 'Casta diva' from *Norma*. In each of these, the slow cantilena (vocal line) is enhanced by gentle decoration in a manner that has often been compared to the piano melodies of Chopin, for instance in the Nocturnes. Also, Bellini knew how to add interest to the vocal line with discreet use of solo in-

struments in the accompaniment, such as the cor anglais for Imogene's aria in *Il Pirata*.

The tenor roles are also demanding, as they are written for a light graceful voice that must also be capable of ringing high notes: Pavarotti's recording of 'A te, o cara' from *I Puritani* sets the standard for modern singers.

The natural emphasis on solo singing in any discussion of Bellini's operas suggests that they do not provide the 'total theatre' experience of later composers; even in his lifetime, he was accused in the London press of writing 'pretty tunes weakened by unskilled orchestral parts'. The plots of his operas are also lacking in dramatic intensity, although the simple village tale of the sleepwalking Amina in *La Sonnambula* is moving, and *Norma* is more integrated in its presentation of the Druid priestess torn between love and duty in a situation similar to Aida. But the mention of Verdi reminds us of the greater variety and power that he was to add to such dramas, beside which Bellini's works can seem slightly pallid, for all their lyrical beauty. Nor can one find in Bellini the fizzing high spirits of his contemporaries Rossini and Donizetti; what Bellini offers is more refined, more static, perhaps more languid. Even today, the purity of his innocent melodies can work its magic and help us understand why audiences of his day, according to the composer Glinka, 'shed tears of emotion and ecstasy'.   P.J.

LEFT: A view of Naples, seen from the Capodimonte, painted by Alexander Dunovy. Bellini moved to Naples in 1819 to pursue his musical studies at the Naples Conservatory.

ALBAN Berg

(b. Vienna, 9 February 1885; d. Vienna, 24 December 1935)

Chronology

The son of a merchant, Alban Berg inherited his musical talents from his mother, a daughter of the Austrian court jeweller. But he was no prodigy, and only started to show his gifts when he was fourteen, composing his first music in 1900, the year in which his father died. Four years later he passed his final school examination, at a second attempt, and entered the civil service.

At this time, Schoenberg advertised for pupils. Berg's brother showed the composer some of Alban's songs, whereupon the older man enrolled him as a pupil. Didactic and dominating by nature, he set about transforming Berg from a promising amateur into a dedicated professional, and at the same time became his mentor and substitute father. Berg was his pupil until 1910.

While adopting Schoenberg's techniques, Berg also found his own voice, and, it has been said, 'developed from a dreamy and sensitive boy into a serious artistic personality'. Thanks to an inheritance in 1906, he could devote himself to composing and was not forced to teach or undertake hack work simply to earn money. In the following year, he met his future wife, Helene Nahowski, and they began a happy marriage in 1911. Yet he lacked artistic confidence and in 1913 suffered a mortifying experience when the première of two of his Five Altenberg Lieder in Vienna was interrupted by ridicule from the audience. Schoenberg, who was conducting, begged people to leave the hall rather than spoil the concert, but it had to be abandoned. Schoenberg himself then censured this music, the first that Berg had written without his guidance, and the Altenberg Lieder were never performed complete in their composer's lifetime. Berg recovered from this setback only slowly.

During the First World War Berg served in the army, but his asthma saved him from active service. He now discovered his gift for musical theatre and in 1917 set about the composition of the opera Wozzeck, completing the score in 1922. Some aspects of his military experience made him the ideal composer for Georg Büchner's play, which portrays the sufferings and final destruction of a despised common soldier and touched him closely.

A currency devaluation now reduced Berg's income, and he had to teach and undertake other work, complaining in 1919 that 'the army, family and earning a living have robbed me of half my life'. Success still eluded him, for the subject and style of Wozzeck were unorthodox and the work was rejected by several opera houses before the Berlin Staatsoper accepted it. Its première there in 1925 was greeted with hostility by critics who wrote of its composer 'poisoning the well of German music' and being 'a musical swindler dangerous to society'. Yet it also found supporters and the public recognized its quality. The numerous performances of Wozzeck that followed marked Berg's arrival as a major composer of his generation. However, he had a mere decade left to live, and composed only a few more works, of which the Violin Concerto is the best known. The score of his second opera, Lulu, was unfinished at his death.

BELOW: *Expressionism in painting: 'Shrine in the Woods' painted in oils by the Austrian Egon Schiele (1890-1918) in 1915. Schiele was acquainted with – and drew portraits of – the Viennese 'trinity': Berg, Schoenberg and Webern.*

Of the three composers of the Second Viennese School, namely Schoenberg and his pupils Berg and Webern, Berg is the only one generally accepted by the public, for the powerful emotional content of his music readily communicates itself even where its syntax and structure are complex. Though his language is often intellectually ingenious in a way which delights theorists, the musical result does not resemble Schoenberg and is even further removed from the etiolated world of Webern. Indeed, it is emotionally rich, though tense even in lyrical passages, and this aspect of Berg is most readily seen in the Violin Concerto which, written in 1935, was his last work.

This concerto bears the dedication 'to the memory of an angel'; she was Manon Gropius, the child by a second marriage of Mahler's widow, and a beautiful and gifted girl who died aged eighteen of poliomyelitis. The work features a twelve-note series which is stated at the start by the soloist, yet these notes do not seem arbitrary in the way that they can with Schoenberg. Instead they climb gently upwards and relate to a G minor key that lies behind the whole work, in spite of the fact that tonality has no place in 'pure' serialism. Furthermore, because the violin seems to represent the dying Manon, the solo writing offers a gentler aspect that contrasts effectively with dramatic orchestral outbursts. Add to these things Berg's prominent use of a Ländler-like Carinthian folk melody in triple time and the chorale tune 'Es ist genug' from J.S. Bach, and one sees that Berg's world was never dominated by theory. The critic Mosco Carner wrote of Berg's 'reconciliation of twelve-note music with tonality' in this music, declaring that he alone had made serialism humane, and Sibelius probably meant the same thing when he called Berg 'Schoenberg's best work'.

Although the Violin Concerto provides the easiest access to Berg, he remains a difficult composer and perseverance is needed to grasp his music. His style is both ornate and tautly economical, with something enigmatic about it, and is already recognizable in earlier works such as his *Seven Early Songs* and Piano Sonata. For an example of his ingenious methods, even in music for the theatre, we need only look at his operas. Thus in Act 2 of *Wozzeck* (1925) the music not only shows the protagonist's mental collapse but also contains a kind of 'symphony' with a sonata movement followed by a fantasia and fugue, slow movement, scherzo and rondo, while Act 3, in which the tormented Wozzeck kills his wife and drowns himself, has a series of orchestral 'inventions' in turn on a theme, sustained note, rhythm, chord, key and a repeated figure. In *Lulu*, each half of the twelve-note series associated with the young composer Alwa contains the same notes, rearranged, as each half of the series associated with his father Dr Schön.

Berg's fascination with the inner workings of composition makes him quite different from a composer like Verdi who thinks in broad lines. Besides his ingenious shaping of notes according to serial patterns, recent research has discovered a cipher in his *Lyric Suite* for string quartet which relates to a woman he loved, Hanna Fuchs-Robettin. The initial letters of her name combine with those of his own in German notation to give the basic melodic motif of the work, H (B natural), F, A, B (B flat).

Such music has power and personality, and undoubtedly came from the heart as much as the head. Nevertheless, *Wozzeck* is not a comfortable theatrical experience and *Lulu* is a lurid tale in which the heroine is murdered by Jack the

ABOVE: *A portrait in oils of Alban Berg painted by fellow composer Arnold Schoenberg (1874-1951) in Vienna in 1910. Schoenberg was Berg's teacher in Vienna between 1904 and 1910 and encouraged his experiments with atonal composition.*

Ripper. This very tall man who 'looked like an angel' was a moralist who criticized Viennese society for hypocrisy, but also said that he valued 'the emphasis on the sensual in modern works . . . an immense strength that lies in us, the pivot of all being and thinking'. C.H.

HECTOR Berlioz

(b. Côte St. André, Grenoble, 11 December 1803; d. Paris, 8 March 1869)

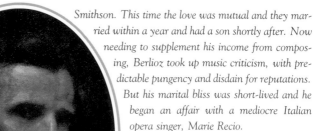

*B*erlioz's parents groomed him for a career in medicine; his feeling for music was tolerated as a hobby. It is said that his first experience of a dissection class was sufficient to bring his medical education to an abrupt end. By eighteen, he had gone to live in Paris and quickly acquired notoriety by standing up at concerts and hurling insults at conductors who dared to tamper with the music they were performing. Disparaging remarks made to its director, the composer Luigi Cherubini, also saw Berlioz's first application to join the Paris Conservatoire summarily rejected. When accepted by the Conservatoire in 1826, he immediately applied for the coveted Prix de Rome but – true to character – elected to flout all the (admittedly archaic) rules associated with the competition. Inevitably, he failed, but his persistence was rewarded with the prize for 1830.

In the intervening years, Berlioz had developed a passion for literature to equal that for music. Goethe prompted the composition of Eight Scenes from Faust but Shakespeare was to prove even more inspirational. Shakespeare also brought Berlioz into contact with the Irish actress, Harriet Smithson, who was playing Ophelia in a touring production of Hamlet. Berlioz's infatuation was not reciprocated and his emotional turmoil found its outlet in that landmark of Romanticism, the Symphonie fantastique.

Ignored by Harriet, Berlioz struck up a relationship with the pianist, Camille Moke, but this foundered when she married the composer Ignace Pleyel (1757-1831), while Berlioz was enjoying his sabbatical in Rome. While there, he satisfied the demands of his tutors at the Conservatoire by regularly sending mundane reworkings of earlier compositions while working on scores which he knew would meet with their disapproval, the overtures Rob Roy and King Lear and the sequel to the Symphonie fantastique, Lélio, among them.

Upon his return to France, he again encountered Harriet

Smithson. This time the love was mutual and they married within a year and had a son shortly after. Now needing to supplement his income from composing, Berlioz took up music criticism, with predictable pungency and disdain for reputations. But his marital bliss was short-lived and he began an affair with a mediocre Italian opera singer, Marie Recio.

Although Berlioz's music had still to find widespread recognition in France, it had been acclaimed elsewhere in Europe, even in conservative Britain. Above all, there was praise for the colourful and original orchestration – the one area in which the composer had received no formal musical education. His genius for orchestration was intuitive and his most lasting contribution to music in general. He enshrined his theories in his 'Treatise on Modern Instrumentation and Orchestration'.

On account of his treatment of Harriet, Berlioz was full of self recrimination after her death in 1854, but it did not stop him marrying Marie. After completing the operas Les Troyens and Béatrice et Bénédict, he concentrated on writing – including his memoirs – and on conducting his music, often with gargantuan forces. His second wife died in 1862 and, five years later, Berlioz was further heartbroken by the death of his son, a ship's captain. His own health now deteriorated rapidly, culminating in his death, aged sixty-five, in March 1869.

RIGHT: Hector Berlioz, a portrait in oils, now in the Louvre Museum, painted in 1850 by the French realist painter Gustave Courbet (1819-77).

BELOW: Berlioz caricatured in 'A Concert in 1846'; a coloured engraving by Andreas Geiger (1765-1856) reflecting the contemporary view of Berlioz's inflated orchestrations.

Hector Berlioz precisely fitted the notion of the Romantic artist of the 19th century: unconventional, rebellious, impetuous and highly-strung. And, true to the Romantic ideal of art and life as one, his music mirrored his temperament – and still polarizes opinion. There are those who hail Berlioz as one of music's great innovators; others hear little more than overblown rhetoric. Did the German poet, Heine, capture the character of the Frenchman when he said Berlioz 'had not sufficient talent for his genius'?

Whatever his technical limitations, there is no doubt that with the *Symphonie fantastique* Berlioz shattered musical boundaries very much as Stravinsky was to do eighty years later with the *Rite of Spring*. Apart from its startlingly vivid orchestration, the work was notable for its use of the *idée fixe*, a musical motif permeating all four movements but subject to extremes of treatment according to the music's mood and to the melodramatic programme which Berlioz devised for the work. The symphony's wild swings of emotion, its nightmarish imagery, and its undisguised depiction of the mental state of its creator, were utterly unlike anything ever composed before. It was an astonishing achievement for a largely untrained composer of just twenty-six and Berlioz never again plunged quite so deeply into the dark abyss of the psyche as here.

Virtually all of Berlioz's music reflects his love of literature, his fascination for the stage or his belief that the human voice – especially the soprano – was the most expressive instrument of all, an interesting sentiment from a master of orchestration. This affection for the soprano voice is nowhere better expressed than in the delicious song-cycle *Les nuits d'été*, to poems by Théophile Gautier). He composed three performed operas, *Benvenuto Cellini*, *Béatrice et Bénédict* (inspired by Shakespeare's *Much Ado About Nothing*) and *Les Troyens* (*The Trojans*), the last a colossal work that occupied him for four years. Scale is also a facet of his major sacred choral works, the *Te Deum* and the *Requiem* or *Grande messe des morts*, the latter calling for two hundred voices (Berlioz preferred seven or eight hundred!), a vast orchestra, sixteen kettledrums and four brass bands.

More modestly scored are the sparkling overtures *Waverley*, *Les Francs-juges*, *King Lear*, *Le Corsaire*, *Rob Roy* and *Le Carnaval romain*. As well as Shakespeare and Walter Scott, Berlioz also found a kindred spirit across the English Channel in the poet, Lord Byron and, in his 'symphony' for viola and orchestra, *Harold in Italy*, Berlioz paints four sound-pictures inspired by Byron's poem *Childe Harolde's Pilgrimage*. Another programmatic symphony was based on *Romeo and Juliet* but Berlioz is to be heard at his most moving and affecting in the charming oratorio *L'Enfance du Christ* and, as mentioned, in the sensuous, elegaic settings of *Les nuits d'été*. Never one to waste a good idea, Berlioz reworked the youthful *Eight Scenes from Faust* into the more substantial *La Damnation de Faust*, part of which – the 'Hungarian March' – remains a popular concert showpiece.   P.H.

LEFT: 'Liberty Guides the People', a painting by Eugène Delacroix (1798-1863) finished in 1830, the year that Berlioz wrote his Symphonie fantastique.

GEORGES
Bizet

(b. Paris, 25 October 1838; d. Bougival, 3 June 1875)

Bizet was born in Paris, the son of a hairdresser turned singing teacher, and originally christened Alexandre-César-Léopold, though he was always known as Georges after a godfather. His mother also had a musical background, and the precociously gifted Bizet was admitted into the Paris Conservatoire at the age of ten. He became a brilliant pianist (although he never played at concerts), studied composition under Jacques Halévy (1799–1862), and also encountered Gounod, who was to be a great support and influence. Bizet was an outstanding student, winning numerous prizes, including one awarded by Offenbach for an operetta. This was jointly awarded to Bizet, with Le Docteur Miracle (1857), and Charles Lecocq (1832–1918). Most importantly for Bizet, he won the Prix de Rome, which took him to Italy for three years. For us, the composition at the age of 17 of his early Symphony in C (lost for 80 years) might be rated as the most exciting event of all.

In Rome, Bizet dutifully produced the expected works – an opera Don Procopio (1858-9), a symphony, Vasco da Gama, and a Te Deum. Nothing much came of this, and he returned to Paris to attempt a career as an opera composer. Les Pêcheurs de perles (The Pearl Fishers) (1863) was well received by the audience, but less so by the critics, and its successor La Jolie Fille de Perth (The Fair Maid of Perth) (1867) went less well all round. Bizet had to make ends meet as a piano teacher and arranger, and this was a depressing period for him. In 1869 he married the daughter of his old teacher Halévy, and although this was to lead to trouble from his domineering mother-in-law, it gave him the incentive to branch out into orchestral music (though he did produce another unsuccessful opera, Djamileh, in 1871). Here he was more successful with the overture Roma, the Petite Suite (Jeux d'enfants) and especially his suite of incidental music to Alphonse Daudet's L'Arlésienne (although the play itself was destined to be a failure).

At last, his career seemed established, and he was awarded the Legion d'Honneur in 1874. Emboldened by this, and by his greater experience, he began work on the opera Carmen, based on Prosper Merimée's novel. This was finished and performed in 1875, but – as is well-known – had a very mixed reception. The subject was attacked as 'obscene', the music as coarse and derivative. This setback affected Bizet's always delicate health, and after a recurrence of his chronic throat condition, he died quite suddenly of a heart attack.

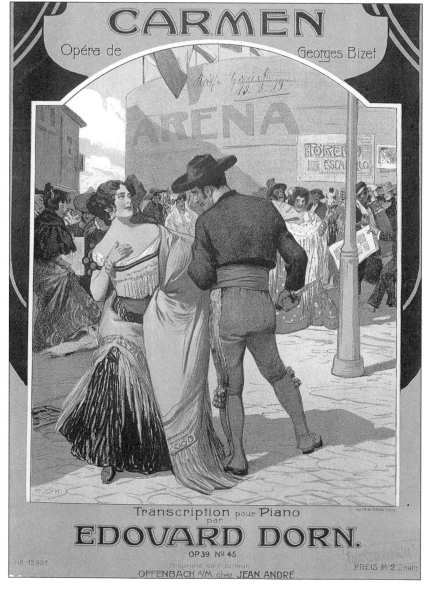

izet is described as having been a lively, energetic man with a sense of humour and a temper – not a very reflective or philosophical character. This can be seen in his music, which is always full of colour and rhythm, beautifully orchestrated, dramatic, but not often moving or thoughtful. Even allowing for the poor libretti which restricted him, it is only in *Carmen* that signs appear of real characterization, and the expression of deeper emotion. Had *Carmen* not been written, Bizet would be seen today as a promising but unfulfilled composer who wrote a few pleasant orchestral pieces and a few flawed operas. As it is, his immortality is assured, but we are still left with the tantalising question of what he might have achieved had he lived longer.

Bizet's operas are his best-known works, but apart from *Carmen* they do not contain much of his best music. The early works – *Le Docteur Miracle* and *Don Procopio* – are pleasant and lively in a Rossinian way, but surprisingly devoid of the tunefulness which is so characteristic of Bizet's later music. With *The Pearl Fishers* comes Bizet's first fully mature music (if we exclude the precocious Symphony), but little is memorable apart from the two famous hits – the duet and the serenade – which unluckily come close together in Act 1. *The Fair Maid of Perth* shows at last Bizet's talent for tuneful, colourful orchestral interludes, but the vocal music is less striking melodically. With *Djamileh* Bizet does only moderate justice to an exotic Eastern setting. Composed only two years later, *Carmen* signals an enormous leap forward. Here at last are dramatic power and characterization, a dazzling orchestral score full of dance numbers, vivid choruses, varied rhythms. And yet, it was an initial failure, and only became popular later in an inauthentic edition.

As regards orchestral music, we have the amazing youthful symphony – written in emulation of Gounod's Second Symphony, but far excelling it. Remarkably, the score was lost for 80 years, and only surfaced for its first known performance in 1935. This charming work, like Schubert or Mendelssohn rather than Gounod, was followed by no orchestral music of quality until *L'Arlésienne* in 1872, with the exception of *Jeux d'enfants*, which was orchestrated from a longer piano duet suite. *L'Arlésienne* needs no introduction; it clearly points the way to *Carmen* with its colour and rhythmic dash, and in the new expressiveness of the more tender episodes. Otherwise, Bizet wrote much piano music (*Jeux d'enfants* much the best of it) and some enjoyable songs.   P.L.

BELOW: *'A Village Bull-Fight', a painting by Spanish artist Francisco de Goya (1746-1828) which brings* Carmen *to mind. Bizet's music brilliantly evokes the colour and drama of Spain.*

ABOVE: *Bernstein conducting Beethoven's Ninth Symphony at the East Berlin Schauspielhaus in December 1989.*

LEONARD **BERNSTEIN**

(b. Lawrence, MA, 25 August 1918; d. New York, 14 October 1990)

A remarkably vibrant and vital figure on the American musical scene throughout his career, he was constantly torn between the demands on his time as one of America's finest conductors and his personal preference for composition. Even within that sphere there was an additional division between his serious, Yiddish based, music and his lighter pieces as so successfully represented by the lastingly successful West Side Story of 1957. It was music in this latter vein, which also includes Wonderful Town (1953) and the ballet Fancy Free (1944), that will surely be his most lasting monument; for he never found a final integrated form for his oft-revised opera Candide (1956), nor went much deeper into a promising vein of choral music that included the Chichester Psalms (1965) and many fine songs. His more substantial and serious minded orchestral works found it hard to shun an exuberant jazz vein (as heard in the exhilarating piano part in the Age of Anxiety Symphony No.2, 1947-9), in spite of their examination of moral and religious issues that were a background to his tumultuous life-style. Beyond conducting and composing, he was a brilliant inspirational pianist, and a compelling lecturer, broadcaster and author. Like so many American composers, of whom Copland is the best example, he never seems to have come to terms with the role of a serious composer who has a taste for the jazz and popular music world. *P.G.*

FRANZ **BERWALD**

(b. Stockholm, 23 July 1796; d. Stockholm, 3 April 1868)

S weden's most talented 19th century composer was not recognized as such until the 20th century. Although a practising musician (an orchestral violinist) as well as a composer, he was forced to pursue numerous other professions to survive, including the management of an orthopaedic institute, a glassworks and a sawmill. So disorganized was his career that his life is still not fully documented. Berwald was of German extraction, and studied for some time in Berlin. His early music, culminating in two operas Estrella di Soria (1862) and The Queen of Golconda (1864), was influenced by Spohr and unsuccessful – so much so that he destroyed much of it. His most original music was composed in the 1840s for orchestra, and includes four symphonies and a violin concerto. Here Berlioz is a clear influence in its melodic and structural freedom and unconventional harmony, together with what can be seen as a prefiguring of modern Scandinavian feeling. This new style was also unacceptable to the public because of its very originality, and Berwald's last works comprise mainly chamber music in a 'safer' Mendelssohnian mode. These elicited the belated offer of an academic post in Sweden, but only a year later Berwald was dead. With the revival of Scandinavian music at the turn of the century, it was not long before Swedish musicians discovered Berwald, whom they belatedly saw as the founder of a national school leading to the music of Hugo Alfvén (1872-1960) and Wilhelm Stenhammar (1871-1927). *P.L.*

ARTHUR **BLISS**

(b. London, 2 August 1891; d. London, 27 March 1975)

B orn in England of an American father and English mother, Bliss had the most conventional of upbringings, including Cambridge, the Royal College of Music under Stanford and ser-

FAR RIGHT: *'Small Girl at the Piano' by Carl Larsson (1853-1919), a painting by a fellow countryman of Berwald.*

ABOVE: *Sir Arthur Bliss in his younger days when he was seen as something of an 'enfant terrible'.*

vice with the Guards in the 1914-18 war. After the war, he reacted as did so many against convention, and his early works such as Rout and Madame Noy, influenced especially by Stravinsky and Satie, earned him the name of the 'enfant terrible' of English music. An extended visit to the USA and the acquisition of a wife and family seem to have led to a change of emphasis. His next major work, the Colour Symphony, although still with its share of 'modern' harmonies, clearly belongs to the Elgarian romantic tradition, and this impression is confirmed by Music for Strings and the succession of dramatic ballet scores which he wrote in the 1930s, including Checkmate (1937) and Miracle in the Gorbals (1944). The 1939 Piano Concerto, written for the New York World's Fair, is more spectacular than inspired and the best of his later music is to be found in the two string quartets of 1941 and 1950. (The earlier clarinet quintet is also enjoyable.) His opera The Olympians was first produced in 1949. He was knighted in 1950 and in 1953 he succeeded Bax as Master of the Queen's Musick. Although he then produced such large-scale works as the Violin and Cello Concertos, these works seem little more than routine utterances when compared with the virile, energetic music written between the wars. *P.L.*

ERNEST **BLOCH**

(b. Geneva, 24 July 1880; d. Portland, Oregon, 15 July 1959)

B loch's father was a prosperous Swiss clock-maker, but young Ernest was never happy in the family business, and spent more time studying music. His early works were over-ambitious operatic and orchestral projects, but in the second decade of the century he found a more personal note deriving from his Jewish background. From this period dates his most popular work, the Rhapsody for cello and orchestra Schelomo (Solomon); his Israel Symphony appeared in the same year, 1916. Like many

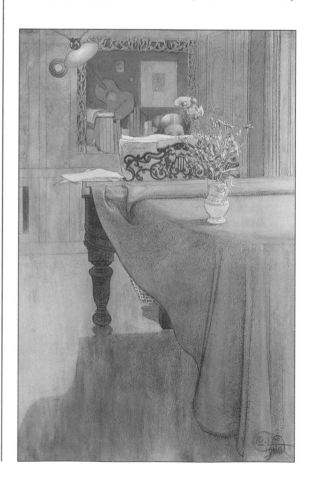

European artists of that period, Bloch sought a new career in the less traditional musical milieu of America, and gradually his works were championed by many varied groups there: especially acclaimed were his Piano Quintet (1923), Concerto Grosso (1925), Sacred Service (1933) and the 1937 Violin Concerto associated with Yehudi Menuhin. Bloch had taken American citizenship in 1924, but spent the 1930s in Europe until the threat of war sent him back to the USA where he spent his last twenty years revered as a teacher, and as an inventive composer, especially of impressive chamber works. Above all, he is respected as giving noble voice to the traditions and aspirations of the Jewish people in an age of uncertainty.   P.J.

LUIGI **BOCCHERINI**

(b. Lucca, 19 February 1743; d. Madrid, 28 May 1805)

The list of Boccherini's works is an extraordinarily long one, and it is ironic that the public associate his name with just one short minuet, the one so memorably featured in the vintage Ealing film The Lady Killers. Boccherini came from a highly musical Italian family, and early in life he appeared as a cellist in Vienna and Paris. In 1768 he journeyed to Madrid, and apart from some years in the employ of the Prussian court, it was in Spain that he spent the rest of his life. However, the royal patronage he initially enjoyed inevitably weakened after Napoleon's forces invaded the country. As a consequence, Boccherini's final years were spent in poverty and sadness; having seen his wife and children die, he himself succumbed to tuberculosis at the age of 62. The vast catalogue of his works contains instrumental and orchestral pieces for various ensembles, and the standard of invention and skill in those that we hear today seems remarkably high. However, it is still difficult to pass a general verdict on one who composed over 100 quartets, 100 quintets, 20 symphonies, and numerous vocal works. His worth is still not fully recognized.   P.J.

WILLIAM **BOYCE**

(b. London, September 1711; d. London, 7 February 1779)

Boyce was a typical English church musician. A simple, kindly man, he began his musical career as a choirboy at St. Paul's and quickly progressed to a series of appointments as organist at various churches and the Chapel Royal. Like Arne, he was much involved in the production of masques, odes and operas, but,

as befitted his profession, had more to do with church music than the theatre. Throughout his life he was afflicted by progressive deafness, which eventually ended his active career. He took over from his teacher Maurice Greene a massive compilation of English Cathedral Music, which remained the standard work until this century. This worthy, respected musician wrote mainly worthy, respected music, some of which is still played today in churches. As with Purcell and Arne, the demise of the ode and the masque have made performance of much of his work difficult, and his music is in any case in a more traditional baroque style than the original Purcell and the charmingly melodic Arne. Consequently he is remembered mainly for the vigorous and refreshing overtures or 'symphonies' to many of his odes and masques. These were rescued from obscurity by Constant Lambert, who also constructed from them a ballet, The Prospect Before Us. And of course Boyce wrote Heart of Oak   P.L..

HAVERGAL **BRIAN**

(b. Dresden, Staffs., 29 January 1876; d. Shoreham, 28 November 1972)

Any composer living as long as Brian did might be expected to have had a wide-ranging career, but his can reasonably be called unique. The conventional events and music of his first 35 years have virtually nothing to do with his extraordinary last 60 years. His early life was humble and mundane, and he was virtually self-taught, but he had striking early success, his English Suite being conducted by Henry Wood in 1907. He also started a career in musical journalism which was to last until 1939. His early music was lively but conventional, as exemplified by some pleasant songs and the overture Dr Merryheart. After the 1914-18 war he ceased to be noticed: from then on, his vast output was simply not played. His works became more and more ambitious, from the opera The Tigers (1918) to increasingly abstruse symphonies and the intimidating operas of his later years – Turandot (1950-1), The Cenci (1952), Faust (1955-6) and Agamemnon (1957) – to say nothing of his enormous lost setting of Shelley's Prometheus Unbound. His first symphony was the breathtakingly grandiose Gothic Symphony of 1919-27 (not performed until 1961), in a relatively accessible if overwhelming romantic style. The remaining 34 (!) were composed at increasing speed, and with increasingly knotty themes and structure, 27 of them after the age of 70 and the last at 95. Although sporadic performances were given in his last years, he was never to receive significant recognition.   P.L.

ALEXANDER
Borodin
(b. St. Petersburg, 12 November 1833; d. St. Petersburg, 27 February 1887)

Alexander Borodin, composer of Prince Igor, one of the greatest of all Russian operas, once said that for him 'music was a pastime, a relaxation from more serious occupations'. Those 'more serious occupations' were the disciplines of science and medicine, in which he also achieved international fame.

The illegitimate son of a Russian prince, Borodin was a very talented child but not, it seems, a musical prodigy. By his teens he could speak German, French, Italian and English, as well as play the piano, flute and cello. With his friend and fellow-student Mikhail Shchiglev he would perform arrangements for four hands of music by Haydn, Beethoven and Mendelssohn. But even in these student days, his enduring passion was for experimental chemistry.

In 1850 he entered the Medico-Surgical Academy at St. Petersburg, where he studied anatomy, botany, chemistry, crystallography and zoology. On graduation he spent a year as house surgeon in a military hospital, followed by three years of more advanced scientific studies in western Europe. In 1862 he succeeded to the professorship at the Academy, and ten years later played a leading role in establishing medical courses for women. He spent the rest of his life lecturing and supervising student work.

How Borodin managed to find time for music remains a mystery, but in 1864 he met Balakirev and, through him, Cui (1835-1918), Mussorgsky and Rimsky-Korsakov. In this way he became a member of the 'Mighty Handful': musically speaking he was the least committed, but the most gifted, of the five composers. As a group they were opposed to the academicians and to the music of Richard Wagner. They saw themselves as Russian patriots, standing for spontaneity and 'truth in music'.

On his appointment as professor, Borodin, now a much-loved and greatly respected figure, moved into a flat at the Academy with his wife, his in-laws, many other relatives and a large number of cats. Here he lived in happy disorder, with friends and students coming and going more or less as they pleased. Heart attacks and cholera in 1882-83 seriously undermined his health, but it was entirely in character that early in 1887 he returned from an important academic engagement to attend a fancy dress ball at the Academy. Wearing a red shirt and high boots, Russia's national costume, he joined the dancing in great good humour and high spirits. Then, at midnight, as the festivities reached a climax, he fell back and within a few seconds died from heart failure.

RIGHT: A portrait of Borodin taken in 1885 near the end of his life when he was Professor at the Medico-Surgical Academy in St. Petersburg.

Chronology

1833 Born 12 November, St. Petersburg
1841 First lessons on the flute
1842 Composes Hélène-Polka
1846 Shares music lessons with Mikhail Shchiglev
1847 Composes 'concerto' for flute and piano
1850 Enters Medico-Surgical Academy, St. Petersburg
1853 Forms group to perform string quintets
1855 Graduates in Medicine. Fantasy on a Russian Theme, for 2 violins and cello
1856 Appointed House Surgeon, 2nd Military Hospital
1857 Attends International Ophthalmic Congress, Brussels
1858 Awarded doctorate; studies medicinal properties of mineral waters; publishes paper on 'Action of Ethyl Chloride'.
1859 First meeting with Mussorgsky
1859-62 Scientific research in Heidelberg. Visits Holland, France and Italy
1862 Appointed Assistant Professor of Chemistry, Academy of Medicine. Meeting with Balakirev
1867 'Opera-farce' The Bogatyrs. Completes Symphony No.1
1868-9 Music critic, 'St. Petersburgski Vedemosti'
1869 Begins work on Prince Igor and Symphony No.2; Balakirev conducts first performance of Symphony No.1
1872 Co-founder School of Medicine for Women
1875-9 Quartet in A major
1877 Visits Liszt in Weimar

Borodin's reputation as a major composer rests on a remarkably small number of works, but they are of such originality and high quality that his place in the annals of Russian music is assured. And not only in Russian music, for his interest in oriental themes was taken up by other musicians in Europe and America, and his quartets encouraged later composers, such as Debussy and Ravel, to follow his example. His achievement is all the more remarkable when it is remembered that, as a 'Sunday composer', music had to take second place to his professional duties, and that many of his scores were amended, and in some cases completed, by fellow-members of the 'Mighty Handful'.

Of the three symphonies, the Third was left unfinished at the time of Borodin's death and was later orchestrated by Glazunov. Probably the most popular, with its abundance of attractive and accessible themes, is the Symphony No.2 in B minor. However, the equally tuneful Symphony No.1 in E is of greater technical interest because in the first movement the form of the music generates the theme – a procedure Sibelius

BELOW: *A religious procession in Kursk painted by another citizen of St. Petersburg, Ilya Repin (1844-1930), in around 1880 when* In the Steppes of Central Asia *was first performed.*

later followed to such telling effect in the first movement of his Second Symphony. The most important of Borodin's other orchestral works is *In the Steppes of Central Asia*, a tone poem in which the slow approach and passing of a Kurdish caravan is most effectively portrayed.

Borodin's surviving chamber pieces include two important string quartets, dating from 1878 and 1880, which are among the most popular in the entire repertoire. The opening movement of the first was inspired by a theme of Beethoven, but in other respects these quartets, with their many beautiful tunes and an almost orchestral use of the instruments, are as far removed from the Germanic tradition as possible.

Prince Igor, in a series of colourful tableaux, tells the story of the capture of Prince Igor and son Vladimir by the Polovtsian leader, Khan Konchak. He entertains his prisoners lavishly and calls on his slaves to perform the famous Polovtsian dances, which provide a barbaric and thrilling climax to the second act. While many of the effects are down to Rimsky-Korsakov and his brilliant orchestration, the flowing melodies and strange, exotic harmonies are Borodin's own. Unorthodox in form and unwieldy in length, it is yet an opera full of fire, splendour and passion, and stands as his greatest single masterpiece.   R.H.

ABOVE: *Vladimir Stasov (1824-1906), Russian nationalist, critic and music historian. This painting of him at his country house is also by Ilya Repin. Stasov was a firm supporter of the 'Mighty Handful'.*

1880 *Tone-poem* In the Steppes of Central Asia

1881 *Death of Mussorgsky inspires setting of Pushkin poem*

1881-7 *Quartet in D major*

1882-3 *Suffers heart attacks and cholera*

1886 *Begins Symphony No.3, left unfinished*

1887 *Dies 27 February, St. Petersburg*

1890 *First performance of* Prince Igor *in St. Petersburg*

JOHANNES Brahms

(b. Hamburg, 7 May 1833; d. Vienna, 3 April 1897)

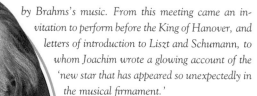

RIGHT: *Portrait of Johannes Brahms by Olga Miller zu Aichenholz painted in 1890. In that year he visited Italy, spent the summer at Ischl, and composed the G major String Quintet.*

BELOW: *'The Return of Dockyard Workers in Hamburg Harbour' painted by Carlos Grethe (1864-1913). Brahms was born in Hamburg, and in his youth used to play in dockside cafés.*

*J*ohannes Brahms learned the rudiments of music from his father, Johann Jakob Brahms, who played the double-bass. An early plan to train his son as an orchestral player was abandoned when it was found that the young musician had a natural gift for the piano. Under the tuition first of Otto Cossel, who wisely opposed the idea that he should be taken on tour as a child prodigy, and then of Eduard Marxsen (1806-1887), he made rapid progress and started to improvise his own compositions when he was twelve years old.

A year later he was sent out to earn money by playing the piano late at night in Hamburg's dockside taverns and brothels. After an unsuccessful attempt to branch out on a concert career, he was obliged to return to these 'places of humble entertainment' to earn a meagre living and keep up his music studies. It was an experience that scarred him for life.

In 1851, he met Eduard Reményi, a colourful young violinist of Hungarian extraction, whose national music and the Zigeuner (gypsy) style fascinated Brahms. Reményi took him to see the famous violinist Joseph Joachim, who was absolutely spellbound

by Brahms's music. From this meeting came an invitation to perform before the King of Hanover, and letters of introduction to Liszt and Schumann, to whom Joachim wrote a glowing account of the 'new star that has appeared so unexpectedly in the musical firmament.'

The encounter with Liszt at Weimar was not a success: his music failed to attract Brahms, who was ill-at-ease in the Liszt household. After this setback he hesitated before following up the introduction to Robert and Clara Schumann. But when he did so, in September 1853, he found a welcome that was warm, friendly and sincere. Schumann was overwhelmed by his music, referring to Brahms as 'the young eagle' and hailing him as a genius in an article published in the 'Neue Zeitschrift für Musik'. He sent the young man with recommendations to Leipzig, where he found two publishers and met Hector Berlioz.

The following year Schumann suffered a nervous collapse and tried to commit suicide. Brahms rushed to Düsseldorf to be by Clara's side: his motives were those of a loyal friend, but before long he fell in love with her. With seven children to care for, and an international concert career to pursue, she greatly valued Brahms's support but kept him at a proper distance. When Robert died in 1856 she and Brahms gently parted: they remained the best of friends, but he seems to have determined never to reveal his personal feelings so openly again.

In 1862 he moved to Vienna, where he lived the rest of his life as a bachelor, increasingly set in bachelor ways. He lived simply, in modest lodgings; he enjoyed his food, but was not extravagant; his clothes were out of fashion and often untidy, but always scrupulously clean; his uncouth manner kept the world at bay, apart from a handful of close and trusted friends.

He came bitterly to regret a blunder made in 1860, when he allowed his name to appear on a 'manifesto' deploring 'neo-German' music theories. Liszt and Wagner were not named in person, but the attack was clearly aimed at them and their followers. In all other respects, his life was uneventful: it revolved around a routine of performances and concert tours, interrupted

BELOW: *Brahms at the age of 20, drawn by J. B. Laurens in Düsseldorf in 1853. At this time Brahms was described as 'youthful, almost boyish looking, a shy but friendly young Apollo'.*

from time to time by holidays in Italy or Switzerland, and – of course – composition and constant revision.

'Go over it again and again until there's not a bar you can improve on' Brahms told his students. His creative power remained undimmed almost to the end, which came not long after he had attended the funeral of Clara Schumann in 1896. He was by then already suffering from cancer, from which he died a few months later at the age of sixty-four.

Tchaikovsky described Brahms as a 'giftless bastard'. Hugo Wolf said that one cymbal clash of Bruckner was worth all four symphonies with the Serenades thrown in. In our own time, Benjamin Britten claimed that he played through 'the whole of Brahms' at intervals to see whether his music was as bad as he thought, only to discover that it was much worse. And yet to most music-lovers, he stands as the last of the great classical composers. Bach – Beethoven – Brahms: his name completes the triad, and there has been no one quite of his stature since. What is it about this enigmatic genius that provokes such opposing views?

It took him twenty years or more to bring his first symphony to the concert platform: therein lies the central clue to his musical personality. He had a strict musical upbringing, and although he fell under Schumann's spell while he was still

Chronology

young and rather immature, he had the wit to see that the new, Romantic style of composition was not for him. With considerable artistic courage he chose conventional forms; he venerated the classical masters, and knew that only by perfecting his own technique would he be able to follow in their footsteps. In a revealing remark to the conductor Hermann Levi, he said: 'You've no conception of what it's like to hear a giant's footsteps marching behind you.'

And so, he was 43 years of age when his Symphony No.1 in C minor was first heard at Karlsruhe on 4 November 1876. Other performances soon followed, and the work was hailed as 'Beethoven's Tenth'. The powerful Viennese critic Hanslick declared that the symphony 'displays an energy of will, a logic of musical thought, a greatness of structural power and a mastery of technique such as are possessed of no other living composer.' These words were written when Liszt, Wagner, Tchaikovsky, Verdi, Dvořák – to name just a few – were at the height of their powers.

Brahms was determined, as always, to create powerful absolute music of great intrinsic beauty. He was also aware that much was expected of him, for his reputation had already been firmly established by works such as the two serenades which, in some ways, were forerunners of the symphonies, and the *St. Anthony Variations* – surely the finest set of orchestral variations ever written. By 1876 he had also produced a magnificent piano concerto, two volumes of *Hungarian Dances*, the delightful *Liebeslieder* Waltzes and

ABOVE: *Clara Schumann (née Wieck) (1819-96). She married Robert Schumann in 1840, the year of this portrait. She became a great advocate of Brahms, who was a lifelong friend and admirer.*

the *Alto Rhapsody*, not to mention the *German Requiem*, that remarkable Protestant statement on the mysteries of death, prompted by the death of his mother in 1865.

Nor was this all, because by the time Brahms had completed his first symphony he was already regarded as an outstanding contributor to mid-19th century chamber music. Two luxuriant string sextets, two piano quartets, exemplifying the critical balance between Brahms's romantic impulse and his austere classical training, and a magnificent piano quintet, were among the works that became a cult in later decades and still hold a well-deserved place in the repertoire of today.

As if this were not enough, by 1867 there was already a vast catalogue of piano music, in which his genius for variation is again clearly demonstrated, and many songs which are, perhaps, more romantic in feeling than his other works. The only thing missing was opera – a form that held no attraction for him and which he made no attempt to master, unlike most of his contemporaries.

What followed the First Symphony was no less remarkable. A second piano concerto, a huge, high-spirited,

LEFT: *A watercolour of
Brahms's apartment in
Vienna where he lived from
1869 to the end of his life.
Note Beethoven's bust
above the piano.*

BELOW: *Part of the score of
the German Requiem
which Brahms finished
writing in Baden-Baden in
1866. It had a cool
reception when it was first
performed in Vienna in
December 1867.*

four-movement work which some critics and performers say is the greatest of its kind; a violin concerto that is a worthy successor to Beethoven's; the *Academic Festival* and *Tragic* overtures; three more symphonies, each of which is a near-perfect model of symphonic structure, the *Four Serious Songs*, and a late flowering of instrumental and chamber music including a sublime clarinet trio and clarinet quintet.

The genius of Brahms presents so many different facets that it is not easy to encompass his life's work in a single sentence. But perhaps the description of him holding the balance between Beethoven, the classical composer turned Romantic, and Schumann, the Romantic who tried in vain to be classical, comes closest to the truth. Brahms could not have laid a more powerful or convincing tribute at the feet of his classical masters, or have provided a richer legacy for generations to come. And with the modern century only three years ahead at the time of his death, who now will say that his fear of chaos in the pursuit of the new for its own sake was without foundation, to be dismissed as the reaction of a master musician who looked more to the past than to the future?

R.H.

BENJAMIN Britten

(b. Lowestoft, 22 November 1913; d. Aldeburgh, 4 December 1976)

RIGHT: *Benjamin Britten in 1960, aged 47, when A Midsummer Night's Dream was first performed in Aldeburgh.*

Chronology

1913 Born 22 November, Lowestoft

1921 Starts piano lessons with Ethel Astle

1927 Head boy at preparatory school. Begins lessons with Bridge

1930 Leaves school, enters Royal College of Music

1932 Sinfonietta for chamber orchestra

1933 A Boy was Born. Leaves RCM

1934 Simple Symphony for strings. Father dies. Visits Europe with his mother

1936 Our Hunting Fathers for voice and orchestra

1937 Mother dies. Friendship with Peter Pears begins. Variations on a Theme of Frank Bridge, performed Salzburg 27 August. Buys Old Mill, Snape, Suffolk

1938 Piano Concerto, performed at Promenade Concert 18 August

1939 Sails for Canada with Pears in May, later settles near New York. Violin Concerto; Les Illuminations

1940 Seven Sonnets of Michelangelo

1941 Paul Bunyan performed in New York 5 May. String Quartet No. 1

1942 Returns to UK with Pears. A Ceremony of Carols. Hymn to St. Cecilia.

1943 Serenade for tenor, horn and strings. Rejoice in the Lamb

1945 Peter Grimes première in London 7 June. Tour of German camps with Yehudi Menuhin. The Holy Sonnets of John Donne. String Quartet No. 2

RIGHT: *'Trench Warfare' portrayed by Otto Dix (1891-1969). Britten's War Requiem of 1962 addresses the horrors of the First World War.*

The son of a Suffolk dentist, Britten received his Christian name as his parents' youngest child. His mother was a singer who gave him music lessons when he was only five, and he immediately made his first attempts to compose. Later he received more formal lessons on the piano and viola, while continuing to produce new compositions including eleven piano sonatas by the age of thirteen. In 1927 he was introduced to the composer Frank Bridge, who took him as a pupil and remained his mentor for some years. On leaving school in 1930, he entered the Royal College of Music in London on a scholarship and John Ireland became his teacher, although he still sought advice from Bridge.

Britten left the RCM in 1933 and soon found a publisher (Boosey & Hawkes) and employment as a composer for the theatre and documentary films, often collaborating with the poet W. H. Auden, who became a friend and whose artistic views, left-wing politics and homosexual lifestyle influenced the young provincial. By 1937, his parents had died and he used a legacy to purchase a house in Suffolk, near the town of Aldeburgh where he later lived and founded the festival.

In 1939, Britten was sharing a London flat with the tenor Peter Pears, and they gave occasional recitals. They then travelled to Canada and North America, where Auden was now living, and after the outbreak of war remained in the US, where they gave concerts and Britten's compositions were performed – though unsuccessfully in the case of his operetta Paul Bunyan, written in collaboration with

Auden and produced in 1941 in New York. Britten was now increasingly homesick and in March 1942 he and Pears sailed for the UK. Several new works followed culminating in the opera Peter Grimes, which at its 7 June 1945 première in London's Sadler's Wells Theatre firmly established him as a major force in 20th-century British music.

The story of Britten's life thereafter is closely bound up with his music and a long series of works, from string quartets to operas, that appeared in the next three decades. He saw himself as a professional with a clear vocation and declared in 1964 that 'it is the composer's duty, as a member of society, to speak to or for his fellow human beings'. Though a lifelong pacifist and internationalist, he was also a practical man and became a joint founder of the English Opera Group, the Aldeburgh Festival, the Britten-Pears School at Snape and the Snape Maltings concert hall. He was also an excellent pianist and conductor, as his many recordings show.

He was a keen sportsman until middle age, tennis and swimming being among his favourite relaxations, and enjoyed holidays that were sometimes combined with concert tours. But a heart condition eventually forced him to undergo surgery in May 1973. The operation was a partial failure and caused a slight stroke that left him handicapped, although a year later he began once again to compose. Towards the end of 1976 his condition seriously deteriorated, Peter Pears was summoned back from a Canadian tour, and Britten died in the arms of the singer with whom he had shared his life and for whom he created much of his music.

Britten's music quickly attained a popularity which was denied to almost every other serious composer of his generation and has, if anything, increased since his death. Several of his operas are firmly established in the international repertoire, and helped to bring about a renaissance of British opera generally. Yet their subject-matter is unorthodox and more than once portrays a doomed outsider figure such as the stubborn, violent fisherman Peter Grimes whose apprentices die, or the writer Aschenbach in Death in Venice with his tormenting unexpressed love for a young boy. Humphrey Carpenter's biography (1992) makes much of the composer's paedophilia, although there is no evidence that it was ever physically expressed, and suggests that his was a guilt-ridden and frustrated personality that was reflected in the subject-matter of these two operas – The Turn of the Screw is another – which uneasily portray the relationship between a boy and a man.

Whatever the truth of this, we may also choose to think of Britten more positively as what he clearly tried to be, and remember the Times' leading article after his death which was headed 'A Dedicated Life'. Above all, he was an integrator, and while his music owes much to British tradition (though to Purcell and folk song rather than Elgar or Vaughan Williams), he also learned from Viennese composers from Schubert to Berg, and from the operas of Verdi with their strong theatricality. His language was so flexible that he could incorporate familiar hymns into his Saint Nicolas and Noye's Fludde and create works such as these for children to sing and play. As a lifelong performer, he never lost touch with audiences in the way that some contemporary composers have done, was

LEFT: *Saint Cecilia by Carlo Saraceni (c. 1585-1620). The patron saint of music has had many musical tributes, among them Britten's* Hymn to St. Cecilia. *Britten himself was born on St. Cecilia's Day.*

never ashamed to write a tune, and went on record as saying that it was 'insulting to address anyone in a language which they do not understand'.

Britten admitted to a special fondness for the human voice, firstly because of his memories of his mother's singing and then because he shared his life with a singer, but he was not exclusively a vocal composer. However, even in such instrumental pieces as the *Sinfonia da Requiem, Cello Symphony* and the three string quartets, he is never abstract, but characteristically vivid and dramatic. His childhood apprenticeship and lessons with Bridge gave him an early mastery of musical form, and the exceptional ear that made him such a fine pianist and conductor also helped him to become a master of instrumentation, so that his scores are invariably clear and effective. Indeed, one of his most popular works is his *Young Person's Guide to the Orchestra* – a piece written to teach children about orchestral sound.

Placed beside Schoenberg or Stravinsky, Britten seems a conservative composer, and given his wish to communicate it could hardly be otherwise. Some think that his choral *War Requiem*, for all its moral message, is too derivative to be a true masterpiece. Britten knew that this was said, and that future historians would also judge his importance. But he declared, 'I believe in roots, in associations, in backgrounds . . . I want my music to be of use to people, to please them, to enhance their lives . . . I do not write for posterity'.   C.H.

MAX Bruch

(b. Cologne, 6 January 1838; d. Friedenau, 20 October 1920)

Like many German children of his generation, Bruch received his first practical music lessons from his mother, who in his case was a singing teacher of some standing, and, following further lessons in theory, he was already composing orchestral and chamber music by the age of eleven and a symphony at fourteen. Though he continued with piano lessons, his future evidently lay in composition and his chief teacher was now Ferdinand Hiller (1811-85), the founder of the Cologne Conservatory and a pianist, composer and conductor.

At the age of twenty, Bruch established himself as a teacher in his native city and also saw the production there of his first opera, a one-act Singspiel on a early comedy by Goethe called Scherz, List und Rache (Jest, Cunning and Revenge). Five years after this he produced a more ambitious romantic opera in three acts called Die Loreley, and a decade later still he turned to Shakespeare's The Winter's Tale for the libretto of his third opera, Hermione (Berlin, 1872). During this time, while still a youngish man, he also composed the Violin Concerto in G minor, Op.26 (1866, revised 1868), which was destined to become his most lastingly popular work, and much else including two of his three symphonies (the last dates from 1887), and much other instrumental and choral music. In the latter category, he had a major success with his choral cantata Frithjof (1864), a work for soprano, baritone, male chorus and orchestra that was inspired by a Nordic legend: he conducted performances of it as far afield as Brussels and Paris, and composed other choral works in the same stirring mould.

Thereafter, Bruch was widely respected, and from 1873 he as able to devote himself principally to composition. But he also pursued a conducting career that took him to many musical centres including Liverpool in the North of England, where he directed the Philharmonic Society from 1880-83 and also married. Though his authoritarian methods made his work in Liverpool less than wholly successful, he remained respected by British musicians and ten years later Cambridge University awarded him an honorary doctorate. On leaving Liverpool, he went on to a similar post at Breslau and stayed there until 1890. In the following year, Germany's recognition of his importance was marked by his appointment as a senior professor of composition at the Berlin Hochschule, a post which he held until his retirement in 1910 at the age of seventy-two. He also maintained his links with Britain, and conducted the Scottish Orchestra (the future Scottish National Orchestra) from 1898-1900.

Although Bruch gained an international reputation, it soon became clear that for all his early gifts he was no Mozart, nor even a second Mendelssohn, although he was closer to the latter in the nature of his talent. His career has been described as leading to anti-climax, and even during his lifetime the public pronounced something of the same verdict in that none of his symphonies, operas or choral works gained a place in the repertoire and it is only the first of his three violin concertos that has survived as a regular concert piece. Living on until the age of eighty-two, he felt some bitterness as his work received only patchy appreciation, and doggedly continued, in the age of Stravinsky and Schoenberg, to compose music that would have been readily understood by Mendelssohn.

RIGHT: This portrait shows Bruch in 1905 when he was Professor of Composition at the Hochschule in Berlin, and aged 67.

BELOW: The Singakademie in Berlin, drawn by K. F. Schinkel in 1821. Bruch worked here in 1871 while he was composing the opera Hermione.

In many ways Bruch was an archetypal Kapellmeister figure of German music, a fine working musician of the second rank, and in considering his music we may remember a remark made about Saint-Saëns, the French composer who was his contemporary (1835-1921) and in many ways his counterpart: 'He was the greatest composer who ever lived who wasn't a genius'. In other words, Bruch's music has everything except the vital spark of individuality and personal depth which marks out the great composers and even lesser ones such as Delius and Satie who were, from some standpoints at least, technically less proficient but had something more special to say.

Yet his best music has real beauty and staying power, and when one listens to his First Violin Concerto (and not least its tender central Adagio in E flat major) it is impossible not to be captivated by its warmth and lyricism as well as the idiomatic writing for the violin. Hearing the eighteen-year-old Richard Strauss's Violin Concerto, completed in 1882, one feels certain that Bruch's First Concerto was his principal model, a compliment from a still finer musician of the next generation. There are also passages in Sibelius's Violin Concerto (1903, revised 1905) which recall Bruch more than any other master, although it would be idle to deny that both Strauss and Sibelius, as well as Bruch himself, also learned from the concertos of Beethoven and Mendelssohn. Another work for violin and orchestra, his *Scottish Fantasy* (1880), reminds us that he felt affinities with folk music: he was proud that his colourful work used real local melodies that he had learned

in Britain. Another eloquent piece, this time based on Hebrew melodies (although he was not himself Jewish), is *Kol Nidrei*, for cello and orchestra (1881).

Yet for all the romantic warmth of Bruch's best music, he never seriously questioned the classical symphonic forms that had served composers from Haydn onwards. During a turbulent era that saw the so-called 'new German school' of Liszt and Wagner apparently casting aside such forms and ideals, Bruch prided himself on remaining loyal to the conservative school of German music and as a result he saw himself become unfashionable. The sacred and secular choral works which constitute a large part of his output, and often won popularity, also fell by the wayside as the German tradition of choral singing itself steadily declined. So did his solo songs, as fewer people sang Lieder in the home in the way that he had known in his boyhood. In all these things, he shows some parallel with his contemporary Brahms. Living on into the 20th century, he was inevitably shocked by the still more radical new music that seemed to sweep aside many of his musical ideals, and the death of his son in the First World War was a major blow from which he never fully recovered.

In every respect, Bruch must be classed as a traditionalist, but he never became a mere academic. Vaughan Williams, who went to Berlin in 1897 to study with him, always remembered his maxim that 'music is written for the ear to enjoy, not the eye', and perhaps through this British pupil he did help to sow some seeds of 20th-century music. C.H.

Chronology

1838 *Max Karl August Bruch born 6 January, son of a civil servant and a singer*
1847 *Compositions shown to Hiller, who accepts him as pupil*
1852 *Wins Frankfurt Mozart Prize with a string quartet. Studies with Hiller and (for piano) Reinecke*
1858 *Teaching in Cologne. Scherz, List und Rache produced there, January*
1861-2 *Travels to various German cities and Vienna*
1862 *Die Loreley performed at Mannheim: living in that city*
1864 *Frithjof given at Breslau*
1865-7 *Music Director at Koblenz. First version of Violin Concerto No.1*
1867 *Moves to Sonderhausen to become court Kapellmeister*
1868 *Joachim performs revised version of First Violin Concerto at Bremen, the composer conducting*
1870 *First and Second Symphonies performed, No.1 in Bremen and No.2 in Berlin*
1871 *Moves to Berlin and lives independently*
1872 *Hermione produced in Berlin. Odysseus, for voices and orchestra*
1873-8 *Living in Bonn*
1878 *Second Violin Concerto (in D minor) given in Berlin*
1880 *Scottish Fantasy given in Berlin. Moves to Liverpool*
1880-3 *At Liverpool, where he also marries*
1881 *Kol Nidrei, for cello and orchestra, given in Berlin*
1883 *Moves to Breslau to conduct the city orchestra*
1887 *Third Symphony (Op.51) given in Leipzig*
1890 *Relinquishes Breslau post*
1891 *Becomes Professor of Composition at Berlin Hochschule*
1910 *Retires from teaching post*
1919 *Death of his wife*
1920 *Dies at Friedenau, near Berlin, 20 October*

LEFT: 'Cologne on the River Rhine with the unfinished Cathedral' painted by Clarkson Stanfield (1793-1867) in 1826 – a romantic view of Bruch's place of birth.

ANTON
Bruckner (b. Ansfelden, nr. Linz, Austria, 4 September 1824; d. Vienna, 11 October 1896)

RIGHT: *Anton Bruckner, a portrait by Ferry Bératon (1860-1900) painted in 1889 when the composer was 65 and had recently completed his Eighth Symphony.*

Chronology

1824 Born in Ansfelden, near Linz

1835-6 First regular tuition on the organ

1837 Death of father; accepted into the choir at the monastery of St. Florian and lives there until 1840

1841 Appointed assistant teacher in Windhaag

1843-5 Teacher in Kronstorf; composes several sacred works

1845 Returns to St. Florian; appointed organist at the monastery in 1851

1849 Requiem Mass, first composition of note

1852 Settings of the Magnificat, Psalm 22 and Psalm 114

1854 Missa Solemnis first performed at St. Florian

*T*he personality of Anton Bruckner presents a paradox. On one hand, he was a man of unshakeable religious faith and convinced of his artistic destiny; on the other, subject to depression and to such self-doubt that he coveted all manner of testimonials to his skills as a musician and his proficiency as a teacher. Worse, he was susceptible to criticism and was all too ready to allow fellow musicians to 'correct' and 'improve' his scores whenever he himself was dismayed by an adverse critical reception.

The perception of Bruckner by many of his contemporaries was equally paradoxical. The composer responsible for some of the most sublime and visionary symphonic and choral music to have been written post-Beethoven was characterized as little more than a simple-minded peasant. The image hardly equates with someone who became one of the finest organists in Europe (and a remarkable improviser) and who emerged with distinction from every aspect of musical education he undertook.

He was also Austrian to the core. Bruckner's family had lived within the environs of Linz since at least the early years of the fifteenth century. His father was a keen amateur musician and his mother sang in the church choir in Ansfelden. At four, Anton Bruckner was playing hymn tunes on the violin; at ten, he was substituting for his father at the organ during church services.

By profession, his father was a schoolmaster and at seventeen, Bruckner followed him into teaching. Between 1845 and 1855, he spent eleven contented and formative years as organist of the monastery of St. Florian, before taking up a similar post at Linz

Cathedral. Although he had determined in his mid-twenties that composing was his goal, his genius was slow to blossom. His first major composition, a setting of the Requiem, appeared in 1849 and was followed by several other sacred choral works of not inconsiderable stature.

In 1854, Bruckner qualified as a high school teacher and, the same year, took and passed an organ examination in Vienna. The following year, he returned to Vienna to begin a course in counterpoint that was to last on-and-off for six years (how much he benefitted from it can be heard, for example, in the final movement of the Fifth Symphony). Back in Linz, he studied harmony, fugue, form and orchestration and, by 1862, was about as technically qualified a composer as it was possible to get. What really lit the creative touchpaper, however, was hearing Wagner's Tannhäuser. Bruckner had always been a devout Catholic; now he worshipped both God and Richard Wagner.

In Viennese musical circles, which were strongly pro-Brahms, this adulation of Wagner bordered on heresy. Critics such as the powerful Eduard Hanslick heaped abuse on Bruckner's music, particularly the Third Symphony dedicated to Wagner.

Though hurt by criticism, Bruckner was undeterred and entered his most productive phase as a composer. Between 1866 and 1896, came the nine symphonies which guaranteed his place among the immortals. Gradually, he also received the academic and critical recognition he sought, culminating in the award, in 1891, of an honorary doctorate in philosophy at the University of Vienna. The country bumpkin had finally been accepted.

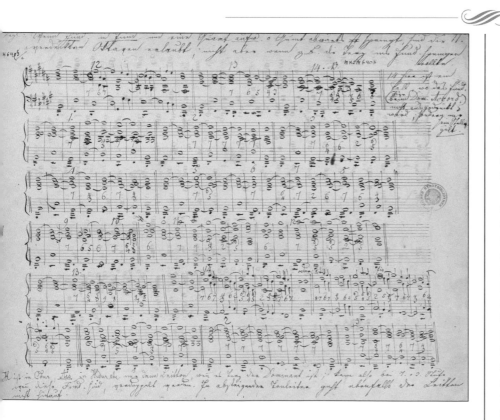

ABOVE: *Manuscript of the unfinished finale of Bruckner's Ninth Symphony which he began to write in 1893. While composing it, Bruckner was aware of his impending death.*

*A*nton Bruckner wrote religious music; not just in the accepted sense of masses and motets, but in his symphonies, each one of which suggests an affirmation of faith. Each contains moments of awesome grandeur and of spiritual ecstasy; there are slow movements whose inner communion evokes an air of radiant benediction. In describing the symphonies in this way, however, it should be emphasized that, though composed by a staunch Catholic, they transcend any single creed or dogma.

It has also been claimed that the symphonies are the orchestral equivalent of Wagner's music dramas and it is true that Wagnerian echoes abound. But the comparison underrates the uniqueness of Bruckner's idiom and the remarkable unity of both style and vision shared by the nine symphonies. Each makes liberal use of massive, chorale-like chords in the brass contrasted with passages of serene mystery. Titanic climaxes are set against spacious, long-breathed melodies of a beauty that disarms all structural criticisms. For this is not flawless music in the sense of, say, Mozart's. Bruckner relies heavily on repeated phrases and there are some jarring discontinuities. Only in the scherzos and in the central sections of the First and Third Symphonies does he depart from 2/2 or 4/4 time. With the exception of the Ninth Symphony (which Bruckner did not live to complete), the scherzos remain rooted in the realm of the rumbustious country dance, full of the whooping hunting horns that Bruckner must have been familiar with since childhood. Perhaps he intended them as an earthy contrast to the other-worldly experience created by the music of, for example, the slow movements of

ABOVE: 'Three Women in Church', a painting by
German artist Wilhelm Leibl (1844-1900) which
reflects Anton Bruckner's simple and devout
religious faith. Leibl identified closely with the
country folk of Bavaria.

the Fourth, Seventh, Eighth and Ninth Symphonies, or the
glorious finale of the Fifth.

All the symphonies are long – eighty minutes in the case of
the Eighth – and all require a commitment on the part of the
listener. It is, though, a commitment amply rewarded time
and again throughout this epic musical pilgrimage.

Bruckner's achievement as a symphonist has overshadowed the fact that he also composed much fine choral
music. There are three settings of the Mass, of which the
third, in F minor, stands comparison with any of the genre, as

does the Te Deum of 1884 which the dying Bruckner suggested could be played as the finale of the incomplete Ninth
Symphony. In addition to these, Bruckner composed several
magnificent psalm settings and a host of very beautiful
motets. His solitary masterpiece in the field of chamber
music is the String Quintet in F Major of 1879, along with an
intermezzo for String Quintet, a movement discarded from
the final version of the Quintet.

Few of Bruckner's early attempts at composition are
played these days, although the Three Orchestral Pieces and
the Overture in G minor merit greater exposure. What we
now know as the First Symphony was predated by two other
essays in the genre, of one of which Bruckner approved the
publication, listing it as Symphony No. 0. He was right to do
so. The work offers much more than curiosity value and
deserves to be heard as part of the whole, towering cycle of
Bruckner's symphonies.   P.H.

ABOVE: Frank Bridge, composer, teacher and inspirer of Benjamin Britten.

BELOW: 'The Painter's Studio' by Jan Vermeer (1632-75), a setting that brings Byrd's secular songs to mind.

FRANK **BRIDGE**

(b. Brighton, 26 February 1879; d. Eastbourne, 10 January 1941)

For a long while Bridge was remembered only as the teacher of Benjamin Britten, but the grateful pupil did a great deal to revive the music of his revered mentor, whose late style was a clear influence upon him. Bridge was a talented viola player, as well as a more than competent conductor and a composition pupil of Charles Stanford. His early music was in an impressionistic English style, with echoes of Debussy grafted on to the usual German romantic base, and a pleasant if not striking gift of melody. The piano quintet, the symphonic suite The Sea, and some nice but conventional songs (including 'Love went a-riding') are typical of this period. As with many composers, but more than most, Bridge was deeply affected by the 1914-18 War, and his music became tougher, bleaker and altogether more 'advanced' – but of course at the same time less melodic and popular. This was most evident in his Third and Fourth String Quartets, which are almost like Schoenberg in their freedom from conventional keys and harmony. The more accessible orchestral music is still very different from the pre-war style: such works as Enter Spring, Phantasm for piano and orchestra and Oration for cello and orchestra are sometimes as uncompromising as Bartók, while still recognizably in the English tradition.   P.L.

FERRUCCIO **BUSONI**

(b. Empoli, Tuscany, 1 April 1866; d. Berlin, 27 July 1924)

A musician of extraordinary range and contrasts, Busoni was born of an Italian father and a German mother. Something of an infant prodigy, he was to become an intellectual of music as well as a virtuoso pianist, a notable teacher, and a striking if enigmatic composer. His earlier works, including the violin and piano concertos (the latter a massive work with chorus), are almost Brahmsian, but with an austerity derived from Liszt's last piano works. By 1907, he was settled in Berlin as teacher and pianist, and had developed his theory of 'Junge Klassität' (young classicism). From then on his music changed, in the Elegies and other works for piano, and the tough if visionary and invigorating operas Arlecchino (1916) and the unfinished masterpiece Doktor Faust (based on the medieval legend, rather than Goethe). The music in this period leaves Brahms well behind. Late Liszt is overlaid with neo-classical elements, and some dabbling in modern devices. Melody – not always Busoni's strongest point – becomes refined, other-worldly, resembling no other music. This is not the music of conflict: rather the result of a lifetime's attempt to combine all the different forms of appeal music can have for the human mind.   P.L.

GEORGE **BUTTERWORTH**

(b. London 12 July 1885; d. Pozières, 5 August 1916)

Perhaps the most serious musical loss of the First World War was the death of Butterworth in the Battle of the Somme at the age of 31. He was educated at Eton and Oxford, where he was much involved in musical activities; after some abortive attempts at journalism and teaching, he belatedly enrolled at the Royal College in 1910, and almost immediately began to produce music in his mature style. Two groups of Housman songs, A Shropshire Lad and Bredon Hill, together with the short Henley cycle, Love Blows as the Wind Blows, showed in 1911-12 his sensitive response to words, and the Housman settings have arguably never been excelled. In 1913 came the orchestral rhapsody based upon the first Housman set, and in 1914 the folk-song-inspired The Banks of Green Willow. These were in the pastoral tradition being developed at the time by Vaughan Williams, but with a personal delicacy of style that was Butterworth's own. With the outbreak of war he enlisted, and was killed in 1916. It is impossible to say what he might have achieved had he lived. English composers are often late developers, but his slim oeuvre, however distinguished, is a limited base from which to make predictions. It can be said at least that he would have been a valuable addition to English music if not a great one.   P.L

WILLIAM **BYRD**

(b. probably in Lincoln, 1543; d. Stondon Massey, Essex, 4 July 1623)

There are comparatively few facts on which to build a biography of Byrd, but fortunately much of his music survives and holds an honoured place in the history of the Elizabethan and Jacobean ages. We know that in 1563 he was organist at Lincoln Cathedral, and that nine years later he and his mentor Thomas Tallis were joint organists at the Chapel Royal. Together they produced a collection of Cantiones Sacrae (Sacred Songs), and Byrd on his own wrote a series of liturgical works, madrigals and songs that make excellent use of counterpoint and a flowing

melodic line. *Outstanding are the three masses and Great Service, but he also wrote original and vivid works for small instrumental groups and for keyboard. Byrd spent the last thirty years of his long life in Essex, apparently unswerving in his allegiance to Catholicism. It seems probable that his reputation as a great musician protected him from the more obvious discomforts of those troubled times.* P.J.

JOSEPH **CANTELOUBE (DE CALERET)**

(b. Annonay, 21 October 1879; d. Gridny, 4 November 1957)

Canteloube came from an old family in the Auvergne, a province of south central France known for its formerly volcanic mountains, forests, vineyards and rich agriculture. From 1901 he studied with Vincent d'Indy at the Schola Cantorum in Paris, but despite this fairly strict academic training he soon came to see himself as a musical spokesman for the music of his native region. One of his two operas, Le Mas (Paris, 1929), has as its title an old Provençal word for a country farmhouse, while the other, Vercingétorix (Paris, 1933), tells of the young Gaulish leader of the 1st century BC, today seen as a pioneer of Gaulish unity, who bravely led an army against Roman invaders but was finally defeated, taken to Rome and executed. Canteloube also edited an anthology of French folksongs (1944) and made several choral arrangements of folk material. However, his most popular music is to be found in the arrangements with orchestra that he made of the songs of his Auvergne region; these Chants d'Auvergne, written between 1923 and 1930, come in four volumes and are skilfully arranged to display colourful dialect words and fine local melodies in a deft and affectionate setting. C.H.

ELLIOTT **CARTER**

(b. New York, 11 December 1908)

Carter was an exceptionally precocious child, and rapidly gained honours in languages, philosophy, mathematics and music. Although his background was wealthy and conservative, he felt attracted to the avant-garde in politics and music, and after studies in Harvard, made his way to Paris to seek guidance from Nadia Boulanger (1887-1979). At the outbreak of war, Carter returned to the USA and composed his first orchestral works, including the ballet The Minotaur (1947). Gradually his style became more severe and neo-classical, with few concessions to lyricism: the four string quartets (1951-1986), and orchestral works such as the Double Concerto (1961) and the Symphony of Three Orchestras (1976) are rightly admired by musicians, but they seem forbidding to unadventurous audiences. However, the concertos written in later life are less angular and dense. Carter's intellectual grasp and unflinching pursuit of the unvarnished truth have won him the highest academic honours, and he is revered by his colleagues as one of America's finest composers. P.J.

MARIO **CASTELNUOVO-TEDESCO**

(b. Florence, 3 April 1895; d. Los Angeles, 17 March 1968)

A leading figure in 'modern' Italian music between the wars, Castelnuovo-Tedesco seems today a fairly mildly flavoured romantic composer. He is best known for his Guitar Concerto and the guitar suite Platero and I, popularized by Segovia, but in fact he composed in a wide variety of forms. His early career was closely bound up with the more progressive Italian music of the day. A pupil of Ildebrando Pizzetti (1880-1968), he became an associate of Alfredo Casella (1883-1947), though his music was never as 'advanced'. He wrote ballets, concertos (three for violin, two for piano and one for guitar), chamber music, and a complete set of 33 Shakespeare songs, as well as two late Shakespearean operas – All's Well that Ends Well (1959) and The Merchant of Venice (1961). Of all this music, the smaller scale songs and piano pieces are considered to be the most successful, despite the popularity of the Guitar Concerto. Castelnuovo-Tedesco's career was abruptly cut short by the rise of Mussolini, which compelled the Jewish composer to start a new life in California, where he was to remain until his death. He wrote a certain amount of film music, some anonymously, but did not significantly add to his reputation. P.L.

FRÉDÉRIC *Chopin* (b. Zelazowa Wola, 1 March 1810; d. Paris, 17 October 1849)

RIGHT: *Frédéric Chopin, a portrait by Eugène Delacroix (1798-1863). Chopin liked Delacroix, and the two men became close friends.*

ABOVE: *Portrait of the French novelist George Sand (1804-76) painted by Auguste Charpentier (1813-80) in 1839, when she was living in Majorca with Chopin.*

*T*he patriotic Polish composer/pianist of popular imagination was, in fact, half-French, and left Poland at the age of 20, never to return. He composed most of his music in France, where he established his legendary reputation as a virtuoso performer by no more than 30 public recitals. Many more performances were given in the salons of French aristocrats. 'I have entered into the best society,' he wrote home from Paris. 'At once you have more talent if you have been heard at the Austrian and English embassies.'

The second of four children of French-born Nicholas Chopin by his Polish wife Justina, Frédéric was a child prodigy. His Polonaise in G was published in 1817 and a year later, at the age of 8, his brilliant piano technique captivated Warsaw's society audiences. Wisely, his father buttressed this natural talent with a sound education – at the Warsaw Lyceum for general studies, and the Warsaw Conservatoire for composition.

By 1830, when he first performed his Fantasia on Polish Airs (Op. 13), Chopin was already being hailed as Poland's national composer. But virtuoso performers such as Paganini and Rummel showed him what could be achieved on the international scene, and in 1829 Chopin left Warsaw for Vienna. Always on the qui vive for something new, his audiences responded warmly to the Polish themes he loved, and which became so characteristic of his music.

From Vienna he went to Paris, where he was lionized and be-came the admired friend of leaders of the Romantic movement such as Berlioz, Bellini, Liszt and Meyerbeer. From his recitals, and by giving lessons to the talented (and pretty) daughters of wealthy families, he made enough money to live in style. After several unhappy love affairs he met the woman novelist George Sand in 1837. By now he was already suffering from tuberculosis, the disease that was to carry him off at a comparatively early age. A warm climate was recommended, and the lovers took up residence in Majorca, where he completed the 24 Preludes.

Winter in Majorca also proved disagreeable, so the couple returned to the comforts of Paris and of George Sand's country home at Nohant. For ten years Chopin lived in elegant seclusion, composing and teaching. But the great romance faded into friendship, and when the Revolution came in 1848 Chopin fled to England. Though desperately ill, he had to give public recitals to earn a living. In 1849 he returned to Paris, where he died on 17 October.

BELOW: *'Almond trees in blossom in Majorca', an oil-painting by the Spanish painter and writer Santiago Rusiñol (1861-1931). This was once a familiar scene for the composer who lived there in a monastery at Valdemosa.*

One of the best introductions to Chopin is to be found in the various arrangements of his music for the ballet *Les Sylphides*, of which probably the best known is that by Roy Douglas, written in 1936. And therein lies an irony, for the orchestration is of a quality quite beyond the grasp of Chopin himself, whose early piano concertos are performed today for their pianistic value, not for their orchestral worth.

His contemporaries regarded Chopin as an outstanding performer as well as a highly original and gifted composer. He had the good fortune to live at a time when the pianoforte itself was being steadily improved. As each technical development came along he took full advantage of it in his unique, brilliant style of pianism and in his own compositions. In this way, performance and composing technique went forward hand-in-hand.

Mendelssohn described him as a 'truly perfect virtuoso', and when Schumann first heard the 'Là ci darem' Variations he uttered the famous cry, 'Hats off gentlemen, a genius!'. From his late teens Chopin wisely concentrated all his energies and abilities on what he did best — writing for the piano and playing to fashionable audiences.

Two major influences are at work in his music. Firstly, there is the Italian *bel canto* tradition reflected in many of his melodies (aptly described as 'singing on the piano'), and the

ABOVE: *The spirit of Chopin — one of the greatest of composers of piano music – is conjured up by this painting by the English artist J.M.W. Turner (1775-1851) – 'Music Party', now in the Tate Gallery.*

vigorous rhythms of the folk music of Poland. It is true that Chopin's mazurkas and polonaises were never meant to be danced to, any more than were his waltzes, more accurately described as 'waltz-poems'. But in taking such dance forms as the frame on which to hang his audacious and glittering inventions, he followed a tradition which dates back to Bach and beyond.

With so many works to choose from it is difficult to draw up a short list for recommended listening. But the two sets of 12 Etudes (the first of which was dedicated to Liszt), and the 24 Preludes, together with the four Ballades he composed towards the end of his short life, lie at the very heart of Chopin's genius. As a man, he may not have been as passionate, as revolutionary or even as romantic as Hollywood would have us believe. But all these qualities, and more, are to be found in his music . . . the richest and most influential legacy to be left to the piano repertoire by any one composer in the history of music. R.H.

AARON
Copland
(b. New York, 14 November 1900; d. New York, 2 December 1990)

Like George Gershwin, who was born two years before him, Aaron Copland was Brooklyn-born and of Russian-Jewish stock; the original of his name was Kaplan, and his shopkeeper father became the president of Brooklyn's oldest synagogue. The fifth child of a large family, he came to music early and soon became a keen concertgoer, also attending ballet performances and exploring world literature. His serious musical studies began when he was seventeen and were chiefly with Rubin Goldmark (1872-1936) (who also taught Gershwin), but it was not long before he chafed under his classically oriented guidance, and when he had saved enough money he set off at the age of twenty for Paris, where he spent four formative years.

In France, his teacher was Nadia Boulanger (1887-1979), who rigorously observed classical principles yet revered some new music, notably Stravinsky's, and this mentor suited him so well that he persuaded other young Americans, such as Virgil Thomson and Walter Piston, to follow in his footsteps. Encouraged by Boulanger, he used his European years to advantage and travelled widely in search of new musical experiences. He returned to the US in 1924 as a convinced modernist, and soon began to get performances, although the conductor at the first performance of his Organ Symphony in January 1925 told his audience, 'If a young man at twenty-three can write a symphony like that, in five years' time he'll be ready to commit murder!'.

RIGHT: Aaron Copland, the pre-eminent 20th-century American composer, portrayed in 1958 during the period when his writing was particularly experimental.

BELOW: A detail from the painting 'Pop and the Boys' (1963) by T. H. Benton (1889-1975) – a graphic reflection of Copland's more homely, hoe-down sort of music.

Copland saw himself not just as a composer but also as a teacher and pioneer. Along with obtaining performances of his own music, he joined a League of Composers and wrote for its journal 'Modern Music', and his ability as a clear-thinking writer was to result over the years in four books between 1939 and 1960, 'What to listen for in music', 'Our New Music', 'Music and Imagination' and (a collection of essays) 'Copland on Music'. He showed a lifelong concern as to the relationship of a composer with society, arguing that industry and art must coexist, and aiming to 'make clear to our countrymen the value attached in all lands to the idea of the creative personality'. He was active in many musical and artistic bodies, finding sponsorship for concerts of new American music and helping to found the Yaddo Festival, the Arrow Music Press and the American Composers Alliance of which he was the president from 1937 to 1945. In the 1940s he twice toured Mexico as a cultural ambassador for the US government. He did some university teaching at Harvard, and his lectures there during 1951-2 were later published as 'Music and Imagination'.

Living as he did until the age of ninety, Copland latterly took little part in public musical life. But although his reputation fluctuated during the musical upheavals that took place in his latter years, he was firmly held in affection by his countrymen, and indeed worldwide. His many honours included the Presidential Medal of Freedom.

Copland once wrote that 'Contemporary music as an organized movement in the USA was born at the end of the First World War', and the British writer Colin Wilson has called him 'a romantic who felt that American music ought to express the essence of America'. Thus he was as much a nationalist as de Falla in Spain and Vaughan Williams in Britain, and for all his classical European training, he quickly saw jazz as a means by which he could form a style that was unmistakably American in the way that Stravinsky's was Russian. The blue notes and syncopations of his orchestral suite *Music for the Theatre* (1925) represent this side of his art, while later works such as his ballets *Billy the Kid*, *Rodeo* and *Appalachian Spring* were to show that other kinds of American folk music could be no less fruitful. The latter work in particular, with its use of the Shaker song 'Simple Gifts', radiates a freshness and rural piety which movingly affirms the deep-rooted values of the American pioneers. So, in a different way again, do his *Fanfare for the Common Man* and *Lincoln Portrait*: in the latter, for speaker and orchestra, he uses passages from the addresses and letters of the former president and melodies from his era. Though he called his orchestral piece *El salón México* 'tourist music', it brilliantly evokes another part of the American continent and has had countless performances following its première in Mexico City in 1937.

For listeners who know only *El salón México* and other popular pieces, Copland's style seems essentially tonal and, in its own quirky and personal way, tuneful. Yet he never lost interest in techniques and musical developments and certain works are tougher in idiom: these range from the chunky Piano Variations (1930) to the acerbic orchestral *Connotations* and *Inscape* (1962 and 1967). From about 1950 onwards, Copland followed Stravinsky's example and adopted some aspects of Schoenberg's serialism, calling it 'an angle of vision . . . not a style', and Leonard Bernstein, who conducted the premières of these two orchestral pieces of the 1960s, felt that in trying to catch up with fashion he had lost something of his spontaneity. But he still also wrote pieces suitable for ceremonial and a wider public, such as *Music for a Great City* (1964), of which he himself conducted the première in London, and always knew that something intended for intellectual listeners would not suit audiences of his ballet and film scores, of which he wrote several between 1930 and 1960.

Copland's music is usually easy to recognize. It frequently has great harmonic and rhythmic vitality, as well as wit, yet can also be dignified and spacious. He wrote sympathetically for voices as well as instruments, although vocal compositions are in a minority in his worklist and there are just two shortish operas, *The Second Hurricane* (1936, written for school performance) and *The Tender Land* (1954). As we come to recognize the independence and identity of the best American music composed in this century, he stands out as a central figure. He is both the successor of Charles Ives and the precursor of Leonard Bernstein and Elliott Carter, very different composers who both admired him. Bernstein said of him in a simple but tellingly eloquent phrase, 'He is the best we have'.

C.H.

LEFT: 'The Reconnaissance Patrol' by William Tyler Ranney (1813-57), an oil-painting of 1851 which portrays the American pioneering spirit that Copland also evokes in The Tender Land and other works.

FRANÇOIS
Couperin (b. Paris, 10 November 1668; d. Paris, 11 September 1733)

*L*ike J.S. Bach, François Couperin was born into a musical family, and his father, Charles Couperin (1638-79), was the organist at the Eglise St. Gervais in Paris, having succeeded to this post in 1661 following the death of his older brother Louis, an organist-composer of some distinction who had occupied it for eight years. This Couperin, Charles's son François, is often referred to as 'Couperin Le Grand' to distinguish him from other musicians in the family with the same Christian name, both before and after him, and to emphasize his pre-eminence in the dynasty.

Charles Couperin probably gave his son his first music lessons, but he died at the date of forty in 1679, when François was ten, leaving the boy as an only child in the care of his mother. His nearest male relative was his uncle and godfather François Couperin (ca 1631-1710), who (according to his nephew) was 'a great musician and a great drunk'; perhaps for this reason, his mother entrusted his musical education to a family friend, the organist Jacques Thomelin who held a court appointment as well as a church post. Such was his progress, and the regard in which his family was held, that the St. Gervais church council agreed that his mother should stay in the church organist's house and that he should inherit his father's post when he reached the age of eighteen.

Couperin married on 26 April 1689. His wife was Marie-Anne Ansault, a well connected person whose friends proved valuable as the young musician embarked on his career; in 1690 he obtained a licence to publish his music. The couple were to have four children, two girls and then two boys, in the period between 1690 and 1707.

When Thomelin died in 1693, Couperin took over his post of 'organiste du roi', and this court appointment, made by Louis XIV himself, doubled the salary he earned at St. Gervais. Since his duties at the Chapel Royal and Versailles were shared with three other organists, and in practice were limited to the first three months of each year, he also remained the organist of St. Gervais and indeed held that post for a further three decades until 1723. The court appointment opened up more than a generous salary and working conditions. He was also engaged to teach the harpsichord to the royal children and was given the resounding title of 'Maître de clavecin des enfants de France'. After only three years at court, he also acquired ennoblement and his own coat of arms, and could sign himself 'le Chevalier Couperin'.

Although not officially the chief court musician, Couperin seems to have been regarded as such from about 1700 and was considered to be without equal as a teacher of the harpsichord and organ. In 1713 he took out a further licence which thereafter covered the publication of his music, beginning with sets of harpsichord pieces and including three of his nine Leçons des ténèbres. He served the 'Sun King' Louis XIV until the monarch's death in 1715 following a reign of seven decades, and in 1717 was created 'Ordinaire de la chambre pour le clavecin' to the court of the boy Louis XV during the regency of Philip of Orléans. In 1716 he published a treatise on harpsichord playing called 'L'art de toucher le clavecin', and then revised it for a second edition in the following year. From about 1730 he suffered from ill health, but it is uncertain what illness this was. He gave up his court appointments, arranging for his daughter Marguerite-Antoinette to replace him, and died three years later.

RIGHT: François Couperin 'Le Grand', a portrait by an unknown contemporary artist which is thought to have been painted around 1695.

BELOW: 'Italian Commedia Players', a painting by Antoine Watteau (1684-1721) dating from 1720. It recalls that Couperin wrote a harpsichord piece entitled 'The Harlequin'; in many ways he and Watteau are artistic counterparts.

Couperin is a major figure of the baroque era and the nearest French equivalent to J.S. Bach, his near-contemporary, who knew and admired his harpsichord music and copied out some of it. It seems that he corresponded with Bach, but scholars will always regret that – as it seems – some of these letters were used as jampot covers and none survives. Indeed, no single Couperin letter remains and contemporary accounts of his personality are rare. But from the occasional prefaces that he wrote for his published works, we gain an impression of a practical man, and the description of his uncle François as 'a great drunk', already quoted above, suggests that he had a sense of humour. So do many of the titles of his harpsichord pieces, like *The Bees*, *The Eel*, *Delights*, *The Nightingale in Love* and, untranslatably, *Le tic-toc-choc*.

Although Couperin began life as an organist, he composed little organ music but instead wrote mostly for the harpsichord. Many of these pieces are short, although he grouped them into twenty-seven sets which he called *ordres* and roughly correspond to suites. He is unlike Bach in that his keyboard style is more rococo than baroque: prettiness rather than sober beauty is the norm and melodic lines are decorated with elaborate ornaments. In this sense, he is the musical counterpart of the great French painter Watteau, who was his younger contemporary and lovingly depicted idealized pastoral scenes with courtly figures engaged in gentle diversions. He shows a sharper wit in *Les folies françoises* in the 13th Ordre, with its depictions of virginity,

ABOVE: 'The Concert' by the Dutch artist Jan van Bijert (1603-71). These are the kind of musical forces that Couperin would have encountered in his early years as an aspiring composer.

modesty, hope, perseverance and so on, and the piece in the 11th Ordre that evokes a company of minstrels finally chased away by their own performing animals.

Most of Couperin's considerable output of vocal, chamber and harpsichord music was composed for the Versailles *Concerts du Dimanche*. Some of his chamber music shows his admiration for the Italian master Corelli, and he jokingly passed off an early trio sonata as Italian until it had been, as he wrote, 'devoured with eagerness' by a French audience. Later, however, his own kind of Gallic elegance is evident: principal works here include *Concerts royaux* and a suite called *Les nations*. His sacred music is more serious in character, but here too there is charm, although his *Leçons des ténèbres*, settings of the Lamentations of Jeremiah, begun in 1713 and written for performances in Holy Week, have a quiet melancholy suited to the final years of the Sun King whom he served. Along with Lully and Rameau, Couperin is the chief figure of French baroque music, and appreciated as such by those composers who have come after him. Ravel's last major piano work (1917) is a suite of six movements called *Le tombeau de Couperin* written in homage to his great predecessor. C.H.

ABOVE: *Emmanuel Chabrier, an undated photogravure portrait of the composer.*

ABOVE: *Luigi Cherubini, a coloured lithograph by Delpech made around 1832 when the composer was head of the Paris Conservatoire.*

RIGHT: *'Saint Cecilia' by Carlo Dolci (1616-86), the patron saint of music painted by a contemporary of Charpentier.*

EMMANUEL **CHABRIER**
(b. Ambert, 18 January 1841; d. Paris, 13 September 1894)

*C*habrier is an unusual figure – a composer of light-hearted enjoyable music who was much respected by more 'serious' musicians, and had a great influence upon them and their successors. A self-taught composer, he spent his life up to 1880 as a lawyer in the French Civil Service, and was regarded by many as a pure amateur. Unlike many amateurs, however, he had originality without lacking skill. An exuberant, pleasure-seeking man, he associated with artists in all fields as well as with contemporary musicians such as Fauré and Massenet. With the production of his lively and original operettas L'Etoile (1877) and Une Education manquée (1879), he decided to take up music seriously, and produced a series of sparkling, and in many ways forward-looking, orchestral and piano pieces such as España, Joyeuse marche and the Pièces pittoresques during the 1880s. His last completed opera, Le roi malgré lui (1887) was to have a great influence through its harmonic originality. Chabrier died prematurely at the age of only 53, but his reputation has grown with the years. Not only did he leave a legacy of perennially enjoyable, witty, colourful music, but he is now recognized as the inspiration behind much later French music – especially Ravel. *P.L.*

MARC-ANTOINE **CHARPENTIER**
(b. Paris, c. 1645-50; d. Paris, 24 February 1704)

*C*harpentier's early life is still little documented, but it is known that he trained in Rome, and his music always retained Italian characteristics. Ironically, his contemporary and all too successful rival, the Italian Lully, was at pains to develop an individually French style. Charpentier held numerous appointments with the aristocracy and at different churches, ending as head of music of the Sainte-Chapelle in Paris. He also collaborated with Molière, most notably on music for Le Malade imaginaire. What he was never able to do was break into the Court circle, where Lully held sway, and made sure Charpentier had very limited opportunities. This also led to his centuries-long obscurity, from which he has only recently been rescued. Charpentier wrote much, and in widely varying forms. His church career produced motets, masses and magnificats in quantity, while on the secular side he is best known for 10 operas, including Les Arts florissants (1686) and Médée (1693). His religious music is grand, highly ornamented, but also capable of 'popular simplicity', as in the Messe de minuit based on traditional carols. His secular music is light and graceful, with frequent wit and humour. *P.L.*

ERNEST **CHAUSSON**
(b. Paris, 20 January 1855; d. Limay, 10 June 1899)

*C*hausson was a reserved, fastidious man, and the high ideals he set himself made composition a painful activity, clouded by self-doubt. This may have sprung from his privileged childhood; his wealthy father had employed a private tutor who demanded the highest standards. After graduating in law, Chausson studied music – again privately with a high-minded teacher, César Franck. The orchestral writing of Chausson bears many signs of the influence of Franck, and also of Wagner whose operas intoxicated so many French musicians of the time. So we find in Chausson heavy chromatic harmonies and opulent orchestration redolent of Tristan; to underline the dependency, his only published opera Le Roi Arthus (1886-95) is on the theme of adulterous love in the Arthurian court. Yet despite being haunted by 'the red spectre of Wagner', Chausson achieved an individual beauty in his works. Violin soloists love his Poème (1896) as do mezzo-sopranos his Poème de l'amour et de la mer (1882); in each case the solo voice soars ecstatically over a swell of orchestral sound. There is also fine music in his Symphony and his handful of chamber works. Chausson was happily married with five children, and generously opened his lovely house to less fortunate friends, such as Debussy. It seems inappropriate that the life of this high-minded composer should have been cut short so suddenly. He lost control of his bicycle while riding downhill, and crashed into a wall, dying instantly. *P.J.*

LUIGI **CHERUBINI**
(b. Florence, 14 September 1760; d. Paris, 15 March 1842)

*T*he musical skills of the young Cherubini, as exhibited in several liturgical works, so impressed the Grand Duke of Tuscany that he paid for the young man to study in Venice. This was the first step in a career that seemed to win him influential patronage and senior posts as a matter of course. In 1784 he visited London and soon won the favours of the Royal Family, being granted the imposing title of Composer to His Majesty. Four years later, he decided to settle in Paris, and there he remained for the rest of his long life, esteemed not only as a composer of operas, such as Medea (1797) and Anacréon (1803), but as an increasingly influential administrator of the newly formed Paris Conservatoire. Here he guided the early careers of the rising generation of French composers, although the most talented of them, Hector Berlioz, regarded Cherubini as a pompous reactionary. Despite this alleged resistance to new ideas, Cherubini continued to write imposing works such as the Requiem in 1836, and must have gained satisfaction from the thought that he had survived the upheavals of the Revolutionary and Napoleonic years to become a respected authority under the restored monarchy, in effect the Grand Old Man of French musical life. *P.J.*

DOMENICO **CIMAROSA**

(b. Aversa, nr. Naples, 17 December 1749; d. Venice, 11 January 1801)

This much-travelled musician must have a claim to be among the most prolific composers in an amazingly prolific century. The complete list of his works would fill many pages: it includes a vast number of operas – perhaps eighty or more – and dozens of choral works, as well as many attractive piano sonatas. Cimarosa came from a poor family near Naples, where he was educated by monks; in recompense, his widowed mother washed the community's robes. Cimarosa's first opera, for the Naples carnival of 1772, was the start of a career of frenzied activity, with over forty operas appearing in ten years. His fame spread beyond Italy, and he spent four years in St. Petersburg at the invitation of Catherine the Great. On his return, he was appointed court musician in Vienna, where his most successful opera was presented in 1792, Il Matrimonio segreto. Cimarosa's final years were marred by unexpected troubles. In Naples, he was condemned for having supported Napoleonic republican ideals, and was imprisoned for four months when the old monarchy was restored. Travelling north to seek more friendly regimes, he was taken ill in Venice, and died there aged fifty-one, leaving a rich legacy of delightful music, still far too little known. P.J.

MUZIO **CLEMENTI**

(b. Rome, 23 January 1752; d. Evesham, 10 March 1832)

At the age of fourteen the young Clementi was brought to England, where his brilliant pianistic skills soon made him famous. Subsequently, he made his home in London, although his insatiable love of travel led him to most European musical centres, where he met such great figures as Mozart and Beethoven. Later, he set up his own London music firm which was the first to publish the latter's works in England, and which also built the new, stronger pianos needed to play them. In fact, Clementi was an indefatigable business man and a lively companion with a wide range of knowledge. He married twice in his later years, each time to a much younger English woman (the first died in childbirth). Finally, he retired to the Midlands where he died aged eighty. Clementi's musical output was largely confined to piano sonatas. Although they are bright and attractive, he longed to emulate Beethoven in writing powerful symphonies, and a recent complete edition of Clementi's orchestral works does include four reconstructed symphonies. But his claims to fame are more widely based: for popularizing the piano; teaching the modern technique of piano playing; helping to found the Philharmonic Society in London; and promoting the works of his great contemporaries. The decision to bury him in Westminster Abbey was well justified. P.J.

ARCANGELO **CORELLI**

(b. Fusignano, 17 February 1653; d. Rome, 8 January 1713)

Born a generation earlier than Bach, Handel and Vivaldi, the precociously gifted Corelli moved from his home near Milan to Bologna, then to Rome, where he soon became rich and famous as violinist and conductor. Apart from a tour of western European cities, he seems to have passed his life in the service of powerful ecclesiastical and royal patrons in Italy, revered as the master violinist of the age. In Rome, he was lodged in a cardinal's palace, and amassed a fine art collection; even his dying wish to be buried next to the great painter Raphael was respected. Corelli's compositions are easy to classify: four sets of trio sonatas, one set of solo violin sonatas, and one set of concerti grossi published posthumously as Opus 6 (this set contains the lovely Christmas Concerto). These works are unfailingly polished and satisfying, and deserve greater renown. Yet Corelli's reputation stretched far beyond composition. He made a major contribution to the development of violin playing, both through his own example and the apostolic work of his many pupils through the 18th century. Moreover, the establishment of the sonata and the concerto grosso – and so ultimately the modern concerto – as viable forms exerted a huge influence on the great composers who succeeded him. P.J.

ABOVE: Muzio Clementi, a miniature portrait by an unknown artist.

ABOVE: Arcangelo Corelli, a portrait of the master violinist by Jan Frans van Douven (1656-1727) completed in 1700.

CLAUDE Debussy

(b. St. Germain-en-Laye, 22 August 1862; d. Paris, 25 March 1918)

RIGHT: *Claude Debussy portrayed by his fellow student Marcel Baschet in Rome in 1884, the year Debussy won the Grand Prix de Rome with* L'Enfant prodigue.

Chronology

1862 *Born, St. Germain-en-Laye, near Paris, 22 August*

1871 *Receiving piano lessons from Mme Mauté de Fleurville*

1872 *Enters Marmontel's piano class at Paris Conservatoire*

1877 *First compositions date from around this time*

1878-9 *Piano studies become less fruitful, enters harmony class*

1880 *Wins prize for harmony. Summer travels with Mme von Meck and her children. Enters Guiraud's composition class*

1882 *Mme Vasnier performs one of his songs at a Paris concert, 12 May*

1884 *Wins Prix de Rome with 'lyric scene'* L'Enfant prodigue

1885 *In Rome from January, but returns twice to Paris. Meets Liszt*

1886 *Reads much literature from Shakespeare to Verlaine, studies Wagner's* Tristan und Isolde

1887 *Symphonic suite* Printemps *criticized by Academy in Paris. Returns to Paris, February*

1888 *Visits Bayreuth to hear* Parsifal *and* Die Meistersinger. *Deux arabesques for piano; publishes some songs*

1889 *Becomes member of Société Nationale de Musique. Petite Suite for piano duet*

*B*orn above his father's china shop, Debussy grew up in humble circumstances: both his parents worked and in 1871 his father (whom he later called 'an old layabout') was sent to prison for a political offence. But he had wealthier god-parents who recognized his musical gift and when he was nine he began piano studies with Madame Mauté, a disciple of Chopin. A year later he entered the Paris Conservatoire, but although he showed some promise as a virtuoso, gradually his lack of progress disappointed his teacher Antoine Marmontel.

From around the age of fifteen Debussy had been composing songs and short instrumental pieces, and in the summer of 1880 he was engaged as a pianist and companion by Tchaikovsky's wealthy patroness Nadezhda von Meck, writing a Piano Trio and other music at this time; she showed some of his work to Tchaikovsky, who criticized the young composer's sense of form. In December 1880 he enrolled in the composition class of Ernest Guiraud (1837-92) at the Conservatoire, and such was his progress that four years later he won the prestigious Prix de Rome.

This award entitled him to a period of residence in Rome during which he was expected to write new works and submit them to the French Académie des Beaux Arts. But although he met Liszt, who played to him and introduced him to the beauties of sacred music by Palestrina and Roland de Lassus (1532-94), he was unhappy during this sojourn at the Villa Medici (1885-87) and irked by his fellow students and the restrictions of student life. He also disliked being separated from a woman whom he loved (the first of several in his life): she was Blanche Vasnier, a singer who had already performed his music. Furthermore, the French Academy criticized his orchestral suite Printemps (1887) for its 'vague impressionism'.

In that year he returned to his parents' house in Paris. During 1888-9 he twice visited Bayreuth and came for a while under Wagner's spell, and was enthralled by the Javanese gamelan orchestra that he heard during the World Exhibition in Paris. He began a relationship with Gabrielle Dupont that lasted some years, but it ended badly and in 1897 she attempted suicide. Two years later, he married her mannequin friend Lilly Texier.

By now, Debussy had made his mark with such masterpieces as his String Quartet and the Prélude à l'après-midi d'un faune, but money remained short and he gave a piano lesson on his wedding day to pay for the reception. Financial success finally came with the production of his opera Pelléas et Mélisande in April 1902. However, once again his private life became strained, and in 1904 he left his wife for Emma Bardac. Lilly then attempted suicide, just as Gaby Dupont had done, and the news of this scandal damaged his reputation, particularly as it was suggested that he was interested in Madame Bardac's money. Both obtained their divorces in 1905, and their daughter Claude-Emma Debussy (nicknamed Chou-Chou), was born on 30 October, a fortnight after the première of his orchestral triptych La Mer. They were married in January 1908. From 1909, Debussy's health gave cause for concern. Eventually it became clear that he was suffering from rectal cancer and he underwent an operation in 1915. For the rest of his life he wore a colostomy device and described the act of dressing himself as 'one of the twelve labours of Hercules'. The outbreak of war in 1914 and the subsequent sufferings of his country much distressed him, but he continued to compose, signing his works proudly with the words 'musicien français'. When he died on 25 March 1918, his daughter wrote that he looked 'oh, so happy!'.

RIGHT: *'The Wave' by Japanese artist Hokusai (1760-1849). The title-page of the published edition of* La Mer, *which was completed in 1905, featured an illustration based on this print.*

Debussy is commonly described as an impressionist composer, and the term links his work with painters from Turner (whom he admired) to Monet, whose water pictures are the visual counterparts of such piano pieces as *Reflets dans l'eau*. However, his music owes as much to literary figures such as Poe, Baudelaire and Mallarmé, with their elements of mystery, and it was a poem by the last of these writers which inspired the *Prélude à l'après-midi d'un faune*. Pictorial subjects suggested some of his titles, such as *Nuages* ('Clouds'), *Brouillards* ('Mists') and *Des pas sur la neige* ('Footsteps in the Snow'). There are bell sounds in his piano pieces *Cloches à travers les feuilles* and *La Cathédrale engloutie* and the orchestral *Ibéria*; this last piece is a brilliant yet affectionate evocation of Spain, a country which fascinated him and also inspired other works. He also liked England, which he knew well; he completed *La Mer* while staying with Emma Bardac at Eastbourne in 1905.

'Music has this over painting', Debussy declared in 1906, 'that it can bring together all manner of variations of colour and light': and, of course, it was in motion rather than static as a painting must be. He believed that his art should be one of 'colours and rhythms' rather than 'the lifeless rules invented by pedants'. By following his instinct and what he called his 'ear', he brought to music a unique world of sensibility. This applies not only to actual harmonies, rhythms and textures in his piano and orchestral pieces, but also to the acute response to words that is a major feature of his vocal music. Yet his art is never merely exquisite in a hothouse way. It can have as much power and drama as Beethoven or Wagner, and in this context one thinks of the elemental force of *La Mer* and the passion of *Pelléas et Mélisande*, an opera that depicts the agonizing jealousy of Prince Golaud over the growing youthful affection between his wife and his half-brother Pelléas. Incidentally, this is Debussy's only complete opera, although he attempted others, both earlier and later.

Debussy founded no school of composition, as Schoenberg did, and had few close imitators in the way that Stravinsky had, so that for some four decades after his death it seemed that he would always stand alone as a master who had fully explored the new worlds he created. However, more recently composers have learned much from his individual use of form, and his 'poème dansé' *Jeux* (1913), which for a long time was neglected by conductors, is now seen as a seminal work of 20th-century music by later composers such as Pierre Boulez because of the way in which a three-note motif flowers into a full symphonic structure.

Debussy's music never seems intellectual in the sense of elaborately contrived; indeed, spontaneity is among its chief features. Melody is another, and although his tunes are sometimes unusual they stick in the mind. This has helped to make him popular today whereas he was once thought too 'modern' for ordinary listeners to appreciate. He now seems the most subtly influential of the 20th century's composers.

C.H.

FREDERICK Delius

(b. Bradford, Yorkshire, 29 January 1862; d. Grez-sur-Loing, France, 10 June 1934)

Frederick Delius was born into a family of Yorkshire wool merchants of Dutch/German extraction. After an academic education at Bradford Grammar School, his father fully expected Frederick to take his place in the family business. In order to learn basic administrative skills, the twenty-two-year-old was sent to Florida in 1884 to manage an orange grove. For Delius, it proved a most beneficial experience, but not in the way his father had intended. Most of the time was spent, in Delius's own words, 'absorbing and translating' both the natural sounds he heard, and the improvized part-songs of the black plantation workers. When his brother arrived to take over the running of the disintegrating orange grove, Delius opted for a career in music and went first to Virginia and then to New York, teaching and playing the violin.

He returned to Europe in June 1886 and in August of that year began a formal musical education at the Leipzig Conservatory. Unfortunately, of the rudiments of musical form, only counterpoint held any interest for him and his distaste for the Austro-German classics hardly endeared him to his tutors. However, he did strike up two important friendships: one with Edvard Grieg, the other with the Australian musician, Percy Grainger.

It was Grieg who persuaded Delius's father that his son should be allowed to pursue a career as a composer, largely on the strength of Delius's first composition of note, the Tropical Scenes for Orchestra, better known as the Florida Suite, which he completed in 1888 but revised two years later. At Grieg's suggestion,

Delius visited Norway and, as in Florida, was overwhelmed by its natural beauty, something he attempted to portray in the magical Over the Hills and Far Away.

In 1897, Delius married Jelka Rosen, who was prepared to tolerate his self-centredness and irascibility in the belief that she was nurturing a genius. The following year, they moved to a beautiful part of France, Grez-sur-Loing near Fontainebleau, and this was to be Delius's home for the rest of his life. The acceptance of his music received a considerable boost when, in 1902, his works were first heard by the eminent conductor, Sir Thomas Beecham. Thereafter, Beecham championed Delius's music everywhere, culminating in 1929 in a highly-successful Delius festival in London. The composer returned to England for the concerts, but by now he was blind and virtually paralysed, the long-term effects of imperfectly-treated syphilis.

The fact that Delius was able to compose at all during his last yeas was entirely due to a fellow-Yorkshireman, a musician called Eric Fenby (b. 1906). Hearing of Delius's plight, Fenby offered his services as an amanuensis (in truth, he was more of a collaborator) and came to live at Grez-sur-Loing where he painstakingly transcribed Delius's grunts and groans into musical notation.

After his death, Delius was at first buried at Grez-sur-Loing but then – in response to a death-bed wish heard only by his wife – disinterred and reburied in the churchyard at Limpsfield in Sussex. Appropriately, Thomas Beecham delivered the funeral oration.

RIGHT: Frederick Delius, a photograph taken in 1910, the year he completed his opera Fennimore and Gerda. He was by then living at Grez-sur-Loing.

BELOW: 'Contes barbares', an oil-painting of 1902 by Paul Gaugin (1848-1903), the French artist who was a friend of Delius when the composer was living in Paris in the 1890's.

elius had no time for music which he described as 'having a palpable design on us'. Few other composers had much influence on him: Wagner, to some extent; Chopin; Debussy; Richard Strauss (he admired the tone poem *Don Juan*); and his long-time friend, Grieg. His dislikes were broad, from Beethoven to Bartók and including his fellow-countryman, Elgar. He pursued his own ideas with scant regard for convention or the musical mainstream.

Evocative as it is, the early *Florida Suite* is very much an apprentice piece. The first flowering of the mature Delius came with *Over the Hills and Far Away*. He preferred to work on several projects simultaneously, not persisting with a work if the ideas dried up. Styles clash in the extraordinary and frequently uplifting *Mass of Life* in which Delius – an atheist – sets texts from Friedrich Nietzsche's 'Also sprach Zarathustra' in preference to the Latin rite.

In *Paris*, Delius produced as atmospheric a sound-picture as it is possible to imagine, using the orchestra to brilliant effect in evoking the fantasy and mystery of the city after dark. Delius's feel for orchestration owed little to others and is evident again in the variations – albeit very loose ones – that go to make up *Appalachia* of 1902, the work which first introduced Beecham to Delius's music.

Delius began to explore the possibilities of opera, beginning with *Irmelin* (1890-92) and *The Magic Fountain* (1893-95) – neither performed in his lifetime – then *Koanga* (1895-97) – which again drew upon his Florida experience. *Margot la Rouge* (1902) was an unworthy effort, but his finest opera is generally considered to be *A Village Romeo and Juliet* (1901), based on a story by Gottfried Keller but, in its tragic

ending, appearing to owe something to Wagner's *Tristan und Isolde*. A fifth opera, *Fennimore and Gerda* of 1910, also has much to commend it.

Of four works composed in 1907, the most significant remains *Brigg Fair*, subtitled *An English Rhapsody* and making free use of a Lincolnshire folk melody collected by Percy Grainger. He followed this with *In a Summer Garden*, capturing the intoxicating mix of sights and sounds of his own garden at Grez. If there is a suggestion of Debussy here, the Englishness of the *First Dance Rhapsody* is wholly evident.

The quintessential Delius is perhaps best captured in two works from 1911-12, the magical *Summer Night on the River* and the folk-inspired *On Hearing the First Cuckoo in Spring*. In contrast to the gentle intimacy of this piece, *The Song of the High Hills* is every bit as magnificent as its subject. More reflective are the *North Country Sketches* of 1913-14.

The First World War saw Delius produce five major compositions, two dedicated to the fallen of that conflict, the uncharacteristically aggressive *Requiem* and the Concerto for Violin and Cello. In addition, there was the strange, darkly primeval *Eventyr* and the *Second Dance Rhapsody*. The Double Concerto was followed by the even finer solo Violin Concerto and Cello Concerto and, thanks to Eric Fenby, Delius was able to bring such late masterpieces as the *Songs of Farewell*, *A Song of Summer*, *A Late Lark*, *Cynara* and the third of his underrated violin sonatas to fruition. And it was Fenby who best summed up Delius's achievement when he said: 'The people who really count are those who discover new ways of making our lives more beautiful. Frederick Delius was such a man.'   P.H.

LEFT: 'Curving Road: View of the Seine' by Alfred Sisley (1839-99), another Englishman who lived in France. This is countryside near to where Delius lived at Grez.

GAETANO Donizetti (b. Bergamo, 29 November 1797; d. Bergamo, 8 April 1848)

RIGHT: *An early portrait of Gaetano Donizetti by G. Induno. This is now in the Civic Museum at Bologna.*

ABOVE: *Manuel de Carrion as the ill-fated Edgardo in Lucia di Lammermoor when performed at the Victoria-Theater, Berlin in 1859. Coloured lithograph by Louis Veit.*

Donizetti, the son of a janitor, was educated at a charity school, where he exhibited enough musical talent to be sent to Bologna for two years of advanced studies. While there he wrote two operas and contracted syphilis, events that foreshadowed in their different ways his later life. Back in his native Bergamo, he applied himself to the composition of four more operas, which from 1821 gained for him a series of posts in the theatres of Rome, Naples and Palermo. The urge to compose seemed compulsive: he completed thirty operas in under ten years!

In 1828 he married Virginia Vasselli, but despite their devotion to one another, their nine years together were marked by many misfortunes. Their first son was misformed, and soon died, while two subsequent children were stillborn. When his wife died after the final delivery, Donizetti was overwhelmed with grief and feelings of guilt. However, that decade of married life in the 1830s had seen its compensation in Donizetti's musical career. His first success, the historical drama Anna Bolena (1830) was soon followed by a rustic comedy in complete contrast, L'Elisir d'amore (The Love Potion, 1832). Its success won the composer a professorship at Naples in 1834, and there he wrote two more operas which gained great fame, Maria Stuarda (1835) and Lucia di Lammermoor (1835) (British royalty and Scottish romance were potent inspirations for many composers of that era).

Donizetti's striking ability to switch from high tragedy to light comedy was again demonstrated in 1836 in two sparkling operas Il Campanello and Betly, but they appeared during an outbreak of cholera in Naples, and audiences were small. The death of his wife in 1837 moved the unhappy composer to leave Naples, and after the première of another work based on English history, Roberto Devereux (1837), he travelled to Paris to make a fresh start. His stay there was successful, as in 1840 he won praise for two strongly contrasted operas – the lively La Fille du régiment and the dramatic La Favorite.

He was invited to Vienna, where he scored another hit in Linda di Chamonix (1842) and was offered the post of Music Director at the Imperial Court. Increasing problems with his health did not impede his amazingly prolific output: by the end of 1843 four more operas had appeared, including the delightful Don Pasquale. It was as if he was aware that little time remained for him. From 1843 till his death in 1848, he suffered increasing mental disorders, and eventually a pathetic disintegration of all his faculties. After two years in a mental hospital, he was granted permission to return to his native Bergamo, where he died following a series of strokes.

BELOW: *Portrait of Gaetano Donizetti painted by Giuseppe Rillosi (1811-80), now in the Theatre Museum at La Scala, Milan. This portrays him at about the time he was writing* Lucia di Lammermoor.

A study of Donizetti's career reveals two surprising facts. Firstly, it is remarkable that a man who lived only fifty years, and through many of those suffered much painful sickness of body and mind, should have completed over seventy operas including several of high quality. Secondly, he seemed able to move quickly from tragedy to comedy and back again, and compose in a few weeks noble, delicate or joyful operas irrespective of his often unhappy personal circumstances and while he himself was racked with pain and grief.

The comedies are especially noteworthy, as his contemporary Bellini never attempted comic operas, and his successor Verdi wrote only two, one at each end of his career. *L'Elisir d'amore*, Donizetti's first complete success in this genre, is still a great favourite; its affectionate picture of simple villagers rings true, and there are many fine solos for the leading singers, such as the tenor's 'Una furtiva lagrima' with its haunting bassoon obligato. Mention must also be made of *La Fille du régiment* (1840), a favourite of Joan Sutherland; and *Don Pasquale*, perhaps his comic masterpiece. The tale of young lovers outwitting an old miser is transmuted into something touching and funny at the same time. A series of inventive solos and duets culminates in a magical last scene containing a serenade and love duet to melt any heart.

As already noted, Donizetti had an extraordinary facility for changing his style to suit the subject, and his several dramatic and tragic works on historical subjects are worthy of their themes. The latter half of the 20th century has seen a revival of his operas based on figures in British history such as Anne Boleyn, Mary Stuart and Robert Devereux, Earl of Essex. They are not all solid gold; stirring scenes are sometimes followed by conventional choruses and hastily composed ensembles. However, they are noteworthy not only for their own sake but for the example they gave to Verdi.

Hitherto unknown works by Donizetti have been recently appearing regularly on CD, and there is a surprisingly high level of invention in them. Yet, for most music-lovers, *Lucia di Lammermoor* reigns supreme. It has taken imaginative producers like Zeffirelli, and singing actresses like Callas and Sutherland, to reveal the full force and beauty of his adaptation of Scott's novel. The romantic yet doom-laden atmosphere is unerringly maintained by the composer, and individual numbers such as the Sextet and the Mad Scene are rightly counted among the treasures of Italian opera.   P.J.

Chronology

1797 Born 29 November in Bergamo

1806 Educated at music school for poor children

1815 Sent to Bologna. Writes first opera

1817-21 Returns to Bergamo with syphilis. Writes four more operas

1821-5 Holds posts in opera houses in Rome, Naples, Palermo. Composes thirty operas over next ten years

1828 Marries despite increasing effects of disease. First child born misformed (two subsequent children stillborn)

1830 First success Anna Bolena performed at Teatro Carcano, Milan

1832 L'Elisir d'amore first performed at Teatro Canobbiana, Milan

1834 Maria Stuarda first performed in Naples. Appointed Professor at Naples

1835 Inspired by Bellini to write Lucia di Lammermoor, first performed in Naples

1836 Cholera in Naples prevents success of short comic operas

1837 Wife and baby die in childbirth: Donizetti inconsolable. Roberto Devereux produced at Teatro S. Carlo, Naples

1838 Leaves Naples for Paris

1840 La Fille du régiment first performed at Opéra-Comique, Paris. La Favorite first performed at Paris Opéra

1842 Feted on visit to Vienna, appointed Music Director of Imperial Court. Linda di Chamonix first performed in Vienna

1843 Increasing mental disorders, but quickly completes four more operas, including comedy Don Pasquale, first performed at Paris Théâtre-Italienne

1845 Mental and physical collapse. Two years in Naples hospital

1848 Returns to Bergamo to die 8 April

LEFT: *The Burgtheater, Vienna, where a number of Donizetti's operas had their first German performances. In Vienna, he was appointed Music Director of the Imperial Court.*

_D_vořák ANTONIN

(b. Nelahozeves, nr Prague, 8 September 1841; d. Prague, 1 May 1904)

_D_vořák might have spent his life as a butcher and innkeeper, like his father, if his parents had not encouraged his precocious musical talent by having him taught the viola, organ, pianoforte and counterpoint. They also insisted on his learning to speak German, essential for professional musicians in Austria-Hungary. But for all this, they prudently made him complete his butcher's apprenticeship. When he was 16, a kindly uncle paid for his studies at the Prague Organ School.

From 1866 he was principal viola with the Prague National Theatre Orchestra, whose director was Smetana. His Czech nationalist music, particularly The Bartered Bride, inspired Dvořák and filled him with a lifelong ambition to write equally successful patriotic operas. However, his first major success came not with an opera but with a choral work, The Heirs of the White Mountain, which made enough money to enable Dvořák to concentrate on composing.

By 1875 his completed works included three operas, five symphonies and many instrumental pieces. He was awarded the Austrian State Prize for Music and won the admiration of Brahms, who became a close friend. He introduced the rising young composer to his own publisher, Simrock, who infuriated Dvořák by printing his first name as 'Ant.' and by his reluctance to

publish longer, and therefore more expensive, works. Nevertheless, their association proved profitable to Dvořák, who became wealthy enough to buy a country estate about 40 miles south of Prague. Several of his choral works, including The Spectre's Bride and St. Ludmila, were written for first performance in England, where Dvořák and his music enjoyed great popularity in the 1880s and 1890s. His Slavonic Rhapsodies and Slavonic Dances, and works such as the 7th Humoresque and 'Songs My Mother Taught Me' became great favourites in late Victorian parlours. Academic honours were showered upon him, while from New York came a pressing invitation to be professor of composition at the National Conservatory of Music.

Dvořák wrote some of his finest music, including the New World Symphony, during his three years in America, where his work was widely acclaimed. Nevertheless he was very homesick, and it was with great relief that he returned to Prague in 1895, to be welcomed as a national hero and treated as the Grand Old Man of Czech music. A crowning triumph came three years before his death in 1904 with the resounding success of his opera Rusalka at the National Theatre in Prague. When he died, thousands took to the city's streets to mourn his loss.

RIGHT: Antonin Dvořák, the great Czech composer. This unsigned crayon drawing is based on a photograph of 1890, taken when Dvořák was 49.

Chronology

1841 Born 8 September at Nelahozeves (Mühlhausen), near Prague

1853 Sent to relatives at Zlonice to learn German and work as a butcher's apprentice while taking music lessons

1857 Enters Organ School, Prague

1859-71 Plays viola, first in local band then with Prague National Orchestra under Smetana

1865 First Symphony (Bells of Zlonice), unpublished until 1961

1870 First opera Alfred, first performance 1938

1873 Marries Anna Cormáková, by whom he has eight children. First success with Hymnus: Heirs of the White Mountain

1874-77 Organist at St. Adalbert's Church, Prague

1875 Austrian State Prize for Music. Death of daughter Josefa inspires Stabat Mater

1876 Begins close friendship with Brahms. Opera Vanda performed, but with little success.

1878 3 Slavonic Rhapsodies and first set of Slavonic Dances bring world fame

1884 First successful conducting tour in England

1885 Purchases estate at Vysova

1885-6 Cantatas The Spectre's Bride and St.Ludmila

58

There are three incorruptible strands, each like a metal thread in a genuine banknote, that run through Dvořák's personality and his music. The first is a fervent nationalism, shared with his elder compatriot Smetana; not for nothing were they known as the co-founders of the Czech school. Secondly, and closely-related, was his intense love of his native countryside. In his music, on the printed page and in performance, one can almost feel – as with the music of Elgar – the shape of the composer's own personal landscape. And lastly, throughout his career, he was fascinated by the natural and spontaneous folk music of his own countrymen and that of other lands.

Some critics say that Dvořák spent too much time trying to force his natural genius into the straitjacket of classical form, and that this accounts for the uneven quality of his work. Others claim that, unlike Brahms, he was unable to shake off his simple, peasant background and that too often, as a result, intuition overcame intellect in his music. But all agree that his greatest gift was for melody – an apparently inexhaustible ability to write memorable and heart-warming tunes.

BELOW: *'Autumn by the Hudson River', an oil-painting by Jasper Francis Cropsey (1823-1900) completed in 1860. This is the kind of 'New World' scene that must have inspired Dvořák.*

ABOVE: *An oil-painting of Dvořák by the Czech painter Souček which hangs in the Dvořák Museum in Prague, an appropriate memorial to one of the heroes of Czechoslovakian culture.*

That is why Dvořák has been described as 'the most inventive and spontaneously musical of all national composers'. You have only to hear the lovely *cor anglais* tune in the *New World* Symphony (No. 9), or Humoresque, or virtually any one of the many Slavonic Dances, to realize that he stands alongside Haydn, Mozart and Schubert as a composer 'whose thoughts and emotions manifest themselves directly in musical forms.'

There are many riches awaiting discovery in Dvořák's symphonies and orchestral works, operas and songs. Also among his chamber and instrumental pieces; notably the F major Quartet (Op. 96) and the 'Dumky' Trio (Op. 90), to quote just two examples. Part of the fascination of such a quest is that you can never be sure what you are going to find, in terms of musical quality.

At its best, Dvořák's music bears witness to 'an inspired creative spirit and to a great mastery of technique', in the words of his fellow-countrymen Otakar Sourek. Or, as Hans von Bülow, the eminent conductor, put it in a letter he wrote to the composer in 1887, ' . . . next to Brahms you are the most God-gifted composer of the present day.' It is a judgement that has, in full measure, withstood the passage of time.

R.H.

1890 Requiem
1891 Honorary doctorates, Cambridge and Prague Universities, Professor of Composition at the Prague Conservatoire
1892 Director, National Conservatory of Music, New York
1893 Symphony No. 9 From the New World
1895 Returns to Prague
1901 Rusalka, his most successful opera, first performed at the National Theatre in Prague. Appointed Director of the Prague Conservatoire. Elected to the Austro-Hungarian Senate
1904 Dies in Prague, 1 May

LÉO **DELIBES**

(b. St. Germain du Val, 21 February 1836; d. Paris, 16 January 1891)

One of the indisputably great ballet composers, Delibes began his career after studying at the Paris Conservatoire as a church organist. Under the influence of his teacher, the composer Adolphe Adam (1803-1856), he began composing operettas, and this led in 1864 to appointment as chorus master at the Opéra. After joining with Minkus in the ballet La Source (1866), his first success came with Coppélia in 1870, to be followed by Sylvia in 1876, both still firm favourites in the ballet repertoire. Now firmly entrenched in theatrical circles, Delibes turned to opera with Le Roi l'a dit (1873), the more serious Jean de Nivelle (1880), and Lakmé (1883) in the popular 'oriental' genre of the time. Here the tradition of Gounod and Bizet is at its finest, full of colour and melody. Delibes also wrote some charming incidental music to Hugo's Le Roi s'amuse, and pleasant songs, including 'Les Filles de Cadiz', but appointment as a professor at the Conservatoire in 1881 prompted his easy-going, diffident nature to lapse into inactivity, and thereafter he wrote only an unfinished opera, Kassya, before his death.   P.L.

ERNÖ **DOHNÁNYI**

(b. Bratislava, 27 July 1877; d. New York, 9 February 1960)

A quintessential product of the Austro-Hungarian dual monarchy, Dohnányi was born in the city now called Bratislava, and was himself known for many years as Ernst von Dohnányi. His music similarly has a modest dash of paprika in an essentially Brahmsian stew. For most of his life, Dohnányi was better known as an outstanding virtuoso pianist and teacher than as a composer. He occupied important teaching posts in Berlin and Budapest, giving support to Bartók and Kodály, and also conducted in Budapest until forced to leave for America in 1944. His last years from 1949 were spent teaching in Florida. Despite this active career, Dohnányi composed a great deal – three operas, two symphonies, two concertos each for piano and violin, chamber music and piano music in quantity. All is well made, if not strikingly original, but his name will live primarily for the delightful Variations on a Nursery Song for piano and orchestra (1913),

the Suite for Orchestra, one or two piano pieces such as the suite Ruralia Hungarica, and the Serenade for string trio. The conductor Christoph von Dohnányi is his grandson.   P.L.

PAUL **DUKAS**

(b. Paris, 1 October 1865; d. Paris, 17 May 1935)

The son of a banker and a musically gifted mother who died when he was four, Dukas learned the piano as a child but only showed special gifts when he started to compose in his early teens. At sixteen he began studying at the Paris Conservatoire and also played the timpani in its orchestra. Debussy (who was three years older) became his friend, and they shared a passion for Wagner's music, but in time his cultural allegiance went to the more conservative side of French music as represented by Franck and his pupil d'Indy. In the early 1890s, Dukas became known as a critic and writer on music, as well as a scholar who contributed to a new edition of Rameau's works. But it was only when he was thirty that he began to find himself as a composer with his Symphony, a noble yet vigorous work, finely orchestrated, that has been called Beethovenian. It had its première in January 1897, and later in the same year he wrote the music for which he is most famous, the 'symphonic scherzo after a ballad of Goethe' called L'Apprenti sorcier. This brilliantly colourful and invigorating descriptive piece is also one whose harmonic subtlety and invention clearly influenced two later works, Stravinsky's Fireworks and Debussy's Jeux. But while most people restrict their experience of Dukas to L'Apprenti sorcier, there are other works that deserve to be heard more often, such as his monumental Piano Sonata (1901), the opera Ariane et Barbe-bleue (Paris, 1907) and the vivid ballet La Péri (1912).   C.H.

HENRI **DUPARC**

(b. Paris, 21 January 1848; d. Mont-de-Marsan, 12 February 1933)

The creator with Fauré of the French mélodie or art song, Duparc also rivals Gustave Charpentier for paucity of output and length of withdrawal from composition. In fact, his case is the sadder of the two, for his output is smaller, amounting to just

16 songs and one or two instrumental pieces, and his silence even longer – no less than 48 years. He was also much the greater composer. Originally destined for the law, Duparc studied with Franck who advised him to compose little but of the highest quality. The implied extreme self-criticism seems to have struck a chord, for Duparc destroyed all his early work composed under Franck's influence. Between 1868-84 he then composed the 16 songs, some with alternative orchestral accompaniments, upon which his reputation now rests. They are romantic, almost Wagnerian, but also unmistakably anticipate the impressionism of Debussy. Texts from contemporary poets such as Baudelaire and Leconte de Lisle are set with great sensitivity in a way hitherto absent from French music. In 1885, afflicted by a nervous complaint, Duparc ceased to compose. He retreated to the country, and devoted himself to his family, painting and literature until his death   P.L.

JOHN **FIELD**

(b. Dublin, 26 July 1782; d. Moscow, 23 January 1837)

Ireland's first notable composer began life as a piano prodigy in Dublin. Taken initially to London for instruction, he visited France, Germany and Russia on concert tours, and it was in Russia that he eventually settled in 1803. He toured Europe as a piano celebrity, famous for his delicate, sensitive playing which contrasted with the current vogue for display. A saturnine, self-indulgent personality, his career steadily declined, and his already intermittent teaching with it. After a final tour, he died in Russia at the age of 55. Field's music almost all involves the piano, and he is most famous for the invention of the Nocturne, of which he wrote 19 in an expressive, ornamental style which later inspired Chopin. He also wrote seven piano concertos, in the superficial but mellifluous manner of the time, and four piano sonatas. The music reflects the piano player rather than the man. It is dreamy and sensitive, with attractive melodics, but lacking in variety. Before the piano pieces were rediscovered in modern times, they were known only through a short orchestral suite arranged by Harty.   P.L.

GERALD **FINZI**

(b. London, 14 July 1901; d. Oxford, 27 September 1956)

Finzi was for some time thought to be only a minor survivor of the English national school, but extensive recordings restored his reputation, which has been steadily growing ever since. Finzi came from a prosperous family with an Italian Jewish background. A shy, withdrawn boy, he was much affected by a series of family bereavements and the death of his teacher in the First World War and became a life-long pacifist. After musical studies in Yorkshire and London, he taught at the RAM for a few years before retiring with his family to the country in 1933 to concentrate on composition and other musical activities, as well as literature and gardening. In 1951 he was diagnosed as having leukaemia, and died at the age of only 55. He was a painstaking composer, often polishing and revising works for years, and it is therefore hard to date them. The influence of Vaughan Williams is discernible, but can be exaggerated. His orchestral music is sometimes delicately pastoral, but can often be forceful and lyrical as in the cello and clarinet concertos. Finzi is at his best with vocal music – the mystical Traherne cantata Dies Natalis and the Shakespearean cycle Let us garlands bring for solo voice with orchestra, the choral In terra pax, and the unrivalled settings of the knotty yet expressive poetry of Thomas Hardy.   P.L.

PHILIP **GLASS**

(b. Baltimore, 31 January 1937)

After studies at the Juilliard School, Glass followed the well-worn path to the studio of Nadia Boulanger (1887-1979) in Paris, but he was not enamoured of the neo-classical styles she admired, nor did he feel sympathy for the Boulez school of avant-garde experiments. However, a meeting with Indian musician Ravi Shankar sparked an interest in oriental music and its prolonged repetitive patterns. Back in the USA, Glass supported himself with odd jobs such as taxi-driving, while forming his own group to try out his own 'minimalist' compositions, which were a conscious reaction against the dry, mathematical formulae of the twelve-tone composers. He achieved sudden recognition in 1976, when his opera Einstein on the Beach – actually five hours of stylized stage scenes – was performed to enthusiastic audiences, who seemed mesmerized by the hypnotic rhythms into an almost spiritual response. Minimalism became a major trend in America, and Glass's subsequent film scores and operas such as Akhnaten (1983) continued to attract large audiences, less for their vocal lines than for the shifting patterns in the orchestra. The 1992 première of The Voyage, bizarre reflections of Columbus, was a media event, further marking the achievement of Glass in breaking down the barriers between 'serious' music and the freedom of modern rock, and attracting new young audiences into the opera houses of the world.   P.J.

ABOVE: Philip Glass, who has brought an experimental body of composition, especially opera, to a wide public.

BELOW: 'Nocturne in Blue and Gold: Old Battersea Bridge' by James MacNeill Whistler (1834-1903) painted in 1865. The 'invention' of the musical nocturne is usually credited to John Field.

EDWARD Elgar

(b. Broadheath, near Worcester, 2 June 1857; d. Worcester, 23 February 1934)

In those later photographs, he appears the epitome of the English country gentleman, the kind of imposing yet avuncular character you would imagine to have composed the Pomp and Circumstance marches or the Cockaigne overture. In his later years, Elgar fitted that image, venerated as Britain's greatest and most famous musical figure and recipient of a host of honours and accolades. But that is the superficial Elgar; other facets of his life and personality were far removed from the optimism and confidence exuded by his 'public' music.

Edward Elgar was the son of a piano tuner from Dover, who arrived in the cathedral city of Worcester in 1841 and married his landlord's daughter. They set up home in the hamlet of Broadheath just outside the city and it was there that Edward was born, in a cottage which is now a museum devoted to the composer. Elgar's father ran a music shop in Worcester and eventually the whole family moved to live above it. Everyone was expected to serve behind the counter and Elgar later recalled the experience as giving him the chance to 'read everything, play everything, hear everything'. However, Elgar senior did not think music was any career for his son and placed him with a firm of solicitors as a trainee clerk.

Elgar was not so easily dissuaded. He taught himself harmony, counterpoint and form and studied theory and scores, including those of Beethoven's symphonies. With his brother, Frank, he formed a wind quintet and, in 1877, paid his first visit to London to hear a concert. He continued to attend concerts there – whenever he could afford the train fare!

In 1878, Elgar was appointed bandmaster of the attendants' orchestra at – of all things – a lunatic asylum. He also took a teaching post in Malvern and began to offer his own compositions to publishers and conductors. There was unanimous rejection: having a provincial background worked against Elgar as, he was convinced, did being a Catholic. Then, during 1886, the daughter of a major-general, Caroline Alice Roberts, came for music lessons. She was nine years Elgar's senior, but the relationship blossomed – much to the Roberts family's disapproval – and in 1889 the pair moved to London and married.

Alice Elgar was convinced of her husband's genius and gave him every encouragement in his composing, even undertaking the laborious task of drawing the bar lines on his score paper – they could not afford to buy the real thing. In 1890, the overture Froissart

RIGHT: *A photograph of Sir Edward Elgar taken in 1903, a year before he received his knighthood. The ultimate accolade – the award of the Order of Merit – followed eight years later.*

RIGHT: *'Cornfields at Fittleworth', Sussex, painted by Edward Wilkins Waite (1854-1924). Elgar lived in a cottage near here between the years 1917-23.*

was accepted for performance at the Three Choirs Festival, that year held in his birthplace of Worcester. In London, though, recognition was unforthcoming and the Elgars were forced to cut their losses and return to Worcester where Edward took a teaching post, at the Mount School in nearby Malvern. Following the birth of a daughter, Carice, Elgar composed the lovely Serenade for Strings for his wife and, inspired by a visit to Germany in 1892, wrote Scenes from the Bavarian Highlands, to her poems. Other works followed, including the cantata Caractacus and, also in 1897, the Imperial March to mark the diamond jubilee of Queen Victoria's reign.

Elgar's status was finally secured by the Variations on an Original Theme (Enigma), performed to an enthusiastic audience on 19 June 1899, two weeks after the composer's forty-second birthday. That success was followed by an invitation to write a work for the Birmingham Festival of 1900 and, for Elgar, that was the chance to bring to fruition a cherished idea – to compose a choral work on Cardinal Newman's devout meditation on immortality, The Dream of Gerontius. He completed the score in the summer of 1900, working in a cottage to the north of Malvern, surrounded by the landscape that he loved. 'The trees are singing my music,' he enthused, 'or have I sung theirs?'

Elgar was in no doubt about the qualities of Gerontius: after the last bars, he wrote: 'This is the best of me – this, if anything of mine, is worth your memory.' Sadly, the first performance at the

Birmingham Festival – like Enigma, under the baton of Hans Richter – was marred by under-rehearsal and Elgar was crest-fallen, but the following year the work was performed to great acclaim in Düsseldorf. Afterwards the 'the welfare and success' of the composer was toasted by no less than Richard Strauss, who referred to him as the '. . . first English progressive'. Elgar was now established as a figure in international music.

Honours at home followed: a knighthood, the freedom of the city of Worcester, and a guest lectureship at Birmingham University. Between 1903 and 1911 Elgar completed two oratorios in a planned trilogy, The Apostles and The Kingdom (the third was never completed), two symphonies and a Violin Concerto for Fritz Kreisler. The 1911 coronation honours saw him awarded the Order of Merit but, for Elgar, there was a certain finality in the accolade. 'There's now nothing left for me to achieve,' he wrote to a friend.

In 1920, his beloved Alice died. Elgar retreated into the study of science, especially biology, and in 1923 left the Sussex cottage he had shared with Alice to return to Worcestershire. He composed little in his final years but did make sketches for a Third Symphony, a commission from the BBC. He also actively discussed writing an opera based on Ben Jonson's play The Devil is an Ass and made a number of recordings for the Gramophone Company's HMV label, including a celebrated one of the Violin Concerto with a sixteen-year-old prodigy called Yehudi Menuhin. Sir Edward Elgar OM died peacefully in his home at 7.45 on the morning of 23 February 1934.

ABOVE: 'The West Front of Worcester Cathedral' painted by Joseph Mallord William Turner (1775-1851). Elgar's family home was in Worcester, and this cathedral was the venue of many Elgarian first performances.

Chronology

A tune like that comes once in a lifetime,' Elgar once mused. He was referring to the central theme of the first of his *Pomp and Circumstance* marches, the tune now familiar as 'Land of Hope and Glory'. The suggestion that words could be fitted to Elgar's great theme came from no less than King Edward VII and Elgar accordingly asked the librettist, A.C. Benson, to supply a text. It is doubtful whether Elgar ever approved of the jingoistic sentiments Benson expressed and, during the First World War, he came to loathe the words attached to his tune, and to regret his failure to make more of it, perhaps in a symphony.

However, there is plenty of other evidence of Elgar's gift for melody: the evocative opening of the Cello Concerto, for example, or 'Nimrod' from the *Enigma Variations*. His musical language was firmly rooted in the tradition of Brahms and, to a lesser extent, Wagner. Elgar was no 'modernist'. In the year that his First Symphony made its debut (1908), Mahler was introducing a Prague audience to the strange sound world of his Seventh Symphony and Schoenberg was completing his influential Five Pieces for Orchestra, one of the first large-scale atonal compositions. No such experimentation is to be found in the Elgar, although in other respects the symphony was both original and idiomatic. Certainly, the composer had fulfilled the requirements he had stated a few years earlier:

'I hold that the symphony without a programme is the highest development of art . . . Perhaps the form is somewhat battered by the ill-usage of its admirers . . . but when the looked-for genius comes, it may be absolutely revived.'

It is interesting that, unlike many symphonists, Elgar did not compose the basic framework of any of his works at the piano. Instead the music came to him quite abstractly, already in the sounds and colours that others would flesh out from their keyboard scores.

The First Symphony was enthusiastically received. The Second, however, met with a lukewarm response and a degree of incomprehension. Elgar completed the score in February 1911 and headed it with a quotation from Shelley: 'Rarely, rarely comest thou, Spirit of Delight.' He dedicated the symphony to the memory of Edward VII who had died the previous year and in the Larghetto Elgar wrote some of his most moving and solemnly beautiful music.

The Second Symphony was more complex, both musically and psychologically, than its predecessor and it may have been that its mood of retrospection mixed with a dark urgency was at odds with the 'coronation fever' of 1911. During the première, which he conducted, Elgar turned to the leader of the orchestra, his close friend, W.H. Reed andremarked, 'What is the matter with them, Billy? They sit there like a lot of stuffed pigs.'

Elgar invested his two concertos with the same ideals as his symphonies. The violin virtuoso Fritz Kreisler had been badgering Elgar to write a concerto for him for some years. Elgar finally completed it in 1910. Kreisler, it is said, was dis-

BELOW: *King Edward VII receiving dignitaries prior to his Coronation, a painting by A.E. Harris. Elgar wrote a Coronation Ode for this occasion which included a version of 'Land of Hope and Glory'.*

ABOVE: 'Midsummer' by Sir James Guthrie (1859-1930), a gentle evocation of Edwardian Britain. In its essential Englishness, the painting brings to mind the unmistakable sound of Elgar.

appointed by what he received; perhaps it was too 'English' for him with insufficient opportunity for display. It is certainly Elgar at his most lyrical and romantic, and a work worthy to stand alongside the violin concertos of Beethoven, Brahms, Mendelssohn and Tchaikovsky. The second of Elgar's concertos, for cello, was his last orchestral masterpiece. Completed in 1919, elegiac, yearning, autumnal, sorrowful, it seems to sum up a life, and an era.

Elgar was also capable of writing the most brilliant lighter music, the dashing overture Cockaigne – In London Town being a particularly fine example. An Italian holiday in 1904, surrounded by the colourful landscape and atmosphere of Alassio, inspired the effervescent concert overture, In The South, while the exuberant Introduction and Allegro for Strings continues to evoke images of the English countryside.

As well as the two symphonies, Elgar composed a work which he carefully described as a 'symphonic study'. The idea first germinated around 1901, but it was some ten years later that Falstaff was completed. This finely-honed work depicts the personality of Shakespeare's character as much as his life, as depicted in the plays but, despite being its musical equal, has never attained the popularity of the Enigma Variations.

The enigma of Enigma remains. 'Its "dark saying" must be left unguessed,' said Elgar, mysteriously. He was equally mysterious about the personality associated with Variation XIII in the work (all the variations characterized friends, relations or fellow musicians). Was it Lady Mary Lygon, as some are convinced, or Helen Jesse Weaver, to whom Elgar was once briefly engaged?

Elgar's contribution to vocal music is dominated by the three great oratorios, with Gerontius the most consistently fine, but The Kingdom and The Apostles touching spiritual and musical heights in many passages. The cantata, Caractacus, is also very fine and of the Scenes from the Saga of King Olaf, written in 1896, the composer himself admitted, 'It always sweeps me off my feet.'

During the First World War, Elgar captured the mood of the time with The Spirit of England, settings of poems by Lawrence Binyon, and then composed music for a children's play, The Starlight Express. But his most important compositions from this period, along with the Cello Concerto, were three exceptional chamber works, a string quartet, a piano quintet and a violin sonata.

Towards the end of his life, the gramophone became a source of consolation to Elgar. One of the composer's Worcester friends, the architect Troyte Griffith, recalled:

'I put on the Stratton Quartet's records of his String Quartet. After the slow movement, I said, "Surely that is as fine as a movement by Beethoven?" He said quite simply, "Yes it is, and there is something in it that has never been done before." I said, "What is it?" He answered, "Nothing you would understand, merely an arrangement of notes." '

Perhaps his fellow composer, Hubery Parry, best summed up Elgar's achievement when, on hearing that Elgar had been awarded the Order of Merit, he commented:

'He is the right person for it. You see, he has reached the hearts of the people.' His music still does. P.H.

MANUEL DE
Falla (b. Cadiz, 23 November 1876; d. Alta Gracia, Argentina, 14 November 1946)

As a composer Manuel de Falla was a perfectionist and in his private life he was no less punctilious. His meals had to be served exactly on time; his clothes perfectly pressed; his shoes brilliantly polished. We are not told to which of his parents he owed these particular characteristics, but his father was a business man from Valencia and his mother, Maria del Carmen, from whom he had his first music lessons, was Catalan.

RIGHT: *Portrait of the Spanish composer Manuel de Falla by his countryman Ignacio Zuloaga (1870-1945). In the latter part of his life, Falla lived in Argentina.*

He was not a child prodigy; indeed, for some time he could not decide whether he wanted to be a composer or a writer. But music ultimately claimed him, and surprisingly it was Grieg's example that filled him with an ambition to create a similar national style and idiom for the music of his native Spain.

For business reasons his father moved the family to Madrid, where Manuel de Falla entered the Madrid Conservatory. Here he triumphantly completed a seven-year course in two years, carrying off the highest prizes in each field of study. Later he became a pupil of one of the champions of Spanish national music, Félipe Pedrell (1841-1922). Falla cherished the hope of retrieving the family fortunes by writing zarzuelas, the Spanish comic operas then at the height of their popularity. Altogether he composed five but only one of them was actually performed, and that with indifferent success.

BELOW: *Daniel Zuloaga and his daughters, a painting of his uncle and cousins by Ignacio Zuloaga. Falla collaborated with Zuloaga and the poet Lorca in producing a festival of Spanish folk songs.*

The first major work which Falla himself was prepared to acknowledge was his opera La Vida breve, which he wrote in 1904. Its reputation preceded him to Paris, where he was befriended and helped by rising young composers such as his fellow-countryman Albéniz, and by Debussy, Dukas and Ravel. On the outbreak of the First World War, Falla returned to Madrid. There followed a comparatively fruitful period with the completion of the ballet-pantomime El Amor brujo (1915), the concert piece for piano and orchestra Nights in the Gardens of Spain, and the ballet The Three-Cornered Hat (1919), of which Diaghilev's London production in 1919 brought Falla international fame.

The following year he went to live in Granada with his sister, where he would probably have stayed had it not been for the outbreak of the Civil War and the murder of his close friend, the poet Féderico García Lorca. Devastated and embittered, Falla retired in 1939 to Alta Gracia de Cordoba in Argentina. He died there on 14 November 1946; his body was reverently transported back to Spain for burial in Cadiz Cathedral.

Few composers enjoy as great a reputation as Manuel de Falla on the strength of so small a number of published works. He constantly revised and polished his scores, giving attention to the minutest detail, and refused to have them publicly performed until he was completely satisfied. Although strongly influenced by the folk music of Andalusia and of Catalonia, and inspired by Grieg's example to draw on his own national musical heritage, it was in the works of Haydn that he found an unerring sense of form and economy of means. These two qualities distinguish Falla from Albéniz, Turina, Granados and other near contemporaries, and single him out as the undisputed master of modern Spanish music.

After moving to Paris, Falla's first major published work was the opera *La Vida breve* (1904-5), for which he won a coveted prize from the Madrid Academy of Fine Arts. To the original version he later added an orchestral *Interlude* and *Danza*, for which the work is now best known. Also in Paris the distinguished Catalonian pianist Ricardo Viñes gave the first performance of *Four Spanish Pieces*; the London debut was given by Falla himself in 1911. By the time the next major work *El Amor brujo* appeared, war had broken out in

Europe and the composer had returned to Madrid, where the new ballet was premièred in April 1915, and in a rescored concert version a year later. From this characteristic work the *Ritual Fire Dance* is frequently performed as a separate item.

In 1916 there followed *Nights in the Gardens of Spain*, dedicated to Ricardo Viñes, and described by Falla not as a 'concerto' but as 'symphonic impressions for piano and orchestra'. He also said that it was his intention to convey a mood and an atmosphere, and not to paint pictures in sound. Nevertheless it is difficult not to conjure up visual images when listening to his wonderfully evocative score.

Also in 1916, Diaghilev heard a preliminary version of music Falla had composed for a pantomime, *El Sombrero de tres picos* (*The Three-Cornered Hat*) and persuaded him to turn it into a full-scale ballet. With sets designed by Picasso and an orchestra conducted by Ernest Ansermet, the great Russian impresario staged Falla's colourful and dramatic work at the Alhambra Theatre in London in 1919. It was this spectacular production that set the seal on the composer's international reputation, which has grown steadily in stature ever since.   R.H.

Chronology

1876 *Born 23 November at Cadiz, Spain*

1896 *Family moves to Madrid*

1898-9 *Completes seven year Madrid Conservatory course in two years*

1901-3 *Writes five zarzuelas (popular operas) of which one is staged*

1902 *Studies under Félipe Pedrell, champion of Spanish national music*

1904-5 *Composes opera La Vida breve, first performance in Nice, 1913*

1905 *Awarded Madrid Academy of Fine Arts prize*

1907 *Moves to Paris: meets and is influenced by Debussy, Dukas and Ravel*

1909 *Cuatro piezas españolas published in Paris*

1914 *Returns to Madrid on outbreak of First World War*

1915 *Ballet El Amor brujo, first performance in Madrid*

1916 *Nights in the Gardens of Spain, first performance in Madrid*

1919 *Ballet version of The Three-Cornered Hat; Diaghilev production in London*

1920 *Fantasia baetica first performed by dedicatee Artur Rubinstein in New York. Moves to Granada to live with sister, Maria del Carmen*

1923 *Puppet opera El Retablo de Maese Pedro, first performance in Paris*

1926 *Harpsichord Concerto first performed by Wanda Landowska in Barcelona. Starts work on unfinished cantata Atlantida (first performance in Milan 1962)*

1936-9 *Shattered by murder of his close friend, the poet Lorca, during Spanish Civil War*

1939 *Leaves Spain to settle in Argentina*

1946 *Dies 14 November. Body returned to Spain; buried Cadiz Cathedral*

LEFT: 'El Jaleo' by John Singer Sargent (1856-1925), the American painter who settled in London in 1884. It reflects the quintessential spirit of Spanish dance that pervades Falla's music.

GABRIEL
Fauré (b. Pamiers, 12 May 1845; d. Paris, 4 November 1924)

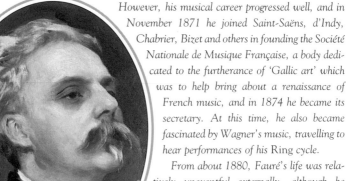

RIGHT: *Portrait of the composer Gabriel Fauré by John Singer Sargent (1856-1925), an internationally famous portrait painter who had studied in Paris.*

BELOW: *Paul Verlaine (1844-96) portrayed in the Café Procope by F. A. Casals. Fauré set Verlaine's poems in his song-cycle La bonne chanson (1894).*

BELOW: *'At the Grand Piano', a pastel drawing by Russian artist Leonid Pasternak (1862-1945). Fauré wrote with special affection and understanding for the piano.*

Born in the southern French département of Ariège, not far from the Pyrenees and the Spanish border, Fauré was his parents' sixth child. His father was a school inspector and later a head teacher, but there were no known musicians among his forbears. However, he showed musical talent by the age of nine and in 1854 he was given a scholarship to a 'School of Classical and Sacred Music' in Paris by its founder Louis Niedermeyer, and stayed there until he was twenty, undergoing the strict instruction that was to prepare him for a career as a church choirmaster and latterly making friends with his piano teacher Saint-Saëns.

After graduating from this school, Fauré became organist in January 1866 of a church at Rennes and stayed there until 1870. Although he shocked his priest by sometimes playing operatic music in church and smoking during sermons, he spent his time usefully, giving a few lessons and composing varying pieces in a search for a personal style. He then took up a post at a Paris church, but left it to spend some months of 1870-1 in the army during the Franco-Prussian War; after demobilization he took on two more church appointments in fairly quick succession, first at St. Honoré d'Eylau and then in October 1971 (following the collapse of the revolutionary Commune that held power for ten weeks of that year) as assistant to Widor at Saint-Sulpice. In 1874 he left this post to deputize for Saint-Saëns at the Madeleine, and when Saint-Saëns resigned in 1877, Fauré became choirmaster.

By now Saint-Saëns was a valued and influential friend, at whose home Fauré met other distinguished musicians such as d'Indy and Chabrier, as well as the writers Flaubert, George Sand and Turgenev. This was also the time of a love affair with Marianne Viardot, the daughter of the singer Pauline Viardot, and they became engaged in July 1877, but she broke off the engagement in October. His turbulent feelings at this time may be reflected in his First Violin Sonata (1876), First Piano Quartet (1879) and the Ballade for piano and orchestra (1881). In March 1883 he married Marie Fremiet, the daughter of a sculptor; they had two sons, born at the end of that year and in 1889. But they do not seem to have been especially happy together, and the composer continued to indulge himself in a few flirtations outside matrimony.

However, his musical career progressed well, and in November 1871 he joined Saint-Saëns, d'Indy, Chabrier, Bizet and others in founding the Société Nationale de Musique Française, a body dedicated to the furtherance of 'Gallic art' which was to help bring about a renaissance of French music, and in 1874 he became its secretary. At this time, he also became fascinated by Wagner's music, travelling to hear performances of his Ring cycle.

From about 1880, Fauré's life was relatively uneventful externally, although he suffered from occasional debilitating depression. His father's death in 1885 prompted the composition of the Requiem, one of his most popular works; but he did not finish it until 1900, by which time his mother had also died. He found a publisher for his numerous songs and other music and became a distinguished teacher as well as holding a post as inspector of music in provincial conservatories. He was a leading figure on the Parisian social scene, and travelled widely. In 1896 he became the senior organist at the Madeleine and succeeded Massenet as teacher of composition at the Paris Conservatoire, where his pupils included Ravel, who liked and admired him. He also wrote music criticism for the Paris paper 'Le Figaro' from 1903-21. In 1905 he became Director of the Conservatoire, and although he suffered from hearing problems he did not retire until 1920, when he was 75. He continued to compose until the year of his death.

Fauré's music is unmistakably Gallic, but in a way utterly different from that of his compatriots Berlioz and Messiaen with its frequent epic and grandiose quality. He avoids their powerful prophetic and rhetorical style and, some would say, consequently fails to produce the fire that we associate with genius. Most of his work is gentle in character, and the unusual serenity of his Requiem is enhanced by his omission altogether of the text, and consequently the terrors also, of the *Dies irae*. Similarly, his song cycle *La bonne chanson* (1894) offers nine love poems by that sensuous poet Verlaine and was inspired by his love for the amateur singer Emma Bardac, whom Debussy was later to marry; but although Fauré himself said that he never composed anything 'more spontaneously', its characteristically refined utterance may be thought a little pallid.

The same problem for the listener with this composer – if problem it is – is no less exemplified by the thirteen piano nocturnes which he composed not as a set, but singly over some forty-five years: the keyboard writing has a rare finesse and the harmonies are such as to interest the connoisseur, but (save in the finest performances) there is a certain sameness about them and they can seem to go on too long in a way which is never true of Chopin's nocturnes.

Given his musical personality, it is hardly surprising that the one really epic work in Fauré's catalogue has failed to survive. This was a 'lyric tragedy' called *Prométhée*, commissioned by the town of Béziers in his native department of Ariège. The first performance on 27 August 1900 went ahead with some success before an audience of around ten thousand. Saint-Saëns told Fauré that his music 'astonished' his colleagues. But despite attempts to keep the work alive, and a revision for orchestra that the composer made with Roger-Ducasse in 1917, the work went into oblivion. His opera *Pénélope* (Monte Carlo, 1913) is also on a Greek theme. It contains much beautiful music and is highly regarded in France; however, it has not gained a place in the international repertoire. In this opera, Fauré showed his debt to Wagner by using leitmotifs, but the generally restrained style is un-Wagnerian, and there are no big choruses to bring the house down, for he disliked the raw emotional force of *verismo* (realistic) opera. People who love Fauré's music do not go to him for such things. Rather, they value him for the reassuring calm of his Requiem, the refinement of *La bonne chanson* and many other songs such as the gently sad 'Après un rêve', the orchestral Pavane, Op.50, with its mood of 'light seductiveness', the *Dolly* Suite for piano duet, the eloquent *Elégie* for cello and piano and some of the piano barcarolles, nocturnes and impromptus. For all their lack of big effects, they have a quietly compelling charm.   C.H.

BELOW: 'Music in the Tuileries, Paris', a painting of 1862 by Edouard Manet (1832-83). This is the sort of fashionable audience for which Fauré wrote in his younger days in Paris. In later years, he was a leading society figure himself.

César Franck

(b. Liège, 10 December 1822; d. Paris, 8 November 1890)

Born in what is now Belgium, Franck was the son of a clerk; his mother's family were German. His father ensured that his gifted son began a thorough musical training at the Liège Conservatoire, but also exploited his precocious talents as a pianist, sending him and his brother Joseph (who played the violin) on a concert tour in 1835, when he was twelve. Franck's earliest compositions date from this time. In the same year the family moved to Paris with the intention of sending the boy to the Conservatoire there, but ran into difficulties over his nationality; finally he gained admission in October 1837 and studied piano, organ and theory.

His three piano trios, Op.1, were completed in 1842 and published by subscription soon after: the purchasers included Chopin and Liszt. But his father still expected him to be a pianist and withdrew him from the Conservatoire in April 1842, taking him back to Belgium to launch him on a virtuoso career. Although he gave several concerts, these plans failed and in 1844 he was seriously ill, perhaps through overwork. The forcing of his gift may have scarred him, and he was also disappointed by the poor reception accorded to his oratorio Ruth when it was given at the Conservatoire in January 1846. Resentful of his father, he left home for good and, ignoring parental opposition, became engaged to Félicité Saillot Desmousseaux; their marriage took place in February 1848.

Though he obtained an organist's post at the church of Notre-Dame de Lorette, Franck was now more of a teacher than a performer, giving lessons privately and in various schools. Once established, this pattern of life persisted for many years; travelling around Paris in a constant round became a drudgery, and the former prodigy seemed destined for obscurity. But little by little, his position improved. In 1858 he became organist of the church of Ste. Clotilde, which soon afterwards gained a fine new Cavaillé-Coll instrument, and in 1872 he was made Professor of Organ at the Conservatoire. By this time he had also begun to teach composition privately: his pupils revered his simplicity and honesty, and his regard for tradition yet open-mindedness towards new music such as Wagner's. During this decade and the next they included such men as Duparc, d'Indy and Chausson. They in turn formed a loyal group known as 'la bande à Franck', which soon became a force in French music, not least because Franck and his pupils saw a future in symphonic and chamber music, then rather neglected in France.

Frank had now composed two more oratorios, Rédemption and Les Béatitudes (1872 and 1879), and three symphonic poems called Les Eolides, Le Chasseur maudit and Les Djinns (1876-84). But the fact that these last pieces written over six years have consecutive opus numbers reminds us that he composed only occasionally. The real flowering of his gifts finally came when he was around sixty and was already widely saluted by his compatriots. The Piano Quintet (1879), the Symphonic Variations for piano and orchestra (1885), the Violin Sonata (1886) and the great Symphony in D minor (1888) are landmarks in French music, as are the organ and piano works of this final and eminently fruitful decade in his life.

RIGHT: A photograph of César Franck taken in Paris during the 1880's, the last decade of his life which was crowned by his greatest compositions.

BELOW: 'The Banks of the Seine', an oil-painting of 1880 by Gotthardt Kuehl (1850-1915). Such a scene would have been familiar to Franck who spent most of his life in the city of Paris.

Franck's music often reveals a spiritual fervour that has affinities with such German masters as Bach and Bruckner, though in another guise it has appeared in the works of a later French master, Messiaen. Perhaps it is no co-incidence that all four of these composers were church organists. When Liszt visited Franck's organ-loft at Ste. Clotilde on 3 April 1866 and heard him play his *Six Pieces* (1862), he declared that they deserved a place alongside the works of Bach. Franck's work also owes something to Liszt, especially his religious music, and the Wagner of *Tannhäuser* and *Parsifal*. D'Indy wrote in his biography of Franck that there was a time when he studied Wagner ardently, and noted themes that showed his influence.

Another link with Liszt is represented by Franck's orchestral tone poems, for Liszt did more than anyone to establish this programmatic form. Indeed Franck's first piece of this kind, *Ce qu'on entend sur la montagne* (ca 1847) shares the same title as a tone poem that Liszt completed a couple of years later, both works being inspired by a poem of Victor Hugo which describes the link between Nature and mankind in religious terms. Furthermore, the cyclic form which Liszt used in his *Les Préludes* and Piano Sonata is a major feature of Franck's music. It involves the transformation of a theme or themes as a work progresses, and we see it in works as dif-ferent as his Violin Sonata and Symphony. For example, in the Sonata, the interval of a major third gives rise to later melodies, while in the Symphony a motto of a falling second and a rising fourth is similarly heard at the start and then

ABOVE: 'The Angelus' by Jean-François Millet (1814-75) painted in oils in 1859. Perhaps the best known of Millet's works, it is also a potent evocation of the deeply religious convictions that Franck held so earnestly.

yields up several fully-fledged themes throughout the work.

The sense of affirmation in Franck's music is so strong that d'Indy wrote of the Symphony's 'ascent towards pure glad-ness and life-giving light', adding that this was 'because its workmanship is solid, and its themes are manifestations of ideal beauty'. He and Franck's other pupils believed that this music inherited the mantle of the great masters from Bach to Beethoven. Franck's influence also spread wider than his im-mediate circle, for the young Debussy attended his organ class at the Conservatoire and his String Quartet (1893), which uses cyclic form, owes something to Franck's String Quartet written four years previously.

Although Franck's music is romantic in its passionate emo-tional content, his was a pure musical spirit. Like his con-temporary Brahms, he was in some ways a guardian of tradi-tion and capable of using apparently archaic devices like canon and fugue quite naturally. The finale of the Violin Sonata begins with a fine example of canon, as the piano plays a sunny, flowing melody and the violin effortlessly fol-lows it with the same tune played a bar later and an octave higher. C.H.

GEORGE
Gershwin (b. Brooklyn, New York, 26 September 1898; d. Beverly Hills, California, 11 July 1937)

*A*merica's most famous composer was born into a Russian-Jewish family in Brooklyn, thereby adding yet another interesting flavour to the stewpot of American music. He first became interested in music at around the age of 10 when the family acquired a piano, taught himself the rudiments of harmony, and started to write in imitation of the popular songs of the day. His first important teacher, Charles Hambitzer, tried to lead him towards more classical tastes, but Gershwin's real sympathies were always to lie within the field of popular music, while his ambitious nature led him into more challenging areas of music-making. He published his first song when he was 18 and had his first big hit with 'Swanee' when he was 20. By 22 he was becoming known for his contributions to popular New York revues and musical comedies, and soon showed a distinctive melodic gift that matched that of his senior by some 13 years, Jerome Kern (1885-1945). But whereas Kern's music lingered in the world of operetta, Gershwin's was given a new brashness and boldness by his use of the jazz strains that began to dominate American music in the 1920s.

At the age of 25 he made his first move into larger musical forms, when his Rhapsody in Blue was presented at the Aeolian Hall by Paul Whiteman in 1924. It was heavily criticized but soon became, and has remained, immensely popular. This had been orchestrated by other hands, but Gershwin continued to study and most of his other large-scale compositions were his own work. In the meantime, with the collaboration of a brilliant lyricist in the shape of his brother Ira Gershwin (1896-1983), he contributed endless classics of popular song to flimsy Broadway shows and, later, to the blossoming field of the Hollywood musical film where such perennials as 'They can't take that away from me', 'They all laughed' and 'Nice work if you can get it' first appeared.

Achieving substance with his enduring Piano Concerto in F and other orchestral works; he aimed to make an equally substantial contribution to the musical theatre. This was realized when he came across the story Porgy and Bess which inspired him to compose what has become the best-known of all American operas; a status it has achieved both because and in spite of its splendid 'arias' which still have one foot in Tin Pan Alley, although part of an integrated score. It was received unenthusiastically at its first performances in Boston and New York, but every subsequent revival has enhanced its reputation. While working on the score of yet another Hollywood film, Gershwin was taken ill and a brain tumour was diagnosed. It was too late to save him. There is little doubt that had he survived this illness, he would have added greatly to the catalogue of American music.

It is only the residual snobbery of the musical establishment that prevents some from seeing that Gershwin's songs, in their own way and style (as with the gems written by Jerome Kern), are worthy of consideration alongside the Lieder of Schubert or Schumann. The same natural gift for finding the best musical settings for words is apparent, as is the effortless gift for melody. It is only the fact that Gershwin's music is tinged with the colours of jazz that makes both his songs and his other music seem slightly to come from the other side of the tracks for the classical world. And, strangely, for the jazz world as well. Ever since it burst upon New York in 1924, *Rhapsody in Blue* has had a cool reception from purists on either side of the musical fence. This has never prevented it from being played and recorded incessantly. Only slightly less popular were his Piano Concerto in F (1925), which is still the most frequently played concerto in the repertoire of American music, *An American in Paris* (1928), *Cuban Overture*, and the less effective *Second Rhapsody*.

Gershwin's music is always jazz-influenced to some extent, even if his jazz expression was often filtered through Tin Pan Alley processes. He wrote as a product of the early years of the urgently developing 20th century, a natural part of its popular culture. And he was mainly successful in bringing such material to the concert platform. With *Porgy and Bess* (1935), after an initially cool reception, he likewise created the greatest American opera. Even though its musical language is that of ragtime, jazz and the blues, and its individual

RIGHT: A portrait of George Gershwin painted by Arthur Kaufmann (1888-1971) in 1936; it is now in the National Portrait Gallery in Washington D.C.

Chronology

1898 *Born in Brooklyn, New York, 26 September*

1916-18 *First songs published and a piano piece,* Rialto Ripples *(1917). Contributes to* The Passing Show *(1917)*

1919 *First big hit with 'Swanee' in* The Capitol Revue. *First complete musical score* La-La Lucille

1920-4 *Contributes to five editions of George White's* Scandals, *songs such as 'I'll build a stairway to Paradise' and 'Somebody loves me'*

1924 Lady, Be Good *produced in New York and London. First performance of* Rhapsody in Blue *at the Aeolian Hall*

1925 *Piano Concerto in F and* Tip-Toes

1927 Strike Up the Band *and* Funny Face

1928 An American in Paris *first performed*

1930 Girl Crazy

1931 Of Thee I Sing *becomes the first musical to win a Pulitzer Prize*

1932 Pardon My English

1933 Let 'Em Eat Cake

1935 Porgy and Bess *first produced in Boston 30 September, and in New York at the Alvin Theater in October*

1937 *Dies in Beverly Hills, 11 July*

LEFT: *Urlee Leandros as Bess, and John McCurry as Crown in the 1952 touring production of* Porgy and Bess, *which was presented at the Titania-Palast in Berlin. William Warfield played Porgy.*

arias are still basically popular songs, the opera has a strength and unity that enables it to stand beside the works of Verdi and Wagner. It is intensely moving, satisfying and vital. But no appreciation of Gershwin would be complete without looking the other way and enjoying the accomplishment of his witty, urbane, yet romantic writings for the Broadway theatre and enjoying those gracefully muscular songs that lie within such scores as *Lady, Be Good* (1924); *Tip-Toes* (1925); *Strike Up The Band* (1927); *Funny Face* (1927); *Girl Crazy* (1930) and others; or such films as *Shall We Dance* (1937) and *A Damsel in Distress* (1937). Occasionally Gershwin was pretentious, occasionally he missed the mark. But, notwithstanding such flaws, the impact of his sadly curtailed output was really tremendous. P.G.

ABOVE: *Russian composer Alexander Glazunov photographed in 1930 by Seidenberg. At this time he was living in France, having left the Soviet Union in 1928.*

ALEXANDER **GLAZUNOV**

(b. St. Petersburg, 10 August 1865; d. Paris, 21 March 1936)

*I*t is a hard fate for a composer to follow closely after a period of acknowledged rich talent. This happened to Glazunov, who grew up when Tchaikovsky and the Russian nationalists were at their peak. Although he was a precociously successful musician, his first symphony making a great impression in 1882, he was never able to carve out a personal style as did Rakhmaninov, for example. Glazunov was the son of a wealthy publisher, and a favoured pupil of Rimsky-Korsakov. He was influenced by Liszt and Wagner as well as the Russian school, but all these influences seem to cancel out, as his music has little clear-cut character. He wrote much until his appointment to head the St. Petersburg Conservatoire in 1905, but then abandoned composing until after leaving Russia in 1928 for Paris. Glazunov wrote eight finished symphonies, a violin concerto, two piano concertos, seven string quartets and two well-known ballets, Raymonda (1897) and The Seasons (1901), as well as a late saxophone concerto. The best music is to be found in The Seasons and the violin concerto, but inspiration is always diluted, and authentic Russian character is generally missing. *P.L.*

MIKHAIL **GLINKA**

(b. Novospasskoye, 1 June 1804; d. Berlin, 15 February 1857)

*T*he founder of Russian classical music was the son of a land-owner, and he developed an early interest in folk-song. He took lessons in piano (from Field), violin and harmony, and sang as an amateur, but worked in the Civil Service until he decided in 1828 to study music seriously. Travelling to Italy in search of musical instruction also helped him to decide, in a fit of home-sickness, that he would endeavour to write in a Russian style. The result, when he returned home in 1836, was his opera A Life for the Tsar (1836). This epoch-making work is not in fact very Russian save in its story and a few Russian tunes, but its very existence was enough to start Russian music on its way, and pro-cure for Glinka the post of Imperial Kapellmeister. His next opera, Russlan and Ludmilla in 1842, is more clearly Russian, anti-cipating future interest in the Orient and magic, and also some typical stylistic traits. It was too original to be a success, and Glinka took refuge in more travel in Europe, especially Spain, which inspired his orchestral work Jota aragonesa. The rest of his career was something of an anti-climax. His lazy, self-indulgent temperament reduced his output and hastened his death. Only the folk-tune-based orchestral work Kamarinskaya and some dis-tinguished songs added to his reputation in his last years. *P.L.*

ABOVE: *Mikhail Glinka, 'the Father of Modern Russian Music', photographed around 1850, shortly after he had written Kamarinskaya.*

CHRISTOPH WILLIBALD VON **GLUCK**

(b. Erasbach, Bavaria, 2 July 1714; d. Vienna, 15 November 1787)

*T*oday the music of Gluck is more honoured in history books than in performance, for of his two dozen operas only a handful hold the stage, and of these only Orpheus and Eurydice (1762) can be considered a repertoire work. The son of a hunts-man, Gluck was the only member of a large family to exhibit musical talent. After studies in Prague and Vienna, he travelled widely with his princely patron to Europe's capitals, including London where he met Handel. During these years, he produced a series of successful operas which led eventually to a court appoint-ment in Vienna, where he received many honours and married the

ABOVE: *Christoph Willibald Gluck, a detail from a Parisian portrait of 1775 painted by Joseph Siffred Duplessis (1725-1802).*

ABOVE: *'Merchant's Wife' painted in St. Petersburg, the birthplace of Glazunov, by Boris Kustodijev (1878-1927). Glazunov became a professor at the St. Petersburg Conservatoire in 1899, and its director in 1905.*

daughter of a banker. Gluck's major contribution to the theatre was his insistence on blending words and music, drama and sing-ing, into a convincing whole. Arias, recitative and ballet were part of an integrated theatrical experience, and opera was not just a string of solos for star singers. Obviously, Gluck was attempting to achieve a kind of music-drama a century before Wagner pro-claimed the same ideal. The last twenty years of Gluck's life saw a fruitful collaboration with the dramatist Calzabigi in a succession of noble operas on themes from Greek mythology, e.g. Alceste (1767), Iphigenie en Aulide (1774), Iphigenie en Tauride (1779). These works, full of grand melody and genuine drama, were acclaimed in Paris and Vienna. Gluck's last years were marred by a series of strokes which prevented him undertaking further composition. *P.J.*

KARL **GOLDMARK**

(b. Keszthely, 18 May 1830; d. Vienna, 2 January 1915)

*T*he son of a Hungarian cantor, Goldmark was largely self-taught in all fields, including music. He studied for a while in Vienna before beginning to earn his living there as a musician. Before long, he was established as a leading figure in musical life. His compositions began with the string quartet of 1860, and in-clude six operas, a symphony, two violin concertos and various other orchestral and chamber works. The two best-known, and the basis of his reputation then and now, are the Rustic Wedding

Symphony of 1877 and the opera Die Königin von Saba (The Queen of Sheba) of 1875. The winning charm of the former, and the rich Wagnerian harmony and tunefulness of the latter were an immediate success, although the opera, like his others, is rarely heard today. The same qualities, without the Wagnerian overtones, are found in the first violin concerto and the concert overture Im Frühling (In Spring). Despite his Hungarian origins, Goldmark's music is directly in succession to Mendelssohn and Schumann, with only occasional reminders of central European folk song.

P.L.

HENRYK MIKOLAJ GÓRECKI
(b. Czernica, Poland, 6 December 1933)

His mother died when he was two and he was brought up by his father who was a railway clerk. During the war members of the family fought in the Polish resistance and several of them died in concentration camps. He studied composition at the Conservatory of Katowice 1955-1960. Later, from 1968, he was to teach there. He became a disciple of the avant-garde composers like Stockhausen and Boulez and wrote a number of scores that were described as both violent and difficult. He married in 1963 and from that time his music relented a little, became more tuneful and moved towards the rhythmic simplicity of works like Three Pieces in Old Style. These display his favourite devices of repetitious phrases, modal harmonies and the sort of harmonic alternations that look back a little towards Orff. Although described by some critics as a minimalist, Górecki denies this categorization and says that he simply writes as he feels. Having been largely unknown, in spite of a substantial output, he suddenly became a popular figure internationally when his Third Symphony (sub-titled Symphony of Sorrowful Songs), by way of classical radio programmes and recordings, suddenly caught the public's imagination and went into the pop charts. It is a potentially monotonous work in three slow movements; the two outer ones are in his medieval, chantingly repetitious vein, while the centrepiece, the popular section, is a setting for soprano of texts, one of which was carved in a concentration camp cell wall near Auschwitz. It achieves its memorability by the sheer strength of feeling that Górecki puts into the music.

P.G.

LOUIS MOREAU GOTTSCHALK
(b. New Orleans, 8 May 1829; d. Tijuca, Brazil, 18 December 1869)

America's first international performer and composer was an exotic bird indeed. Born in New Orleans of an English Jewish father and a French Caribbean mother, he studied in Paris with various well-known musicians, and caused a sensation as a pianist and composer of exotic creole-based works like Le Bananier. Admired by Chopin and Berlioz, among others, he returned to undertake triumphant concert tours of North and South America, where he added sentimental pieces like The Dying Poet (1863) to his composing repertoire. The rest of his short life was passed in more frenetic tours and periods of recuperation in the Caribbean. Here he produced spectacular fantasies on national airs, an opera Escenas campestres and his two extraordinary symphonies A Night in the Tropics and In Montevideo where the syncopated rhythms and unexpected melodies anticipate jazz some 40 years ahead of its time. Gottschalk finally ran out of time himself, as the result of his wild, self-indulgent life-style, at the early age of 40.

His reputation did not long survive his death, but his music still makes entertaining listening and certainly has more to offer than just curiosity value.

P.L.

ENRIQUE GRANADOS
(b. Lérida, 27 July 1867; d. English Channel, 24 March 1916)

Born in Catalonia of a Cuban father and a mother from the north of Spain, Granados has no clear regional affiliation. The most refined and expressive of the Spanish national school, his music is full of the national character, but can never be accused of simple pictorialism. He studied in Spain and Paris, and early came under the influence of Felipe Pedrell (1841-1922), the founder of Spanish music. A brilliant pianist, he also founded concert series and an academy in his native Barcelona, though teaching was not to his taste. Although he composed in all forms, his orchestral music has not stood the test of time, and of his seven operas only the last, Goyescas (1911), was a real success. Ironically, this work indirectly led to the death of him and his wife, when their ship was sunk during the First World War as they returned from the first performance in New York. Granados will be best remembered for his piano music and songs, though their quality is uneven. The piano music starts with the popular Spanish Dances of 1892-1900, and ends with his masterpiece, the suite Goyescas, which represents various pictures by Goya. This suite was developed into the opera of the same name, which also contains the beautiful Intermezzo – his most successful orchestral piece. His best songs, full of life and character, are the collection of Tonadillas, recreating an 18th-century Spanish form.

P.L.

ABOVE: American virtuoso pianist and composer Louis Moreau Gottschalk – this photograph was taken in 1858 when he was living in the Caribbean.

BELOW: 'The Guitar Player' by Auguste Renoir (1841-1919), a painting that evokes the Spanish character of the musical world of Enrique Granados.

CHARLES
Gounod (b. Paris, 18 June 1818; d. St. Cloud, 10 October 1893)

Charles Gounod grew up in a cultured background. His father was a talented painter, who died when his son was only four years old, and his mother a distinguished pianist. Recognizing his exceptional ability, she arranged to have him taught by the Czech/French composer Antonin Reicha (1770-1836), among whose other pupils at various times were Berlioz, Liszt and César Franck. After a period of further study at the Paris Conservatoire he won the Grand Prix de Rome in 1839 for his dramatic scene Fernand.

The city of Rome made a great impression on the young composer. He was profoundly moved by 16th century church music, making a special study of Palestrina, and became deeply religious. Before returning to France he visited Vienna (where two Masses were commissioned by the Karlskirche) and Berlin and Leipzig, where he stayed with the Mendelssohn family and learned to admire the choral music of J.S. Bach.

Back in Paris, as organist of the Eglise des Missions Etrangères, he found his congregations responding coolly to Palestrina and Bach, rather than their favourite Rossini. He considered entering the church, studied theology and took to signing himself 'Abbé Gounod'. But after 'five years of silence' he gave up the idea of priesthood, and turned his attention to more worldly matters. Like most ambitious young French composers of his day, he sought success in the theatre, writing a great deal of incidental music and a number of operas. At his fourth attempt he hit the jackpot with Faust (1859), which almost overnight made him the most famous composer in France. He followed it up with Mireille (1864) and Roméo et Juliette (1867), both of which were first performed at the Théâtre-Lyrique in Paris.

With the outbreak of the Franco-Prussian War in 1870 Gounod took his family to England. He lived for five years in London, shocked Victorian society with a notorious extra-marital affair, and founded a choir (later to become the Royal Choral Society) which he conducted at the grand opening of the Royal Albert Hall in 1871.

During his last years Gounod wrote a number of religious works which appealed especially to English tastes, and for which he was able to command very substantial fees. Some of his operas, notably Faust, remained box-office successes, his pious, sentimental songs were extremely popular and his masses and oratorios were performed all over Europe. His appointment in 1888 as Grand Officer of the Légion d'honneur set the seal on Gounod's worldly success, and if he did not die a contented man at the age of 75, he certainly died a rich one.

RIGHT: Charles Gounod in 1875 when he was celebrated as the composer of Faust (1859) and many other popular operas.

BELOW: The Rev Père Lacordaire portrayed by Théodore Chasseriau (1819-56). Gounod was an ardent follower of the priest who founded the Brotherhood of St. John the Evangelist.

Gounod's first attempt to make money in the French theatre was *Sapho*, a three-act opera in the style of Gluck. First performed at the Paris Opéra in April 1851, it failed to attract public support. Three years later, his second opera, a more ambitious five-act work entitled *La Nonne sanglante*, was taken off after only eleven performances. In 1858 he did rather better with a comic opera, *Le Médecin malgré lui*, based on Molière's comedy. But real success eluded him until, on 19 March 1859, at the Théâtre-Lyrique, the curtain rose on the first night of *Faust*.

It was an immediate hit. The audience loved the seductive tunes and rousing choruses, and overnight Charles Gounod became the toast of Paris. The five-act opera concentrates upon the love of Faust and Marguerite and, in the ten years following its first performance, sung recitatives and a complete ballet sequence were added. It is in this extended form that it is presented to modern audiences.

Gounod was unable to match the triumph of *Faust*, but had he written nothing else, his place in French music would still be assured. Among his other major successes on the operatic stage are *Mireille* (1864), a romantic love story in a Provençal setting, and *Roméo et Juliette*, which was first performed in 1873. This work is more highly regarded in France than else-where, as are his many songs which, some critics say, surpass those of Fauré which they inspired.

The oratorios and cantatas Gounod wrote during the latter part of his career are not religious works in the true sense, but are rooted in the sentimental religiosity which flourished in England, and in other countries in western Europe, from the middle of the 19th century onwards. Popular in its day, to our ears the music seems more appropriate to comic opera than to the liturgy. One such work is the *Messe solennelle de Sainte Cécile*, written in 1882, in which (with the exception of the *Benedictus*) the melodic line unfolds in a predictable way, and much of the chorus work is either in drab unison or laid out in harmonic patterns lacking all interest. Lush arpeggios from the harps and meaningless interventions by the brass complete the sorry picture, and one might be forgiven for wondering whether music of such relentless triviality could have been written by the creator of *Faust*.   R.H.

BELOW: *A painting (1866) by Mariano Fortuny y Carbo (1838-74) of the visions conjured up as the Spanish pianist J. B. Pujol plays his composition 'Fantasy on Gounod's Faust'.*

EDVARD *Grieg* (b. Bergen, 15 June 1843; d. Bergen, 4 September 1907)

Grieg was descended from Alexander Greig, a Scotsman who settled in Bergen in the mid-18th century. He prospered, acquired a fishing fleet, twice married Norwegian girls, became British consul, and changed his name to Grieg to make it easier for Norwegians to pronounce. By the time his great-grandson was born, the Griegs, respected and well-to-do citizens, had become closely involved in the musical life of Bergen.

Like many leading composers, Grieg was first taught music by his mother, an accomplished pianist. The Norwegian violinist Ole Bull persuaded Grieg's parents to send him to Leipzig, where he contracted pleurisy which permanently undermined his health. He also found the teaching at the Conservatoire pedantic and dull.

Leipzig was followed by three happy years in Copenhagen where he worked with the Danish romantic composer, Niels Gade (1817-1890) who was greatly influenced by Mendelssohn. Rikard Nordraak (1842-1866), composer of the Norwegian national anthem, became another close friend. Through him Grieg came to appreciate the peasant songs and dances of his native land. In their unusual harmonic structures and strong rhythms he found his own personal idiom as a composer, and determined with Nordraak to create a new and independent Norwegian school of music. But in 1866, while Grieg was wintering in Rome, he received news of Nordraak's death – a blow that left him so grief-stricken that there were fears for his life.

When at last he recovered, Grieg returned to Scandinavia to embark upon his life's mission. He married his cousin, the soprano Nina Hagerup, whom he had met during the idyllic years in Copenhagen. Theirs became a lifelong musical partnership. She was the inspirer and interpreter of many of his songs, and for nearly forty years they were to travel throughout Europe giving innumerable concerts and recitals.

The years of tireless work composing, conducting, arranging concerts of Norwegian music and teaching, did not go unrewarded. Grieg became a national figure, and his fame spread abroad. His work was admired by composers as widely different as Liszt, Brahms and Tchaikovsky – who met the Norwegian and described Grieg as a man 'of uncommon charm, blue eyes, not very large, but irresistibly fascinating.'

Although a miniaturist, and often under-valued as a result, Grieg had the satisfaction of seeing his life's work fulfilled. As the years passed he became a source of encouragement and support to younger composers, some of whom became close personal friends, notably Sibelius, Nielsen, Delius and Percy Grainger.

In recent years the marketing departments of many record companies have hyped various composers in turn in order to promote sales. Edvard Grieg has so far escaped the treatment, yet his A minor piano concerto continues to stay at, or near, the top of the classical charts. First performed on 3 April 1869 in Copenhagen with the composer as soloist, it is a work which, with its fresh and spontaneous lyrical quality, continues to enchant audiences all over the world. Such universal appeal would have delighted Grieg, who wrote music in order to reach the widest possible audience.

'The world of harmonies was always my dream world,' said Grieg on one occasion, and that he 'discovered the hidden harmonies' of Norwegian folk music is a less fanciful claim than many of its kind. From these harmonies, which Debussy not too unkindly described as 'bonbons stuffed with snow', he allowed his own melodies to take shape. The result is that his compositions have a close affinity with, but are not directly based upon, the folk songs and dances of his native land. Grieg, like Vaughan Williams, is a striking example of a national composer whose originality is firmly rooted in his own background and tradition.

Although he wrote incidental music for *Sigurd Josalfar* and Ibsen's *Peer Gynt*, and actually embarked on an opera *Olav Trygvason*, which remained unfinished at the time of his death, Grieg was at his best in works of a smaller scale. Nowhere is this more clearly demonstrated than in his orchestral suites, derived either from stage works or from his considerable output of piano music. The *Lyric* and the *Holberg* suites are delightful examples of their kind, as are the popular *Norwegian Dances*.

Grieg's many songs are less well-known than they deserve. 'When I compose a song', he said, 'my concern is not to make music but, first and foremost, to do justice to the poet's intentions.' Such integrity makes doubly difficult the task of translating Norwegian texts into more familiar languages in a way that makes sense musically as well as linguistically, but it does not explain why his other settings, of German poems for example, are so neglected today. His gift for melody, his inventiveness and his graceful style are perfectly suited to the form, and young artists who have the courage to explore this neglected corner of the singer's repertoire will certainly reap a rich reward.   R.H.

LEFT: 'The Elements' by Thomas Cole (1801-1848), a painting of 1828 that evokes the mysterious world of Peer Gynt and the 'Hall of the Mountain King'.

GEORGE FRIDERIC
Handel (b. Halle, 23 February 1685; d. London, 14 April 1759)

It was one of the remarkable coincidences of musical history that the two great figures of the 18th century, Bach and Handel, should have been born within a month of each other in the same year, 1685. The coincidence stops there, however. Bach remained rooted in Germany and church music, Handel spread his wings in the world of Italian opera and finally settled in England. The two never managed to meet, though one or two half-hearted efforts were made, and Bach died in 1750, while Handel lived on to 1759, when Mozart was three years old.

Furthermore, while Bach came from a long line of musicians and was expected to take up the trade, Handel was the first in his family to show any definite musical gift. His father was a barber-surgeon in the university town of Halle, twenty miles north of Leipzig (where Bach was to flourish), and he wanted his son to take up law. To turn his mind from musical notions he forbade any indulgences in that direction, but Handel's mother secretly smuggled a small keyboard into the attic where the young genius taught himself the rudiments of music. At the age of seven he went with his father to the court of the Duke of Sachse-Weissenfels where he played the organ and so impressed everyone that even his father was persuaded. Handel studied for three years with an organist in Halle, lived for a time in Berlin, then became an assistant organist at the local Domkirche. His father still wanted Handel to pursue law and he was sent to study it, but when his father died in 1697, the composer took the decision to live by music. In 1703 he made his way to Hamburg.

In Hamburg he obtained an orchestral post as violinist and harpsichordist, met Telemann, fought a duel with a rival composer, and had his first opera Almira performed at the Hamburg Opera in 1705. The next year he decided to travel and was to spend the next thirteen years moving between Florence, where Rodrigo was staged in 1707, Rome, where he became friendly with Alessandro Scarlatti, Venice, Naples, to Hanover where he became Kapellmeister to Elector George of Brunswick. He was allowed a year's leave to visit London where he staged Rinaldo (1711) and Il Pastor fido (1712), returned to Hamburg where he was restless, and again got permission to go to London which he now saw as his spiritual home. He overstayed his leave

RIGHT: 'Georg Friedrich Haendel' (one of the many versions of the spelling of his name), an anonymous portrait in the Civic Museum of Bologna. This likeness was based on a portrait painted by Balthasar Denner in the late 1720's.

BELOW: 'A Performance of The Emperor of India', painted by Handel's famous contemporary, William Hogarth (1697-1764). This type of painting of a portrait group engaged in social activity in a domestic setting is known as a 'conversation piece'.

but when Queen Anne died in 1714, his Hamburg employer came to England as King George 1.

At first King George remained annoyed with Handel for deserting his Hamburg post but was reconciled in 1715 when Handel wrote his now famous Water Music for one of the King's royal processions down the Thames. For the next decade Handel was to dominate the English opera scene, producing one work after another, and in 1726 he became a naturalized Englishman. But in 1728 he found himself being outshone in popularity by a new work called The Beggar's Opera, which was based on a libretto by John Gay. It drew away his audiences so tellingly that his own company lost £50,000 and went into liquidation. The worry caused a stroke from which he took many years to recover.

After 1741 Handel, in the face of new fashions, left the opera field and added to his attainments by achieving success in the choral field. In 1738 he had written the oratorios Saul and Israel in Egypt. In 1742 came his biggest success of all in any genre, Messiah, first performed in Dublin, which in a short time was to become and remain the world's most rightly popular oratorio. This was followed by Samson and Judas Maccabaeus (with 'See the conquering hero comes' a top hit of the time), the flood of choral works only being interrupted for the composition of the Music for the Royal Fireworks suite in 1749 to commemorate the Peace of Aix-la-Chapelle. In 1752 his failing eyes were unsuccessfully operated on and he became totally blind, but he still conducted and produced a yearly performance of Messiah. It was after one of these performances that he collapsed and later died. He was buried in Westminster Abbey and 3,000 people attended his funeral.

BELOW: By contrast, here we see the lower social orders in Handel's time vividly portrayed in Hogarth's painting of the Annual Fair at Southwark in 1733. It conjures up the world of The Beggar's Opera, the popular work by John Gay which damaged Handel's own fortunes.

RIGHT: *A view of London and the River Thames by Canaletto (Giovanni Antonio Canal) (1697-1768). This scene vividly captures the setting for Handel's Water Music, which was written for a royal party on the Thames in 1715.*

The operatic world that Handel entered was dominated by a clique of fashionable and well-paid singers who saw themselves as God's gift to the musical world and thought little of composers. The score could be altered and decorated at their whim. In later years Verdi was to find the same situation and rebelled against it with good effect. Handel, in spite of all his influence, was never able to outwit the singers and so composed to meet their needs. His operas were, therefore, conventional in many ways, but his great genius allowed him to use the Italianate conventions well, inserting superb arias that no-one could deface, writing expressively and deeply, and, as he grew more experienced, tightening the format so that it became harder for performers to flout his desires. Even if they represent, according to popular taste, the lesser side of his genius, they are constantly re-

vived and recorded for the pleasure of those who like the stylized music of his period. An occasional hit like the famous Largo from *Serse* (1738) keeps Handel's operatic reputation alive in more general terms. If he never moved far from the Neapolitan style that had been created by his friend Alessandro Scarlatti, he injected much strength and purpose into the tradition, and his operas are found to be well-constructed and dramatically effective.

For most, Handel is known as the composer of those two lively suites, the *Water* and *Fireworks* music, whose well-formed, muscular tunefulness offer a foretaste of the work for which he is best-known and most-loved, the imperishable *Messiah*, a score of unabating splendour and memorability. It was almost rivalled by his other choral writings, the large and splendid oratorios on biblical subjects which are so essential

the operas, beyond the established oratorios and the better-known orchestral works, there is a wide range of orchestral music to be discovered – concerti grossi including the well-known *Alexander's Feast*, and concertos for all manner of instruments, including two important sets of organ concertos. Handel's music can be greatly enjoyed in some delightful, if naughtily orchestrated, ballet suites put together by that great Handel lover, Sir Thomas Beecham – *The gods go a-begging* and *Love in Bath*. Beyond these, again, a vast range of chamber music and instrumental writings await the listener.

Handel's musical worth probably ranks him somewhere alongside that other great professional, Joseph Haydn. Both practical and earthly geniuses, they were writers of formal works that reflect the age of elegance (on the surface at any rate), yet which are far from dull. Handel's music is very much alive, friendly, full of good spirit and deep beauty.

P.G.

a part of the English choral tradition, plus such refined works as the *Chandos* anthems. There was no clear stylistic break between his operatic and his choral writing and the oratorios remain basically operatic by nature. The transition from one area of music-making to another was dictated almost entirely by commercial rather than artistic considerations.

It has often been said that Handel's dominance of the 18th century British musical scene was a tragedy in that it over-shadowed the work of much worthy native genius. If so, at least it had the effect of eventually forcing British composers to turn back to their own true inheritance and rediscover the early roots of a national style. Meantime Handel's own music, robust and straightforward, less intellectual on the one hand and less emotive in certain works than Bach's, has a solid, professional value that brooks no argument. Beyond

JOSEPH Haydn

(b. Rohrau, 31 March 1732; d. Vienna, 31 May 1809)

RIGHT: A portrait of
Joseph Haydn painted
when the composer was in
London in 1792 by
Thomas Hardy (1757-
c.1805). Kept in the Royal
College of Music, London,
it is said to be one of the
best portraits of the
composer.

BELOW: 'The Freyung in
Vienna, a View from the
South-East' (showing the
Schottenkirche), a painting
by Bernardo Bellotto
(known as Canaletto the
Younger) (1720-80).
Haydn lived in Vienna for
many years and was made
an Honorary Citizen.

Franz Joseph Haydn was born in a small village on the Austro-Hungarian border. His father was a wheelwright and a great lover of music; his mother, who had a fine voice, had served as a cook, and he had a younger brother Michael, who also became an excellent musician. Music and singing were therefore very much part of his simple family background from which, however, he was soon uprooted. The organist of St. Stephen's Cathedral, Vienna, happened to hear Haydn sing and immediately recruited him.

So, at the age of eight, he found himself in the capital of the Empire, singing in the Cathedral Choir and taking part in palace concerts. But as soon as his voice broke he was dismissed and left to fend for himself. Wandering the streets of the city, he made a meagre living, copying parts and playing the violin at dances. After working as accompanist at the Italian composer Nicola Porpora's music academy, he got a job at a minor court and then disastrously married Anne Marie Keller, a wig-maker's daughter, who plagued his life for forty years.

He had by now composed his first symphony – a youthful and immature work, the shortcomings of which he very well knew. Since he could not afford to take lessons, he decided, with characteristic good sense and determination, to teach himself harmony and counterpoint and improve his musical knowledge and technique. He carried out these intentions to such good effect that in 1761 he was invited to join the private orchestra of Prince Paul Anton Esterházy, head of the richest and most powerful family in Hungary, who were great patrons of music and the arts.

Haydn's duties as Vice-Kapellmeister were numerous and demanding. He had charge of the court musicians, and was responsible for their musical standards and general behaviour; he had to attend the court twice daily to receive instructions, and was obliged 'to compose such music as the Prince may require'; he was responsible for the care of all the court's musical instruments and for training the 'female singers, so they shall not forget in Eisenstadt what they have learned in Vienna'; he also had to conduct the court orchestra, to arrange operatic performances and to take part in chamber works to entertain the Prince and his guests.

Within a year Prince Paul died, and was succeeded by his brother, Nikolaus. In 1766 he promoted Haydn to Kapellmeister, and at Esterháza started to build a new palace, modelled on Versailles, with a marionette theatre and a 400-seat opera house as magnificent as it was isolated. 'There was no one near to confuse me,' said Haydn, 'so I was forced to become original.'

ABOVE: *A representation of the production of Haydn's opera* L'Incontro improvviso *in the private theatre at Esterháza in 1775. The composer himself can be seen seated at the harpischord.*

With a vast output of works of all kinds, fame crept up on him unawares. Foreign editions began to appear and commissions came in from abroad. After meeting Mozart, he developed a great admiration for his music and the men became firm friends.

In 1790, with the death of Prince Nikolaus, musical activities at Esterháza were suspended and Haydn's duties at the court came to a halt, although he retained his title and salary. In 1791 he accepted an invitation from the impresario Salomon to visit London, and stayed in England for eighteen months or more. On his return to Vienna he taught Beethoven for short time – not a happy experience for either man. In 1794 there came a second invitation to England, and this visit was even more triumphant.

By 1795 music had returned to Esterháza, but the family allowed Haydn to concentrate on his work as a composer. The final years were as productive as ever, with six splendid settings of the Mass as well as two oratorios – The Creation and The Seasons. Thereafter his health began to fail, and he died in Vienna the day after Napoleon's troops entered the city in May 1809.

RIGHT: *Haydn's employer from 1762-90 was the Hungarian nobleman Nikolaus I, Prince of Esterhazy, a great patron of the arts.*

ABOVE: *'The Deposition' by Rembrandt (1606-69) painted in 1655. Religious music was a major part of Haydn's output, and many of his late masterpieces are masses or oratorios.*

I t is not so long ago that the works of Haydn, almost overwhelming in number, were treated with a benign affection and respect but without a real understanding of their true place in the development of western classical music. Recent scholarship has done much to make amends and, incidentally, to correct the more patronizing view of the man himself. Today we see a musical hero – a titan – and not merely an amiable figure cosily nicknamed 'Papa' by his colleagues.

When Haydn arrived on the scene, the symphony was still at an early stage of development. While he was quick to acknowledge a profound debt of gratitude to C.P.E. Bach, many of Haydn's own early symphonies were scarcely more than overtures, having little in common with the larger-scale, richer and more expressive works of his mature years. The three famous symphonies composed at Esterháza during the

1760s, *Le Matin*, *Le Midi* and *Le Soir*, charming and as original as they are, do not have either the substance or the structure of their successors ten years later, composed during the so-called 'Sturm und Drang' ('Storm and stress') period.

With the Esterháza orchestra completely at his command Haydn was able to experiment, trying out all manner of effects with different combinations of instruments, enriching the whole time his orchestral palette and adding to the fund of witty, profound, and elegant musical ideas. Haydn did not, as is sometimes claimed, invent the modern symphony, but the form certainly reached full stature under his hands, with his constant search for new methods of expression within a strict classical structure, and his wonderful gift for melody and harmony.

Similarly, the two great sets of quartets, Op.20 of 1771 and Op.33 of 1781, show a remarkable development of style during the intervening ten years. Admittedly, the first set may well incorporate material written earlier in his career (Haydn was never one to waste a good idea), but the second set, composed after he had entered the Esterházy household, has a sustained quality not matched by the earlier works.

Another claim sometimes made on Haydn's behalf is that he invented sonata form, but this, also, goes much too far. What he actually achieved was impressive enough. Again, by comparing his early compositions with those written at the height of his creative powers, we can see clearly that he took sonata form as it existed at the time, and over the years strengthened and refined the principle of contrast and development of musical ideas to great effect.

The importance of opera in Haydn's life and work was not recognized until recent research on the Esterházy papers (now in the Hungarian National Library) revealed the astonishing fact that between 1775 and 1790 he was responsible for no fewer than 88 new operatic productions. More than 20 of these operas or *Singspiele* were from his own pen, for performance either in the main court theatre or the marionette theatre. How he managed to find time for all his other compositions is almost beyond comprehension. The important thing for modern audiences is that these works contain a great deal of beautiful music, which is now being heard again after nearly two centuries of neglect.

From 1790, with the death of Prince Nikolaus and the suspension of musical activity at Esterháza, Haydn turned his attention from opera to choral music, producing during the final years such masterpieces as the *Heiligmesse*, the *Nelson* Mass and the *Theresa* Mass, as well as his two great oratorios, *The Creation* and *The Seasons*. To this same period belong the Sinfonia Concertante and the twelve last great symphonies, including the well-known *Surprise*, *Military*, *Clock*, *Miracle*, *Drum Roll* and *London* symphonies. All these reveal the liberating influence of Mozart to whom Haydn, in his turn, gave a deeper understanding of the importance of classical structure. It was one of the most fruitful and most moving friendships between composers, based on an affection founded on mutual respect and an instinctive recognition of genius, one to the other.

Haydn needs no hyperbole. He was probably one of the most prolific composers who has ever lived, and certainly one of the greatest. We know that a number of his works have been lost, either destroyed by fire or simply mislaid, but there remain 104 symphonies, 83 string quartets, 52 piano sonatas, concertos for many different instruments (including the baryton, a bass string instrument much favoured by his patron, Prince Nikolaus Esterházy), a huge number of songs, operas, choral and chamber music, four oratorios, 14 masses and many other sacred works. These stand testimony to a genius that encompassed all musical forms of his time, and upon whose shoulders rests the progress of classical music during the 19th century and beyond.   R.H.

1797 *Composes Austrian national anthem*
1798 The Creation *and Nelson* Mass
1800 *Death of Haydn's wife*
1801 The Seasons
1804 *Nominated honorary citizen of Vienna*
1806 *Death of Michael Haydn*
1809 *Dies 31 May in Vienna*

BELOW: *A performance of the great oratorio* Die Schöpfung (The Creation) *given in the Hall of the University of Vienna on 27 March 1808 in honour of the composer who was present. Aquatint by Balthasar Wigand (1771-1846).*

GUSTAV
Holst (b. Cheltenham, 21 September 1874; d. London, 25 May 1934)

Holst was born in Cheltenham of a family of Swedish and German extraction, long since thoroughly anglicized. Both his parents were musical, and he was taught the piano and found a post as an organist before going to the Royal College of Music from 1893-1898, where he was taught composition by Stanford and also learned the trombone. At the RCM he met Vaughan Williams, who was to be a life-long friend and strong influence. On leaving, he spent five years as a professional trombonist, before his marriage in 1901 forced him to seek the relative security of teaching posts. In this field he built up a satisfying, but exhausting, workload at James Allen's and St. Paul's Girls' Schools (1903-20 and 1905-34), Morley College (1907-24), and later at Reading University and the RCM.

So far he had had little time for composing, and his works were in a semi-Wagnerian style, but under the influence of Vaughan Williams and their shared interest in folk song collecting, he began to develop his own approach. His intellectual curiosity also opened him to other more exotic influences: three of his best early works, the Beni-Mora Suite, the choral Hymns from the Rig-Veda and the opera Savitri (1916) sprang from a holiday in North Africa and an interest in Sanskrit literature. More related to folk-song were the Suites for military band and the St. Paul's Suite, written

for the school orchestra. Then, almost out of the blue, came his most famous work, The Planets, composed between 1913 and 1916, and the product of a casual conversation on astrology. Nothing in his work so far had foreshadowed a work like this, and with hindsight it can now be seen that it is unique in Holst's output, even though various future fingerprints of his appear here for the first time. It was to make his reputation, but a very misleading one, in that his public was always to await a sequel which was never to appear.

The First World War led to Holst's being sent to the Near East for war work, but on his return a performance of The Planets in 1919 established him as a leading composer. From now on teaching and composing jostled for his time, but in 1923 a serious fall left him with physical disabilities which were to limit his work, and may possibly have shortened his life. A series of austere works – the Fugal Concerto & Overture, and the Choral Symphony (a chilly representation of Keats) – were blamed on the effects of the fall, but his more extrovert operas The Perfect Fool (1922), At the Boar's Head (1925) and The Wandering Scholar (1934), and such pieces as Hammersmith, contradicted this idea. Late works such as the Hardy-inspired Egdon Heath for orchestra and the Humbert Wolfe songs showed him at his best, but in 1934 his health finally gave way, and he died aged 59.

Despite the immense teaching burden Holst undertook, he wrote a remarkable amount of music. Some drew inspiration from his teaching, such as the *St. Paul's* and *Brook Green* Suites, but most of his best work was the product of his enquiring, unconventional mind. Even the relatively early *Beni-Mora*, *Hymns from the Rig-Veda* and *Savitri* already show the influence of modal folk-song melody, and the remote mystical element which all his music is liable to contain even at its most approachable. The folk-song content is most obvious in the Suites for band and *At the Boar's Head*, but in the neo-classical Fugal Concerto and *Egdon Heath* it has been transmuted into an individual melodic style quite unlike the parallel work of Vaughan Williams.

Holst's mysticism made him choose the Hindu Rig-Veda or the Hymn of Jesus as texts, but his music is ideally suited by its austerity and purity of style to the expression of such ideas. Sometimes, as in *The Planets* and the Choral Symphony, such influences as Strauss and Debussy are not fully absorbed, but this happens rarely. *The Planets* is a unique example of Holst indulging all his new-found skills and tastes in a piece of late romantic display, combined in 'Saturn', 'Venus' and 'Neptune' with passages of the mature mystical Holst to come.

Holst's later music used to be seen as cold and arid, but it now appears austerely lyrical and coolly romantic. There is more emotion in the impressionistic picture of *Hammersmith* or the restraint of the *Ode to Death* than listeners of the 1930s were able to appreciate, and the economy of means and wil-

ABOVE: *An oil-painting of Holst in 1911 by Millicent Woodforde, now in the National Portrait Gallery, London. It shows the composer in his music room in the house where he lived in Barnes, on the outskirts of London.*

lingness to experiment no longer seem to be a sign of intellect overriding emotion.

Holst's operas, other than the one-act *Savitri*, are not a great success, although all contain good music, including the well-known ballet music in *The Perfect Fool*. The dramatic representation of human life was not his forte, and he was better suited by his many masterly part-songs, as well as the Four Songs for voice and violin, the Twelve Songs by Humbert Wolfe, and the remarkable choral works, the Choral Fantasia, the *Ode to Death* and the *Hymn of Jesus*, where his calm reflectiveness finds full expression.

By comparison with the vocal music, the orchestral pieces are generally less personal. Many are occasional and teaching pieces; *The Planets* is more of a *tour de force*; the neo-classical works, although enjoyable, seem to be exercises in the style of Stravinsky or Hindemith; only *Egdon Heath* and *Hammersmith* show the real individual Holst. Holst is an unusual case – a composer of a handful of popular pieces, whose most characteristic work appeals to a totally different audience. He has probably had more influence on modern British music than any composer of his generation.   P.L.

ABOVE: 'The Crucifixion part of the Isenheim Altar by Mathias Grünewald (c.1460-1528). The painter's life was portrayed in Hindemith's opera Mathis der Maler, while he based his Mathis der Maler Symphony on the three panels of this very altarpiece.

ABOVE: A portrait in oils of Paul Hindemith painted relatively late in life by Gartmann.

HAMILTON **HARTY**

(b. Hillsborough, 4 December 1879; d. Hove, 19 February 1941)

A major figure in British music as a conductor, Harty has also a claim to fame as accompanist and composer. Initially a church organist in his native Ulster, he moved to London to seek his fortune in 1900, and established a reputation as an outstanding accompanist. His first compositions in 1907 were a Comedy Overture, and a setting of Keats's Ode to a Nightingale sung by his wife, the soprano Agnes Nicholls. He then cemented his reputation with a Violin Concerto (premièred by Szigeti in 1909) and the tone poem With the Wild Geese. Harty had also been developing a career as a conductor, and the offer of the musical directorship of the Hallé Orchestra in 1920 meant that composing had to take second place to his increasing success in this field. Thereafter he wrote only a revision of his early Irish Symphony, based on traditional tunes, and his valedictory tone poem The Children of Lir (1939), when he was already mortally ill. Harty's music is in the German romantic tradition, but with a strong Irish melodic influence which gives it real individuality. Most successful are With the Wild Geese and the lively and tuneful Violin Concerto, but all the music is well-written and enjoyable. P.L.

PAUL **HINDEMITH**

(b. Hanau, 16 November 1895; d. Frankfurt, 28 December 1963)

A fine example of the volatility of reputation, Hindemith was in his time considered a daring avant-garde satirist, a respected pedagogue, a dangerous social agitator, a leading figure in modern music, and an old man writing in an outmoded style. Needless to say, it was the world which was changing, and Hindemith who was (up to a point) standing still. In early life, Hindemith was a viola player in German orchestras and chamber groups (and remained a leading soloist). His first works were two one-act satirical operas and his Kammermusik – abrasive neo-classical works that made him an enfant terrible. In 1927, he acquired respectability as teacher at the Berlin Hochschule, where he developed his famous Gebrauchsmusik (utility music) as a teaching aid. This idea was to colour his reputation for the rest of his life. With the advent of the Nazi party, Hindemith became persona non

grata again. A satirical opera Neues vom Tage in 1929, a work with a libretto by Brecht, and his opera Mathis der Maler (Matthias the Painter) about the artist's view of society, led to him leaving for the USA. Here he taught and produced a succession of works (Nobilissima Visione, the Requiem, Die Harmonie der Welt) regarded by some as valuable masterpieces and by others as boringly conservative. P.L.

ARTHUR **HONEGGER**

(b. Le Havre, 10 March 1892; d. Paris, 27 November 1955)

Honegger was born in Le Havre, attended the Paris Conservatoire (where he was taught by Widor and d'Indy), and was initially one of the French group known as 'Les Six', but this was the extent of his French affiliation. He was the child of Swiss immigrants to France, and as he became older this heritage became increasingly dominant. Honegger became involved with Milhaud, Poulenc and the other members of 'Les Six' in 1920, when he produced his elegant string work Pastorale d'été. This was to be his only Gallic piece, for in 1924 came the very serious oratorio Le Roi David, which was popular with the public but was evidence of his separation from the French group. Another surprise came in 1924 with the abrasive orchestral piece Pacific 231, representing a railway locomotive, in which Honegger seemed to become an out-and-out modernist. This impression was strengthened in 1928 with the 'symphonic movement' Rugby, but yet another change of direction saw him becoming more romantic, although with a neo-baroque rhythmic undercurrent. A series of five symphonies from 1920 to 1951 were more and more easy-going and melodic, the Fourth Symphony (Deliciae Basiliensis) being positively cheerful. His oratorio Jeanne d'Arc au bûcher (1934) and the charming Christmas Cantata (1941) both reflect this more direct style. Although Honegger ended his life teaching in Paris, he was now established as an ally of Hindemith in the German tradition. P.L.

HERBERT **HOWELLS**

(b. Lydney, 17 October 1892; d. Oxford, 23 February 1983)

Howells was one of the many English composers between 1920 and 1960 to hail from the Severn valley. His music has echoes of Vaughan Williams, traces of Elgar and even of Delius, but is more restrained and pastel-coloured than any of them; he never lost an early love of folk song. He gravitated like so many to the Royal College in London and was Stanford's favourite pupil. There followed a series of teaching posts: the RCM in 1920, St. Paul's Girls' School (following Holst) from 1936, and London University from 1954. His music was less conventional and more individual than this might imply. His early works included a piano quartet, three string quartets and a clarinet quintet, and a more romantic and uninhibited piano concerto. This work received a mixed reception in 1924 for alleged 'modernism' and the hypersensitive Howells gave up composing for several years. The death of his young son from polio in 1935 paradoxically renewed his wish to compose, and the Concerto for strings and an unaccompanied choral Requiem were at once a therapy and a renewal of creativity. In 1938 he turned the Requiem into his best-known work Hymnus Paradisi (not performed until 1950) and the remainder of his work was to follow this style – choral, contemplative and marked by delicacy and restraint. He also wrote about 65 songs, including 'King David' and the cycle 'In Green Ways'. P.L.

JOHANN NEPOMUK **HUMMEL**

(b. Pressburg, 14 November 1778; d. Weimar, 17 October 1837)

Austrian composer and pianist, Hummel was very fashionable and influential at the time when Franz Schubert was struggling to make a living and a name in Vienna. His music, if not profound, is immediately attractive, graceful and well-written, and full of vitality. His family had moved to Vienna in 1785 and Hummel obtained a post as conductor at the Theater an der Wien. His piano-playing, brilliant and impressive, was admired by Mozart who took him on as a pupil for a while. He toured Europe as a performer from 1788 and was in London 1790-92. Back in Vienna he studied with Albrechtsberger, Haydn and Salieri and found himself in friendly rivalry with Beethoven. He became Konzertmeister to the Esterházys until he became Kapellmeister to the Stuttgart court in 1813. From 1814 to his death he worked in Weimar. Hummel was always very influential in the musical world and seems to have been generally admired both as a man and musician, his technical skills having an influence on future generations of pianist composers like Schumann and Chopin. His piano writings were charmingly brilliant and included several concertos and sonatas. In recent years the world has discovered the delights of a Trumpet Concerto that is now regularly played and recorded. He wrote ballets, incidental music, church music and chamber music, all worth a hearing, and was the author of an influential treatise on piano-playing.   P.G.

ENGELBERT **HUMPERDINCK**

(b. Siegburg, 1 September 1854; d. Neustrelitz, 27 September 1921)

Humperdinck is famous for two things – writing the opera Hänsel und Gretel, and lending his name to the well-known popular singer. There are other things to say about him, but nothing as interesting as these two! He was the son of a schoolteacher, destined to be an architect, but insisting on learning music. On a musical trip to Italy in 1879 he met Wagner, and was invited to assist with the first production of Parsifal. He naturally became something of a Wagnerian disciple as a result, though the influence on his music is limited to harmony and orchestration. He taught for some years in Spain and Germany, but in 1900 he ex-

ABOVE: 'La Gare Saint Lazare' by Claude Monet (1840-1926). One of the few successful musical portrayals of trains is Honegger's Pacific 231.

panded some songs which he had written for a domestic play into the opera Hänsel und Gretel. The combination of delightful folk-like tunes with rich Wagnerian sound was an immediate success. He subsequently tried for some years to make a living from composing alone. Alas, although he wrote five more operas, some also on fairytale themes, only Königskinder (1910) was at all successful. He reverted to teaching in Berlin and writing some pleasant incidental music for Shakespeare and other plays. All Humperdinck's music is attractive and tuneful, but it is only in Hänsel und Gretel that he found the recipe for immortality.   P.L.

JOHN **IRELAND**

(b. Bowdon, 13 August 1879; d. Rock Mill, Sussex, 12 June 1962)

Ireland is an elusive composer, perhaps because he seems to have found life and happiness elusive himself. He was trained in the heart of the English musical establishment at the turn of the century. A pupil of Stanford, he was a church organist for some years, and then a composition teacher at the RCM. His own works start in the late 1890s with solid Brahmsian chamber music, but Debussy's influence is soon to be found in the early piano music and the violin sonatas and piano trios. This uneasy blend of styles hardly changes to the end of Ireland's life, and is never visited by any recognizable English influence, even when he is setting English poetry or picturing English scenes for the piano. The result is often tantalisingly unsatisfactory. Most of his best music dates from 1915-1925; the lively if disorganized Piano Concerto, the evocative landscape of Mai-Dun (reflecting Ireland's interest in legend and prehistory), the London Pieces for piano, and some good songs including 'The Land of Lost Content' (Housman) and the inevitable but indestructible 'Sea Fever'. Too much of the rest of his music is impressionistic in the wrong way. The harmony never stands still, and the music cannot be grasped. The tuneful London Overture of 1936 is an honourable exception, but otherwise Ireland's lack of a precise vision is all too evident.   P.L.

CHARLES EDWARD *Ives*

(b. Danbury, Connecticut, 20 October 1874; d. New York, 19 May 1954)

Ives's roots were deeply traditional. Connecticut was founded as a Puritan settlement early in the seventeenth century and then, in 1788, became one of the original thirteen states of the USA. Furthermore, his father George Ives directed what General Grant called 'the best band in the Army' and was well steeped in hymns and national songs: later, his son was to say that there was 'something about the way Father played hymns . . . the fervor would at times throw the key higher'.

Taught first by his father, Charles learned not only the classical compositional techniques of Bach but also the bolder American side of Danbury's musical world, and already as a boy he began to experiment in the way that we associate with his mature music, for example sketching a pair of 'fugues in four keys'. By the age of twelve, he was composing regularly as well as playing drums in his father's band, and at fourteen he became a paid church organist. His musical life already reflected his temperament, which veered from vigour to withdrawnness.

In his later teens, Ives went on to other schools and another organist's post, and finally to Yale University from 1894-8. There his professor of music was Horatio Parker, who persuaded this unorthodox young man that he must write more conventionally if he hoped for a future as a composer. Though Ives resented such disciplines as having to write what he called 'a stupid fugue', he also recognized that there was more to real originality than simply being different, and his First Symphony, which occupied him during these university years, shows his command of a broadly romantic idiom which at times suggests Dvořák.

Nevertheless, after leaving Yale, Ives took up an altogether different career, first moving to New York and joining the actuarial section of an insurance company and then teaming up with his colleague Julian Myrick to develop sales techniques. Thereafter he earned his living in insurance and composed in his spare time,

although for a while he still played the organ in a church, and some of his music was played there. In 1905, he began to court Harmony Twichell and they were married on 9 June 1908.

By now, Ives had composed several important works in the challenging idiom that was his alone, among them the two orchestral pieces called The Unanswered Question and Central Park in the Dark, which he also entitled Two Contemplations. They date from 1906, a time when Ives and his colleague Myrick began to think of running their own business. They initially set up an insurance agency called Ives & Co., which led in January 1909 to another called Ives & Myrick.

The next four decades brought Ives prosperity as a businessman, and although he composed only patchily, during the 1920s national interest in his music began steadily to grow. However, his earliest publications – of his Concord Sonata for piano (1911-15) and a song collection amounting to over a hundred songs – were done at his own expense in 1919 and 1922 respectively. His Third Symphony (The Camp Meeting), written in 1904, won a Pulitzer Prize in 1947; but the Fourth (1910-16) was not played until 1965. However, during 1931-2 the conductor Nicolas Slonimsky performed his Three Places in New England in the US and France, and also The Fourth of July in Paris, and in 1932 Aaron Copland mounted a performance of seven of his songs at the Yaddo Festival. Even so, the difficulty of his music deterred all but the most dedicated musicians – as when an orchestral work had such independent rhythmic writing that more than one conductor was needed. He retired from business at the end of 1929. Ten years later he saw his Concord Sonata hailed by the critic Lawrence Gilman as 'the greatest music by an American'. Latterly his health deteriorated: his heart had given trouble since his thirties, and eventually he became diabetic. He died five months before his eightieth birthday.

RIGHT: *Charles Ives won the Pulitzer Prize for his Third Symphony in 1947, but the Second was not premièred until 1951. The photograph by Eugene Smith was taken in 1950.*

BELOW: *'Lee Shore', Cape Cod, painted in 1941 by Edward Hopper. This is the sort of New England scene that inspired some of Ives' most American music.*

An earlier American composer, the European-trained Edward MacDowell, once declared that 'the weakness of our music is its borrowing . . . What we must arrive at is the youthful optimistic vitality and the undaunted tenacity of spirit that characterizes the American man'. In this sense, Ives is the unchallenged pioneer figure of American art music. Towards the end of his life, Schoenberg called him 'a great man [who] responds to negligence by contempt' and Stravinsky found that he offered a 'fascinating . . . new awareness of America'. Leonard Bernstein wrote of 'Ives's brave resolve to be American, to write American music in the face of an indifferent and uncaring world'.

Yet Bernstein also noted his 'wicked sense of humor' and called him 'eccentric', remarking that his Second Symphony (1902) had everything from Beethoven to 'Turkey in the Straw' (a famous American song dating from 1834) and resembled a charming lace-trimmed Christmas card that could explode when you opened it. Aaron Copland suggested that 'perhaps he was too far in advance of his own generation'. His music has been called uneven and amateurish, a sort of 'anything goes' style that mixes things of value with meaningless muddle that no amount of performance artistry will disguise. Faced with the piano part in his song 'Soliloquy', where the player is asked to play an impossible chord spreading over more than six octaves, one may wonder what this

ABOVE: An aerial view of the skyscrapers of Manhattan, a hand-coloured photograph taken in 1924. Ives spent much of his life as a citizen of New York and died there in 1954.

has to do with practical sound. But Ives's only answer was, 'My God! What has sound got to do with music?'.

In forming his language, Ives drew not only on European tradition (which, after all, gave him the orchestra) but also on American popular music, from barn dances to hymns and Stephen Foster's ballads, although black idioms and jazz play little part. His music commonly reflects his patriotism and has a recurrent philosophical strain. For him, it was something 'approving and reflecting moral goodness' which could and should carry a 'message' even if it did occasionally 'pull the ear, hard' – as when he asked orchestras to play two pieces simultaneously despite their different keys and tempos. Literature often inspired him, and he named the movements of the Concord Sonata for piano after the American sages Emerson, Hawthorne, the Alcotts and Thoreau. Humour was another lasting aspect of this unique composer whom Bernstein admiringly called 'an authentic primitive'. Among his American successors, John Cage and Elliott Carter both owed him much.

C.H.

LEOŠ
Janáček (b. Hukvaldy, Moravia, 3 July 1854; d. Moravská Ostrava, 12 August 1928)

RIGHT: *Leoš Janáček was producing his most successful operas,* The Cunning Little Vixen *and* The Makropulos Affair, *when this portrait was taken in 1925.*

*B*oth Janáček's grandfather and father were teaching musicians, and he was the fifth of nine children born to a poor though respectable Czech family. At the age of eleven, he was sent to the Moravian capital Brno to be a chorister at the city's Augustinian monastery: it played an important part in his training, as did its choirmaster Pavel Křížkovský (1820-1885), himself a composer of importance in Moravia's musical life.

Janáček himself expected to follow in the family tradition. On ending school life in 1869 he gained a scholarship to a teacher training institute and after graduation taught in a school for two probationary years. But thereafter he asserted his musical interests to a greater degree. He founded a choral society in 1873, and in the following year he began to study at the Prague Organ School; some sacred and organ pieces date from this time. In 1875, he returned to his old monastery school at Brno to teach and conduct the choir, for whom he wrote an Exaudi Deus with organ accompaniment that was his first published work. He also conducted other choirs, performing Mozart's Requiem and Beethoven's Missa Solemnis. In 1877 he was again studying in Prague, and gained the encouragement and friendship of Dvořák. His institute now recognized that this was no ordinary trainee and in October 1879 it allowed him to travel on a year's study leave, first to the Leipzig Conservatory and then on to its counterpart in Vienna six months later.

Yet although in his mid-twenties, he had not yet found himself as a musician. Nor had he settled down personally. Always a man of strong emotions, in 1879 he had fallen in love with his pupil Zdenka Schulzová, the daughter of the director of the Teachers' Institute. She was eleven years his junior and only fifteen when they were married in July 1881. Their marriage lasted many years, but was to have its ups and downs. However, it brought Janáček additional confidence, and he made ambitious plans to turn Brno into a musical centre comparable with Prague. He taught, conducted, studied folk music and founded and edited a journal. In 1884 a new theatre opened in the city and three years later Janáček started his first opera Šárka, but its librettist (who wanted Dvořák) finally eventually refused permission for him to use the text. This was not the only setback of these years. His wife did not share his enthusiasm for everything Czech, and although their daughter Olga was born in 1882 they lived apart from 1882-4, partly, it seems, because Janáček invited his mother to live with them. A son born four years later died in infancy, and thereafter the marriage cooled.

BELOW: *Part of the original manuscript score of* Jenůfa, *his first operatic success which was premièred in Brno early in 1904.*

It was not until he approached fifty that Janáček found his own voice with his opera Jenůfa, which occupied him from 1894-1903. Its successful première in Brno on 21 January 1904 was a milestone in his life. In that year he resigned from his post at the Teachers' Institute to run his Organ School and give more time to composition. Over the next decade or so, he composed the operas Osud (Fate) and Mr Brouček's Excursion to the Moon (1917) but neither received a performance. Other works on a smaller scale included Along an Overgrown Path (1908), fifteen piano pieces that recalled his childhood, and Pohádka (1910), a 'fairy tale' for cello and piano. Finally in May 1916, Jenůfa was performed in Prague, and at sixty-one Janáček found himself hailed as a genius.

Thereafter, Janáček took on a new lease of life. He composed four more operas as well as the vocal cycle The Diary of One Who Disappeared (1919), the First String Quartet (1923), the wind sextet Mládi with its title meaning 'youth' (1924), the Glagolitic Mass and the powerful, five-movement Sinfonietta for orchestra (both 1926). However, his private life remained disturbed, for in 1918 he fell in love with Kamila Stösslová, a married woman nearly forty years younger than himself. Although he did not seriously contemplate leaving his wife for her, she inspired the song cycle mentioned above, as well as his portrayal of operatic heroines. Kamila seems to have paid little attention to his passion, but received almost daily letters from him, which are the 'Intimate Letters' that inspired his Second String Quartet, written in the year of his death.

Janáček is one of those composers whose stature remains a matter of argument among his fellow musicians, although no one denies his immense individuality. For much of his life, he was considered by his contemporaries (when considered at all) as an eccentric, a mere 'folklorist' whose musical methods were idiosyncratic and too crude to be of significance beyond local Moravian circles. But when Jenůfa reached Prague in 1916, it became clear that there was more to him than that. Nevertheless there is much of the primitive about his most characteristic music, whether it be the operas, the Glagolitic Mass, the Diary of One Who Disappeared, or the massive Sinfonietta with its blaring trumpets. He frequently used everyday speech rhythms as the basis for musical ones, did not hesitate to repeat little figures over and over again, and wrote for orchestra in a way that is as brash as it is powerful.

Indeed, there are few expressive half-tones in Janáček's music, for his aim often seems to have been to express raw emotions as nakedly as possible. Thus there is an emotional naïvety about the opera Kátya Kabanová (1921), which tells of an unfaithful wife in a Russian village who, in shame, finally drowns herself in the Volga: the story seems novelettish because no character, not even the heroine herself, is painted in depth by either the libretto or the music. However, Ian Horsbrugh's book on the composer (1981) finds that here 'a tragedy is enshrined in music of supreme beauty' and so reminds us that Janáček continues to divide opinion.

His choice of subject here undoubtedly reflected his own liberal views as to women's rights. Women are often the central figures of his operas, and in this sense he may be an important contributor to positively changing attitudes on female emancipation. However, the powerful mother-in-law in Kátya Kabanová is a most unsympathetic character, while Emilia Marty, the protagonist of The Makropulos Affair (1925), is a femme fatale who reduces men to feebleness as well as being three centuries old and weary of life. Mr Brouček's Excursion to the Moon (the first of two operas: the second takes him to the fifteenth century) is also a satire on bourgeois complacency, although dressed as a fanciful extravaganza. There was always something of the rebel about this composer, and even the song cycle The Diary of One Who Disappeared fully sympathizes with the young man who abandons respectable village life for a gipsy girl. Indeed, he told Kamila Stösslová, 'I thought only of you. You were Zefka'.

Janáček was a great letter-writer and a diarist, and from his correspondence we learn of his methods. At the time of writing The Makropulos Affair, he wrote, 'Everything flies about, completely boundless. Many motifs. Don't know yet how to get them into order'. A description of him at work by the secretary of the Brno Conservatory is no less informative: 'The whole morning I could hear his piano but in a most unusual way. [He] kept banging out a few notes of a theme as loudly as possible, repeating it many times unchanged or with only slight alteration. The verve of his playing made one realize how much he was carried away.' C.H.

LEFT: The Charles Bridge over the River Moldau in Prague, looking towards Prague Castle and St. Vitus' Cathedral. Janáček studied in Prague, and the 1916 production of Jenůfa here established Janáček's musical reputation.

RUGGIERO Leoncavallo (b. Naples, 23 April 1857; d. Montecatini Termi, 9 August 1919)

The probable date of Leoncavallo's birth in Naples was 23 April 1857, although in later life he cited 8 March of the following year. His father was not only a magistrate but also a novelist, and these literary interests were inherited by the son, who in later life always preferred to write his own libretti. In fact, young Leoncavallo followed his years as a precocious child at the Naples Conservatory by going to Bologna University in 1876 to study literature and law. His musical talents were not forgotten, however; he completed his first opera Chatterton, but plans for a production of this eventually collapsed.

The disappointed composer consequently began almost ten years of travel, earning a living as pianist and songwriter in various cities as far apart as Cairo and London. In the mid-1880s he settled temporarily in Montmartre in Paris and planned an ambitious trilogy on life in Renaissance Florence, called Crepusculo (Twilight) doubtlessly influenced by Wagner's Ring. When he returned to Italy, Leoncavallo was annoyed that the publisher Ricordi showed no interest in his music, but requested only a libretto for an opera Puccini was planning, Manon Lescaut. To increase Leoncavallo's chagrin, in the event Puccini rejected the libretto, so the craving for fame and fortune was still unsatisfied.

Mascagni had won sudden renown in 1890 for his short, violent opera Cavalleria rusticana, so Leoncavallo decided to attempt a similar feat. Moreover, he was successful. I Pagliacci, a tale of murderous jealousy among a troupe of touring actors, was an instant success in 1892. Leoncavallo based his libretto on a real-life killing (the case had been tried before his own father), and both words and music have the ring of truth and genuine emotion. Sadly, this was something Leoncavallo never achieved again.

The following year, the first part of his cherished trilogy was

RIGHT: *Ruggiero Leoncavallo, a photograph of the composer taken in 1905 during his fallow years when continued success eluded him.*

RIGHT: *'Behind the Curtain', an oil-painting by Ludwig Knaus (1829-1910) completed in 1880. This might well have been the setting for the story of I Pagliacci (1890), which tells of jealousy and murder among a group of travelling players.*

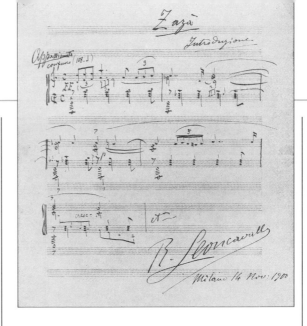

finally produced, but it was deemed to be boring by his critics. His next project met an even sadder fate, for when Leoncavallo decided to write an opera called La Bohème *in which his own Bohemian life in Paris could be profitably recalled, he did not realize that Puccini was well advanced on his opera of that same title. Leoncavallo's* La Bohème *has many merits, but it never recovered from being produced a year after Puccini's masterpiece had won universal acclaim.*

In 1900, Zazà, *another story of theatrical affairs, failed to restore Leoncavallo's waning fortunes, and in desperation he undertook a commission from an unexpected source – Kaiser Wilhelm II. However, the Germanic historical drama* Der Roland von Berlin *was unsuccessful even in Berlin, and the composer increasingly was forced to find quick success by writing operettas, and travelling widely to promote them. The onset of war in 1914 found the formerly easy-going Leoncavallo an embittered, sick man, and in his remaining five years there was little to cheer him as it became obvious that nothing of his was going to remain in the operatic repertoire apart from that single triumph he had written a quarter of a century earlier –* I Pagliacci.

To the average music-lover, the name of Leoncavallo is memorable only for his short opera of 1892, *I Pagliacci*, which has been a major favourite with audiences since its birth. Even if we add the little song 'Mattinata' which he wrote for the tenor Enrico Caruso to record, it leaves his reputation resting on barely one hour of music. Many must have wondered if his other stage works are so inferior that they have virtually withered in the shadow of their thriving companion piece. The answer is not simple. Some of the most ambitious of Leoncavallo's projects have hardly been seen in public since their hurried withdrawal after unsuccessful premières; even among opera enthusiasts, very few have seen *I Medici* (1893), *Der Roland von Berlin* (1904), or *Edipo Re* (1920). Critical reviews of the time condemned them for heaviness, lack of melody and theatrical clumsiness, unexpected faults in the composer of *Pagliacci*!

With regard to the creation of *La Bohème*, Leoncavallo was unlucky, as his opera on the subject is attractive in its own right, and may well have held the stage had not Puccini's superior work appeared a year earlier. Listening to Leoncavallo's version today is a slightly confusing experience, for he has concentrated on Marcello and Musetta, so that Rodolfo and Mimi are subsidiary characters; moreover, Marcello is now a tenor and Rodolfo the baritone. However, it is worth recalling that in its early years this *La Bohème*, with Caruso in the leading role, was almost as popular with audiences as Puccini's version was.

Two other Leoncavallo operas deserve rescue from neglect: *Zazà* (1900), the story of a Parisian actress's affair with a married man, and *Gli Zingari* (1912), based on Pushkin's story of gypsy life. At present, however, neither is easily seen or even heard on CD.

And so we come back to *I Pagliacci*, which is perhaps the greatest success of the verismo school of Italian opera. Its plot tells of the murder by a jealous actor of his unfaithful wife, committed during a performance of a comedy. Leoncavallo's skill in fashioning his own libretto is admirable. He makes full use of the 'play within a play' device, and the contrast in the final scene between the trivial songs of the comic players and the violent outbursts of the enraged Canio is wonderfully effective. He also incorporates a wide range of emotions in the space of two brief scenes, and his gifts of melody and varied orchestration have justly made such numbers as the Prologue and 'Vesti la giubba' ('On with the motley') universal favourites. Perhaps only the solo aria for Canio's bored, frivolous wife is inadequate; the other participants, including the simple village audience, spring to life. For once, at least, Leoncavallo's talents were used to their full extent.

P.J.

Chronology

1857 *Born in Naples 23 April (others suggest 8 March 1858)*

1867 *Student at Naples Conservatory*

1876 *Graduates in music. Goes to Bologna to study law. Meets Wagner*

1878 *Having failed to get* Chatterton *produced, begins years of travel (Cairo, Marseilles, Paris, London) as pianist and songwriter*

1882 *Settles in Montmartre and plans historical trilogy of operas*

1889 *Publisher Ricordi rejects music but requests libretto for Puccini (Manon Lescaut); Puccini rejects it*

1890 *Seeks quick success with* I Pagliacci

1892 *Triumphant first performance under Toscanini in Milan at the Teatro dal Verme*

1893 *First part of Florentine trilogy produced without success*

1894 *Another set-back – he discovers Puccini is also writing an opera on theme of* La Bohème. *Legal disputes*

1897 *Leoncavallo's* La Bohème *produced in Venice a year after Puccini's successful première*

1900 *Zazà first performed in Milan*

1904 *Commission from Kaiser,* Der Roland von Berlin, *a failure. Writes song 'Mattinata' for Caruso*

1906 *Turns to operettas. Tours USA*

1912 *Gli Zingari fairly successful in London*

1914-18 *More trivial operettas. Increasing ill-health and bitterness*

1919 *Dies at Montecatini, 9 August*

1920 *Last serious opera* Edipo Re *produced posthumously*

FRANZ
Liszt (b. Raiding, 22 October 1811; d. Bayreuth, 31 July 1886)

RIGHT: Franz Liszt as a young man, painted in oils in 1839 by Henri Charles Lehmann. At this time many women found him irresistible.

Chronology

1811 *Born at Raiding, 22 October*

1817 *First piano lessons*

1820 *First concert, at Sopron*

1821-3 *In Vienna, taught by Czerny and Salieri. Gives concerts and meets Schubert and Beethoven. Moves to Paris, December*

1824 *First visit to England; plays to George IV*

1825 *Don Sanche performed in Paris, October*

1827 *Death of Adam Liszt, spiritual crisis. Returns to mother in Paris*

1831 *Hears Paganini, March*

1832 *Hears Chopin and they later become friends*

1835 *Goes to Switzerland with Marie d'Agoult; teaches at Geneva*

1838-47 *Transcendental Studies. Recommences virtuoso career and travels widely*

1844 *Parts from Marie; takes their three children to Paris for their education*

1847 *Meets Princess Carolyne von Sayn-Wittgenstein in Kiev*

1848 *Settles with Carolyne at Weimar and accepts full-time conducting appointment there*

1850 *Conducts première of Wagner's Lohengrin, August*

1853 *Piano Sonata. Visits Wagner in Switzerland*

1857 *Completes Faust Symphony and conducts première in September; also conducts that of Dante Symphony in Dresden, November*

1858 *Gives up Weimar post but remains there for a while*

Although born in what is now Hungary, Liszt came from a German-speaking family, his father being a minor official in the service of Prince Esterházy. Adam Liszt also played the cello, and began to teach his son the piano when Franz was about six. His progress was such that by the age of nine he had already given concerts and composed short pieces. Wealthy patrons then made it possible in 1821 for him to continue his studies in Vienna, where his teachers were Czerny for piano and Salieri for composition. Finally in 1823, the Liszts settled in Paris and the boy pianist gave further concerts there and made three visits to England (where he played for George IV) during 1824-7. His one-act opera Don Sanche was first performed in Paris in October 1825. But the pace of this career proved too much, and in 1827 he went through a spiritual crisis that was aggravated by his father's death, even considering the priesthood as a vocation.

Instead, he set up house with his mother in Paris and began to teach the piano. He also read widely and got to know such leading artistic figures as Victor Hugo and Berlioz. In March 1831 he heard the celebrated violinist Paganini play and determined to become his pianistic equivalent, devoting long hours to the perfection of his already dazzling keyboard technique. His meeting with Chopin, whom he first heard in 1832 and who became a friend, was also influential.

He now began a ten-year relationship with Marie d'Agoult, who left her husband in 1835 to elope with Liszt to Switzerland, where he taught at the Geneva Conservatoire; their daughter Blandine was born in December of that year, their daughter Cosima (later Wagner's wife) in 1837 and their son Daniel in

1839. From 1838, he recommenced his life as a travelling virtuoso pianist and for several exciting but exhausting years he performed in countries ranging from Ireland to Russia and Turkey. Several women featured in his life, but he spend his summers in Germany with Marie and his children until they parted in 1844.

In 1840, Liszt began also to conduct, and following his appointment as Music Director at Weimar and the commencement of a new relationship with Princess Carolyne Sayn-Wittgenstein, he and she settled in this German city in 1848. Thereafter he gave up most of his pianistic career in favour of a new life as a composer and conductor.

Gradually, Liszt found his Weimar post less congenial, and he gave it up in 1858, moving eventually to Rome (where he and the Princess went their separate ways) and living there from 1863 in semi-retirement. In 1865 he received minor orders and became an Abbé. But four years later, he started once again to spend part of each year at Weimar, where he was much sought after as a teacher, also spending time in Rome and Budapest, where he was made a Royal Hungarian Counsellor. His daughter Cosima married Wagner in 1870, and he visited their home at Bayreuth shortly before the première there of Wagner's Ring cycle in 1876. During this last part of his life, he continued to travel, and gave friendship and advice to many younger composers including Grieg, Franck, Debussy, Albéniz and Borodin. In 1886 he revisited England to hear his orchestral works enthusiastically received and also played to Queen Victoria at Windsor. He then went on to Antwerp, Paris, Weimar, Luxembourg and finally to Bayreuth, where he developed pneumonia and died six days after hearing Tristan und Isolde.

ABOVE: A photograph by the celebrated French photographer Nadar, taken in 1865, the year Liszt took minor orders in the church and became known as the Abbé Liszt.

Liszt is a principal figure of the romantic movement. Like his friends Wagner and Berlioz, he was inspired by grand subjects, and there is an epic quality about such music as the *Faust* and *Dante* Symphonies. Although he could write delicate, intimate miniatures such as his six *Consolations* (1850), some of his greatest keyboard music storms the heights of virtuosity, and it is no coincidence that he called twelve of his most difficult pieces *Studies of Transcendental Execution*, or that Schumann called them 'studies of storm and dread for at most ten or twelve players in the world'. In this mood, Liszt as a composer-pianist was described by Charles Hallé as 'all sunshine and dazzling splendour, subjugating his hearers with a power that none could withstand'. Music such as his *First Mephisto Waltz* for piano solo and his *Totentanz* for piano and orchestra also have more than a touch of *diablerie* and leave a whiff of sulphur behind them.

Yet even here we meet the religious element which was fundamental to Liszt's nature throughout a life that people may sometimes have thought worldly and even vain. As a practising Catholic, he composed a large number of sacred works during his later life, some on a large scale such as his oratorios *The Legend of St. Elizabeth* and *Christus*, the Hungarian Coronation Mass and a Requiem. His *Via Crucis* (1879) is in fourteen sections describing the Stations of the Cross: it was rejected by a publisher and only received its first performance on Good Friday 1929 in Budapest. Besides his music actually for church use, there are other works that take

BELOW: *Countess Marie d'Agoult, with whom Liszt lived from 1835-1844 and who bore him three children They parted on bad terms.*

ABOVE: *'Waterfall near Tivoli', an oil-painting by Martin von Rohden (1778-1868). Such a scene might have inspired Liszt's* Années de pèlerinage *Book 2, which is subtitled 'Italie'.*

a moral tone, and his noble yet gentle symphonic poem *Orpheus* has as its theme the civilizing influence of art. Pope Pius IX once visited Liszt in Rome and asked to hear him play, telling him that the authorities 'ought to employ your music to lead hardened criminals to repentance', adding that he believed that one day such methods would be used.

Liszt wrote many songs, and his pianistic tone poems, such as his three sets of *Années de pèlerinage*, also show his keen response to pictorial and literary themes. He established the symphonic poem as a musical form, and also developed cyclic form, with its transformation of themes as a work progressed: we see this at work in his symphonic poem *Les Préludes*, his great one-movement Piano Sonata and his *Faust* Symphony. The atonal (keyless) opening theme of this Symphony reminds us that he was a remarkable innovator. He composed a *Bagatelle without Key* and sometimes ended a piece on a dissonance, and one of his pupils asked of his *Csárdás macabre* (1882), 'Is one allowed to write such a thing and to listen to it?'. His compatriot Bartók believed that his contribution to music was more important even than that of Wagner.   C.H.

ABOVE: *Aram Khachaturian photographed at a World Youth Festival held in Berlin in 1959.*

ABOVE: *A photograph of Zoltán Kodály by Lazlo Vamos taken in 1962, just a year after Kodály had completed his only symphony.*

RIGHT: *'The Dancer Marietta di Rigando' painted in 1904 by Max Slevogt (1868-1932). Lalo's Symphonie espagnole is one of several works that sets out to capture the spirit of Spain in music.*

ARAM **KHACHATURIAN**

(b. Tiflis (Tbilisi), 6 June 1903; d. Moscow, 1 May 1978)

Although Khachaturian is known as a Russian composer, he really should be thought of as Armenian. His music is dominated by Armenian themes and rhythms, which give it an unmistakable character, even though in other ways it follows the Russian nationalist tradition. He was the son of a bookbinder, and destined to be a scientist, but taught himself enough music to gain entry relatively late into the Moscow Conservatory, where he was taught composition by Miaskovsky. His first real success came with his First Symphony in 1934, when he was already over 30. This was quickly followed by the Piano Concerto which is still his most popular orchestral work. Khachaturian's career flourished in the 1940s, when as a respected member of the Union of Soviet Composers he produced the statutory political choral works, as well as his popular ballet (about a collective farm) Gayane (1942) – containing the well-known Sabre Dance and other colourful and exciting music. Two more symphonies, a cello concerto, incidental music to Masquerade (1940) and a successful ballet, Spartacus (1954), added to his reputation, though he was briefly (and amazingly) out of favour for 'formalism' during the political purges of 1948. In his last years he concentrated on film music, and produced little of consequence.   P.L.

ZOLTÁN **KODÁLY**

(b. Kecskemét, 16 December 1882; d. Budapest 6 March 1967)

One of the founders of modern Hungarian music, Kodály occupies a position between Dohnányi and Bartók, with both of whom he was closely associated. He was brought up in a musical family, and after studying at Budapest University he spent much time in collecting folk songs, which was to affect him and his music for the rest of his life. He also travelled widely in Europe, and with Bartók was much influenced by Debussy. His composing career began with the orchestral Summer Evening in 1906, and shortly thereafter he began his other lifelong career in teaching.

Despite other activities, he still had time to compose steadily: the years 1908-1915 were dominated by chamber music, including two string quartets and a sonata for solo cello. Then the choral Psalmus Hungaricus in 1923 was followed by the folk operas Háry János (1926) and The Spinning Room (1932). In 1931 came his best-known orchestral work, Dances of Galánta. There were still more works to come – the Peacock variations, the Concerto for Orchestra, a final opera Czinka Panna (1948) – but most of his later life was occupied by a vast output of choral music for schools. Kodály appears to have been an unusual combination of saint and administrator, and his greatest influence in Hungary was as the inspirer of musical education and folk song research. His own music is more characterful than Dohnányi's but less individual than Bartók's. Unmistakably Hungarian and saturated with characteristic folk themes, it can at its best be invigorating and captivating, but the lack of Bartók's originality and drive is clear in his lesser pieces.   P.L.

EDOUARD **LALO**

(b. Lille, 27 January 1823; d. Paris, 22 April 1892)

Lalo's Spanish-sounding name, and that of his best-known work, the Symphonie espagnole for violin and orchestra, give the impression that he was a man of the south. In fact he was born in Lille, at the other end of France; his family had left the Spanish Netherlands generations before. For some years, Lalo's career was that of a chamber musician and teacher, and he wrote only some under-appreciated chamber music. His first attempt at larger-scale composition, the opera Fiesque, was a failure in 1866, and it was only when he wrote two works, a violin concerto and the Symphonie espagnole, for the Spanish violinist Sarasate in 1873-4 that he achieved success. There followed a cello concerto, an oriental ballet Namouna (1881-2), a symphony, a second more popular opera Le Roi d'Ys (1888) and finally a virtually unknown piano concerto. Lalo's music achieved only moderate success partly because of its uneven quality, but also because it was thought to be 'German' as was that of Franck. This accusation seems odd to us today. In fact, his best music is very French in being either operatic (Le Roi d'Ys) or in pseudo-Spanish vein (the delightful Symphonie espagnole).   P.L.

CONSTANT **LAMBERT**

(b. London, 23 August 1905; d. London, 21 August 1951)

An enigmatic and confused figure, Lambert was perhaps the most versatile, yet most distracted, English musician between the wars. He was equally talented as composer, conductor and critic, but his career problems and early death from alcoholism seriously reduced his legacy. A member of an artistic family, Lambert studied at the London RCM (with Vaughan Williams among others), and he achieved remarkable early success when Diaghilev commissioned the ballet Romeo and Juliet from him in 1926. This was followed by another ballet, Pomona, and his orchestral masterpiece The Rio Grande. The jazz influence in this work and in the unconventional Piano Concerto of 1931, as well as his involvement with Walton in Façade, marked him out as a member of the avant-garde. In 1934 his astringent book 'Music Ho!' was in part a plea for English music to be less insular and pay more attention to international activities. He had by now begun to compose in a more traditional, though by no means English nationalist, style, as in his great choral masque Summer's Last Will and

Testament (1935) and the ballet Horoscope (1937). Ballet occupied more and more of his time on account of his need to earn his living as a conductor, and this, with his drinking, drastically reduced his time for composing. Only the short orchestral work Aubade heroique of 1942 and the ballet Tiresias of 1950 were to come before his premature death.   P.L.

GEORGE **LLOYD**

(b. St. Ives, 28 June 1913)

Lloyd is an unusual composer for our time, and he has had an unusual life. His music is old-fashioned, in the sense that it is tuneful, accessible, often lighthearted, not very experimental. His life, on the other hand, has been shot through by reverses, changes of course, violent alterations of routine. Lloyd was a violin student with Albert Sammons in the '30s, but soon gravitated to composing. His First Symphony emerged at the age of 19, and his first opera, Iernin, on a Cornish subject, in 1933. Two more symphonies and another opera, The Serf, followed before the war, which was to prove traumatic for him, as he was shell-shocked during an Arctic convoy. Composing proved a valuable therapy, and this is the origin of his Fourth and Fifth Symphonies (1946). Another opera, John Socman, written for the 1951 Festival of Britain, proved too great a strain, and precipitated a breakdown as a result of which he spent three years market-gardening. After a gradual resumption of composition, he produced seven more symphonies, as well as four piano concertos and a large oratorio, The Vigil of Venus. Lloyd's music is an unexpected product of his unpredictable life. The style is unabashedly romantic, not strikingly derivative, owing something to Walton, something to Bax – and something perhaps to Eric Coates.   P.L.

JEAN-BAPTISTE **LULLY**

(b. Florence, 29 November 1632; d. Paris, 22 March 1687)

'The father of French opera' was the son of an Italian miller. Lully left his native land in his teens as a valet with an aristocratic French family. Once settled in Paris, he devoted himself to the mastery of dancing and the composition of ballets to exhibit his skills, many of which were written in collaboration with Molière. Lully prospered in the court of King Louis XIV, achieving

ABOVE: 'Allegorical Picture of the Royal Family' painted by Jean Nocret (1615-72) in 1670. The King is Louis XIV of France (1638-1715), the employer of Lully in the late 17th century.

virtual domination of French theatrical life. He took French citizenship and married a rich French lady in 1662. He composed untiringly throughout his life, mainly ballets but also several operas and choral works. It was while performing one of the latter that he stabbed his foot with the staff he used for conducting; the subsequent infection proved fatal. Lully's reputation as a court intriguer has unfairly harmed his musical standing, but in the last quarter of this century the trend towards authentic performances of old music has effected the revival of several of his half-forgotten stage works, such as Le bourgeois gentilhomme (1670) and Atys (1676). On stage and on disc they have proved to be extremely stylish and effective.   P.J.

WITOLD **LUTOSLAWSKI**

(b. Warsaw, 25 January 1913; d. Warsaw, 7 February 1994)

Lutoslawski studied composition at Warsaw University in the years preceding the Second World War and soon showed a flair for bold orchestral scoring. Wider recognition of his talents was impeded by the war years – during which he played piano in a café – and the subsequent imposition of a Communist régime in Poland. Paradoxically, the Polish authorities seemed to compensate for political restrictions by increasingly allowing artistic licence, and Lutoslawski was hailed for his forward-looking Concerto for Orchestra (1956) and the Funeral Music (1958). In the '60s, he even employed improvisation and serial techniques to powerful effect in Livre pour orchestre (1968) and the Cello Concerto (1970). Subsequently, he was in growing demand as a lecturer in many countries, which may have restricted his time for composition; his output is not extensive, but obviously each work has been subject to much thought. In 1983 he produced his Third Symphony, which had taken ten years to complete and was considered his masterpiece. The advancing years did not diminish the powers of this dignified and respected composer, and the ongoing series of Chain pieces testify eloquently to his continuing emotional and intellectual appeal.   P.J.

ABOVE: Edouard Lalo photographed in Paris, probably in the 1860's when his gift for composition began to flower.

ABOVE: Jean-Baptiste Lully portrayed by Paul Mignard (1639-91). The painting is now in the Musée Condé in Chantilly.

GUSTAV Mahler

(b. Kalište, Bohemia, 7 July 1860; d. Vienna, 18 May 1911)

For many years after his death, audiences were more likely to recall Mahler's interpretation of a Mozart or Wagner opera than a performance of one of his own symphonies. Mahler's stock as a conductor stood considerably higher than as a composer. The current popularity of his music is in part due to the generation of European conductors which succeeded Mahler and who proved such persuasive advocates of his cause: conductors such as Bruno Walter, Otto Klemperer, Jascha Horenstein and Willem Mengelberg. And it is surely no accident that the wider appreciation of Mahler has coincided with, first, the advent of the long-playing record and, more recently, compact disc.

The fashion for his music, however, is deeper-rooted than mere sonic spectacle. In embracing the banal and the brutal along with the beautiful, Mahler's symphonic canon, if anything, has gained in relevance. It is nothing less than a voyage across the ocean of human experience.

Gustav Mahler was one of fourteen children, seven of whom died in infancy. His father was a small-town brewer, running the equivalent of today's off-licence. Although something of a bully – he is known to have mistreated his wife – he appears to have encouraged his son's evident musical gifts and, at ten, Gustav Mahler was giving his first recital. He gained admission to the Vienna Conservatory and, in 1880, produced his first composition of merit, the song-cycle Das klagende Lied (The Song of Lament), based on a medieval folk legend. Thereafter, folk poetry

was always to prove an inspiration to the composer. Despite graduating in composition, financial pressures forced Mahler to pursue first-and-foremost a career as a conductor. He became an exceptionally good one, intolerant of anything less than the highest standards, and rapidly moved up the conducting ladder despite frequent rows with opera-house managements and several abrupt departures. He finally attained the highest post in Austrian music, that of director of the Vienna State Opera, but only at the expense of converting from Judaism to Catholicism.

In 1901, he married Alma Schindler and came to enjoy his happiest years, although controversy was never far away. In 1907, when he had held the Vienna Opera post for ten years, anti-semitic elements conspired to force his resignation. He accepted contracts in the United States, becoming, first, Conductor of New York's Metropolitan Opera, then of the city's Philharmonic Orchestra.

Mahler was a fatalist, and not without justification. The 'three blows of fate' which he had scored into his bleakly tragic Sixth Symphony proved all too prescient: the first he came to see as his resignation from the Vienna State Opera; the second, the death of his daughter, which left him heartbroken; and the third, the diagnosis of his own chronic heart disease. He died in Vienna in May 1911, his reputation as a conductor universally accepted. Despite the enthusiasm of such as Alban Berg, Arnold Schoenberg and Anton Webern – the core of the so-called 'second Viennese school' – as a composer, Mahler's time was yet to come.

RIGHT: A photo portrait of Mahler taken in 1892, when he was Kapellmeister at the Stadttheater in Hamburg, and contemplating his Second Symphony.

All of Mahler's major compositions belong to one of two musical forms, either the symphony or the song-cycle, and there is a close relationship between the two: a number of vocal pieces reappear in the symphonies. They are also bonded by Mahler's fascination for folk poetry, especially the collection known as Das Knaben Wunderhorn (The Boy's Magic Horn). This was no pot-pourri of rustic trivia; instead, Mahler discovered in it potent images of the macabre and the supernatural, a mixture of satire and allegory which fired his

imagination and, in the melancholy tale of 'Der Tamboursg'sell' (The Drummer-boy) perhaps a metaphor for his own personality. Altogether Mahler set twenty-one of the Wunderhorn poems, twelve in the eponymous song-cycle which occupied him from 1892 until 1901.

Mahler's First Symphony was first performed before an uncomprehending audience in Budapest in 1889. It was four years before the next performance, by which time the composer had added a title The Titan. Far from aiding under-

Chronology

1860 *Born in Kalište, Bohemia*
1871 *Enters Prague Gymnasium*
1875 *Accepted into Vienna Conservatory*
1878 *Leaves conservatory and matriculates at Jihlava*
1880 *Das klagende Lied*
1883 *Appointed second conductor at Cassel's court theatre*
1884 *Lieder eines fahrenden Gesellen*
1885 *Appointed second conductor at Deutsches Landestheater, Prague*
1886 *Becomes second conductor under Nikisch at Leipzig*
1888 *Resigns Leipzig post to become music director of the Budapest opera*
1889 *Death of father (18 February) and of mother (4 October); Symphony No. I premièred in Budapest*

RIGHT: The State Opera in Vienna, a coloured etching of 1900 by Rudolph van Alt (1812-1905). Mahler became Kapellmeister here, and later Director.

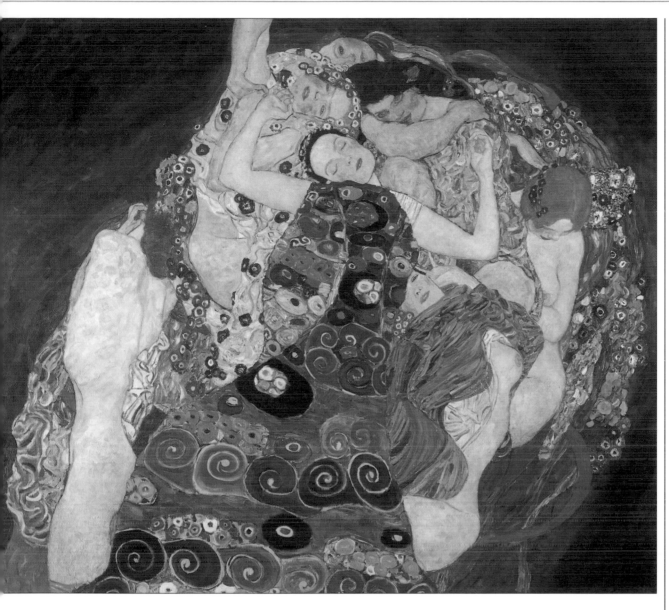

ABOVE: 'The Virgin' by Gustav Klimt (1862-1918), painted in 1913. Klimt and Mahler became friends in Vienna in the 1890's; both strove to discover new forms of artistic expression.

standing, it seemed to compound the bewilderment. He scrapped the title in 1896, at the same time deleting the second movement which he had entitled 'Blumine' (flowers).

With his Second Symphony, Mahler attempted nothing less than a depiction of the Apocalypse – and comes as close as anyone to achieving it – in music of spectacular theatricality but undeniable sincerity. Is there an audience anywhere that does not hold its breath as the last trump is announced on the off-stage brass and the massive forces of orchestra, soloists and choir begin their inexorable progress to one of the most thrilling climaxes in music?

The pantheistic Third Symphony of 1895 glories in the delights and mysteries of the natural world and its mood of radiant innocence is maintained by the Fourth Symphony, the shortest and most lyrical of the cycle. The Fifth Symphony marks a fundamental change of outlook, its stern opening fanfare heralding a funeral march of unrelieved grimness. However, light does eventually flood the darkness in the form of Mahler's best-known symphonic movement, the wistful and nostalgic Adagietto for harp and strings. There is no such balm in the Sixth Symphony. The sleigh bells of the Fourth are crushed under the boots of some invading army; the slow movement is an aching tragedy; the scherzo a dance of demons; and the finale, with its three 'blows of fate', admits only the finality of death.

Mahler followed this with the extraordinary Seventh Symphony, with its startlingly original scoring and the elusive, strange quality of its two 'Night Musics'. With the Eighth, he composed a paean for the human soul and music's first entirely choral symphony, managing to juxtapose the medieval hymn 'Veni creator spiritus' with the closing scene from Goethe's *Faust*.

The song-cycle to ancient Chinese texts, *Das Lied von der Erde* (*The Song of the Earth*) was to all intents and purposes Mahler's ninth symphony but superstition led him to avoid numbering it as such. It is exquisite music, encompassing youthful hedonism, the transience of beauty, mortality and, in the concluding 'Abschied' (Farewell), an utterance of almost unbearable poignancy and resignation.

While in many ways valedictory, the Ninth Symphony we know today also showed how forward-looking Mahler was in his music and we can glean some idea of the direction he was taking from the late Deryck Cooke's performing version of the unfinished Tenth Symphony.   P.H.

PIETRO Mascagni

(b. Livorno, 7 December 1863; d. Rome, 2 August 1945)

RIGHT: *A photo portrait of Mascagni taken in the 1930's when he was the Director of La Scala Opera House, Milan.*

Mascagni's early years seemed to be the stuff of romantic fiction. His father, a baker in Livorno, opposed his son's musical inclinations, so studies were pursued secretly, aided by a sympathetic uncle who even gave young Pietro lodging when the father evicted the boy. Eventually some early cantatas won round the opposition, and secured Mascagni funds to study in Milan under Ponchielli; one of his new friends there was Puccini.

However, Mascagni did not take kindly to scholastic routine, and after two years left to follow a more congenial life as part of a touring opera company, eventually marrying and settling in Cerignola in 1887. The turning-point of his career soon followed. He was persuaded to enter a competition for one-act operas, and completed at great speed a version of Varga's Cavalleria rusticana, *a tale of violent passion in a Sicilian village. In 1890, it won first prize, and suddenly Mascagni was whirled into the public gaze, as the opera was acclaimed around the world.*

It is to Mascagni's credit that he did not attempt, in the years that followed, merely to repeat the same type of verismo melodrama. His next opera, L'Amico Fritz *(1891) was a gentle romance set in Alsace, and scored a moderate success, but the rest*

BELOW: *Mafalda Salvatini as Santuzza in the 1920 Berlin production of* Cavalleria rusticana. *The opera found instant fame after its première at the Teatro Costanzi in Rome in 1890.*

of the decade saw nothing but disappointments, despite his conscious attempts to vary the themes: Iris *(1899), for instance, features a Japanese heroine five years before Puccini's* Madama Butterfly. *Further indignities followed. He made a disastrous tour of the USA with an inadequate company, which ended with his arrest in Boston for unpaid bills. An academic post in Italy was taken away from him for negligence, and his new operas achieved no place in the repertory, although a strange version of the Lady Godiva tale, Isabeau (1911) was a succès de scandale when it was performed in South America and Italy.*

The last thirty years of Mascagni's life can be briefly summarized. His last two operas of note, Lodoletta *(1917) and* Il Piccolo Marat *(1921), made little impression, and, as if to compensate, he became a prominent supporter of Mussolini's Fascist régime, providing fanfares and marches for nationalistic rallies, and usurping the La Scala directorship from Toscanini. Inevitably, Mascagni's star waned with Mussolini's. The golden anniversary performances of* Cavalleria *with Gigli in 1940 were overshadowed by the war, and when the Fascist régime fell, Mascagni was reduced to living in a cheap hotel in Rome, where he died shortly after the end of hostilities.*

Mascagni's career has much in common with that of Leoncavallo: one tremendous success as a young man, followed by decades of increasing frustration, desperately trying to find a new formula. Fate was kind in one respect – in each case the triumphant opera was only one act, lasting about one hour, so they were naturally combined to provide a full evening of verismo, the 'heavenly twins' Cav. and Pag.

The sordid yet strangely moving tale of Sicilian village life that Mascagni used for *Cavalleria rusticana* was a perfect vehicle for the young composer's talents. Nobody could claim that his orchestration was subtle or that his melodic gift was distinguished, yet his lack of refinement is here an advantage. The hero is a swaggering bully and most of the other characters are one-dimensional stereotypes, so the regular blare of the brass section or the wooden repetitions in Alfio's song seem apt for the setting. We can detect the lack of academic knowledge resulting from Mascagni's early departure from college, but we can also admire the professional 'know-how' he picked up while on tour with an opera company. The effect of the soaring Intermezzo is something many a learned composer failed to achieve.

Mascagni's next opera, *L'Amico Fritz*, was a praiseworthy attempt to write in a more delicate, affectionate style. The setting is Alsace, the characters are genial and the music consistently pretty. The Act Two Cherry Duet in the orchard is more than that: it is a lovely lyrical inspiration, and helps to keep the opera in the Italian repertoire. Also, what other opera specifically requires a middle-aged tenor as its hero?

Mascagni's other operas have never gained wide fame, but extracts from them are still popular items in Italy. The intermezzi he regularly placed in these works, hoping to emulate his *Cavalleria* inspiration, retain a melodic charm and keep alive the titles of otherwise neglected operas such as *Guglielmo Ratcliff* (1895) and *Le Maschere* (1901). Moreover, in his later works Mascagni can achieve individual scenes of power: for instance, the Hymn to the Sun which opens and closes his Japanese opera *Iris* lifts the atmosphere of an otherwise sordid story.

Surely that is how Mascagni's *oeuvre* will be recalled: a dozen or so effective extracts from unsatisfactory complete works, plus one total success which even after a century shows no signs of fading.   P.J.

BELOW: *The brooding Sicilian landscape of* Cavalleria rusticana *is called to mind by 'Juno's Temple in Agrigento' painted in 1830 by Caspar David Friedrich (1774-1840). Mascagni's opera ushered in the new realistic style called 'verismo'.*

Chronology

1863 *Born 7 December at Livorno, son of baker.*

1876-81 *Secretly follows music course against parental opposition*

1881 *Early works win him sponsors; goes to Milan*

1882-4 *Studies at Milan Conservatory under Ponchielli. Befriends fellow student Puccini*

1887 *Settles in Cerignola and marries*

1889 *Is persuaded to enter competition; composes Cavalleria rusticana at speed*

1890 *Wins first prize and instant fame. Cavalleria rusticana first performed at Teatro Costanzi, Rome*

1891-2 *Subsequent operas L'Amico Fritz and I Rantzau less popular*

1895 *Director of Pesaro Music College, but Guglielmo Ratcliff and Silvano fail*

1898-1901 *More successful with Japanese opera Iris (first performed Rome, 1898) and Le Maschere*

1903 *Disastrous tour of USA; arrested in Boston for debt. Dismissed from Pesaro post*

1911 *Isabeau a temporary success in South America and Italy*

1917 *Sets Lodoletta after Puccini loses interest; first performed in Rome*

1921 *His last noteworthy opera Il Piccolo Marat first performed in Rome. Becomes prominent Mussolini supporter through 1920s*

1929 *Replaces anti-Fascist Toscanini at La Scala Opera House, Milan*

1940 *Golden anniversary performances of Cavalleria rusticana with Gigli overshadowed by war*

1945 *Dies in Rome, poor and in disgrace, 2 August*

JULES
Massenet (b. Montaud, St. Etienne, 12 May 1842; d. Paris, 13 August 1912)

RIGHT: *Photograph of Jules Massenet by Nadar, a pioneer photographer, taken in Paris in 1890 when Massenet was teacher of composition at the Conservatoire.*

BELOW: *'Goethe in the Roman Campagna', an oil-painting by Johann Heinrich Wilhelm Tischbein (1751-1829). Goethe (1749-1832) was the author of the novel Werther upon which Massenet based one of his best-known operas.*

The child of a master foundryman in a city three hundred miles south-east of Paris, Massenet was brought up in the capital after his family moved there in 1842, receiving his first music lessons from his mother, who also taught other children in order to supplement the family income. He attended the Paris Conservatoire from the age of eleven and made steady progress, principally under the guidance of the composer Ambroise Thomas (1811-1896), so that in 1863 he won the coveted Prix de Rome, giving him three years at the Villa Medici when he also got to know Liszt. In the meantime he had done some piano teaching and gained experience of the theatre and popular music by playing as an occasional percussionist in the Paris Opéra orchestra and as a café pianist.

After his return from Rome to Paris, he married his piano pupil Constance de Sainte-Marie on 8 October 1866, and in the following year, thanks to the recommendation of Thomas, his opera La Grand'tante received its première at the Opéra-Comique. This was the first of a whole series of operas that Massenet was to write during the remaining forty-five years of his life: the last première in his lifetime was that of Roma in Monte Carlo in 1912. The story of Massenet's life is one of success. His career first flowered with his oratorio Marie-Magdeleine in 1873, but it was the opera Le Roi de Lahore four years later that marked him out as a major composer. His greatest single success came in 1884 with Manon, based on the Abbé Prévost's novel (used also by Puccini in Manon Lescaut) telling of a courtesan and her idealistic young lover, the Chevalier des Grieux. Another courtesan, this time from fourth-century Egypt, is the eponymous central figure of Thaïs (1894). However, he also drew masculine portraits in Le Cid (1885), Werther (1892) and Don Quichotte, this opera (1910) being his last major success. His fame was widespread, and his operatic premières were sometimes outside France, for example in Vienna (Werther) and London (La Navarraise). He also spent many years as a teacher of composition at the Paris Conservatoire, taking up this post in 1878 and holding it for the rest of his life. His other compositions include sacred music, three ballets, incidental music for the theatre and many songs.

POUSSETTE

JAVOTTE

ROSETTE

Like all good opera composers, Massenet was a master both of vocal writing and of orchestration, and his melodious scores are both refined and theatrically effective although conservative compared with those of his compatriots Bizet and Berlioz – to say nothing of Wagner. It is usually said that he was at his strongest in portraying women, and combining in these portraits elements of the discreetly erotic and the moral, or even religious. In this sense, the characters of Manon and the reformed courtesan Thaïs suited his talent. So did the heroines of *Hérodiade* (1881) a version of the biblical Salome story, and *Sapho* (1897), a portrayal of yet another *femme fatale* in the person of the artist's model Fanny Legrand who is loved by the country boy Jean Gaussin. He never lost his taste for such protagonists, as the titles of *Thérèse* (1907) and *Cléopâtre* (1914) remind us.

Massenet also drew masculine portraits in *Le Cid, Werther* and *Don Quichotte*, this last opera (1910) being his last major success. However, the central figure of *Le Jongleur de Notre-Dame* (1902) is another reformed character: a four-teenth-century entertainer who, reproached for singing a drinking song outside an abbey, becomes a monk. Later, shamed by his lack of formal education, he again uses the talents he possesses to dance and sing before a statue of the Virgin Mary. Another monk thinks him sacrilegious, but the virgin extends her arm to bless him as he dies at her feet. The composer called this work a miracle play and 'my faith'.

Nevertheless, in other moods he complained about the public taste that demanded these religious themes from him although admitting in a letter to his fellow-composer Vincent d'Indy that 'the public likes it and we must always agree with

ABOVE: *Design for a performance of Massenet's best known opera,* Manon *(1884), at the State Theatre, Basel, in 1985. The scenery and costumes were designed by Mauro Pagano (1951-88) – this particular example shows designs for the Act 4 gambling scene.*

the public'. Occasionally one senses that there was another more rebellious element in this polished man of the theatre. For example, he chose an influential and controversial novel by Goethe as the basis for his opera *Werther*, reading it on a trip to Germany and writing of it, 'Such rapturous and ecstatic passion brought tears to my eyes. What moving scenes and thrilling moments it would bring about!'. *Werther* is a young man who falls in love with the already engaged Charlotte and leaves her house in distress; after her marriage he finds that he cannot stay away and, returning, asks for her husband's pistols and kills himself to escape from his passion. Even so, along with this strong drama, *Werther* also ex-emplifies the characteristic gentler aspects of Massenet's art, as in the delicate 'moonlight' love scene in Act 1, while the children's songs which open and close the action portray a mood of contented bourgeois domesticity that ultimately remains undisturbed by the hero's tragedy. As always with Massenet, passion gives way to propriety. Debussy wrote that music was for him 'never the cosmic voice heard by Bach and Beethoven, but rather a delightful occupation . . . his harmonies are like enlacing arms . . . Fortune, being a woman, certainly ought to treat Massenet kindly'.   C.H.

FELIX
Mendelssohn (b. Hamburg, 3 February 1809; d. Leipzig, 4 November 1847)

RIGHT: *Portrait in oils of Felix Mendelssohn, painted by Eduard Magnus. It shows the composer towards the end of his life.*

Grandson of an eminent Jewish philosopher, and son of a successful banker, Felix Mendelssohn enjoyed all the comforts of a prosperous middle-class household and all the benefits of a highly-cultured society. He was the second of four children, of whom the eldest, Fanny, was almost as accomplished a pianist as her brother. But as well as his genius for music, which included an astonishing musical memory, Felix displayed in later life great ability as an illustrator and painter and as a writer, and all the charm and social graces to be expected from so secure a background.

He received his early education from his parents; he learned French and mathematics from his father, while his mother gave him art and music lessons, which included elementary piano training. His prodigious gifts soon became apparent, and by the age of nine he had made his debut as a performer, and was receiving tuition in harmony from Karl Zelter (1758-1832).

It was Zelter who took him to meet Goethe, whereupon a warm friendship developed between the 72-year old poet and the 12-year old composer. He had already written a large number of works, some of them of remarkable maturity. By the time he enrolled at Berlin University in 1826 he had completed a comic opera Die Hochzeit des Comacho (1825), and the overture to the incidental music to A Midsummer Night's Dream, which remains one of his best-loved orchestral compositions.

In 1829 he gave the first performance of the St. Matthew Passion since the death of Bach, prompting Berlioz to remark, 'There is one God – Bach – and Mendelssohn is His prophet'. Later during that same year he performed Beethoven's Emperor piano concerto for the first time in England, and went on to tour Scotland where he was inspired to write the Hebrides overture.

The adulation of the English public was shared by audiences throughout Germany, Austria and Italy. Appointed conductor of the Lower Rhine Music Festival 1833-6, he also became the conductor of the famous Gewandhaus Orchestra, Leipzig in 1835. Two years later he married Cécile Jeanrenaud by whom he had five children, and there followed a period during which he composed many of his most celebrated works including the violin concerto.

Success followed success, but years of overwork took their toll. The shock of his sister's death in May 1847 was so great that he collapsed. For a few months he seemed to rally, but then a further collapse occurred in October, and he died in Leipzig in November of that same year. Queen Victoria was 'horrified, astounded and distressed' when she heard the news. 'The greatest musical genius since Mozart,' she declared, 'admired . . . esteemed . . . looked up to and revered.'

BELOW: *'Recollections of the Journey from Mürren to Lauterbrunnen', an aquatint from 1847 by Mendelssohn, who was an accomplished amateur artist.*

Felix Mendelssohn was one of the most remarkable of all musical child prodigies, whose early works can be favourably compared with those of Mozart at a similar age. The twelve string symphonies he composed between the ages of 12 and 14 show that he was already a master of melody, and indicate a rapid development of style and technique. High-spirited and delightful, Mendelssohn's youthful works also reveal an inexhaustible harmonic and melodic invention – a quality that runs through his entire output.

For Mendelssohn wrote music to charm the ear. That is one of the reasons why, unlike many of the great composers, he won great critical acclaim during his brief lifetime and was feted throughout Europe, especially in England. His social graces soon made him a court favourite and his music, notably the oratorio *Elijah*, first performed in Birmingham in 1846, influenced the musical taste of Victorian England in a manner unmatched by that of any other composer.

Among his early triumphs are also to be found the String Octet (1825), written at the age of sixteen, and the overture of *A Midsummer Night's Dream* which he composed a year later, and upon which much of the later incidental music is based. This is the most original and astonishing of all Mendelssohn's scores for he achieves his magical effects with total economy of means and, as one critic has put it, displays an 'arrogant mastery' in the use of his orchestra.

ABOVE: *The composer at the age of 12 painted by Karl Begas (1794-1854). It was at this time that his teacher, Carl Friedrich Zelter, took Mendelssohn to meet Hummel and the poet Goethe, with whom Mendelssohn formed a warm friendship.*

Other overtures include *The Hebrides (Fingal's Cave)*, *Calm Sea and Prosperous Voyage*, *The Fair Melusina* and *Ruy Blas* – all of which represent Mendelssohn's most significant contribution to the development of orchestral form. For it was from works such as these that the idea of a symphonic, or tone, poem emerged, to become a source of inspiration for Liszt, Dvořák, Richard Strauss and other composers.

This is not to undervalue the five symphonies, of which the Third (*Scottish*) and Fourth (*Italian*) are best known, or the many choral and organ works he composed. Mendelssohn won immediate renown, however, with his piano music, particularly the 48 *Songs Without Words*. Once regarded as sentimental trifles, these pieces are now taking up their proper place in the repertoire once more. The two piano concertos are also regaining recognition, but they are not to be compared with the violin concerto, Mendelssohn's most celebrated single contribution to classical orchestral music – and deservedly so. R.H.

OLIVIER
Messiaen (b. Avignon, France, 10 December 1908; d. Paris, 28 April 1992)

RIGHT: *Olivier Messiaen photographed by Heidi Meister in Paris in 1963, the year he returned to liturgical composition.*

Chronology

1908 *Born in Avignon*
1916 *First composition, La Dame de Shalott, after Tennyson*
1919 *Enters Paris Conservatoire; taught composition by Dukas, organ by Dupré*
1926-9 *Wins five first prizes at the Conservatoire*
1928 *Le Banquet céleste, for organ*
1930 *First orchestral work – Les Offrandes oubliées. Trois mélodies, to poems by his mother, wins a first prize from the Conservatoire*
1931 *Appointed organist of the Paris church of the Trinité; marries Claire Delbos; composes Apparition de l'église éternelle*

Olivier Messiaen defies categorization. His music belongs to none of the recognized 20th century schools, yet has been immensely influential. Messiaen's musical vocabulary is an eclectic one, embracing plainchant and medieval isorhythms, the modal system devised by the Ancient Greeks, and gamelan music of Indonesia (and much other oriental music), numerology and the world of birdsong. In the majority of his compositions, these all come together with one unified and overriding purpose: to sing the praises of God.

Messiaen's family was inclined towards literature rather than music. His mother, Cécile Sauvage, was a poet; his father a Shakespeare scholar and English teacher. At eleven, Olivier was accepted into the Paris Conservatoire where his tutors included the organist, Marcel Dupré, and the composer, Paul Dukas. While there, Messiaen developed an interest in oriental music, especially that of India, and made his first attempts at notating birdsong. What he later described as his 'most decisive influence', however, was a parting gift before he left for Paris: the score of Debussy's opera, Pelléas et Mélisande.

Messiaen graduated from the Conservatoire in 1930 and, the following year, began what was to become a lifetime's association as organist of the Trinité church in the heart of Paris. He had been composing for the instrument since 1928, all his works motivated by liturgical texts or religious imagery. The nine meditations of La Nativité du Seigneur of 1935 brought him acclaim, and this remains his best-known composition.

In 1936, Messiaen took up teaching posts at the École Normale de Musique and at the Schola Cantorum. With four other young composers, he founded the group known as Jeune France but any aims they may have formulated were foiled by the outbreak of war. Messiaen was conscripted into the French Army and captured at Nancy in 1940, spending the next two years in Stalag VIIIA prison camp in Silesia. While there, he composed one of his most enduring masterpieces, Quatuor pour la fin du temps (Quartet for the end of time) for piano, clarinet, cello and violin, the instruments dictated by the musical talents of his fellow internees.

Upon his release, Messiaen was appointed to a post at the Paris Conservatoire and in the ensuing years was to become the influential tutor of several major names, Boulez, Stockhausen, Xenakis, Alexander Goehr and George Benjamin among them.

Messiaen remained a major figure in contemporary music for the remainder of his life, if outside the mainstream. His research into birdsong resulted in a kaleidoscopic aviary of music, with Oiseaux exotiques perhaps the most accessible of his explorations. In his later years, when most composers opt for economy, Messiaen composed several gargantuan works, culminating in a four-and-a-half hour opera on the life of St. Francis of Assisi.

LEFT: *'The Stained Glass Window' by Odilon Redon (1840-1916) painted in 1904. It reminds us that Messiaen was organist at the Trinité church in Paris for much of his life.*

Messiaen's music is a celebration, if not of divine love, then of human love. He liked to describe it as 'the music of hope' and saw its purpose as 'shedding light on the theological truths of the Catholic faith'. For Messiaen, that was not the cue to compose drab, lugubrious anthems or turgid chorales. He expressed the joy of faith rather than the fear of faith, with music where rhythm and colour are everything.

Throughout his career, Messiaen maintained the rich tradition of French organ music, as established by the likes of Vierne, Tournemire, Widor and his own tutor at the Conservatoire, Marcel Dupré. The catalogue of his organ works begins with the six-minute meditation of *Le Banquet céleste* of 1928 and concludes with the two-and-a-half hour *Livre du Saint-Sacrament*, composed while in his seventies and surely the longest single solo work ever written for the instrument.

Messiaen's first orchestral work was *Les Offrandes oubliées* of 1930, a piece which, while poignant, also gave a foretaste of the cloying, even mawkish sentiment which could infiltrate his music. He composed little else for orchestra until after the Second World War, when he received a commission from the conductor, Serge Koussevitzky for the Boston Symphony Orchestra. The result was the *Turangalîla-Symphonie* which, both in terms of its length and the forces used, is a sound-painting on the grandest scale. The title is derived from two Sanskrit words which, together, Messiaen interpreted as a 'song of love' or a 'hymn to joy'. The ten-

movement symphony, constructed around two cyclic themes, is an ecstatic celebration of erotic love, as embodied in another of Messiaen's key influences, the Tristan legend.

Not all of Messiaen's music was conceived on such a scale, or is dependent on such a panoply of effects, as his song-cycles *Poèmes pour Mi*, *Cinq rechants*, *Chants de terre et de ciel* and the enigmatic *Harawi* demonstrate. A formidable intellect can be detected at work in taxing piano compositions such as the *Vingt regards sur l'Enfant-Jésus* and *Visions de l'Amen* and – above all – in the seminal but now rarely-played *Mode de valeurs et d'intensités*.

A modal system was fundamental to Messiaen's inimitable musical language. By working with a group of 'modes of limited transposition', as he described them, Messiaen was able to harness harmonic forces. Essentially, the octave is spanned by regular patterns of pitch intervals. With two modes at work, a chromatic texture became possible, and it

ABOVE: 'St. Francis of Assisi preaching to the Birds', a fresco in the Church of San Francesco by Giotto di Bondone (1266-1337) which reflects Messiaen's musical interest in birdsong.

is these 'chromatic modes' which are responsible for the distinctive atmosphere and flavour of much of Messiaen's music, along with his novel use of rhythm – characterized by its irregular metre – and his rich, chromatic harmonies, which owe much to Debussy.

Messiaen's music can be exciting and entrancing. It also has elements of questionable taste and judgement: the sugary sanctimony of the *Trois petites liturgies*; the kitsch of *Aux canyons des étoiles*; and the triteness that occurs, for example, in *Turangalîla*. If the quality of some of his music can be disputed, however, its sincerity is never in doubt. P.H.

ABOVE: *A photograph of Edward MacDowell, one of America's most successful pre-modernist composers. He was the first professor of music at Columbia University, New York.*

EDWARD **MACDOWELL**

(b. New York, 18 December 1860; d. New York, 23 January 1908)

An important American composer, of the same generation as Elgar and Parry, MacDowell was one of the first from the New World to be reckoned alongside these and other European composers of the time. Born of a Scottish-Irish father and a mother who encouraged his musical talents from the start, he went to the Paris Conservatoire and later to Germany where he studied in Frankfurt under Joachim Raff (1822-1882). He became acquainted with Liszt who took a great interest in his excellent piano music and recommended the publication of his works by Breitkopf & Hartel. He taught at Darmstadt where he married one of his pupils, Marian Nevins, in 1884. After various moves and musical posts he returned to the USA in 1888 where he was welcomed as 'the greatest musical genius that American has produced'. When Columbia University established a musical department in 1896, MacDowell was offered its directorship, but he fell out with the authorities and soon after his mental faculties began to decline. He spent his final years gripped by insanity. Perhaps Grieg was the most obvious influence on his two fine piano concertos, written in 1882 and 1889 and still much admired. Most of his work was of a romantic nature, with titles taken from history and mythology. His failure was in not finding a truly American style. Amongst his vast pianistic output, his Woodland Sketches (1896) have remained lastingly popular. *P.G.*

FRANK **MARTIN**

(b. Geneva, 15 September 1890; d. Naarden, 21 November 1974)

Of French Huguenot extraction, Martin was the son of a Swiss Calvinist minister, and was introduced to music by a performance of Bach's St. Matthew Passion *heard at the age of 10. In 1915 the conductor Ernest Ansermet introduced him to the music of Ravel and Debussy, and his early music imitated them. After a spell working with Dalcroze, the inventor of eurhythmics, he became director of a modern music school in 1933, and this coincided with his discovery of the music of Schoenberg. The resultant new style transformed his career, and after the success of his Piano Concerto No.1 and Symphony in 1934 and 1938, he finally won a world reputation with the oratorio Le Vin herbé in 1941. This began, at the age of 51, his most fruitful period, with his most popular piece the Petite symphonie concertante for harp, harpsichord and piano, the oratorio In terra pax to celebrate the end of the war, and the Six Monologues from Jedermann, all written between 1943 and 1945. This music fuses the different influences of Schoenberg, Debussy and late Stravinsky into an individual blend of delicate, mildly dissonant, rhythmically alive music with its own refined attractiveness. Martin composed for another twenty years, writing two operas, another oratorio, concertos for violin, piano and harpsichord and a Requiem, but his reputation rests on the music between 1941 and 1945.* *P.L.*

BOHUSLAV **MARTINŮ**

(b. Polička, 8 December 1890; d. Liestal, Switzerland, 28 August 1959)

Martinů was a cobbler's son from Bohemia, an infant prodigy on the violin and at composition. His studies with Suk at the Prague Conservatory were none the less mediocre, and by 1918 he was still only a violinist in the Czech Philharmonic with little reputation as a composer. In 1923 he went to Paris to study

with Albert Roussel (1869-1937), the start of a lifetime's wandering. In Paris he was influenced by neo-classicism, especially Stravinsky, and also by jazz, though his music was always to remain distinctively Czech. He stayed in Paris until 1941, writing copiously with little success until he won a prize for a string sextet. Although his music made some headway after this, the German invasion forced another move to the USA, where he remained until 1953, after which he divided his time between the USA, France and Switzerland, with only one brief visit to Czechoslovakia. Martinů wrote a vast amount of music in all forms, including ten operas, five symphonies plus the Fantaisies symphoniques, seven string quartets and so on. Inevitably, it is uneven in quality, but his rhythmical energy and exuberant, mildly dissonant style produced several successes. From the Paris years come the opera Julietta (1936) and the Concerto for double string orchestra, piano and timpani (1938), while America produced the series of symphonies, and the orchestral Frescoes of Piero della Francesca (1953). His last years can boast the opera The Greek Passion (1961) and the choral Epic of Gilgamesh, as well as much distinguished chamber music. *P.L.*

PETER **MAXWELL DAVIES**

(b. Manchester, 8 September 1934)

A leading figure in British avant-garde music, Maxwell Davies was born in Manchester and attended both the University and the School of Music there. He was contemporary with Harrison Birtwistle (1934-) and Alexander Goehr (1932-), and all were much influenced by Boulez (1925-), Nono (1924-) and

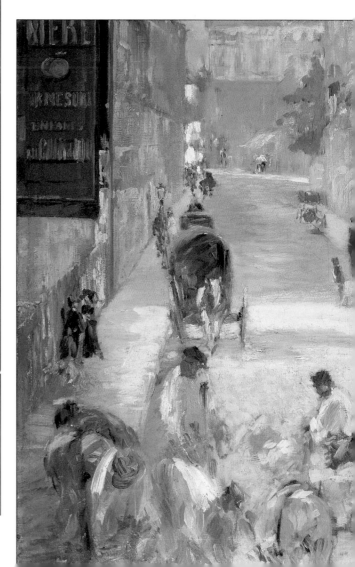

RIGHT: *'La Rue Mosnier aux Paveurs', an 1878 painting that conjures up the Paris of Meyerbeer's time by the artist Edouard Manet (1832-83).*

Stockhausen, as well as the father-figure Schoenberg. Maxwell Davies became Director of Music at Cirencester Grammar School in 1959, and this experience encouraged him to write more dramatically. Study at Princeton with Roger Sessions (1896-1985) followed, and on return in 1967 he formed with Birtwistle the influential Pierrot Players (later the Fires of London) to promote contemporary music. For them he wrote pieces of 'music theatre', the dramatic song cycle 8 Songs for a Mad King and Vesalii Icones for dancer and (oddly-constituted) ensemble. Since 1970 Maxwell Davies has been based in Orkney, and this remote, austere environment is reflected in his work, such as the opera The Martyrdom of St. Magnus (1977). He owes much also to medieval music and even to 1920s foxtrots in his dramatic expressionist compositions such as the opera Taverner (about the 16th-century composer) (1970), and the three symphonies (1976, 1980, 1983). His music is tough, with complex rhythms, unconventional sounds and angular melodic lines, but his more recent compositions such as the series of concertos are less formidable and more approachable, as is his attractive Orkney Wedding. P.L.

───── ⚭ ─────

GIAN CARLO **MENOTTI**

(b. Cadegliano, 7 July 1911)

Menotti achieved enormous popularity in the 1940s and 50s by building upon the operatic world of Puccini, Mascagni and Debussy and producing highly professional works that found a way of translating operatic conventionality into modern dress and situation without losing its links with the musical past. His work might well be diagnosed as smart, clever, Hollywoodish, but it also

had a strength and dramatic quality that gripped the audiences of the post-war years; notably with his great full-length success, The Consul (1950), with its pertinent background of secret police and political wheeler-dealing. This confirmed the talents shown in two popular short pieces, The Medium (1946), a seance set to well-orchestrated music, and The Telephone (1947), a delightful one-acter built around one of the curses of modern life. Most lastingly of all he produced a modern Christmas classic, tunefully sentimental, in Amahl and the Night Visitors (1951), followed by The Saint of Bleecker Street (1954). Menotti had begun to compose at the age of 10, studied in Milan, then studied and taught at the Curtis Institute in Philadelphia 1927-33. Although retaining Italian citizenship, he became a thoroughly American musician. He has continued to write prolifically, if not with the popular success of those halcyon days, also working as an effective librettist for works by Samuel Barber and others. P.G.

───── ⚭ ─────

GIACOMO **MEYERBEER**

(b. Berlin, 5 September 1791; d. Paris, 2 May 1864)

Meyerbeer, originally named Jakob Beer, was the eldest son of a prosperous Jewish banker. After studies in Germany, he used his inherited wealth to tour the opera houses of Europe and introduce himself to leading composers such as Beethoven and Rossini. In 1830, Meyerbeer won fame himself when he persuaded the Paris Opéra to produce Robert le diable. The huge success of this spectacular grand opera led to a series of similar triumphs, full of theatrical effects and crowd-pleasing arias: Les Huguenots (1836), Le Prophète (1849), L'Africaine (1865). As Mendelssohn noted, Meyerbeer catered for every taste. The newly prosperous Parisian audiences were thrilled by the lavish crowd scenes, the lurid melodrama, the opulent ballets; they were not troubled by the contrived plots of Eugène Scribe, or the lack of credible characters. It was a later generation of critics such as Wagner and Bernard Shaw, who began the savage onslaught on Meyerbeer's operas that has so eclipsed his reputation, and made modern revivals so rare. It is true that, as Shaw wrote, Meyerbeer created effects without causes, and that his music seems shallow by comparison with the masterpieces of Verdi and Wagner. Yet estimable composers such as Rossini, Bizet and Dvořák admired his work and as recent productions of L'Africaine have shown, several scenes and solos can still make their mark if sung with distinction. P.J.

───── ⚭ ─────

ABOVE: The German-Jewish composer Giacomo Meyerbeer photographed in the 1860's. In his day, Meyerbeer was considered one of the greatest composers of opera in Europe.

OTTO **NICOLAI**

(b. Königsberg, 9 June 1810; d. Berlin, 11 May 1849)

Early proficiency at the piano prompted young Nicolai to leave his provincial home and travel to Berlin for further studies. While still in his twenties, he secured posts as organist in Rome, conductor in Vienna, and opera director in Berlin. It was in the Austrian capital that he inaugurated the Philharmonic concerts which are regarded as the foundation of one of the world's supreme orchestras, the Vienna Philharmonic. During his short life (he died of apoplexy at the age of thirty-eight) he composed two youthful symphonies, an attractively tuneful Mass, and five operas, of which only one has achieved lasting fame. This is The Merry Wives of Windsor (1847), based on the same Shakespearean subject as Verdi's Falstaff, which has naturally overshadowed it. Yet Nicolai's opera has great charm of its own and is full of graceful melodies, some of which are widely known through the ever popular overture. P.J.

ABOVE: Otto Nicolai, composer and founder of the Vienna Philharmonic: a lithograph portrait of 1842 by Kriehuber.

DARIUS
Milhaud (b. Aix-en-Provence, 4 September 1892; d. Geneva, 22 June 1974)

Milhaud's family were Jewish, comfortably off and cultured. When just two years old, he already showed an interest in music, but his real musical studies began at the age of seven with violin lessons, and soon after this he started composing. At ten, he gave his first concert as a violinist, and at eighteen, he was already writing the sets of songs (settings of poems by Francis Jammes and Léo Latil) which were his Op.1 and Op.2, as well as his opera La Brebis égarée (which he called 'a novel in music'), although he did not complete the latter until 1915. He had entered the Paris Conservatoire in 1909 as a violin student, but while there he decided that he wanted above all to be a composer; his teachers included Paul Dukas and André Gédalge (1856-1926). His first work to be publicly performed dates from these student years and was a Violin Sonata (1911); a String Quartet dates from the following year.

At the outbreak of war in 1914, Milhaud was rejected for military service on health grounds, but in 1916 he travelled to Rio de Janeiro as the assistant to his friend Paul Claudel, a poet and diplomat who had been appointed as a French minister. The music of South America made a deep impression on the young composer, and so did the teeming life of the Brazilian rain forest: both were to be reflected thereafter in his music, not least the ballet L'Homme et son désir (1918), for which Claudel provided the scenario.

In November 1918, Milhaud returned to Paris and joined the friendly circle of composers called Les Six, whose father figure was Satie (though he was not one of the group) and whose literary spokesman was Jean Cocteau. However, he usually went his own way and his prolific and sometimes dark-hued invention was far removed from the spareness of Satie or the gamin charm of Poulenc. In 1920, during a visit to London, he first heard jazz, and this too was to play a major part in his music; he followed up this experience on a visit to the US in 1922. During the next few years, performances of new pieces gave him the reputation of 'an unprincipled exploiter of fashionable oddities', an artist who, for the French establishment, lacked the serious spirit of a Franck or Debussy and was criticized for being insufficiently self-critical.

During the 1920's and 1930's, Milhaud composed an enormous amount of music and travelled in Western Europe as well as Russia and Syria although increasingly handicapped by rheumatoid arthritis. But in 1940 the German occupation drove him and his wife Madeleine (whom he had married in 1925) to California, where he took up a teaching post at Mills College, Oakland. In August 1947 he returned to Paris and taught at the Conservatoire, while also keeping up some American teaching at Oakland and Aspen, Colorado. His Jewish background led to the commissioning of his opera David, composed for the three thousandth anniversary of the founding of Jerusalem, and he travelled and moved to Geneva. His last work dates from 1972 and was a cantata, Ani maamin, composed for the 1973 Israel Festival.

RIGHT: Darius Milhaud, a photo portrait by Karsh, taken in Paris in 1950 when Milhaud was once again teaching at the Conservatoire.

BELOW: Anton Dolin in the rôle of Beau Gosse in the 1924 Ballets Russes' production of Le Train bleu by Milhaud and Cocteau at the Théâtre des Champs-Elysées. Choreography was by Bronislava Nijinska.

Milhaud is difficult to sum up as a composer. The sheer quantity of his output means that hardly anyone can claim to know it all (*Ani maamin* was his Op.441), and his style is unusually wide-ranging. Indeed it incorporates such different elements as the folk styles of Provence (the *Suite Provençale*) and Latin America (*Saudades do Brasil*), as well as jazz idioms (the ballet *La Création du monde*), to say nothing of the epic aspects of his opera *Christophe Colomb*, first performed in Berlin in 1930. Here the composer and his librettist (Claudel) employ huge forces including a Greek-style chorus and aim to conjure up something between a symbolic drama and a medieval mystery. The aim, Claudel said, was to create action taking place 'in a region midway between the spectators and a world of thought made visible', and Milhaud certainly demonstrated his serious intentions in this ambitious, grandiose work, which is cast in 27 scenes and requires 45 soloists, a large chorus and orchestra, and cinematographic projection. The critic Rollo Myers called it 'perhaps his masterpiece'. He was to follow it over the ensuing years with other big operas with epic subjects, such as *Maximilien*, *Médée*, *Bolivar* and *David*, the last dating from 1952 and receiving its première in Jerusalem two years later.

Yet the view of Milhaud as a musical playboy who would try anything once (and sometimes more than once) is not entirely wrong, and it stuck to some extent throughout his long life, particularly since he was so prolific that it is hard to view his work as a whole – there are, for example, twelve symphonies, eighteen string quartets and five piano concertos. Of course, no one reproaches him for the uninhibited Gallic high spirits of such works as his ballet *Le Boeuf sur le toit* and his *Scaramouche* suite for two pianos. Yet the polytonality which he made something of a trademark (writing in two or more keys simultaneously in what he called 'complex combinatory writing') does not often come off in performance and seems more interesting to the eye than to the ear.

Milhaud's symphonies, written between 1939 and 1961, are a long way from the kind of structured drama that we find in Beethoven or Sibelius, and can be so discursive as to seem inconsequential, as in the fourth movement of the Second. On the other hand, they also offer a wayward beauty and languor-ous charm, to say nothing of an infectious joy of a kind that is rare in the music of this century. Milhaud was sometimes a bold experimenter: for example, he composed mini-operas and chamber symphonies, while his String Quartets Nos.14 and 15, written in 1948-9, are designed to be performed separately or simultaneously as an octet. That boldness sometimes succeeds and is refreshing even when it does not. When he is at his best, for example in *La Création du monde*, his music has great power and humanity.

C.H.

LEFT: 'The Thracian Girl Carrying the Head of Orpheus', an 1865 oil-painting by Gustave Moreau (1826-98). Milhaud wrote his own version of an Orpheus and Eurydice story, Les Malheurs d'Orphée, in 1925.

CLAUDIO
Monteverdi (b. Cremona, 15 May 1567; d. Venice, 29 November 1643)

Monteverdi's father was a local apothecary who for some years had a shop in the square outside Cremona Cathedral. He seems to have enjoyed some standing and eventually the authorities were to allow him to use the title of doctor. Claudio was his eldest son, and brought up in modest circumstances. However, he received a good musical education under the cathedral's able if somewhat conservative director of music, Marc'Antonio Ingegneri (1547-1592), although he does not seem to have sung in its choir. Precocious from the start, he was only fifteen when his first music was published, by a Venetian firm: this was a volume of three-voice motets, in other words sacred vocal pieces.

As a young man, Monteverdi soon began to look for work outside Cremona and found it initially as a freelance string player. However, by 1591 he held a salaried post in the rich court of the Duke of Mantua. This seems to have been an influential time for him, not least because the music there was directed by an innovative Netherlander called Giaches de Wert (1535-1596): indeed, his Third Madrigal Book of 1592, settings of secular poems for five voices, represented a change of direction away from a conservative idiom towards a more forcefully expressive one.

When Wert died in 1596, Monteverdi expected to be appointed to his post as maestro di cappella to the Mantua court, but instead it went to an older colleague, Pallavicino. However, he in turn died late in 1601, and Monteverdi then succeeded him in the following year, accepting duties that included organizing and composing music for state occasions and festivities. In the meantime, he had also married Claudia de Cattaneis, a singer at the court, on 20 May 1599. They were to have three children between 1601 and 1604: the second child, a girl, died in infancy, but the other two, who were boys, grew up to become respectively a doctor and a monk. Claudia herself was to die young, in September 1607, the year of Orfeo, and Monteverdi grieved for her long and deeply.

By now his reputation as a musician was high, not least because his first opera, Orfeo, had been produced in February 1607 at Mantua, and two years later it was published in Venice. He had already been criticized, by the monk and musical theorist Giovanni Maria Artusi, for the bold musical language of his published madrigals, and defended himself in the preface to the Fifth Book (1605), saying that although his style was not conventional it rested 'on foundations of truth' such as had served the artists of ancient Greece, whose culture his renaissance contemporaries much respected. In 1608, his opera L'Arianna was given at Mantua with great success, and two years later he published a famous setting of Vespers, the Vespro della Beata Vergine for voices and instruments, that he dedicated to the Pope, Paul V.

When Duke Vincenzo of Mantua died in 1612, Monteverdi along with other musicians lost his post, and spent a year in his native Cremona. But then he heard of a coming vacancy as maestro di cappella at St. Mark's Cathedral in Venice, where the incumbent had died, and went there at once, performing some of his church music for the cathedral authorities and obtaining the eminent post which he was to hold for many years. He was highly respected and well paid, and in return did much to raise the musical standards and standing of San Marco, writing sacred music for the church and operas for other Italian cities as well as madrigals, culminating in 1638 in his last set, the Madrigali guerrieri et amorosi. An outbreak of plague in Venice in 1630-1 seriously damaged the city's morale and music, and he composed a Mass of thanksgiving when it ended. By 1632 he had become a priest. His last major work was the opera L'Incoronazione di Poppea (1642).

RIGHT: Claudio Monteverdi, an oil-painting by Bernardo Strozzi (1581-1644). Like Monteverdi, Strozzi became a priest and lived in Venice in the 1630's.

BELOW: 'Procession on the Piazza San Marco' 1496, painted by Gentile Bellini (1429-1507), an important member of the Venetian School. Monteverdi became maestro di cappella of San Marco in 1613.

Chronology

Monteverdi is usually thought of as a major innovator, someone who helped to change the exploratory musical climate of the Renaissance into that of the more confident, humanistic baroque, just as Beethoven, two centuries later, bestrides classicism and romanticism and was both a guardian of old values and a prophet of new ones. Yet the truth is less simple. He was no lone innovator, but rather belonged to a steady progressive movement in which such men as Giaches de Wert also played a part. It has been said that 'his greatest gifts lay in finding how traditional means could be applied to novel ends'. His church music is in no way revolutionary, although that is no criticism and his celebrated setting of the *Vespers* has the same towering stature as Bach's Mass in B minor and Beethoven's *Missa Solemnis*.

Outside church music, Monteverdi's greatest gift was that of creating vivid musical images, whether in his very numerous madrigals – which commonly use texts calling out for colourful and dramatic treatment – or in his operas. It is, above all, in the field of opera that he stands as a pre-eminent father figure. As a form, opera was only a decade old when he composed his *Orfeo* (1607): yet this work in a prologue and five acts is elaborately structured, with an orchestra of some fifteen wind and string instruments plus a keyboard 'continuo' or backing. It even has an overture, like many later operas, and the music enhances and illuminates the text.

After the première in 1608 of Monteverdi's *L'Arianna*, a courtier wrote that Ariadne's lament for Theseus was such that 'no hearer was left unmoved, nor among the ladies was there one who did not shed a few tears'. The composer said that he aimed to create emotional expression musically, and that 'contrasts are what move our souls: that is the aim of all good music'. Of his madrigals, he said that he wanted above all 'to create on the basis of truth' and to satisfy both the ear and the intelligence. They usually have a harmonic texture, and even a tune with a chordal clothing such as is common in later music but was unusual in his time, as well as a conversational exchange between voices. In his operas, right through from *Orfeo* to *L'Incoronazione di Poppea*, a masterpiece written when he was over seventy, his characters come over as real people and not just melodious cardboard figures. Indeed, *Poppea* is surprisingly modern in its realism and lack of conventional moral tone.   C.H.

WOLFGANG AMADEUS

Mozart (b. Salzburg, Austria, 27 January 1756; d. Vienna, 5 December 1791)

The Mozart family had its roots in the Bavarian city of Augsburg, where they had a bookbinding business. Leopold Mozart did not follow his brothers into the family trade, becoming instead an above-average court musician, one of the hundreds who plied their skills around the ecclesiastical and secular courts of Europe. The mid-18th century found Leopold in the service of the church court in Salzburg and it was there, in January 1756, that the last of seven children was born, a son whom he and his wife named Wolfgang Amadeus. Of the previous six children, only one had survived more than a few months, a girl born in 1751 and named Maria Anna, though this was always abbreviated to the diminutive Nannerl.

Nannerl had proved to have inherited the musical talent of her father and, by the time of her brother's arrival, was already an accomplished harpsichordist. However, Nannerl's gifts were nothing compared to those rapidly displayed by her brother. Almost as soon as he could reach the keyboard, Wolfgang was picking out tunes. At four, he was receiving tuition from his father and was soon playing the violin with the proficiency of children three times his age. By the time he was six, he was composing minuets and other short pieces. The extraordinary thing was that these were not childish doodlings but competent miniatures that displayed an innate sense of structure and balance.

Music historians differ on whether Leopold Mozart nurtured his son's genius or exploited it. The truth is probably a mixture of both, although it is true that the events of the next few years were to have a detrimental effect on Mozart's later development, not as a musician but as a person. In January 1762, when he had just turned six, Wolfgang embarked on his career as a professional musician. He accompanied his father and sister to Munich and, in September, on to Vienna. They found the Austrian capital already buzzing with news of the amazing Mozart children.

Over the next three years, Leopold Mozart toured Europe with his wunderkinder, performing in Brussels, The Hague, London and Paris, as well as towns throughout Germany. Mozart's childhood was a succession of long stagecoach journeys and weeks spent in lodging houses. When he was not performing or taking lessons from his father, he was composing and, by the age of twelve, had written three operas, half-a-dozen symphonies and around one

hundred other works. In September 1767 he was asked by no less than the Emperor to write a comic opera and, within a few months, had completed La Finta semplice (The Pretend Simpleton). However, jealous court composers conspired to ensure that it was not performed for over a year, by which time the Mozarts were touring in Italy.

Leopold Mozart and his son returned to Italy in the autumn of 1772. Wolfgang was asked to write an opera for the Christmas carnival in Milan and the result, Lucia Silla, was an enormous success, and played for a further twenty-five performances. But, by the time the Mozarts returned to Salzburg, there was a new incumbent on the Archbishop's throne. Prince Archbishop Colloredo was nothing like as tolerant as his predecessor of employees' absenteeism. Leopold Mozart resumed his role as court musician and encouraged his son to accept a similar post. Wolfgang, however, had other ideas.

In 1774, he completed the most accomplished of his teenage operas, La Finta giardiniera (The Pretend Gardener) and then wrote Il Rè pastore (The Shepherd King) to a request from Archbishop Colloredo. Much against his father's wishes, Mozart continued touring and it was with his mother that he set out again in 1777. In Mannheim, he encountered and made friends with the Weber family and fell in love with one of the daughters, Aloysia.

The following year marked a turning point in Mozart's life. The Paris audience which had feted him as a child was now indifferent. He did some teaching there, but composed little, principally the Symphony No.31 (now known as the Paris Symphony) and the ballet music Les Petits riens. Tragically, his mother died while they were in Paris.

Mozart returned to Salzburg where his father had secured him a post at the court. He wrote his most ambitious opera to date, Idomeneo, but was then despatched to the Prince Archbishop's secondary residence in Vienna. He was treated as little better than a servant and soon found himself at odds with his employers. Colloredo ordered the dismissal of this 'vile wretch'.

Mozart remained in Vienna, striking up a friendship with Haydn and once again encountering the Webers. Aloysia had run off with an actor, but now it was her younger sister, Constanze, who caught his fancy and in August 1782, they married. Leopold Mozart was furious; he regarded the Webers as little more than dissolute bohemians, and the fact was that – much as he may have loved Constanze – Mozart had married someone as feather-headed as himself when it came to organizing the rudiments of life. Between 1782 and 1790, he enjoyed great success both with his operas and with his concert performances yet was forever falling into debt. Like Beethoven, Mozart was constantly moving house, except that in Beethoven's case it was usually because he had fallen out with his landlords; with Mozart, it simply seems to have been the product of an itinerant childhood and adolescence.

For good and bad, Leopold's influence over his son had waned, but it was still a terrible blow when Wolfgang learned of his father's death early in 1787. Three years later, Mozart bade an emotional farewell to his old friend, Haydn, who was on his way to visit London. Mozart was worried that his health might not be up to such a long journey. Ironically, Haydn was to outlive Mozart.

On 5 December 1791, Wolfgang Amadeus Mozart died after a fit of delirium, and probably from uraemia, although the notion that he was poisoned by a jealous rival or as a result of a masonic conspiracy (Mozart was a Freemason) still has its advocates. Constanze was too distraught to organize a decent funeral and the Mozarts' friends proved broken reeds. The greatest composer of his generation – some would argue of all time – was buried in an unmarked pauper's grave in Vienna. He left unfinished a setting of the Requiem Mass, a commission from a 'mysterious stranger' (actually, a nobleman who had the endearing habit of commissioning music and then passing it off as his own). For Mozart, already slumped in a morbid depression, this was merely the harbinger of his own demise. Tragically it proved to be just that.

LEFT: Antonio Salieri (1750-1825), the Italian composer who ruled the roost in Vienna in Mozart's time. He was said, almost certainly unfairly, to be intensely jealous of Mozart and possibly even his murderer.

BELOW: 'Vienna Seen from the Belvedere' c.1759-61, a detail of a painting showing some of the landmarks that would have been familiar to Mozart, painted in oils by Bernardo Bellotto (1720-80). The spire is of St. Stephen's Cathedral where Mozart was married.

Chronology

BELOW: *Constanze Weber (1763-1842), Mozart's widow painted by Hans Hansen in 1802 before her re-marriage to Georg Nikolaus Nissen.*

Other composers have shared some of Mozart's gifts but none has been blessed with them all. He had the most astonishingly accurate ear, a phenomenal memory, innate style and judgement, all served by a matchless melodic invention, harmonic ingenuity, complete command of the technicalities of counterpoint and the like and an extraordinary virtuosity. Music simply flowed from him and, once committed to paper, it was rare for him to make more than a few corrections (unlike, for example, Beethoven, almost all of whose major compositions involved considerable reworking, as his sketchbooks reveal).

Essentially, Mozart saw himself as a composer of operas and as a concert pianist. The outcome of the former was half-a-dozen of the world's greatest operas and, of the latter, twenty-seven piano concertos of which at least ten are masterpieces.

The first of the truly great operas is *Idomeneo*, first performed in March 1781. The characters are wooden, the libretto – by a cleric at the Salzburg court – inept, but the music is inspired. In *Die Entführung aus dem Serail*, Mozart produced a comedy of delicious wit, but it was when he began his collaboration with the librettist Lorenzo da Ponte that Mozart elevated opera to a new plane. *Le Nozze di Figaro* is the best *opera buffa* (loosely translated as comic opera) ever written, not just for its unforgettable melodies but for its flesh-and-blood characters. *Don Giovanni* is more of a tragi-comedy, with some of Mozart's darkest music, while *Così fan tutte* is the most purely beautiful of the later operas.

Mozart's last opera, written to a commission from an unscrupulous impresario called Schikaneder, was *Die Zauberflöte* (*The Magic Flute*) whose surreal plot centres on the adventures of the bird-catcher, Papageno, and at whose heart is the timeless theme of the struggle between light and darkness. It is superficially a fairy-tale, but with deeper, even bizarrely ritualistic undertones.

Mozart wrote piano concertos to play at his own concerts, the first when he was just eleven, the twenty-seventh and last in the year of his death. Most of the early concertos are light-

weight pieces, although with notable exceptions such as the E flat K271, written for a Mademoiselle Jeunehomme. Although still 'public' music, Mozart reserved the finest of his piano concertos for some of his most profound and personal statements: the poetic A Major K488; the romantic C Major K467; the sombre K491; and the poignant K595.

He also wrote a vast quantity of solo piano music, much of it for teaching purposes or merely trivial, but numbered among the seventeen sonatas are jewels such as the C Major K330 and the A Major K331, with its finale, the evergreen Turkish Rondo; the C Major K545; the C Minor K457 and the B flat K570. The Fantasia in C minor K475 is an exceptionally forward-looking piece, while the two-piano sonata K448 is a kind of miniature keyboard symphony.

Of over 200 chamber works composed by Mozart, around a half are of the highest quality. Of the twenty-three string quartets, the six dedicated to Haydn (Nos. 14 to 19) stand out, as do the three written for the cello-playing King of Prussia, Nos. 21-23. Mozart's favourite instrument among the strings was the viola and he enjoyed nothing better than to play it with friends in chamber ensembles. It is a pleasure reflected in much of his chamber music, the string quartets and quintets, and the works for wind and strings: the beguiling

Clarinet Quintet, for example, and the piquant Oboe Quartet. For many, the summit of Mozart's achievement in chamber music is the Divertimento for String Trio K563.

With the notable exception of the Requiem, Mozart's sacred music – like Haydn's – is more festive than devotional. The exuberant *Coronation* Mass K317, the majestic C Minor Mass K427, the vocal pyrotechnics of the cantata *Exsultate, jubilate* and the jewel-like perfection of the motet *Ave verum corpus* are typical. There is also a heartfelt setting of the Vespers, the *Vesperae solennes de confessore* K339, and an early, largely overlooked masterpiece, the *Litaniae de venerabili altaris sacramento* K243.

Mozart composed a wealth of lesser orchestral pieces – principally serenades and divertimentos – which frequently show an inspiration way above their ostensible status. The evergreen *Eine kleine Nachtmusik* is a case in point, as is the highly-original *Serenata notturna* K239, the *Haffner* serenade K250 – written for a wedding feast – and the splendid Serenade for 13 wind instruments K361.

In addition to his piano concertos, Mozart composed five for violin of modest accomplishment, four entertaining horn concertos, one for flute and harp, and others for flute, oboe and bassoon individually. All, however, are excelled by the

ABOVE: *Setting by Simon Quaglio for a production of* The Magic Flute *staged in Munich in 1818. This set is for the Queen of the Night's appearance.*

glorious Sinfonia Concertante K364 and by the heart-easing Clarinet Concerto K622, a work whose lyricism and sunny disposition suggest nothing of the morbid depression affecting Mozart at the time of its composition, 1791.

Mozart's symphonies, like his piano concertos, usefully map out his development as a composer. The first of note are Nos.25 and 29, works of sparkling vitality and invention. The splendour of the *Paris* Symphony, No.31, belies his unhappy second visit to the city, and No.35 the *Haffner*, No.36 *Linz* and No.38 *Prague* are also works of infectious high spirits and glorious melody.

All, however, are overshadowed by the triptych of symphonies which Mozart wrote in what was an astonishingly creative year, 1788. What suddenly inspired him to write these three masterpieces, we shall never know; suffice to say that in the E flat No. 39 K543, the G Minor No. 40 K550, and the C Major No. 41 K551, Mozart supplied the crowning glories of 18th century instrumental music.   P.H.

MODEST PETROVICH
Mussorgsky (b. Karevo, Pskov district, 21 March 1839; d. St. Petersburg, 28 March 1881)

RIGHT: The best-known portrait of Modest Mussorgsky painted by the Russian artist Ilya Repin (1844-1930) in 1881, the year of Mussorgsky's death. His heavy drinking has taken an obvious physical toll.

'An elegant piano-playing dilettante,' was Alexander Borodin's verdict on first meeting Modest Mussorgsky. Borodin was then 'a green military doctor' and Mussorgsky an 18-year old junior officer in the Preobrazhensky Regiment. The youngest son of a music-loving wealthy landowner, he had shown exceptional musical ability as a child. At seven he could easily play short pieces by Liszt, and at 13 he composed his first published work, a Porte-Enseigne Polka for his fellow cadets. Despite Borodin's verdict, music soon became more important to Mussorgsky than a military career, and in 1858 he left the regiment in order to concentrate on studying musical form with the composer Mily Balakirev.

Mussorgsky became one of a group of five nationalistic Russian composers known as 'The Mighty Handful' or 'the Five', the others being Balakirev, Borodin, Cui, and Rimsky-Korsakov. Borodin's initial impression that Mussorgsky was not fully dedicated tended to linger, perhaps because he left so many of his compositions unfinished, perhaps because his heavy drinking and frequent nervous illnesses sapped his powers of concentration, or perhaps because he never seemed able to settle in a job or home.

In 1863 the liberation of the serfs ruined the Mussorgsky family estates, and he was obliged to take a fairly lowly post in the civil service. For a time he lived in an idealistic 'commune' in St. Petersburg with five like-minded companions. In 1867 he left the civil service to make a precarious living as a music teacher and accompanist, but a year later he had to return to a ministry post, where his superiors tolerated his frequent absences due to dipsomania and nervous breakdown until 1880, after which he lived with friends who subsidized him. In all these years he was projecting, working on, revising and sometimes abandoning a number of operas, notably Salammbo (1863-66) and Sorochintsy Fair (1874-80). His completed scores included many fine songs as well as two of the best-loved works in the classical repertoire, Night on the Bare Mountain and Pictures at an Exhibition and one of the greatest of all Russian operas, Boris Godunov, begun in 1869, was a great success when it was first performed in 1874. Mussorgsky was barely 42 when he collapsed and died in the Military Hospital at St. Petersburg. After his death many of his scores were completed and 'revised' by Nikolay Rimsky-Korsakov and others, but in this century what Mussorgsky had originally written was restored.

BELOW: A scene of troops embarking during the Russo-Turkish War, 1877-8, painted by Apollonowitsch Sawizki (1844-1905). Mussorgsky served in a Guards regiment in the Russian Army between 1856 and 1858.

Chronology
1839 *Born 21 March, Karevo, Pskov Province, Russia*
1848 *Performs John Field concerto before large gathering in family home*
1849 *Piano lessons with Anton Herk*
1852 *Enters Guards Cadet School, St. Petersburg*
1856 *Joins Preobrazhensky Regiment of Guards. First meeting with Alexander Borodin*
1857 *Begins studying musical form with Balakirev*
1858 *First nervous disorder. Resigns army commission*
1860 *Orchestral scherzo in B flat major first performed. Complete nervous breakdown*
1863 *Takes post as junior clerk in Ministry of Communications*
1864 *Joins commune in St. Petersburg*
1865 *First attack of delirium tremens. Leaves commune*
1867 *First songs published. Composes Night on the Bare Mountain. Leaves government service*
1868-9 *Composes opera Boris Godunov. Forced by penury to seek government post once more*
1871-2 *Revises Boris Godunov*

'Mussorgsky's nature is not of the finest quality;' wrote Tchaikovsky in a letter to his patron Nadezhda von Meck, 'he likes what is coarse, unpolished and ugly.' Another contemporary, Anatol Liadov, said that 'it was easy enough to correct Mussorgsky's defects; but that when this was done the result is no longer Mussorgsky.' As for the composer himself, he had no time for 'art for art's sake': he believed that art is a means of communicating with people and not an end in itself. He rejected the lyrical romanticism of his early compositions and came to regard 'pure beauty' and technical fluency with angry contempt. 'I want to speak to man in a language of truth,' he declared.

These very Russian sentiments have given Mussorgsky's detractors plenty of ammunition over the years, and the frequent attempts by Rimsky-Korsakov and others to 'improve' his music have done little to enhance his reputation. But the veneer has since been stripped off, and the rough-hewn integrity of the original works has been revealed, with all their imperfections and all their power.

So far as Western audiences are concerned, the list of such works consists of no more than two highly original and powerful operas, *Boris Godunov* and *Khovanshchina* (which, along with many other scores, the composer failed to complete); an orchestral piece *Night on the Bare Mountain*, described by Mussorgsky as 'an operatic scena without voices' and which was to be made familiar to millions by Walt Disney in *Fantasia*; a piano suite *Pictures at an Exhibition*, orchestrated at least five times by other composers,

ABOVE: *Boris Godunov, Tsar of Russia 1598-1605, the subject of Mussorgsky's best-known opera which was first performed in its complete version in 1874. This impression is by Ilya Glazunov (1930-).*

including Ravel; a large collection of songs, including the ever-popular 'Song of the Flea', and some piano arrangements of works by Beethoven, Glinka and others.

It is a musical legacy made all the more remarkable by the fact that the composer started his career as an amateur, and drank himself into an early grave before his full potential had been realized. The clue to his genius – for it is nothing less – is the way in which his music responds to the sense and the meaning of words, to the drama and emotion those words convey and to the way in which they are delivered. In his operas and in his songs, words and music are totally fused and, unfettered by academic rules, Mussorgsky achieves a clarity of expression and a stark, dramatic power few other composers can match. R.H.

1871 *Begins work on unfinished opera* Khovanshchina
1873-4 Boris Godunov *produced at St. Petersburg*
1874 *Composes* Pictures at an Exhibition. *Begins work on new opera* Sorochintsy Fair
1875-6 *Fits of dementia due to heavy drinking*
1877 *Completes 4 Songs and Dances of Death*
1879 *Composes 'Song of the Flea'. Concert tour of southern Russia*
1880 *Finally dismissed from government service*
1881 *Collapses and dies, St. Petersburg, 28 March*

CARL Nielsen

(b. Nørre-Lyndelse, 9 June 1865; d. Copenhagen, 3 October 1931)

RIGHT: Carl Nielsen photographed in 1910 when he was conductor of the Royal Theatre Orchestra in Copenhagen.

Chronology

1865 Born on 6 June in the village of Nørre-Lyndelse on the island of Fyn

1873 Becomes violinist with an amateur orchestra; tuition in both violin and trumpet. First composition, a polka for violin

1879 Leaves home to join military band in Odense

1883 Introduction to the composer, Niels Gade, in Copenhagen

1884-6 Tuition at the Copenhagen Conservatorium

1888 Composes a string quartet and string quintet; Little Suite for orchestra his first composition to be performed publicly

1889 Joins the second violins of the Royal Chapel Orchestra

1890-1 Visits Germany, France and Italy. Meets and marries the sculptress, Anne Marie Brodesen

The most important figure in Danish music came from humble beginnings. Carl Nielsen was born in the village of Nørre-Lyndelse, on the island of Fyn and some ten miles south of Odense. His father was a housepainter who doubled as the village musician, playing the violin and cornet, while his mother was a fine singer. Much of the youngster's musical education was to come from such down-to-earth sources. At eight, he was playing violin in an amateur village orchestra and, as well as taking violin lessons, learning the trumpet. Around this time, he also composed his first piece, a polka for violin.

In 1879, though just fourteen, Nielsen was selected to join a military band in Odense and his musical horizons were broadened further by making the acquaintance of beer-cellar pianist who introduced him to the music of J. S. Bach, Haydn, Mozart and Beethoven. The impact was such that Nielsen rapidly formed a string quartet with other musicians from the army band so that he could explore the chamber music of the Viennese masters. During 1882 and 1883, he composed chamber music of his own, a string quartet and violin sonata, and also wrote some quartets for brass instruments.

Nielsen was accepted into the Copenhagen Conservatorium in 1884, having made a great impression on the then leading figure in Danish music, Niels Gade (1817-1890). Coming from a poor family, money was to prove a problem for Nielsen for much of his life. During his two years at the Conservatorium, he supplemented his grant by playing violin in the orchestra of the Tivoli, Copenhagen's famous pleasure gardens.

Despite some success as a composer – his Little Suite became the first Nielsen composition to be heard publicly, at a performance in the concert hall of the Tivoli gardens in September 1888 – there followed three very lean years. Then, in the autumn of 1889, Nielsen won a competition to join the violins of the Royal Chapel Orchestra. Life became sweeter still for him while in Paris in 1891. He met the Danish sculptress, Anne Marie Brodesen, and was married within a month.

Nielsen completed his First Symphony in 1892 and, at the première that March, before an audience which included the Danish royal family, the composer had to step out from his place among the second violin desks to receive an ovation.

Successful as his music was, it was insufficient to keep a family of three young children. Often reluctantly, Nielsen was forced to maintain a parallel career as a conductor. He became conductor of the Royal Theatre Orchestra for six years from 1908 but soon found that not all the critics were enamoured with his interpretations. While his Third Symphony was receiving wide acclaim, Nielsen was quitting the Orchestra amid some acrimony. He enjoyed much greater satisfaction from directing Copenhagen's Music Society, a post which he held from 1915 until 1927.

Nielsen continued to compose prolifically, despite a worsening heart condition. All Denmark celebrated his sixtieth birthday in 1925, but the rest of the world remained largely indifferent to his music. The last music that Nielsen heard was a radio performance of the Violin Concerto on 1 October 1931. Two days later, he died, aged sixty-six. That same evening, as it had so many times since the première in 1906, his opera, Maskarade, was delighting the audience in Copenhagen's Royal Theatre. Danish audiences had long known what Nielsen's music had to offer the world; eventually, the world would discover it, too.

BELOW: View from Frederiksborg Castle, painted in 1834-5 by Danish artist Christen Købke (1810-48). Købke specialized in painting landscape scenes around Copenhagen and his works would have been known to Nielsen.

ABOVE: *An evocative painting 'And beautiful, white clouds float past' by the Danish artist, and contemporary of Nielsen, Sophus Hansen (1871-1959) which was completed in 1908.*

At the heart of Nielsen's achievement lies his cycle of six symphonies, at least three of which number among the most potent musical statements of the 20th century. In its own way, each of the six is a tribute to the indomitability of the human spirit. There is struggle, most emphatically in the heroic Fourth (*The Inextinguishable*) and Fifth Symphonies. In the latter, a sidedrum is instructed to play as loudly as possible in an effort to disrupt the progress of the symphony, a starkly effective metaphor. The Fourth, too, is an epic struggle for survival (though not specifically concerned with the First World War, the time of its composition – 1915-16 – was surely not coincidental).

The bold opening of the First Symphony shows a composer already confident of his powers as a symphonist. The Second – the four movements of which characterize the human condition in the form of 'four temperaments' – is equally fine. The Third – the *Sinfonia espansiva* – is heartwarming and inspiring, with the breezy optimism of its first movement set against the delicacy of the second and the dance-like third. The finale is noble and triumphant and, like the remainder of the work, flooded with glorious melody.

The freshness and sincerity of purpose of the *Sinfonia espansiva* is characteristic of all of Nielsen's music. There is barely a trace of sentimentality or self-indulgence, rather an arresting clarity and candour of expression. He harvested much from the fertile soil of Danish folk music; adopted the refinement of Mozart and the structural discipline of Brahms; but, unlike so many of his contemporaries, found little that appealed in Wagner.

Nielsen's technical mastery, in terms of rhythm, harmony and counterpoint, can be appreciated from the very first of his major compositions. The First Symphony is a pioneering example of 'progressive tonality', where the work begins in one key but ends in another. Even in the works of his maturity, fresh ideas abound, witness the Fifth Symphony, or the rejection of the finality of tonal progression as embodied in the Sixth, the most subjective and enigmatic of the cycle.

In the orchestral field, Nielsen was also responsible for three supremely well-crafted solo concertos, for violin, clarinet and flute, and for several other fine pieces: the majestic *Helios* overture, for example, and the evocative *Imaginary Journey to the Faroe Islands*. He composed two operas, the Biblical *Saul and David* and the effervescent 18th century farce, *Maskarade*. There is a delicious humour, too, in the Wind Quintet which he composed for five musician friends. The music for each was designed to match the character of the player.

Nielsen wrote with consummate skill for the piano and organ – his last composition, the serenely lofty *Commotio* was for the latter – and proved as skilful in handling voices as instruments, as his delightful *Hymnus amoris* demonstrates.

P.H.

JACQUES *Offenbach* (b. Cologne, 20 June 1819; d. Paris, 5 October 1880)

RIGHT: *A portrait of Jacques Offenbach by the famous Parisian photographer Nadar, taken in 1876, four years before Offenbach's death.*

BELOW: *Offenbach's reputation soared after the scandalous production of* Orpheus in the Underworld *at Les Bouffes-Parisiens in 1858. It was revived and augmented at the Théâtre de la Gaité in 1874.*

Although of German-Jewish origins, Offenbach has come to be thought of, through his addiction to Paris and its ways, as a quintessentially French composer. His father's real family name was Eberst but he had adopted Offenbach, the town of his birth, as a working name shortly before he married and worked in Cologne as musician and cantor. A young family of Offenbachs were soon pressed into musical service and Jacques (then Jakob) took the cello as his particular instrument. In 1833 he was admitted to the Paris Conservatoire, in spite of the prejudices of its temperamental director Luigi Cherubini (1760-1842), who had turned down many distinguished foreign applicants. However, finding academic ways little to his liking, he left his studies to become a member of the orchestra at the Opéra-Comique.

He began to compose dance music and songs and made a reputation as an eccentric cello virtuoso, visiting London in 1844 in that role. Continued success as a performer contrasted with his lack of success as a composer, the airy and witty music that he wrote being viewed with some suspicion by the Parisian musical theatre establishment. To overcome this he leased and opened his own theatre, Les Bouffes-Parisiens, a tiny place where he produced one-act trifles limited in scope by the whims of the licensing laws. Finding a larger theatre he finally made an impression with his scintillating and shockingly satiricial Orphée aux enfers (Orpheus in the Underworld) (1858) and thereafter produced a constant stream of lively, witty, melodious operettas that became the vogue of Paris, Vienna, Berlin, London and New York alike.

Johann Strauss and Arthur Sullivan were two composers heavily in debt to Offenbach for their inspiration. He was not a good business man and had constant financial difficulties, as well as a struggle against ill-health. In 1876 he made an ill-fated visit to the USA, where audiences were slightly disappointed to find that the man who had scandalized the musical world with his Orpheus was really quite a mild and likeable fellow. Like most comedians he wanted to be taken seriously and spent his last months writing a 'grand' opera, Les Contes d'Hoffmann, which was only produced in 1881 after his death. The greatest compliment he could have received came from Rossini who dubbed him 'The Mozart of the Champs-Elysées', a pleasant assertion of both the genius and the Frenchness of the composer from Cologne

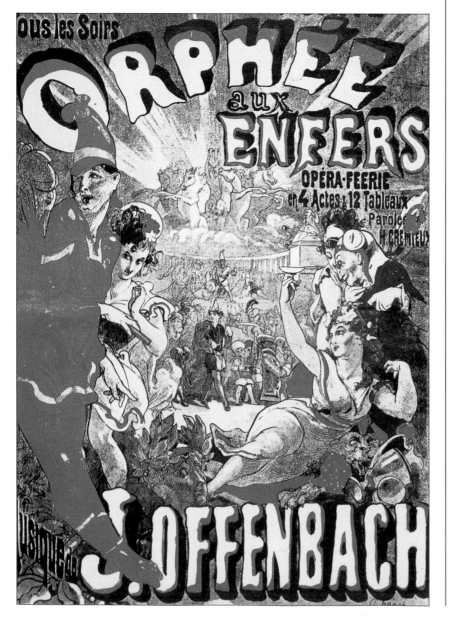

Almost certainly inspired by tuneful operas by the likes of Donizetti and Nicolai which he heard while in the orchestra pit at the Opéra-Comique, Offenbach was the main founder of operetta (light opera with dialogue), a genre which led toward the musical theatre of the 20th century and a distinctly separate world of popular music. His best-known full-length works in this vein are *Orphée aux enfers* (1858); *Geneviève de Brabant* (1859) (very popular in London); *La Belle Hélène* (1864); *La Vie Parisienne* (1866); *Barbe-bleue* (1867); *La Grande-Duchesse de Gérolstein* (1867); *La Périchole* (1868) (one of his finest works), and *Les Brigands* (1869). He also composed over a hundred lesser productions from the early *Les Deux aveugles* (1855) (which Sullivan found a source of inspiration) and *Ba-ta-clan* (1855), to *Pomme d'api* (1873) and after, all full of many delights.

Much of his vast repertoire remains undiscovered despite a strong revival of interest in his achievement in his centenary year in 1980. *Les Contes d'Hoffmann* (1881) has won its own place in the grand opera repertoire, first in many edited versions by various hands, but latterly as Offenbach intended it to be heard. Much of its music has the light quality of his operettas but it is genuinely operatic in scope and shows his capability of writing very satisfyingly and rewardingly for the voice. Much of his music was uniquely comic, many of his best numbers in the style of the lively can-can dance with which the world particularly associates him; but he also had a fine lyrically romantic strain in his writing, heard at its best in *La Périchole* – for instance in the well-known and charming 'Letter Song'. The same lyrical quality is also to be found in his little-known cello music (some written in collaboration with Friedrich von Flotow [1812-83], the composer of *Martha*), which, along with many isolated songs, is still largely unknown territory.

An ideal way to sample the joyful quality of Offenbach's music is through the ballet *Gaîté Parisienne* which Manuel Rosenthal compiled from excerpts from the operettas in 1938. There is a very special quality to Offenbach's writing. While basically simple and ever tuneful, there is an unexpected turn to his melodic lines, ever searching, quirkish and individual, and a touch of wistful melancholy runs through even the most lively works. Although he did not have the advantage of a regular librettist, as Sullivan did with Gilbert, writers like Henry Meilhac and Ludovic Halévy (the son of the opera composer Fromental Halévy, and librettist for Bizet's opera *Carmen*) did provide some admirable texts which enabled Offenbach to show his genius in giving their words so many joyfully ingenious musical twists and turns.

P.G.

LEFT: 'At the Moulin Rouge' by Henri de Toulouse-Lautrec (1864-1901) evokes the atmosphere and spirit of Offenbach's opéra-bouffe *La Vie Parisienne* (1866).

127

ABOVE: *Munich-born Carl Orff photographed in the 1930's at around the time Carmina burana was first performed.*

ABOVE: *Dr. Hubert Parry in 1892. In 1894 he was made Director of the Royal College of Music, and in 1900 he became Professor of music at Oxford.*

RIGHT: *A page from the manuscript of the song collection Carmina burana dating from 1250. Orff's settings of poems from this text is his best-known work.*

CARL **ORFF**

(b. Munich, 10 July 1895; d. Munich, 29 March 1982)

*B*orn into a military family, Orff learned the piano, organ and cello as a boy and soon began to compose, studying at the Munich Academy of Music and graduating in 1914. As a composer, he now came under the influence of Debussy and Strauss, but he earned his living for some years in theatre music and teaching. In 1924 he helped to found a school in Munich 'for gymnastics, music and dance', and in 1930 he commenced the so-called Schulwerk that was his lifelong contribution to musical education. Orff was the conductor of the Munich Bach Society from 1930-3, and in 1937 came the première in Frankfurt of his choral masterpiece, the Carmina burana. This extraordinary work shows his skill with solo voices and choirs and his ability to deploy fresh, strong material. The individual numbers are astonishingly vivid solo and choral settings of lusty and colourful poems in Latin or German dialect that are taken from a thirteenth-century manuscript at the Benedictine abbey of Benediktbeuren, near Munich. He wrote other music, including a Catulli carmina (settings of the Latin poet Catullus) in 1943 and a Trionfo di Afrodite (Milan, 1953) that also has ancient texts: these two works were intended to complement Carmina burana in a triptych called Trionfi which was performed as such in Salzburg in 1953. His operas included Der Mond (1939), Die Klüge (1943) and Antigonae (1949). *C.H.*

GIOVANNI PIERLUIGI DA **PALESTRINA**

(b. Palestrina, 1525; d. Rome, 2 February 1594)

*A*fter a youth spent in various Roman church choirs, Palestrina was appointed choirmaster of the Sistine Choir by Pope Julius III, although he later lost the post because of his married status. In fact, his career was marked by several changes of

post, apparently caused by disputes with his patrons. Of particular significance to him were the decisions of the council of Trent to exclude secular and unliturgical elements from church music, as two of Palestrina's masses fell within this ban. His progression as choirmaster in the leading Roman basilicas was interrupted when the sudden deaths of his wife and sons in an epidemic temporarily persuaded him to seek solace in a priestly vocation, but he soon abandoned this course to re-marry, and this alliance with the widow of a fur merchant brought him more wealth than his musical attainments, and enabled him to publish his works. Among these are several of the greatest polyphonic liturgical settings, marked by flowing vocal lines and a rapturous beauty of sound. His Lamentations, his Mass of Pope Marcellus (1567), and his Litany of the Virgin Mary are random examples of the mastery shown in hundreds of vocal works, secular as well as sacred. *P.J.*

HUBERT **PARRY**

(b. Bournemouth, 27 February 1848; d. Rustington, 7 October 1918)

*N*eatly bridging the gap between the Victorian Mendelssohnians (he studied with Sterndale Bennett and Macfarren) and the renaissance at the end of the 19th century. Parry occupied positions of immense influence for many years. Director of the RCM for 24 years, Professor at Oxford, he and Stanford helped English music to find its own voice after centuries of imitating Germany. After an abortive sally into business, Parry started late as a musician, but soon made up for lost time. From his early piano concerto (1880) to the famous 'Jerusalem' (1916) he kept up a constant flow of works in most forms. His Victorian music is mostly in the Brahmsian idiom, tinged with Wagner, which was fashionable at the time. Shaw used to poke fun at his solemn oratorios, but such works as Blest pair of sirens and the Coronation anthem I was glad show vigour and tunefulness, if also a stodgy texture. Four of his five symphonies also date from this period, and show a refreshing English forthrightness, if no great melodic interest, as do his many settings of English Lyrics. With the distinguished Symphonic Variations of 1897, however, a new individuality is added to the Brahmsian base. The choral Soul's Ransom and Nativity Ode are often inspiring, and the Fifth Symphony (1912) has Elgarian overtones. *P.L.*

KRZYSZTOF **PENDERECKI**

(b. Dębica, near Cracow, 23 November 1933)

*A*fter private study, in 1955 he entered the Cracow Conservatory to which in later life he was destined to return as Rector. His memories of wartime horrors seem to underlie the intensely dramatic works that first made his reputation: Threnody for the Victims of Hiroshima (1961) and the awesome St. Luke Passion (1966). These employ difficult avant-garde techniques yet communicate in a vivid way. However, subsequent compositions such as his 1968 opera The Devils of Loudun and various large-scale religious works were criticized for being less substantial, and, as if to win back audiences, from 1978 he wrote for some years in a more accessible, tonal style. It was not only in the world of music that Penderecki had difficulty in maintaining his reputation. When democracy made its painful return to Poland, his principles and patriotism were called into question. By the mid eighties he had reverted to harsher experimental techniques in concertos for cello and for viola, and his 1986 opera The Black Mask was written in the violent style of his early works. *P.J.*

GIOVANNI BATTISTA **PERGOLESI**

(b. Jesi, 4 January 1710; d. Pozzuoli, 16 March 1736)

*F*rom the time that he entered the Naples Conservatory at the age of fifteen until his death only eleven years later, Pergolesi fully employed his talents, producing a stream of comic operas, orchestral works, church cantatas and instrumental sonatas. He never enjoyed good health; he suffered from tuberculosis, and was troubled by a misformed leg. Considering these handicaps, it seems remarkable that he was so prolific, although it must be remembered that several works originally attributed to Pergolesi are now considered not to be his. The speed of composition seems to have militated against lasting success, and today comparatively few of his works are regularly performed. Noteworthy is the comic opera of 1732 La Serva padrona, a lively domestic scene which anticipates Mozart's Figaro. A few of Pergolesi's choral works are also heard, especially Salve regina and the Stabat Mater composed in the year of his death. Almost two centuries later, the music of Pergolesi was given new currency when Stravinsky adapted several of his pieces, including some of doubtful authenticity, for his witty ballet Pulcinella.   P.J.

WALTER **PISTON**

(b. Rockland, Maine, 20 January 1894; d. Belmont, 12 November 1976)

*P*iston was a respected composer and influential teacher in the middle decades of the twentieth century. However, his reputation never spread widely outside his native America, and even there, in recent years, his strong but conservative compositions have been less frequently performed. Piston's career centred on Boston, and the great symphony orchestra of that city, under its outstanding conductor Serge Koussevitzky, gave the first performances of many of his works, some of which they had commissioned. In his student days, Piston had graduated in Art, and was largely self-taught in music, but by 1919 was so advanced that he was admitted to Harvard, and apart from the almost obligatory years in Paris studying with Nadia Boulanger, it was here that he spent most of his life, progressing from student to teacher to professor by 1944. Piston's compositions, nearly all in traditional form, range over fifty years: they include several concertos, much chamber music, and above all eight symphonies, of which numbers 3 and 4 are especially admired. He won many honours, wrote authoritative text books, and taught such luminaries as Leonard Bernstein and Elliott Carter, yet his own works have not reached a wide popular recognition (with the possible exception of the 1938 ballet The Incredible Flutist) despite their undeniable mastery of form and technique.   P.J.

Above: Walter Piston photographed in the 1950's. He was a notable teacher of music as well as a composer.

AMILCARE **PONCHIELLI**

(b. Paderno Fasolaro, 31 August 1834; d. Milan, 16 January 1886)

*P*onchielli's career coincided with that of Verdi, and the growing mastery of the latter largely overshadowed the operatic efforts of the organist from Cremona. In all, Ponchielli composed nine operas, and the quick success of the first, I promessi sposi (The Betrothed) (1872), was difficult to repeat. In fact, the only work of Ponchielli to hold the stage today is La Gioconda (1876), a complex melodrama of Venetian intrigue, with libretto by Boito; it provides fine singing roles for several characters, as well as introducing the popular ballet Dance of the Hours. Nothing else from his mainly operatic output seems likely to preserve his reputation. Ponchielli held the post of professor at the Milan Conservatory at the time of his death from pneumonia at the age of fifty-one. His pupils included Puccini and Mascagni.   P.J.

Above: Krzysztof Penderecki photographed in 1973 when he was commissioned by the Chicago Opera to write an opera for the United States' Bicentennial celebrations.

NICCOLÒ
Paganini (b. Genoa, 27 October 1782; d. Nice, 27 May 1840)

'The people have all gone crazy,' wrote a reporter of Paganini's first recital in Paris . . . 'it was a divine, a diabolic enthusiasm.' The pop star of his age, Paganini drew the masses wherever he appeared, and there was scarcely a town in all of Europe where he did not perform. Audiences and critics (most of them) raved about the miraculous, inconceivable playing of 'the greatest violinist the world has known'. His personality was magnetic, his appearance fabulous, and his playing 'great and incomparable'.

Taught – or rather forced – to play the violin by his father, Niccolò Paganini rapidly mastered all its techniques and developed some of his own. At 15 he made his first concert tour in northern Italy, and at 23 he composed his famous 24 Caprices for solo violin. His many other compositions included six violin concertos, many sonatas for violin, and violin and guitar, as well as Variations on themes by Rossini.

In 1805 Paganani became music director at the court of Princess Elisa of Lucca, sister of Napoleon. But his fame and fortune were made as a travelling virtuoso. A brilliant showman, he tuned his violin to produce astonishing effects, and exploited pizzicato and staccato as never before. He travelled by coach the length and breadth of Europe, including Britain, taking with him his young son Achilles, and visiting the remotest towns, often giving three concerts a week. During his tour of Germany, Poland and Bohemia in 1828-31, for example, he visited some 40 towns and cities. Undoubtedly this ceaseless travel, overwork and other excesses ruined his health and caused his early death. Afflicted by cancer of the larynx, by 1828 he was described as 'a heap of bones', and after 1834 he gave few recitals. With pulmonary tuberculosis added to his other ills, he returned to Parma, the scene of his first success as a virtuoso, where he bought a villa for his retirement and undertook to reorganize the Court orchestra for the Archduchess. But his plans met with fierce opposition from the musicians and courtiers, and as a consequence came to nothing.

In his last years Paganini was frustrated, lonely and desperately ill. He invested in a casino in Paris ('The Casino Paganini') and lost heavily when it was forced to close down. In search of warmth and health he retired to Nice, where he died in 1840, leaving a large fortune to his sisters, his son Achilles and his erstwhile lover Antonia Bianchi, together with 22 rare instruments, including eleven Stradivari, two Amati and four Guarneri violins.

RIGHT: A portrait of Niccolò Paganini, probably dating from around 1830, when he was at the height of his powers.

BELOW: Nicolo Zaganini, the Great Virtuoso, a scene from a Paganini burlesque produced at the Carltheater, Vienna in 1831. This contemporary watercolour is by Johann Christian Schoeller.

Chronology

1782 *Born 27 October, Genoa, son of a shipping clerk*
1787 *Learns to play the mandolin*
1789 *Begins learning the violin; forced by his father to practise from morning to night*
1794 *Plays during Mass at S. Filippo Neri and wins 'universal admiration'*
1795 *Studies composition under composer Antonio Paer*
1801 *Moves to Lucca with violinist brother Carlo*
1805 *Composes 24 Caprices for solo violin*
1805-13 *Director of Music for Princess Elisa of Lucca, sister of Napoleon*
1810-28 *Successful debut in Milan, followed by triumphant concert tours of Italy*
1817 *Concerto No.1 in E flat*
1822-3 *Seriously ill – no recitals*
1824 *Begins liaison with singer Antonia Bianchi*
1825 *Son Achilles born*
1827 *Created Knight of the Golden Spur by Pope Leo XII*
1828 *In Vienna: 'never has an artist caused such a terrific sensation within our walls as this god of the violin'. End of affair with Antonia Bianchi*
1829-34 *Successful recital tours in Austria, Germany, Poland, France, England, Scotland, Ireland*
1833 *Asked for a viola concerto, Berlioz composes Harold in Italy, which Paganini never plays*
1834 *Cancer of larynx causes decline of his career*
1835 *Returns to Parma: director of Court Orchestra*
1838 *Failure of the Casino Paganini in Paris*
1839 *Sick and broken, retires to Nice*
1840 *Dies Nice 27 May*

From an early age Paganini was groomed by his father to be a virtuoso performer and, with the example of Leopold Mozart very much in mind, he was forced to undergo a strict training regime. This involved many hours of practice each day, first on the mandolin and then – from the age of seven – the violin. Young Niccolò showed great aptitude for the instrument and developed an astonishing performing technique. This included fingered octaves, multiple trills and harmonics, triple and quadruple stopping, ricochet bowing and other dazzling embellishments.

As he reached maturity Paganini realized that he stood to make a fortune with his spectacular new style of playing, and that it made good sense to compose new pieces to show off his skills and artistry rather than to embroider works from the existing repertoire. Before he reached his 18th birthday he had already written a violin sonata and, although composition did not come easily to him, he managed to produce in the course of a busy lifetime a very large number of works for the violin, including unaccompanied pieces, sonatas, string quartets and concertos for violin and orchestra.

A close contemporary, François Fétis, said of Paganini's manuscripts that 'their merit was to be found *only* in perfect execution. As compositions, they have only a transitory existence, and will never hold a place in serious music.' Later generations have not entirely endorsed this severe view, because much of Paganini's music does have a quality and a character that lift it above the level of mere virtuoso trickery and meretricious effect. The first two violin concertos, for example, are among the many compositions well worth listening to as music, and not simply as highly advanced technical exercises.

One of the oddities of musical history is that Paganini is more famous today for music he did not write, than for the music that he did. Among those works which one way or another he inspired is *Harold in Italy*, which he commissioned Berlioz to compose for viola and orchestra, and then refused to perform because he thought the solo part was not spectacular enough. And that spiky, grotesque scrap of a tune in A minor – the last in a set of 24 Caprices for unaccompanied violin that he composed in 1805 when only 23 – has yielded a whole crop of variations by other composers, including Brahms, Schumann, Liszt, Rakhmaninov and, nearer our own times, Lutoslawski, Boris Blacher, John Dankworth and Andrew Lloyd Webber.   R.H.

FRANCIS

Poulenc (b. Paris, 7 January 1899; d. Paris, 30 January 1963)

Though his family were important pharmaceutical manufacturers, the musical talents of Francis Poulenc soon made it clear where his own future lay. They were fostered by his mother, a fine amateur pianist, and as a Parisian schoolboy at the Lycée Condorcet he also became aware of poetry and the theatre, and at the age of fourteen was bowled over by Stravinsky's ballet Le Sacre du printemps. In 1915 he began piano lessons with Ricardo Viñes, the artist who gave first performances of several works by Debussy and Ravel, but the potential influence of Debussy's impressionism was tempered soon afterwards by his meeting with another composer of that generation, the iconoclastic Erik Satie, whose artistic philosophy embraced both the profoundly simple and the irreverently smart. Along with other young composers who later became known as Les Six, Poulenc supported this hitherto rather lonely figure, and dedicated to him his first published work, the Rapsodie nègre for voice and instruments, written when he was just eighteen.

The strong individuality and sharp wit of this music gave Poulenc early fame, and he responded by writing fairly prolifically: although he had to do military service during 1918-21, he managed to compose several pieces during this time including the three Mouvements perpétuels for piano and the song cycle Le Bestiaire. However, he then decided that he needed more instruction in composition and a broadening of his musical horizons. He took lessons from 1921-4 with Charles Koechlin, and in 1921 he also visited Vienna (with Milhaud) to meet Schoenberg and his pupils Berg and Webern, and Italy in 1922 to visit the composer Alfredo Casella (1883-1947). His position as a leading young French composer was reinforced in 1924 when his ballet Les Biches, commissioned by Diaghilev, had a triumphant première in Monte Carlo.

The next decade saw Poulenc as a leading figure on the Parisian artistic and social scene, and he bought a large, comfortable house called 'Le Grand Coteau' at Noizay, on the Loire in Touraine. In 1936 the death of a friend in a car accident prompted him to return to the Catholic faith of his childhood. Thereafter, he was to compose several religious choral works, some of which have the theme of penitence. The dramatic Concerto for Organ, Strings and Timpani (1938) shares this mood, as does the three-act opera, concerned with the martyrdom of Carmelite nuns, which crowns this aspect of his career, his Dialogues des Carmélites, first produced at La Scala, Milan, in 1957.

From 1935 onwards, Poulenc frequently appeared as a pianist with the baritone Pierre Bernac, who became his major interpreter and the singer for whom he created many of his solo songs. During the Second World War and the German occupation, he remained in France and demonstrated a quiet opposition to Nazism in compositions asserting his patriotic feeling: for example, his Violin Sonata of 1943 is dedicated to the memory of the Spanish poet Lorca, shot by Fascists. After the war years, he remained active in musical life and travelled with Bernac on overseas tours including visits to the US. He had a considerable success with his comic opera Les Mamelles de Tirésias in 1947, and the one-woman, one-act opera La Voix humaine in 1958. He had began work on an opera on Cocteau's La Machine infernale when he died in Paris of a heart attack.

RIGHT: A photographic portrait of Poulenc taken in Paris when he was making his international reputation.

Chronology

1899 Born Paris, 7 January

1904 Begins piano lessons with his mother

1913 Sees Stravinsky's Le Sacre du printemps

1915 Piano lessons with Ricardo Viñes

1917-18 Rapsodie nègre; meets Satie and sees his ballet Parade; meets Auric, Honegger and Milhaud, also to become members of Les Six

1918-21 Military service; compositions include Mouvements perpétuels and Le Bestiaire, Sonata for Two Clarinets, Sonata for Piano Duet, Suite in C for piano, Six Impromptus for piano

1921-4 Composition lessons with Koechlin; Promenades for piano

1922 Sonata for Clarinet and Bassoon; Sonata for Horn, Trumpet and Trombone

RIGHT: 'Concert champêtre' by Frenchman Raoul Dufy (1877-1953) painted in 1949. Poulenc's Concert champêtre for piano or harpsichord and orchestra was first performed in 1929.

Although he was influenced by other composers ranging from Mozart to Chabrier and Stravinsky, Poulenc's work has a strong personality of its own that is immediately recognizable and stands refreshingly apart from the more intellectual trends of twentieth-century music. The French critic Roland-Manuel once summed it up as 'sometimes verging on triviality but never falling into vulgarity'. Even a religious work such as his setting of the *Gloria* (1959) has a 'Laudamus te' that can only be described as infectiously bouncy, and the healthy earthiness of such music reminds us of his comment that his Catholic faith was 'that of a country priest'. Indeed, his unquestionable religious sincerity existed quite happily alongside a *gamin* humour which was always among his strongest musical characteristics. One of his friends suggested that he was 'half monk and half street urchin': even his appearance was slightly droll, and Cocteau once likened him to a puppy. Listening to his song cycle *Chansons gaillardes* of 1926, immensely vivid settings of bawdy anonymous seventeenth-century poems with a title literally meaning 'Ribald Songs', one remembers his remark that he disliked rude stories but enjoyed obscenity.

Thus, for many people the most typical Poulenc remains the playfully inventive composer of the *Mouvements perpétuels*, the saucy song cycle *Chansons gaillardes*, his ballet *Les Biches*, the tuneful Piano Concerto (1949) and the *Gloria*. Nevertheless there are other sides to him that are no less powerful, such as the quiet dignity and grandeur of the *Dialogues des Carmélites*, which ends with the nuns going to execution by the guillotine. The humanity of his art, as well as its musical ingenuity, is perfectly illustrated by his wartime choral cantata *Figure humaine* (1943), which shows his knowledge of Bach's chorales and is a sombre setting of a text

by his favourite living poet, Paul Eluard. Eluard, Poulenc declared, endowed his music with true lyricism, and the song cycle *Tel jour, telle nuit* (1937) is another thoughtful and deeply expressive masterwork. Similarly, *La Voix humaine*, written for the fine singer-actress Denise Duval, portrays a woman bidding a forty-minute agonized farewell on the telephone to the lover who is leaving her for another: monotony is wholly avoided in this skilful composition, and Cocteau, who wrote the libretto, congratulated the composer on finding 'the only way to say my text'.

In his honest expression of ordinary emotions ranging from sadness to jollity, Poulenc was unusual among 20th-century composers, and he also showed himself equally at home in vocal and instrumental music: among his last works (in 1962) were two strikingly expressive wind sonatas with piano, one for clarinet and the other for oboe. It may be said that in an age of musical theories and weighty propaganda, he instead offers clarity, vivacity, persuasiveness and tenderness of a quality and consistency that are in the finest traditions of French thought.   C.H.

SERGEY
Prokofiev

(b. Krasnoye, Ekaterinslav, 23 April 1891; d. Moscow, 5 March 1953)

Prokofiev's life was as varied as his music. He was taught piano by his mother, who also encouraged his evident gift for composition, so much so that, at nine, he had composed an opera. When he was eleven, he studied with the composer, Glière (1875-1956), and two years later, in 1904, entered the St. Petersburg Conservatory. There, he studied counterpoint with Lyadov and orchestration with Rimsky-Korsakov, and, subsequently, piano. Several compositions from this period were published. He became a brilliant pianist and, in 1914, won for the prestigious Rubinstein prize, audaciously choosing to play his own First Piano Concerto.

That same year, Prokofiev went to London where he met the director of the Ballets Russes, Serge Diaghilev. As he had with another gifted Russian composer, Igor Stravinsky, Diaghilev commissioned a work from Prokofiev. The outbreak of war, and subsequent events in Russia, scuppered that plan although Prokofiev reworked the material as the Scythian Suite. It was but one of several abrasive works he produced in this period as he experimented with spiky discords and developed an often brutal style of piano writing.

In sharp contrast, Prokofiev's First Symphony of 1917 was a clever, but affectionate pastiche of Haydn, full of sparkling melodies. This Classical Symphony remains one of Prokofiev's best-loved works. However, the new regime in Russia was not to Prokofiev's taste. In 1918 he went into exile, first in the United States, where the Chicago Opera commissioned the opera The Love for Three Oranges.

Encouraged by Diaghilev's interest in his music, Prokofiev settled in Paris in 1920 and continued to live there for the next sixteen years. But he was never wholly enamoured with life in the west and, returning to the Soviet Union for a visit in 1933, was delighted by the reception he received. His works were still being played in the concert hall and, moreover, there came a major commission from the Kirov Ballet in Leningrad (which materialized as the wonderfully lyrical Romeo and Juliet) and an invitation to write the music for a satirical comedy film, Lieutenant Kijé. Full of delicious tunes and very easy-on-the-ear, these enduringly popular works represented a notable change of style for Prokofiev. Three years later, he was back living in Moscow with his wife and two sons.

He could have chosen a more propitious moment: Shostakovich's Lady Macbeth of Mtsensk had just been savaged by Stalin's apparatchiks and – incredibly – Romeo and Juliet was to suffer the same fate. However, Prokofiev remained in the Soviet Union and, like Shostakovich, weathered the vagaries of officialdom (essentially dictated by the whim of Stalin). He composed the obligatory patriotic rhetoric but matched it with works of enduring artistic merit, not least the Fifth Symphony, which so deeply affected the war-weary Moscow audience at the first performance in 1945, and the magnificent opera based on Tolstoy's 'War and Peace'. Sergey Prokofiev died on 5 March 1953, but the event was overshadowed by another passing – that of Josef Stalin. Prokofiev, the eternal ironist, would surely have appreciated the piquancy of that.

Prokofiev's huge talent allowed him to compose with facility in every genre, and in several styles. The tune-smith responsible for the deliciously tongue-in-cheek *Lieutenant Kijé* also wrote some of the thorniest music of the 20th century. The seven symphonies, beginning with the *Classical* of 1917 and ending with the Seventh of 1952 supply telling markers to the directions his music took. The pastiche of the First was replaced by the machine-age modernism of the Second and the searing energy of the Third, which drew on material from his opera, *The Fiery Angel*. The Fourth is softer-edged but equally pungent. It, too, borrows from one of Prokofiev's operas, *The Prodigal Son*.

The opening of the Fifth Symphony marks the serenity after the storm, a broad sigh of relief. It is easy to understand why the Moscow audience at the first performance in January 1945, allowing themselves to believe for the first time that the end of the war was in sight, embraced the noble optimism of this work. The Sixth Symphony finds Prokofiev in a reflective and elegaic mood, while the Seventh recalls the deft humour of the *Classical* Symphony.

Given his virtuoso status, it is no surprise that Prokofiev wrote himself some formidably taxing piano music, principally the five concertos and ten sonatas, but also the compelling *Visions Fugitives* and *Sarcasms*. Among the concertos, the witty Third rightly remains the most popular.

BELOW: *Napoleon's army during the retreat from Moscow in 1812, a scene portrayed by January Suchodolski (1797-1875) in 1859. Prokofiev wrote an epic opera on this theme,* War and Peace.

ABOVE: *A portrait of Sergey Prokofiev painted by Piotr Konchalovsky (1876-1956) in 1934, shortly after he had completed his popular film score,* Lieutenant Kijé.

Prokofiev's two violin concertos are in sharp contrast to the spiky savagery of so much of his early music. The First is contemplative, even unexpectedly nostalgic; the Second, sumptuously lyrical.

Though judged a rebel and an iconoclast in his youth – and there is much astringent, steely and even barbaric music to support that – Prokofiev ultimately followed in the romantic Russian tradition of Rimsky-Korsakov, Borodin and Tchaikovsky, as his two greatest ballet scores – *Romeo and Juliet* and *Cinderella* – amply testify. While those ballets remain in the standard repertoire, Prokofiev's operas are rarely performed now – understandably so with the epic *War and Peace* but less so in the case of *The Love for Three Oranges* or *The Prodigal Son*. Also noteworthy among his eight operas is *The Gambler*, based on Dostoyevsky's novella.

Prokofiev also displayed consummate skill in the field of chamber music, most notably in the eloquent Cello Sonata and in the two sonatas for violin and piano. But for most his name will remain most readily associated with the immortal children's musical fable, *Peter and the Wolf* and the thrilling and colourful cantata which emerged from the music he wrote for Eisenstein's film *Alexander Nevsky*.   P.H.

1939 *Cantata,* Alexander Nevsky

1941 *Begins opera* War and Peace; *composes three piano sonatas (Nos. 6, 7 and 8) during the war years and music for Eisenstein's* Ivan the Terrible

1944 *Fifth Symphony, premièred Moscow, January 1945*

1945 *Ballet,* Cinderella, *with choreography by Rotislav Zakharov, premièred at the Bolshoi Theatre, Moscow on 21 November*

1945-7 *Symphony No. 6; Piano Sonata No. 9*

1946 *Commences opera,* The Stone Flower *(not performed until after his death, Moscow, 1954)*

1948 *With Shostakovich, is condemned for 'formalism' by Stalin's cultural apparatchik, Zhdanov*

1951-2 *Symphony No. 7*

1952 *Completes his last opera* War and Peace; *first complete performance, Leningrad, March 1955*

1953 *Dies in Moscow on 5 March*

GIACOMO
Puccini
(b. Lucca, 23 December 1858; d. Brussels, 29 November 1924)

The son of Michele Puccini (1813-1864), a teacher, church organist and composer, Giacomo Puccini was the fifth of seven children. He was only five when his father died, but followed in his family's long musical tradition by studying first with his uncle and then with Carlo Angeloni, both of whom had themselves studied with his father. At ten, he joined the choir in his father's old church of San Martino and by 1873 he was playing the organ there and elsewhere: his first compositions were organ pieces written from his eighteenth year onwards. However, he was already attracted to opera and after seeing Verdi's Aida in 1876 he made up his mind to break with family tradition and make his future in the musical theatre: later he was to say that this occasion 'opened a musical window' for him. In 1880 he entered the Milan Conservatory and remained there for three years as a pupil of Bazzini and Ponchielli, both of whom had written operas themselves, and in these student years learned to know both the poverty and the lively Bohemianism that he was later to depict in La Bohème.

Encouraged by Ponchielli, Puccini entered a competition for a new one-act opera with his Le Villi, but did not win it. However, Fortune then smiled on him when a wealthy Milan music-lover invited him to a party and he sang and played it in the presence of influential people including the composer-librettist Boito and the publisher Ricordi. As a result of their admiration, Le Villi was successfully performed at the city's Teatro del Verme in May 1884, while Ricordi agreed to publish it (revised as a two-acter) and commissioned Puccini to write another opera. But the libretto of Edgar did not suit him; it was five years before he finished the score and the work failed when it finally reached the stage in April 1889. Later, he called it 'a mistake'. By this time, he had also begun a long love affair with Elvira Gemignani, a married woman, whom he finally married on the death of her husband in 1904. She was to outlive Puccini by six years, dying in 1930. They are buried together at Torre del Lago.

Despite the failure of Edgar, Ricordi maintained his confidence in Puccini and even helped to write the libretto of his next opera, Manon Lescaut. Produced in Turin in February 1893, this marked the real beginning of the composer's triumphant career, and after a London production in the following year, Bernard Shaw hailed Puccini as Verdi's natural successor. Thereafter the story of his life is largely that of his music and his continuing success. However, it was not wholly untroubled. For example, while Tosca was adored by the public, some critics attacked it for what they saw as its brutality, and in 1904 the first night of Madama Butterfly, at La Scala, Milan, was greeted with noisy hostility, although the composer then made some revisions and it succeeded thereafter. However, interest in his work was now widespread, and it was an American audience who first saw his 'western' opera La Fanciulla del West, given in 1910 at the Metropolitan Opera in New York under Toscanini, with Caruso and Emmy Destinn as Dick Johnson and Minnie. His last opera, Turandot, was not quite finished (the present ending, based on his sketches, was by Franco Alfano) when he died in Brussels following treatment there for throat cancer.

Chronology

1858 Born Lucca, 23 December
1864 Death of father Michele Puccini, January; studies with uncle and then Carlo Angeloni, director of local Istituto Musicale Pacini
1869 Chorister at church of San Marino
1873 Playing as church organist
1876 Sees Verdi's Aida at Pisa
1880 Enters Milan Conservatory, studies with Bazzini and Ponchielli
1883 Leaves Conservatory; his Capriccio sinfonico performed there 14 July by student orchestra
1884 Le Villi performed at the Teatro da Verme in Milan; meets future publisher Ricordi
1886 Elvira Gemignani gives birth to their son, Antonio
1889 Edgar performed in Milan, but unsuccessfully
1891 Acquires house at Torre del Lago, his home for thirty years
1893 Manon Lescaut succeeds at Turin, February
1896 La Bohème first performed at Teatro Reggio in Turin
1900 Tosca given in Rome at Teatro Costanzi, January
1904 Madama Butterfly given at La Scala, Milan, February. Elvira's husband dies leaving her free to marry Puccini

Puccini once wrote: 'the Almighty touched me with his little finger and said, "Write for the theatre, but mind, only for the theatre!" '. The immense popularity of his operas – and perhaps above all *La Bohème*, *Tosca*, *Madama Butterfly* and *Turandot* – is due to his powerful sense of drama as much as to his rich vein of vocal melody and colourful orchestration. At the start of his career, he learned the lesson of *Edgar* and thereafter chose his own subjects and librettos – and librettists, notably the excellent team of Luigi Illica and Giuseppe Giacosa for the first three of the above-mentioned operas. Indeed, he knew exactly what suited him and would draw most from his own particular gifts, declaring that 'the basis of an opera is its subject and dramatic treatment'. Like Wagner, he also thought of an opera as a whole, taking an active interest not only in its music and text but also in staging, costumes and even lighting, which he once said should be planned 'with an attentive ear'! His stage directions are much more elaborate than those to be found in a Verdi score.

Another major feature of Puccini's operatic scores is his ability to paint a picture in orchestral terms, whether the Wild West in *La Fanciulla del West*, the Japanese countryside in *Madama Butterfly* or Turandot's Peking. No less a Frenchman than Debussy said of *La Bohème*, 'I know of no one who described the Paris of that time so well'. He also added: 'If

BELOW: *A panorama of the city of Rome painted by Kaspar van Wittel (1653-1736). In the foreground is the Castel San' Angelo, from the battlements of which Tosca hurls herself to her death in one of the most dramatic climaxes in opera.*

ABOVE: *The score of Puccini's unfinished opera* Turandot, *published by Ricordi in 1926 when it was first heard at La Scala, conducted by Arturo Toscanini and with Rosa Raisa in the title role.*

one didn't keep a grip on oneself one would be swept away by the sheer verve of the music'. The love music for Rodolfo and Mimi in this opera has the glow of young love itself, and yet it is not a simply cosy picture that Puccini draws, for these are poor and hungry young people, while in Act III the lovers part and in the final act Mimi dies in Rodolfo's arms.

Doomed loves and dying heroines are central to Puccini's world, and we at once think of Manon, Mimi and Butterfly, and Tosca too, although her suicide at the end of the opera is a magnificent dramatic gesture. Certainly Princess Turandot survives, but only after the self-sacrifice of the faithful servant Liù who is a far worthier character. It has been said that Puccini's operas amount to 'a compulsive exploration of the relationship between sex and suffering', and there is some justice in the remark. But for most of us, their power lies as much in fine melodies finely sung as in their dramatic content, and as Shostakovich (himself an opera composer) once said, these are above all 'great operas'.   C.H.

HENRY Purcell

(b. London, [?] 1659; d. London, 21 November 1695)

RIGHT: A pencil drawing of Henry Purcell by Godfrey Kneller (1646-1723), now in the National Gallery, London.

BELOW: 'Dido and Aeneas', a picture by P. N. Guérin (1774-1833) which is now in the Louvre, Paris. Purcell's opera on the same subject was first produced in 1689.

As with England's greatest poet, William Shakespeare, we know very little about England's greatest composer, Henry Purcell – not even the exact date and place of his birth. Tradition holds that he became a chorister in the Chapel Royal at the age of six, that he composed 'Sweet tyranness, I now resign' when he was nine and a Birthday Ode for Charles II two years later. What is certain, because we have documentary evidence, is that his voice broke in 1673 and on 10 June of that year he was appointed 'Keeper, maker, mender, repayrer of the regals (portable organs with reed pipes), virginals, flutes, recorders and all other kinds of wind instruments whatsoever . . . without fee, to his Majesty . . .'

Four years later the composer of the King's violins, Matthew Locke, died and Henry Purcell, eighteen, was chosen as his successor. Among his other duties he would have been required to compose airs and dances for court occasions, but unfortunately none of this music seems to have survived. In 1679 he succeeded John Blow as organist at Westminster Abbey, and we know that by the following year Purcell's reputation as a composer for the court, chamber and the stage was firmly established.

Yet uncertainty about his private life persists. He was married in 1681, it is believed, to a lady whose surname is assumed to have been Peters, because one of his daughters was baptized Mary Peters. Of his six children, three died in infancy. To these meagre biographical details add that the famous society artist Sir Godfrey Kneller painted his portrait, and you have virtually all that is known about the composer.

Apart, of course, from his music. As an outstandingly gifted court musician, Purcell was called upon to produce music for most royal occasions. In addition to anthems for the coronation of James II and the funeral of Queen Mary, he wrote more than a score of Odes and Welcome Songs. His prodigious output included settings for 70 or more anthems and services, numerous hymns, psalms, canons and sacred songs, as well as over 200 songs and catches, and a hundred or so instrumental and chamber works. But probably his greatest talent was for the theatre, then in its post-Puritan heyday. In the last few years of his short life he produced songs, dances and overtures for about 40 plays, as well as composing five 'semi-operas' and the first great English opera, Dido and Aeneas.

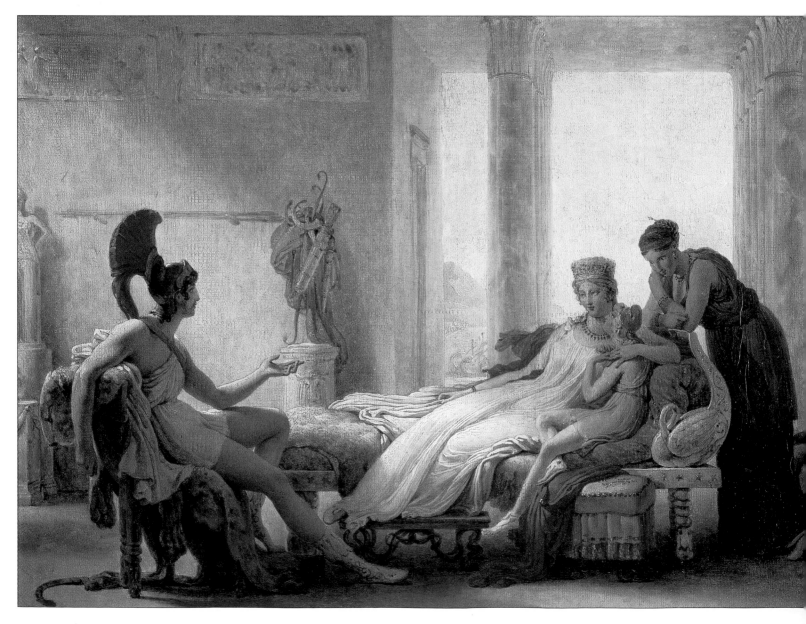

LEFT: *Music making in Purcell's period portrayed in 'The Chamber Music Trio' by Robert Tournières (1667-1752).*

Chronology

If 'the greatest and most original of all English composers' had been born in the middle of the 18th, instead of the 17th century, there can be little doubt that the best of his music would be as familiar to us today, and as highly regarded, as that of Handel, Haydn or Mozart. But, of course, Henry Purcell wrote music within the conventions and forms of his time and for the media then to hand.

Masques and elaborate allegories, virtually impossible to stage under modern conditions, were what his patrons and audiences demanded, which explains why he wrote only one opera, as we would understand the term today. His huge output of music for the theatre is for the most part to be found in plays which would strike us as unimaginably tedious and incomprehensible, while most of his choral works are suitable only for small choirs and demand in performance a high level of technical skill and musical intelligence.

Purcell himself acknowledged a debt to his Elizabethan and Jacobean predecessors by copying into a manuscript book works by Orlando Gibbons (1583-1625), Byrd, Tallis and other old masters. He did this of his own volition and not, as has sometimes been suggested, as part of his duties at Westminster Abbey. He soon developed his own authentic style. His sense of drama served him well when writing odes and anthems for great state occasions and incidental music for the stage; his unfailing fertility of invention and total grasp of key-relationship are shown in his instrumental and keyboard music; his instinctive response to the sound of words and of word-rhythms is clearly revealed in his choral music and in his many songs, some of which are extremely bawdy. His earthy sense of humour, spontaneity of manner and lack of self-consciousness won him great popularity among his contemporaries who, not long after his death, dubbed him 'Orpheus Britannicus'.

Beyond the *Ode on Saint Cecilia's Day*, celebrated dramatic music such as *King Arthur* (1691) and *The Fairy Queen* (1692), his one true opera *Dido and Aeneas*, and music which arrangements by Benjamin Britten and others have made familiar to modern audiences, there remain hundreds of pieces still awaiting rediscovery. There could be no better way of marking the tercentenary of Purcell's death in 1995 than by returning many of these neglected works to their proper place in British musical life. R.H.

SERGEY
Rakhmaninov (b. Semyonovo, Russia, 1 April 1873; d. California, 28 March 1943)

RIGHT: *A photograph of Sergey Rakhmaninov taken in the 1920's when he was living in the United States.*

BELOW: *The Russian Revolution of 1917, led by Lenin, portrayed here with Bolsheviks in 1905 by Valentin Alexandrovich Serov (1865-1911), drove Rakhmaninov from his native land.*

Sergey Rakhmaninov came from an old and aristocratic family. His father and grandfather, both officers in the Imperial Guard, were highly gifted pianists, and Sergey evidently inherited their musical ability. At the age of nine he entered the St. Petersburg Conservatoire, but failed to make progress. He was transferred to the Moscow Conservatoire to study the piano under the strict tutelage of Tchaikovsky's friend Nicolai Zverev; other tutors included Alexander Ziloti and Anton Arensky.

For his graduation exercises Rakhmaninov composed a three-act opera, Aleko, which won a gold medal and was successfully staged in 1893 at the Bolshoi Theatre in Moscow. A year earlier he had won almost instant fame with his celebrated Prelude in C sharp minor which, to his increasing irritation, became a signature tune that followed him wherever he went throughout his threefold career as composer, concert pianist and conductor.

After the failure of his First Symphony in 1897 Rakhmaninov lost all confidence in his creative ability, and was cured only by the patient counselling of Dr. Nicholay Dahl, a psychiatrist and hypnotist who was also a talented amateur musician. When he resumed composition there followed a period of great activity and success. 1901 saw the completion of his Second Piano Concerto –

perhaps the most popular of all his works – and then came two more operas (The Miserly Knight and Francesca da Rimini), the Second Symphony, the Third Piano Concerto, the choral symphony The Bells, the Vespers, and a host of brilliant songs and piano pieces. He gave the first performances of many of these works, either as soloist or conductor.

The Bolshevik Revolution of 1917 was a crux in Rakhmaninov's life and career. As an aristocrat who had grown up in Tsarist Russia he was out of sympathy with the new regime, and possibly in some danger. In 1918 he and his family quietly left Russia, never to return. They settled first in Stockholm, but then embarked to make a new life in America. To earn a living he devoted most of his energies to his career as an international concert pianist, and his last 25 years were a gruelling round of concert tours and recording sessions in North America and Europe, involving constant travel. His Fourth Piano Concerto, begun in 1914, was not completed until 1926, and his public had to wait another eight years for the great Rhapsody on a Theme of Paganini. Had he been able to give more of his genius to posterity as a composer, and less to his contemporaries as a concert performer, who knows what other great works we might now be enjoying?

Like Richard Strauss, his near contemporary, Sergey Rakhmaninov was a 19th century romantic composer who survived well into the present century without coming to terms with it. 'I cannot cast out the old way of writing and I cannot acquire the new,' he once confessed; 'I have made intensive efforts to feel the musical manner of today, but it will not come to me.'

Rakhmaninov himself believed that he owed much to the music of Rimsky-Korsakov, although he was never a pupil of that composer. After the failure of his early studies at St. Petersburg Conservatoire, during which time his parents' marriage also failed, he was sent to Moscow where the influence of Tchaikovsky was paramount. He helped and encouraged the young pianist-composer, who certainly shared the older man's belief in the vital importance of melody. 'Melodic invention,' according to Rakhmaninov, ' . . . is the real aim of every composer. If he is incapable of inventing melodies that endure, his chances of mastering his material are very slender.'

The First Symphony, which received a disastrous first performance in 1897 at the hands of a drunken Glazunov, Rakhmaninov later described as 'weak, childish, strained and bombastic'. But already the composer's very individual style was apparent, and his own melodic gifts were clearly shown not only in this work, but also in the First Piano Concerto which followed in 1891. However, it was not until after his nervous breakdown that Rakhmaninov produced the first of his popular masterpieces, the Second Piano Concerto. Now the lyrical melodies and sumptuous harmonies were allowed full rein, and the idiomatic piano writing was matched by orchestration more subtle and more refined than in any of his previous large-scale works. He had arrived as a composer and his fame grew, first in Russia and then throughout the outside world.

The Second Symphony (1907) and Third Piano Concerto (1909) were among the many works composed during a period of remarkable creativity, followed by two major choral works, the *Vespers* (1910) and *The Bells*, a choral symphony completed in 1913. Other works for recommended listening, apart from his songs and the celebrated *Variations on a Theme of Paganini*, include the tone poems *The Rock* and *The Isle of the Dead*, and works for piano. Many of these he recorded on piano rolls, now available as modern recordings, which stand as a remarkable testimony to his outstanding gifts as a performer.   R.H.

BELOW: *'The Isle of the Dead' by Arnold Böcklin (1827-1901), painted in 1886, inspired Rakhmaninov's tone poem of the same name. He first saw the painting in Paris in 1907 while performing there in concerts organised by Diaghilev.*

MAURICE *Ravel*

(b. Ciboure, St. Jean-de-Luz, 7 March 1875; d. Paris, 28 December 1937)

RIGHT: Maurice Ravel photographed in 1937 in the last year of his life.

Chronology

The name of Maurice Ravel is frequently linked with that of Claude Debussy and, true, their lives overlapped (Debussy was born in 1862 and died in 1918), both were French and both made a significant and lasting contribution to music. There the similarity ends for, both in the style of their compositions and in the manner of their lives, there are few parallels.

Maurice Ravel was born in the Basque region of France, in a suburb of the port of St. Jean-de-Luz. His father, who was Swiss by birth, had won a prize for piano-playing in his youth but had settled on a career as a mechanical engineer. Although Ravel was always proud of his Basque origins, he spent very little of his life in the region. At just three months, his mother took him to live in Paris and that was to remain his home for the next forty-six years.

In 1889, Ravel entered the Paris Conservatoire, studying piano and, under the influential tuition of Gabriel Fauré and Emmanual Chabrier, composition. In 1895, Ravel took a two-year sabbatical from his studies but he had already developed a confident and distinctive technique of composition. His first major work was the wistful Pavane pour une infante défunte for piano (as with so many of his piano compositions, it was later orchestrated) and this was followed by the glittering Jeux d'eau of 1901.

However, there was disappointment for the young composer when he entered for the coveted Prix de Rome. He was rejected by the Conservatoire's adjudicating panel four times, in 1901-3 and 1905, despite including among his submissions the macabre and fantastic Gaspard de la nuit, now regarded as one of the undisputed masterpieces of 20th century piano music. Ravel's rejection caused a furore beyond the confines of the Conservatoire and led to the resignation of its director in disgust.

By 1914, however, Ravel's reputation was second only to Debussy. He was renowned for his piano-playing and music criticism as well as his composing and was at the heart of music-making in France, although he never accepted any official posts. At the outbreak of war, he attempted to enlist but was rejected as being underweight (he was of slight stature). Instead he became an ambulance driver, only to be discharged after eighteen months as medically unfit. During the war, he was devastated by the death of his mother.

During the 'twenties, Ravel continued to enjoy great success, not least with the infamous Boléro. In 1932 he suffered concussion in a road accident which led to the onset of Pick's disease and bouts of locomotor ataxia (a type of incoordination affecting balance, speech and gait). Sadly, he wrote nothing after the Don Quixote songs of 1934 and underwent an operation in 1937. It was unsuccessful and he died in a Paris hospital in December that year.

BELOW: 'Daphnis et Chloé', a set design by Léon Bakst (1866-1924) for Ravel's ballet which was first performed in 1912. Bakst, a Russian, worked closely with Diaghilev designing sets and costumes for the Ballets Russes in Paris.

As befitted the son of a Swiss engineer, Ravel's music was never less than exquisitely crafted. The polish, precision and ear for detail may suggest a soulless beauty but this could not be further from the truth, witness the nightmarish quality of Gaspard de la nuit, the intoxicating atmosphere of Rapsodie espagnole, the frenzy of La Valse or the simmering anger of the Piano Concerto for the Left Hand.

Ravel established his style of composition early in his career and, by-and-large, stuck by it – unlike, for example, his friend Stravinsky. It shows a great respect for classical disciplines, but little involvement with classical forms. His only 'traditional' orchestral works are the two piano concertos and he wrote, for example, no piano sonatas, despite his mastery of the instrument. The sonata, trio and quartet only occur in his chamber music which – it must be added – is remarkably fine: the beguiling String Quartet only leaves one wishing Ravel had composed more for this combination, while the Introduction and Allegro for Harp, Flute, Clarinet and String Quartet, with its lace-like textures and arcadian sonority, seduces with its charm.

Another characteristic of Ravel's music is its economy, a typically Gallic response shared by other French composers to what they perceived as Germanic excesses. At fifty-six minutes, Ravel's longest work is the ballet Daphnis et Chloé, a sumptuous and magical score written for Diaghilev's Ballets Russes. Though he may have preferred to work on a limited scale, there was nothing small about Ravel's ambition. He pursued fresh paths in piano composition, much like Chopin a century earlier. Colourful pictorial imagery figures strongly in almost all his music both for the orchestra and for the piano, music liberally spiced with unconventional and bewitching harmonies. Ravel possessed a remarkable ear for sound and his touch as an orchestrator was unmatched.

Ravel also excelled as a composer of vocal music, where his output includes two enchanting operas and several song-cycles, among them the sensuous Shéhérazade to poems by Tristram Klingsor (the Wagner-esque pseudonym of the writer Léon Leclère). The choice of subject matter reflects Ravel's fascination with the orient and the style of the composition displays a clear debt to Debussy.

Ravel's first opera, a one-act farce in the style of an Offenbach opéra-bouffe entitled L'Heure espagnole met with an indifferent reception. A second opera, L'Enfant et les sortilèges, to a libretto by the French writer, Colette, concerns itself with a naughty child who gets his come-uppance when household objects and animals begin to talk. It is a delightful fantasy, scored with chamber-like translucency and synthesizing styles as diverse as Massenet, Puccini, Monteverdi and jazz.

Yet, despite the superior qualities of so many of Ravel's compositions, it is the ballet, Boléro, which remains his best-known work. The variety he sustains from a solitary 32-bar tune over a period of seventeen minutes can only be admired. It is a pity the piece has become so hackneyed; even Ravel eventually tired of audiences' insatiable appetite for the work.   P.H.

ABOVE: *Jean-Philippe Rameau portrayed in a crayon study by I. Godefroy.*

ABOVE: *Ottorino Respighi in 1920 when he was professor at Santa Cecilia.*

BELOW: *'The Colosseum', an oil-painting by Camille Corot (1796-1875) which brings to mind Respighi's 'Pines of Rome'.*

JEAN-PHILIPPE **RAMEAU**

(b. Dijon, 25 September 1683; d. Paris, 12 September 1764)

The culmination of French baroque music, Rameau's works can in some ways be called French versions of Bach. The two men were almost contemporary, and both immensely widened the scope of the baroque style. Both were devoted to music to the extent that they were not sociable or popular characters, despite happy marriages. Both have had to wait for recognition – Bach until the 19th century, and Rameau effectively until the present day. Rameau was born in Dijon, the son of an organist. He also was an organist for most of his life, but he seems to have been more interested in written works such as his 1722 'Traité de l'harmonie' rather than in performing music. Up to 1733 he was best known for his varied harpsichord music, but at that late stage he was encouraged by a rich patron to embark on opera composition. The first, Hippolyte et Aricie (1733), was a succès de scandale, as his changes to Lully's traditional forms provoked dispute and pleasure in equal proportions. He was to write 22 more operas, including Les Indes galantes (1735) and Le Temple de la gloire (1745), up to the end of his life, when he was ironically involved in the querelle des bouffons (comedians' quarrel) when he was cast as the conservative against the new Italian style of Pergolesi. His contribution to opera was to introduce flexibility, drama and expressiveness, in anticipation of Gluck. His varied dance divertissements were another lively innovation.   P.L.

OTTORINO **RESPIGHI**

(b. Bologna, 9 July 1879; d. Rome, 18 April 1936)

A composer of strange contrasts, Respighi varies between the noisy vulgarity of Feste romane and the intimacy of the song 'Il Tramonto'; between the slick modernity of Pini di Roma and the delicacy of the Trittico Botticelliano. Much can be explained by his education. After study in Bologna, Respighi visited Russia, where as well as playing violin in orchestras he studied with Rimsky-Korsakov, and Berlin, where Bruch was his teacher. But the major influence was Richard Strauss' opera Salome. Returning to Rome in 1913 as teacher and eventually director of the Accademia di Santa Cecilia, he was torn between the colourful orchestration he had learned and his natural classicism and scholarship. Throughout his composing career these poles alter-

nately attract. His range is wide, his achievement variable: two successful operas, Belfagor (1923) and La Fiamma (1934), out of seven, some lovely songs, one or two quietly classical orchestral pieces, a great deal of fine orchestration not always well used, and perhaps loveliest of all the Lauda per la Nativita del Signore, a rapt Christmas cantata. Variable, but not negligible.   P.L.

JOAQUIN **RODRIGO**

(b. Sagunto, 22 November 1901)

It may have been the tragic accident of losing his sight at the age of three that helped to sharpen this Spanish composer's ear and turned his mind towards music. Despite this great handicap, he studied composition in Valencia and in 1927 went to Paris to learn from Dukas at the Schola Cantorum. He also received encouragement from Falla, while his marriage to a pianist in 1933 provided him with an alternative pair of eyes. The Spanish Civil War was a sad period during which he again left Spain, living first in France and then in Germany. It seems that the elegiac slow movement of his Concierto de Aranjuez for guitar and orchestra (1939) was inspired by these difficult times. Its eloquent beauty, together with the Iberian sparkle and energy of the outer movements, made this concerto for the most Spanish of instruments an instant success. In 1947 a Manuel de Falla Chair of Music was created for Rodrigo at Madrid University, and since then he has received many honours both in Spain and abroad. His music, particularly his works for guitar and orchestra, has an immediate appeal that is uncommon in 20th century music, although it is also limited in expressive range and conservative in language. Besides instrumental works, he has written a ballet and two operas and a number of songs, but as yet they are little known.   C.H.

EDMUND **RUBBRA**

(b. Northampton, 23 May 1901; d. Gerrards Cross, 13 February 1986)

When Rubbra left school at 14 and became a railway clerk, no-one could have foretold that in later life he would spend twenty years as a lecturer in music at Oxford University. He was encouraged by his working-class parents to follow his musical inclinations, and by means of single-minded dedication and various scholarships he reached the Royal College of Music, where he studied under Gustav Holst. In the mid-1930s came the first of the eleven symphonies which made his reputation as a serious, individual composer in the English tradition. His symphonic argument is unadorned by colourful decoration, and seems at first to be austere, but his admirers find an elevated spiritual tone in such works as the sixth and ninth symphonies. This is confirmed in the many choral works on religious themes written after his conversion to Catholicism in 1948. Rubbra also composed concertos and much chamber music, and even in his final work, the Sinfonietta for Strings Op. 163, he showed no decline in his ability to convey a direct, sincere message.   P.J.

ERIK **SATIE**

(b. Honfleur, 17 May 1866; d. Paris, 1 July 1925)

A born outsider, of mixed Scottish and French blood, Satie's fate was to stimulate a reaction against existing styles rather than create a style of his own. After an abortive career at the Paris Conservatoire, Satie wrote three sets of piano pieces, Sara-

bandes, Gymnopédies and Gnossiennes (1887-90), which show clearly what is to come. Designed to eliminate Wagnerian harmonic excess and emotionalism, they emerge as static, almost monotonous, but hypnotic pieces – an anticipation of today's minimalists. Next came a spell as a café pianist, during which Satie wrote some entertaining songs, and also made some useful friends including Debussy. He then resumed studies at the Schola Cantorum with d'Indy and Roussel. Their more sympathetic reception stimulated a more active composing period, especially of small piano pieces such as Sports et divertissements (1914). A meeting with Cocteau then encouraged him to large-scale works including the ballet Parade (1917), and the cantata Socrate (1918). His irreverence and facetiousness were well suited to surrealism, Dadaism, and the many other 'isms' of the time. Satie is credited with influencing Debussy, Ravel, Poulenc and others by his detached, epigrammatic, sometimes frivolous style. However, his own music, although often charming and sometimes amusing, seems to have discarded so much, that there is very little of substance left. P.L.

DOMENICO **SCARLATTI**

(b. Naples, 26 October 1685; d. Madrid, 23 July 1757)

The son of Alessandro Scarlatti (1660-1725), the distinguished opera composer, Domenico's career was to follow a very different course. Born and trained in Italy by his father, Scarlatti spent years on the usual circuit of appointments as organist or choirmaster, and eventually became master of the music at St. Peter's Rome from 1715-19. During this period he wrote the expected masses and cantatas, as well as no fewer than 14 operas and 12 concerti grossi. All this music is more than competent, but it is rarely heard today. The turning-point came in 1719, when Scarlatti was appointed as court harpsichordist and teacher to the King of Portugal. Not only did his appointment remove him from his father's influence, but it exposed him to Iberian music and also concentrated his mind on the harpsichord, on which he was a vir-

tuoso performer. His main responsibility was to teach the King's daughter, Maria Barbara, a fine player; he did this until 1728 when she married the Crown Prince of Spain. Scarlatti followed her to Madrid where he spent the remaining 28 years of his life. During this whole period he produced the great series of 550 sonatas on which his reputation now rests. Stimulated by his pupil's skill, he not only vastly developed the technique and resources of the instrument, but also in the process laid down the basics of what was to become sonata form. The sonatas' variety and expressive range are astonishing, as is the almost modern evocation of Spanish rhythms and melodic outlines. P.L.

ALFRED **SCHNITTKE**

(b. Engels, Volga, 24 November 1934)

During the 1980s the name of Schnittke rose to prominence in a remarkably short time, and recordings of his numerous compositions proliferated until he seemed to be filling the gap left in Russian music by the death of Shostakovitch a decade earlier. This was ironic, as for many years the Soviet authorities had blocked performances of Schnittke's music, which they considered as displaying the ugliest features of Western European art. The fact that he was half-German, and had studied in Vienna, only increased their suspicions of his radical tendencies. His experiments with electronics and passages of violent discord go side-by-side with parody and conventional rhetoric, so that critics as well as audiences have confused reactions. Even sympathetic reviewers of the spate of recent Schnittke CDs have found him 'insufficiently self-critical' and 'relying on effects more than argument', while still describing him as 'marvellously inventive'. After serious health problems in the 1980s, Schnittke moved to Cologne where his prodigious output continued, and was regularly championed by the leading Russian musicians of our time. Among his many orchestral, choral and chamber works, special praise has been lavished on his Fifth Symphony, his two concertos for cello, and his Viola Concerto. P.J.

NIKOLAY ANDREYEVICH
Rimsky-Korsakov

(b. Tikhvin, 18 March 1844; d. Lyubensk, 21 June 1908)

Chronology

1844 Born Tikhvin, 18 March
1850 Piano lessons with local
teachers
1855 'Overture' for solo piano
1856 Enters Naval College at St.
Petersburg; continues piano
lessons
1859 Piano lessons with
Théodore Canille; begins
acquaintance with
symphonic repertoire
1861 Canille introduces him to
Balakirev, Cui and
Mussorgsky
1862 Graduates from college;
leaves Russia as
midshipman for lengthy tour
to US, South America,
Europe including London
1865 Returns to Russia and
completes First Symphony
(October), première in
December under Balakirev
1868 Second Symphony (Antar)
– later twice revised

ABOVE: 'Eunuch', a
costume design by Léon
Bakst (1866-1924) for the
Ballets Russes production
of Sheherazade at the
Paris Opéra in 1910.

As a member of a distinguished family, whose father had governed a province, Rimsky-Korsakov was born with advantages, and he wrote in his autobiography, 'Chronicle of my Musical Life', that musical ability came to him very early: 'Before I was two I could distinguish all the melodies my mother sang to me, and at three or four I was expert at beating time on a drum to my father's piano playing'. He started learning the piano at the age of six and soon showed an interest in the sheet music in his home, including Glinka's opera A Life for the Tsar, while his earliest composition was an 'overture' for piano written when he was eleven. However, there was a naval tradition in his family, and as music was not yet considered as a career, even by himself, in 1856 he followed his elder brother's example and entered a school for naval cadets in St. Petersburg where his brother, a full twenty-two years his senior, was to become headmaster shortly before Rimsky graduated in April 1862.

His student years still left time for music, however, including taking more piano lessons, seeing various operas and attending orchestral concerts that included Beethoven symphonies and the music of his compatriot Glinka, music that fascinated him by its Russianness and brilliant orchestral colour. In his last year at the Naval School, when he was seventeen, his piano teacher introduced him to three young Russian composers who had already made their names, Balakirev, Cui and Mussorgsky. Balakirev had a strong sense of his vocation as a prophet of Russian music, and on being shown Rimsky's first attempt at a symphony he insisted that the young naval student should finish the work. By 1862, two and a half movements had been written under Balakirev's guidance.

The pull of music was now so strong that Rimsky wished to abandon his service career, but his family refused him permission to do so, and instead he served at sea as a midshipman for over two years, travelling to cities including New York, Rio de Janeiro and London – where he attended operatic performances at Covent Garden and completed the slow movement of his symphony. Returning to Russia as (in his own words) 'an officer-dilettante who sometimes enjoyed playing or listening to music', he renewed his friendship with Balakirev and finally completed his symphony in October 1865, whereupon Balakirev conducted it at a concert on New Year's Eve. For the rest of the decade, he managed to combine continuing naval duties ashore with an existence as a musician producing several new compositions including his programmatic Second Symphony, subtitled Antar. In July 1871, although still a naval lieutenant without formal training in composition, he accepted a post at the St. Petersburg Conservatory, teaching himself in secret to stay ahead of his students.

Rimsky finally resigned his naval commission in May 1873, when a government navy minister who was a friend created for him a well-paid post of Inspector of Naval Bands that he held from 1873-84. Shortly before this, in July 1872, he married Nadezhda Purgold, who was a fine pianist as well as a beauty. She supported her husband thenceforth in his career. Thereafter, he advanced in skill and renown, producing compositions in several genres but principally operas and symphonic music. He also selflessly devoted skill and energy to the music of his Russian friends, notably Mussorgsky, who died in 1881 leaving his music in some disorder. Rimsky prepared it for performance and publication. He also helped, after Borodin's death in 1887, to finish the orchestration of his opera Prince Igor. At times he suffered from something of a creative block as regards his own music, but he recovered and such fine works as the symphonic suite Sheherazade and the opera The Golden Cockerel belong to the latter part of his life. As a teacher, he had pupils who were to achieve much, including Glazunov and Stravinsky, who held him in much affection. His death in June 1908 was from angina pectoris.

RIGHT: 'The Tsar's Palace', a curtain design by
Natalija Gontcharova (1881-1962) for a 1914
Moscow production of The Golden Cockerel.
Rimsky's last opera makes spectacular demands
upon the stage designer.

Rimsky was one of the group of composers called The Five, who followed the lead of Glinka and helped to create a truly Russian voice in music: the others were Balakirev, Borodin, Cui and Mussorgsky. Drawing on the deep resources of folk music, and also the liturgical music of the Orthodox church (Rimsky often said how he loved church music), they forged an idiom which often set aside the classical procedures of the German-Austrian composers from Haydn to Beethoven in favour of other values. Thus Mussorgsky's extraordinary directness shocked many musicians of the time, and even Rimsky himself toned it down when preparing *Boris Godunov* for publication, although today we prefer the composer's original ideas. Rimsky himself was a master of glittering orchestration of a kind that is generally foreign and uncongenial to German traditions (although he was fascinated by Wagner's instrumentation when the *Ring* cycle reached St. Petersburg in 1889), and did not reach France until her composers learned from him. Later, though, Ravel recommended his pupils to take him as a model. This

wonderfully colourful instrumentation is a major feature of such works as his *Spanish Capriccio*, *Sheherazade* and the opera *The Golden Cockerel*, and as far as his teaching and influence are concerned, they are abundantly evident when we listen to Stravinsky's ballet *The Firebird*. Indeed, Rimsky became something of a father figure and mentor to Stravinsky, whose own father had died in 1902. Generations of students, and not only in Russia, similarly have learned from his book, 'Principles of Orchestration'.

It is also worth remembering that Rimsky was no narrow nationalist, as we can see from the Spanish and 'Arabian Nights' settings of the *Spanish Capriccio* and *Sheherazade*. His opera *Sadko* is set in 'Novgorod, and the bottom of the sea' and includes a 'Viking Song' and an 'Indian Song'. The latter is hauntingly melodious in an exotic way and has been sung and played in countless instrumental arrangements, as has the even better known 'Flight of the Bumble Bee', a brilliant orchestral interlude that derives from his opera of 1900 *The Tale of Tsar Saltan*.   C.H.

GIOACCHINO ANTONIO
Rossini (b. Pesaro, 29 February 1792; d. Paris, 13 November 1868)

RIGHT: *A portrait of the young Rossini painted by Vincenzo Camuccini in 1820 when Rossini was enjoying considerable success following* The Barber of Seville *and* La Cenerentola.

Chronology

1792 *Born in Pesaro*

1804 *Writes the six Sonate a quattro*

1806 *Enters the Liceo Musicale in Milan*

1808 *Writes his first opera* Demetrio e Polibio

1810 *Commissioned to write* La Cambiale di matrimonio *for the Teatro San Moise in Venice*

1812 *Bolsters his growing reputation with* L'Inganno felice *(Venice);* Ciro in Babilonia *(Ferrara);* La Scala di seta *(Venice); and* La Pietra del paragone *(Milan)*

1813 Il Signor Bruschino; Tancredi *and* L'Italiana in Algeri, *all first performed in Venice*

1816 Il Barbiere di Siviglia *first performed in Rome, and* Otello *in Naples*

1817 La Cenerentola *first performed in Rome;* La Gazza ladra *first given at La Scala, Milan*

1822 *Marries Isabella Colbran. Visits Vienna where he meets Beethoven and is distantly admired by Schubert*

1823 Semiramide *first performed in Venice. Visits London; received by King George IV; conducts his works at the Haymarket Theatre and elsewhere*

RIGHT: *'Under the Orange Trees', a painting by Joaquin Sorolla y Bastida (1863-1923) done in 1903. It is a fitting evocation of the gaiety of Rossini's Seville.*

*R*ossini had humble origins; his father was an inspector of slaughter-houses and held the official position (though nobody seems to be quite sure of the duties involved) of Town Trumpeter of Pesaro and he also played in local theatre orchestras; his mother was the daughter of a baker. His childhood was an unsettled one. His father, owing to his political opinions, was sent to prison for a while, so his mother, who had a good singing voice, was forced to augment the family income by occasionally singing in various opera houses. While his parents were thus occupied, Rossini was boarded out with a pork butcher in Bologna. Later, when the family moved to Lugo, his father, restored to freedom, found time to teach him the elements of french horn playing and he studied singing with a local priest.

The next move was to Bologna where he studied singing, harpsichord and composition with Padre Tesei and taught himself the violin and viola. Before he was fourteen, he had been apprentice to a smith, worked as theatre singer, horn-player, accompanist and chorus-master. In 1806 he was accepted as a student at the Liceo Musicale in Bologna where he studied singing, solfeggio (forms of vocal exercise), counterpoint, cello and piano. On the whole he had a pretty thorough and practical grounding in music. He had long aspired to be a composer, and in 1804 had written some splendidly tuneful and assured sonatas for string quartet while on holiday with a musical friend.

His contacts with the opera world inspired him to develop mainly in that direction and even his occasional works for orchestra and instrumental ensembles have an undeniable operatic nature. In 1808 he wrote a cantata which was performed at the Liceo Musicale and, at the same time, composed his first opera, Demetrio e Polibio. His first operatic commission came in 1810 when he produced La Cambiale di matrimonio, an assured work with a remarkably fine overture (always a Rossini speciality, many of them surviving their attached operas). Others followed in the next two years including the sparkling one-acter, again with a superb overture, La Scala di seta. In 1812 came the supreme accolade of a commission from La Scala, Milan, a resounding success called La Pietra del paragone; followed by three successful works written for Venice, the last of which, L'Italiana in Algeri, has remained a performing favourite. He was now

approached by the impresario Barbaja and asked to provide two operas a year for Naples. It was through these productions that he met the singer Isabella Colbran, formerly Barbaja's mistress, who lived with him for several years before they married in 1822. Rossini felt he had a special flair for opera buffa, an opinion fortified by Beethoven when they later met, and he now wrote Il Barbiere di Siviglia. It was a bold decision as an opera of the same name by Paisiello was already an established favourite and Rossini was seen as a usurper. But, after a shaky reception following its first performance in 1816, its superior qualities soon established it as Rossini's finest operatic endeavour.

Rossini, in spite of lazy habits that led him to many last minute crises, was a prolific creator and operas came in rapid succession until 1829 when, after the production of his expansive Guillaume Tell at the Paris Opéra, he suddenly decided to write no more operas. Various reasons have been given – a disenchantment with the opera world in general included – but it seems that he simply wanted to enjoy a full retirement, being a dedicated gourmet and having made his fortune. The last years were spent in Paris, writing countless songs, piano and instrumental pieces which he referred to as 'The Sins of Old Age' and one characterful choral masterpiece, Petite Messe Solennelle. Having been born in a Leap Year on 29 February, a joke which he always enjoyed, he died, a superstitious man, on Friday the 13th.

ABOVE: Here, by contrast, we see Rossini in comfortable old age; this portrait was taken in 1860 while he was living in retirement in Paris. He called his works from this period 'The Sins of Old Age'.

Rossini's essentially operatic genius was typified by the classic comedy Il Barbiere di Siviglia (The Barber of Seville) which has never lost its magic and appeal. Typical of Rossini's approach, it sports an overture originally written for a far more serious work, yet which now sounds entirely suited to The Barber and is a minor masterpiece in its own right. The opera itself boasts frequently sung arias like the barber's 'Largo al factotum' and Rosina's scintillating cavatina 'Una voce poco fa'. In like vein La Cenerentola (Cinderella) has also remained popular. A number of Rossini's overtures, with their cumulative crescendos as trademark, crop up in numerous concerts and recordings, while the operas are sometimes barely known at all. Others enjoy sporadic revival, with William Tell a cumbersome vehicle to stage but full of enjoyable music. The operatic vein is evident not only in worthy choral works like the Stabat Mater (1831-41), the unduly neglected Missa di Gloria (1820) and the charming Petite Messe Solennelle (1863), but also the String Sonatas, and some virtuosic compositions for orchestra with clarinet and other solo instruments. Similar characteristics can be found latterly in the diverse items discovered in several volumes of 'Sins', many of them woven into modern ballet scores like La Boutique fantasque, which was orchestrated by Respighi. Rossini's sure touch in orchestration, his love of strong melody and bold strokes, makes his music stand out in the Italian opera field as the strongest and liveliest of its kind, and certainly the wittiest.   P.G.

1824 Settles in Paris
1825 Composes Il Viaggio a Reims for the coronation of Charles X; first performed at the Théâtre-Italien, Paris
1826 Le Siège de Corinthe first performed at the Paris Opéra
1828 Le Comte Ory utilising music from Il Viaggio a Reims first performed at Paris Opéra
1829 Guillaume Tell first performed at Paris Opéra. Decides to stop writing opera
1832 Meets Olympe Pélissier who becomes his mistress (legally separated from Colbran in 1837 who dies in 1845)
1836 Returns to Bologna to become consultant to the Liceo Musicale
1846 Marries Pélissier
1848 Moves to Florence
1855 Returns to Paris where he spends the rest of his life
1867 Writes Petite Messe Solennelle
1868 Celebrates his '19th' birthday and dies in November
1887 His remains taken to the church of Santa Croce in Florence to be buried

CAMILLE
Saint-Saëns
(b. Paris, 9 October 1835; d. Algiers, 16 December 1921)

*I*nternationally famous as a virtuoso pianist, organist and conductor, Camille Saint-Saëns claimed that he lived in music 'like a fish in water'. He composed over 300 works, including 13 operas, and he was the first major composer to write music specifically for the cinema. He was also a prolific writer and championed earlier French composers, such as Rameau, as well as the Romantics – Liszt, Berlioz and Schumann. Wagner was another of his heroes, but in later life he attacked him for his 'Teutonizing influence on French music'.

Like so many composers, Saint-Saëns displayed Mozartian talents. Blessed with perfect pitch, a prodigious memory and tireless energy, he began composing when he was barely three, and at ten he was dazzling Paris audiences with brilliant recitals of Bach, Mozart and Beethoven. At 13 he became an organ student at the Paris Conservatoire. Though he failed to win the coveted Prix de Rome, in 1852 his Ode à Sainte Cécile made his name as a young composer. His First Symphony came a year later (an earlier work, the Symphony in A of 1850, is not numbered, and was not published until 1974). His music won the admiration of Berlioz, Rossini, Bizet, Liszt and Fauré, all of whom subsequently became his friends.

As a supreme virtuoso, Saint-Saëns was feted all over the music-loving world, travelling ceaselessly throughout Europe, Russia and the USA, accompanied only by his servant Gabriel and his pet dogs. With his beaked nose, neat beard, bowler hat and frock coat, he was a familiar and much admired figure in England, where the oratorios and cantatas he composed for music festivals were always well received, especially when he was able to conduct them himself.

His private life was less happy. The marriage to 19-year old Marie-Laure Truffot was a failure, and their two sons died in infancy. He contemplated suicide when his mother died in 1888, and became a solitary wanderer, spending his days in lonely flats and hotel rooms. In later life he frequently visited Algeria in search of sunshine, rest and the company of boys.

Wherever he went he was honoured as the grand old man of French music, but in France itself his reputation started to fade. Younger composers condemned his facile 'wedding cake' music, while he was appalled by Debussy and by modern works such as Stravinsky's Rite of Spring. But, oddly, it was Saint-Saëns who made possible the first production in France of Mussorgsky's Boris Godunov – music as far removed from his own as could be imagined.

RIGHT: *Saint-Saëns portrayed around 1895. He was a well respected figure and had received an Honorary Doctorate at Cambridge in 1893.*

BELOW: *'Young Girls at the Piano' painted by Auguste Renoir (1841-1919) in 1892. They might be trying out some of Saint-Saëns' extensive piano repertoire.*

RIGHT: *Something of the vitality and quirkish spirit of Le Carnaval des animaux is to be found in this 1910 painting, 'Tropical Jungle with Apes', by French artist Henri Rousseau (1844-1910).*

Camille Saint-Saëns wrote his first symphony at the age of sixteen and remained an active composer throughout his long life. However, it was at the organ that he first established his reputation, and he held the key post of organist at La Madeleine for twenty years. He was also an accomplished pianist: his mastery may be judged from his own writing for the instrument – notably the five piano concertos, each of which he premièred in turn. His playing reflected many of his characteristics as a composer: these include a technical ease, a clarity, a fluency in performance, an elegance, a brilliance and – it has to be said – a lack of emotional depth, which has given rise to charges of superficiality. In his own words, he pursued 'the chimera of purity of style and perfection of form', while Berlioz said of him, 'He knows everything, but lacks inexperience'.

In writing three violin concertos and the well-known Introduction and Rondo Capriccioso Saint-Saëns sought the advice of his friend, the Spanish violinist Pablo de Sarasate. In 1871 he founded with Bizet and Lalo a society to promote French orchestral music, and composed four symphonic poems, including *Le Rouet d'Omphale*, to further the cause. Within a few years Saint-Saëns triumphed in every musical field except the theatre. Success here eluded him until the 1890 Paris production of his opera *Samson et Dalila*, first performed in Weimar thirteen years earlier, which captivated audiences with its lush melodies and orientalism. This remains, together with the Third (*Organ*) Symphony, the Second and Fourth Piano Concertos, the irresistible *Le Carnaval des animaux* (publication of which, with the exception of 'Le Cygne', he barred during his lifetime) and lesser pieces such as *Danse macabre*, among the most popular of his works. Much less well-known, but equally rewarding, is his chamber and instrumental music which includes a set of variations for two pianos on a theme of Beethoven, a considerable quantity of music for solo violin, and a septet for trumpet, piano and strings.

When you consider the critical attention accorded to his music over the years, there seems to be a problem of where to place Saint-Saëns. According to one unkind reviewer, 'he seems to have said to the great composers "you have the best tunes; I want them."' But this does less than justice to a composer whose work is full of invention, gaiety, charm and Gallic wit – qualities which do not necessarily endear him to the more sober-minded critics.   R.H.

Chronology

ARNOLD
Schoenberg (b. Vienna, 13 September 1874; d. Los Angeles, 13 July 1951)

Schoenberg was born of Viennese Jewish parents, the son of a shopkeeper. He learned the violin, but was self-taught as a composer until he received lessons from Alexander Zemlinsky (1871-1942) in his teens. Left with few resources by his father, and already married to Zemlinsky's sister, he had to earn his living as a scoring hack, and in 1901 as music director of a cabaret, though by then he had written or was writing two major works in traditional post-Wagnerian style, the string sextet Verklärte Nacht and the cantata Gurrelieder. On the basis of these, and Richard Strauss's recommendation, he obtained a teaching post in Berlin at the Stern Akademie until 1903 when he returned to Vienna. Here he taught privately (Berg and Webern among others), and with Zemlinsky (and under Mahler's presidency) founded the Society of Creative Musicians to promote new music.

His own music was becoming more and more extreme in its chromaticism, and already attracting hostility. His first Chamber Symphony and two string quartets undermined traditional key structures, and in 1909 with the 3 Piano Pieces Op.11 he embraced atonality. There followed the song cycle The Book of the Hanging Gardens, the 5 Orchestral Pieces Op.16 and the so-called 'monodrama' Erwartung. At the same time he was developing a career as an expressionist painter, and in 1911 he published a textbook 'Harmonielehre', confirming that for him music, life and art were indivisible. Even more controversy was caused by Pierrot lunaire, a song cycle for voice and chamber ensemble, for which he developed a type of vocal delivery called Sprechstimme (speech-song), which occupied a middle ground between song and declamation.

During the First World War, Schoenberg alternated spells in the Army with starting what was to be an unfinished oratorio, Die Jakobsleiter, and with more theoretical works which produced his 'twelve note' system. This aimed to replace diatonic keys with a 'row' of all twelve semitones as the basis of 'serial' musical development. In retrospect this can be seen as the final takeover of theory from emotion in composition, though Schoenberg himself more or less combined the two. The first piece in this style, the 5 Piano Pieces Op.23, the Serenade Op.24 and the Piano Suite Op.25 appeared in 1923. In the same year Schoenberg's wife died and he remarried. From 1925 to 1933 he taught at the Berlin Academy, and while there he produced the Orchestral Variations, a comic opera Von Heute auf Morgen (1930) and a third string quartet, and began Moses und Aron.

With the advent of the Nazis in 1933, Schoenberg re-embraced Judaism, which he had abandoned in 1898, and took refuge in the USA, where he was a professor at the University of Los Angeles from 1936 to 1944, and took American nationality in 1941. By now, he was able to write in any or all of his styles, producing a second Chamber Symphony, a violin concerto, a piano concerto and a fourth string quartet among other works. As a teacher, he was demanding, but not doctrinaire, insisting that his pupils should get a good musical grounding rather than that they follow his theories. He was forced by financial circumstances to continue teaching privately and lecturing until his death.

Musicians would probably agree that Schoenberg was the most influential composer, if not the greatest, of the 20th century. But would listeners? It is now 85 years since the beginning of Schoenberg's experiments with atonality (the destruction of harmony based on keys), and there is no sign yet of this style becoming generally accepted by the public, let alone popular. His influence is undoubted, but many outside the musical profession, and some within it, would question whether that influence has been a fruitful one. Many 20th century composers, including Stravinsky and Britten for example, flirted with some of Schoenberg's theories, but were always careful to keep their feet on tonal ground. Those who sold their souls to serialism had to be content with being admired by their colleagues, but decried by the general public.

Schoenberg's music is too easily approached on the basis of compositions before and after 'the fall' i.e. the advent of atonality. This is simplistic. Certainly the early music (up to 1909) is all approachable, if over-indulgent, romantic music, taking Wagner's harmony further even than Mahler or Richard Strauss or Scriabin. *Verklärte Nacht* is a good example, portraying a night of love in suitably rich textures. *Gurrelieder* and *Pelleas und Melisande* are similarly romantic, with a tendency to going somewhat 'over the top'.

After this the music changes quickly, even bewilderingly, and it is a matter of personal taste as to how far you consider the intellectual theories and organization obscure the real musical impulse beneath. The 5 Orchestral Pieces Op.16, for instance, repay close attention, but the Piano Pieces Op.11

Chronology

1874 *Born in Vienna*
1890-5 *Works in bank*
1895 *Lessons from Zemlinsky*
1898 *Verklärte Nacht; converts
to Christianity*
1901 *Marries Mathilde
Zemlinsky. Director of
Berlin cabaret 1901-3;
teaches in Stern Akademie
Berlin*
1903 *Gurrelieder; Pelleas und
Melisande*
1905 *Returns to Vienna. String
Quartet No. 1*
1906 *Chamber Symphony No. 1*
1908 *String Quartet No. 2*
1909 *Develops theory of
atonality: 3 Piano Pieces
Op. 11; The Book of the
Hanging Gardens; 5
Orchestral Pieces Op. 16;
Erwartung completed (first
performed in 1924 in
Prague)*
1910 *First painting exhibition*
1911 *'Harmonielehre'*
1912 *Pierrot lunaire; belated
success of Gurrelieder*
1917 *Starts Die Jakobsleiter*
1923 *'12-note' system: Piano
Pieces Op. 23; Serenade
Op. 24; Piano Suite
Op. 25. Death of wife*
1924 *Marries Gertrud Kolisch*
1926 *Succeeds Busoni at Berlin
Akademie*
1927 *String Quartet No. 3*
1928 *Starts Moses und Aron
(first performed in 1957 in
Zürich)*
1930 *Von Heute auf Morgen
first performed in Frankfurt*
1933 *Leaves Germany; re-
embraces Judaism*
1936 *Appointed professor at Los
Angeles University. Violin
Concerto; String Quartet
No 4*
1939 *Chamber Symphony No. 2*
1941 *Takes US nationality*
1942 *Piano Concerto*
1944 *Retires on small pension*
1951 *Dies in Los Angeles*

or Op.23 seem arid and unmelodic, even after repeated listening. As with many pioneers, Schoenberg's later music is often more accessible, as if he no longer feels the need to prove his theories. *Moses und Aron* and the late concertos often seem not far from later Stravinsky. There is no question that Schoenberg was a talented composer, but his chosen route was perhaps not calculated to do himself – or music generally – the greatest justice. P.L.

FRANZ
Schubert

(b. Vienna, 31 January 1797; d. Vienna, 19 November 1828)

The names and careers of many great composers were linked with the city of Vienna – Beethoven, Brahms, Bruckner, Gluck, Haydn, Mahler, Mozart, Schubert, to mention but a choice few – but of these only Schubert was born and bred a Viennese citizen. He was born in the Himmelpfortgrund in a house now known as 54 Nussdorferstrasse, kept today as a Schubert museum. It was made up of a number of small apartments, the Schuberts renting two of these, with his father's schoolrooms on the ground floor. Here Franz Schubert senior, a schoolmaster from Moravia, survived just above the poverty line, and produced a large family, of which few survived into adulthood.

By the time in 1801 that Franz Schubert junior was old enough to go to his father's school, it had moved to better premises and, in 1803, he became a full-time pupil, mainly taught by his elder brother Ignaz. He showed early signs of his musical genius, soon outstripped what musical help the local choirmaster could give him, and, in 1808, was taken along to a city school which trained choristers for the Chapel of the Imperial Court. He impressed the examiners, who included Salieri, sufficiently to be admitted. A bleak five years followed, Schubert being subjected to the usual prison-like routine that seems de rigueur in choir schools, but at the same time he was learning a good deal of his craft from playing Haydn and Mozart in the school orchestra and making his first acquaintance with the works of Beethoven.

In 1812 his voice broke, but he was allowed another year at the school providing he attended to his general academic studies. Meanwhile he became a pupil of Salieri, a fact he always proudly proclaimed in later life, while Salieri was equally pleased to report that his star pupil knew 'all that there was to know about music'. It was during this period that Schubert wrote his first mature songs and his first symphony, which was played by the school orchestra when he finally left. At this stage, the young composer had plenty of encouragement and looked set for a highly successful career. His father, though, was still slightly uneasy about his musical prospects, and persuaded Schubert to join his teaching staff.

Reluctantly Schubert remained a teacher for three years, loathing it intensely. He did manage, during that time, to get to his fourth symphony, and to write numerous songs, several quartets, masses, and five operas. It was strange, in regard to this last activity, that Schubert, a natural writer for the voice, never had any substantial success with his operas.

In 1816, weary of teaching, he decided to take his chance in the

musical world. He applied for another music-teaching job but failed to get it. At least he managed to get paid, for the first time, for a cantata that he had written, proudly noting the 100 florins received in his diary. He made an influential friend in Franz von Schober, one of the first of many to give him free lodging, and met the well-known singer Michael Vogl, who was to help to spread his name around. Through an acquaintance with the poet Johann Mayrhofer he also began to collect a number of literary friends, a circle in which he seemed much happier than in musical surroundings. By 1817 he had written such potential hits as 'Die Forelle' and 'An die Musik'. Increasingly influenced by Beethoven, his fourth symphony, regarded as being quite daring for its time, was given an amateur performance, and an Overture in the Italian Style, influenced by Rossini's visit to Vienna, became his first music to be given a professional performance in 1818. He was paid to write a one-act opera Die Zwillingsbrüder, not performed until 1820, and wrote music for Die Zauberharfe, the overture of which he later used for Rosamunde. During the next two years he supplemented his income by teaching the daughters of Count Esterházy, made his first journey outside Vienna, and wrote his inspired Piano Quintet, with variations based on 'The Trout'.

By 1821 he was hovering on the brink of becoming a successful composer, but his work was still considered too modern. At last a break-through came when his first songs, 'Erlkönig' and 'Gretchen am Spinnrade', were published by Diabelli, in response to a public demand for them. The following year, after a customary bout of drinking, he was led astray by some inebriated friends and visited a brothel. He contracted syphilis here and by 1823 his health was seriously undermined. From this time on his life seemed to go downhill. He still achieved virtually no success with his operas and he was constantly hard-up. Occasional rays of hope did light the horizon. His score for the play Rosamunde, only staged for two nights, was greatly praised and the music became widely popular. It was printed in 1824, along with the song-cycle Die schöne Müllerin. Throughout his life Schubert was a devout admirer of Beethoven, yet, living within walking distance of the great man, he could never pluck up the courage to make his acquaintance.

In spite of continual help from friends, Schubert dogged by ill-health, a liking for alcohol, and a strange inability to promote himself with people of influence, could never really get his act together. He never achieved a lucrative or important musical post or joined the musical establishment, as lesser composers like Hummel and Salieri did. His music was still considered too difficult and his 'Great' C major Symphony was turned down on these grounds.

His final year, 1828, followed the same pattern of hope and despair that had marked the last five or so. He produced the wonderful songs that were eventually published as Schwanengesang and such light-hearted items as 'Der Hirt auf dem Felsen'. In March the first public all-Schubert concert was given at the Musikverein. It gained little press attention because Paganini was the focus of attention that week. By October he was seriously ill and he eventually died of a fever at three o'clock on Wednesday, 19 November. He left behind only a few clothes, a few pieces of music and some manuscripts which his brother Ferdinand kept. He was buried next to Beethoven at whose funeral he had been a pallbearer in 1827. On his gravestone the poet Franz Grillparzer's epitaph reads 'The art of music here entombed a rich possession but even fairer hopes'.

ABOVE: 'Schubert at the Piano', an imaginative portrayal of the composer painted in 1899 by the Austrian Gustav Klimt (1862-1918). This painting was destroyed during the Second World War.

Chronology

1797 Born in a suburb of Vienna

1804 First regular music lessons

1808 Becomes a member of the Vienna Imperial Court Choir and a student at the Stadtkonvict where he studies composition, singing and organ

1809 Becomes first violinist in the school band

1811 Writes his first song 'Hagars Klage'

1812 His mother dies

1813 Leaves the Stadtkonvict but continues to study with Salieri. Writes his First Symphony and has it performed at the school. Begins an opera Des Teufels Lustschloss (completed 1814)

1814 Begins to write some of his finest songs, such as 'Gretchen am Spinnrade'. Becomes an assistant teacher at his father's school

BELOW: 'Schubert with his Friends' (Johann Baptist Jenger, left, and Anselm Hüttenbrenner) – a crayon drawing of 1827 by Josef Eduard Teltscher (1801-37). Jenger and Hüttenbrenner were both accomplished musicians.

BELOW: 'Oak Tree in the Snow', a painting of 1827 by Caspar David Friedrich (1774-1840) which captures something of the bleak atmosphere of Schubert's song-cycle, Winterreise.

During Schubert's lifetime, none of his symphonies was published, only one of his 19 quartets, only one of seven masses, none of his operas, and only 187 songs out of a total of 600 written. A few more items had been published by 1830 but he was still a composer mainly unknown to the world outside Vienna. A compilation of musical favourites published in London in 1837 had plenty of Hummel, Kalkbrenner, Kuhlau and Moscheles in it, but no Schubert. The 'Great' C major Symphony was performed under Mendelssohn in 1839; but was not until the 1850s that any true appreciation of his genius began to grow. The first book about him appeared in 1865, the year that the *Unfinished* Symphony was first performed. When the English critic and musicologist, George Grove heard the C major Symphony performed in London in 1856 he had believed it to be Schubert's only symphony. Following the publication of Kreissle's biography in 1865 he visited Vienna, with Arthur Sullivan as companion, to discover the rest and the complete score of *Rosamunde* still lying in the cupboard where it had been placed after its two performances. In 1879 Grove first published his

famous 'Dictionary of Music' and it was his splendid article on Schubert that led to the world's true appreciation of the composer's genius being established. His so-called 'complete' works were in print by 1897, but even as late as the 1950's his Ninth Symphony was still mistakenly printed and performed as the Seventh.

The world now acknowledges Schubert as probably its greatest songwriter and here lies the chief glory of his output, notably in the three song-cycles, *Die schöne Müllerin*, *Winterreise* and *Schwanengesang*, and also in many individual items that seem the quintessence of the Viennese spirit in song, and among the finest unions of words and music. It is strange that, in spite of his genius for songwriting, he had so little success with opera. It is true that he never came across the magic libretto that so often inspires a composer, yet despite this, his operatic music is full of delights and still awaits full discovery.

The rest of his compositions veer bewilderingly between the imperfect and perfection. Within his works we can sense an uncertainty at times, a lack of the formal discipline and overall vision that marks the greatness of Beethoven (a comparison of the symphonies of Beethoven and Schubert illustrates the truth of this) but suddenly we are confronted with music of inspired genius that has never been surpassed. This we find particularly in his chamber music, where he was clearly more at home, notably in the String Quintet in C, in the two fine Piano Trios, in several of the Quartets, and, of course, in the spontaneity of the *Trout* Quintet. His piano music is often uneven; the sonatas, now admired and played by many leading pianists, can seem rambling; and there are no concertos. Yet the Impromptus are magical and the riches to be found in the masses of waltzes and dances he wrote are quite staggering.   P.G.

1815 Writes around 140 songs including 'Erlkönig', 'Die Nonne' and 'Heidenröslein'

1816 Writes the Fourth and Fifth Symphonies. Leaves school and goes to live with his poet friend Franz von Schober

1817 Composes two overtures 'in the Italian style' inspired by Rossini

1818 Works as tutor to the Esterházy family. His first orchestral work to be publicly performed – an Overture in C. Singer J.M. Vogl gets him an operatic commission – Die Zwillingsbrüder

1819 Opera finished. Visits Upper Austria with Vogl and writes the Trout Quintet

1820 Die Zwillingsbrüder performed at the Kärntnertortheater, Vienna and incidental music for Die Zauberharfe used at the Theater an der Wien

1821 'Erlkönig' sung in public for the first time by Vogl. Completes two acts of Alfonso und Estrella

1822 Calls on Beethoven, meets Weber, and some songs published. The Unfinished Symphony presented to the Musikverein of Graz

1823 Rosamunde produced at the Theater an der Wien. Completes the song-cycle Die schöne Müllerin; the opera Fierabras completed

1824 Spends another summer as tutor to the Esterházy family and falls for the daughter Caroline

1825 Sends Goethe three settings of his poems but gets no reply

1826 Applies for post as vice music director to the court but turned down. Sets Shakespeare's 'Hark, hark the lark' and 'Who is Sylvia'

1827 Writes song-cycle Winterreise, two piano trios and Impromptus, Op.142

1828 Increasingly ill; unsuccessful negotiations with publishers; writes String Quintet; writes songs later included in Schwanengesang. Dies at the age of 31

ROBERT
Schumann (b. Zwickau, 8 June 1810; d. Endenich, 29 July 1856)

RIGHT: *A portrait of Robert Schumann, a sketch drawn in 1853 by J. B. Laurens. By this time, Schumann's health was failing; he only had three years to live.*

Robert Schumann was the youngest son of August Schumann, a prolific author and translator of Romantic literature, and a 'notable citizen and bookseller' of the town of Zwickau, in Saxony. Successful as he was, he suffered from attacks of severe nervous anxiety. Robert's mother, who gave him his first music lessons, lived in 'an exaggerated state of romance and sentimentalism', and was herself subject to sudden, violent passions. When Robert was only 16 years old, his sister committed suicide and, not long after, his father died suddenly. With so unstable a family background, small wonder that all his life he was haunted by fears of madness and suicide.

Although Schumann's father had encouraged his musical aspirations, his mother sent him to study law at Leipzig. But when it became clear that he had no aptitude for law and was happy only when making music, she agreed to let him train as a concert pianist. In 1828 he became a pupil of Friedrich Wieck in Leipzig, and found himself a fellow-pupil of Wieck's nine-year-old daughter Clara, who was already a pianist of outstanding ability.

A permanent injury to Schumann's right hand (whether the re-sult of wearing a wooden splint to improve his fingering technique or the outcome of treatment for syphilis is disputed to this day) put paid to any performing ambitions, but Schumann had already dedicated himself to composition. With Carnaval he revealed himself as one of the greatest of all composers for the pianoforte. By this time, he and Clara were in love. But her father bitterly opposed the match, and it was not until permission had been obtained from a court of law that they were finally able to marry in 1840.

Most of his life Schumann was also an influential music journalist. As the editor of the 'Neue Zeitschrift für Musik' he championed the Romantic composers. He was among the first to recognize the genius of Chopin and of Brahms, and he unearthed the manuscript of Schubert's 'Great' C major Symphony. He also taught composition at the Leipzig Conservatoire; travelled with Clara on her concert tours; supported a family of seven children, and attempted unsuccessfully to conduct the Düsseldorf choir and orchestra. By 1854 his mental health finally broke down, and he tried to drown himself in the Rhine. His last two years were spent in a private asylum at Endenich.

BELOW: *Clara Schumann (née Clara Wieck) also portrayed in 1853 by J. B. Laurens. She was a fine pianist who did much to promote Schumann's music.*

The earlier part of Schumann's composing career, and in many ways the most successful, divides into chronological blocks like a timetable. First there is the decade of the 1830s, during which he wrote keyboard music (Op.1 to Op.23). In 1840, the year of his marriage to the celebrated concert pianist Clara Wieck, he composed no fewer than 183 songs. The following year he concentrated on symphonic works, completing his First Symphony and the first movement of what, ten years later, was to become his Fourth Symphony. In 1842 he turned his attention to chamber music, and in 1843 choral music became his main concern. Thereafter the pattern becomes less clear, but the compulsion to compose larger-scale works – the result, some say, of urging by his wife – remained with him for the rest of his life.

When Schumann was rebuked for not following orthodox form, he replied, 'As if each idea did not come into existence

ABOVE: *Robert Schumann as a young boy, a miniature painted by an anonymous artist. Even in his youth, Schumann displayed a colourful temperament and leanings to Romanticism.*

with its form ready made! As if each work of art had not its own meaning and consequently its own form!' These were revolutionary ideas at a time when even Schubert, whose works Schumann much admired, was virtually an unknown composer.

In our own times, Stravinsky said that 'Schumann is the composer of childhood . . . both because he created a children's imaginative world and because children learn some of their first music in his marvellous piano albums.' Nowhere is this aspect of Schumann's genius more clearly seen than in the early *Papillons* and in the later (1838) *Scenes from Childhood*, collections of short, romantic, atmospheric piano pieces which often have some literary or autobiographical association. In *Carnaval* his twin personalities, the impetuous Florestan and the more contemplative Eusebius, make their appearance together with characters from the *Commedia dell'arte* and elsewhere, while in *Davidsbündlertänze* he invokes the League of David, a fictional brotherhood

ABOVE: *'Woman at the Window', an oil-painting of 1822 by Caspar David Friedrich (1774-1840). Friedrich, a contemporary German artist and important exponent of Romanticism in painting, worked in Dresden where Schumann also lived between 1845 and 1849.*

based on real people, to fight bourgeois academicians and unimaginative Philistines.

The songs and song-cycles of the miraculous year of 1840 (*Liederkreis, Frauenliebe und Leben* and *Dichterliebe*, among many others) are an endless source of delight, as are the four symphonies, despite some lack of enterprise in their orchestration, and the chamber music. But perhaps the best introduction to the music of Schumann remains the A minor Piano Concerto – an evergreen work that has opened the door to classical music for countless music-lovers.   R.H.

Chronology

1810 Born 8 June, Zwickau, Saxony
1820-8 Educated Zwickau Lyceum
1826 Sister's suicide; father's sudden death
1828 Enters Leipzig University to study law
1829 Transfers to Heidelberg University; neglects studies
1829-31 Papillons
1830 Abandons law; studies piano under Friedrich Wieck
1832 Hand injury
1833 Fears madness; contemplates suicide
1833-44 Editor of 'Neue Zeitschrift für Musik'
1834 Creates fictional 'League of David' to fight musical Philistines. Composes Carnaval
1836 In love with Clara Wieck, whose father opposes marriage. Death of Schumann's mother
1837 Davidsbündlertänze and Fantasiestücke
1838 Discovers original score of Schubert's Ninth Symphony in Vienna
1839 Court overrules Friedrich Wieck's marriage ban
1840 Marries Clara
1841 Symphony No. 1 (Spring)
1843 Professor of Composition, Leipzig University
1844 Joint concert tour in Prussia and Russia with Clara. Nervous breakdown
1845 Settles in Dresden
1846 Piano Concerto in A minor first performed by Clara Schumann. Symphony No. 2, first performance conducted by Mendelssohn. Failing health – 'constant roaring in my ears'
1849 Uprising in Dresden. Moves to Düsseldorf
1850-1 Conducting career fails. Symphony No. 3 (Rhenish)
1851 Symphony No. 4 (begun in 1841)
1853 Meets Brahms; acclaims his genius in 'Neue Zeitschrift für Musik'
1854 Attempts suicide. Admitted to private asylum at Endenich, near Bonn
1856 Dies 29 July, Endenich

RIGHT: 'The Cross in the Mountains' by Caspar David Friedrich (1774-1840), an altar painting of 1808 that echoes the spirit of Schütz's religious music.

ABOVE: Heinrich Schütz was pre-eminently a composer of choral music; the artist of this portrait is unknown.

ABOVE: Louis Spohr, a pastel portrait by an unknown artist, done around 1807 when Spohr was touring in Europe as a violin virtuoso.

HEINRICH **SCHÜTZ**

(b. Köstritz, 8 October 1585; d. Dresden, 6 November 1672)

*S*chütz was born exactly one hundred years before Bach and Handel; his mastery of choral writing as revealed in such works as his Christmas Oratorio or his superb settings of the four Passions makes it reasonable to mention him in the same breath as these illustrious successors. Ironically, Schütz was drawn to the Law for several years, until music studies in Venice and an appointment as choirmaster in Dresden convinced him that his true vocation lay in providing worthy music for state and religious ceremonies. In these duties he enjoyed a privileged status, and he might have remained in Dresden permanently but for Saxony's participation in the Thirty Years War. Financial problems arising from this, and the grief occasioned by the deaths of several close relatives, led him to Copenhagen for a few years, but in 1635 he found his way back to Dresden and remained in that area for the rest of his long life. Despite deafness, he continued until old age to produce masterpieces that superbly combined Italian vocal freedom with Lutheran piety, as in The Seven Words from the Cross or the German Magnificat. Schütz can also claim to be the first German to compose opera and ballet scores, but it is his endlessly inventive choral works that ensure his lasting reputation. *P.J.*

ALEXANDER **SCRIABIN**

(b. Moscow, 6 January 1872; d. Moscow, 27 April 1915)

*B*lessed with an extraordinary musical memory and a strong urge to be a piano virtuoso, Scriabin abandoned the military career planned by his parents and joined the Moscow Conservatory. He was not happy with traditional studies, however, and eventually left to follow his own individual ways, earning a living by giving piano lessons until he was granted an annuity by a generous patroness. By now, Scriabin had developed a taste for the heady mystical teachings of Madame Blavatsky, and his orchestral works began to reflect their incoherent blend of pantheism, ecstasy and fascination with the powers of darkness. Between the ages of 23 and 31 he produced three long symphonies for large forces, then followed them with The Poem of Ecstasy (1908) and Prometheus, The Poem of Fire (1910), demanding even greater

numbers of performers. In recent years, several distinguished conductors have promoted and recorded these ambitious works without securing a regular place for them in the repertoire. Similarly, his many piano works have been championed by such master pianists as Horowitz without achieving wide popularity. It seems ironic that the unconventional creator of such grandiose work should have met his death in such an apparently trivial manner: a pimple on his lip turned septic, and within days the unfortunate Scriabin had died of blood poisoning. *P.J.*

LUDWIG (LOUIS) **SPOHR**

(b. Brunswick, 5 April 1784; d. Kassel, 22 October 1859)

*S*pohr was a highly rated early romantic composer, contemporary in Germany with Beethoven and Weber, but his music is not like theirs, and he does not appear to have been much in sympathy with them. He was nevertheless to be one of the early supporters of Wagner, and his music adds some pre-Wagnerian harmonies to a Mozartian or Schubertian base, but with no sign of the drama and emotion usually found in the early romantics. Spohr was a child prodigy as violinist and composer. For most of his life he was a travelling violin virtuoso and conductor, and in the latter capacity he is credited with the introduction of the baton. In later yeas he partially settled down as Kapellmeister in Kassel, though he continued touring, especially to England where he was much admired. He wrote a lot of music, including five operas, nine symphonies, 15 violin concertos, and four clarinet concertos which are rarely heard today. Nor is his oratorio The Last Judgement, but his chamber music is revived and shows his charm at its greatest. Most popular are his Septet, Octet and Nonet. *P.L.*

CHARLES VILLIERS **STANFORD**

(b. Dublin, 30 September 1852; d. London, 29 March 1924)

*A*lways referred to by his resounding full name, Stanford was a formidable figure as teacher and man, but perhaps less so as a composer. He was born in Dublin, but educated at Cambridge and in Germany, and the Irish strain is a minor, if important, element in his work. For many years he occupied a more influential position in English music than anyone, even Parry, as he was composition professor at the RCM from 1883 and professor of music at Cambridge from 1887 until his death. Virtually every important English composer of the time (save Elgar) passed through his hands. He also composed nearly 200 works. Stanford's music is strongly influenced by Brahms, especially in his seven symphonies and concertos for clarinet, violin (two), cello and piano (three), but his style remains vigorous and individual, with a fund of melody. The distinctive Irish tinge is more noticeable in his often delightful songs: he shared with Vaughan Williams the ability to write songs which were indistinguishable from genuine folk material, as in 'A soft day' and 'The fairy lough'. His ten operas are little heard, but his church music is widely played, and his two sets of Sea Songs remain popular. *P.L.*

KARLHEINZ **STOCKHAUSEN**

(b. Burg Mödrath, nr. Cologne, 22 August 1928)

*A*n orphan by the age of fourteen, Stockhausen developed his musical skills during the uncertain and painful years of the Second World War. His studies were interrupted by military service and manual labour, but by 1950 he had graduated in music in Cologne. At once he became a prominent member of the avant-garde, and throughout the 1950s the name of Stockhausen was identified with the most extreme experiments, involving electronic sounds, 'total serialism', and granting performers freedom to play what they chose. In these ventures, Stockhausen was fortunate to receive the support of liberal authorities in Darmstadt and Cologne, for works such as Kontra-Punkte (1953) and Gruppen (1957) generally bewildered or antagonized audiences, who listened in vain for any conventional elements of melody, rhythm or harmony. Throughout his career, Stockhausen has travelled widely as a lecturer and tireless propagandist for his theories. Since the mid-1970s, he has pushed his 'spatial multi-media concepts' to the limit in a vast project called Licht (Light), a cycle of seven lengthy 'operas', one for each day of the week, employing a bewildering range of effects and dramatic styles. This modern creation is taking considerably longer than its Biblical model; only three 'days' are finished, and the whole enterprise is not due for completion before the end of the century.   P.J.

ARTHUR **SULLIVAN**

(b. London, 13 May 1842; d. London, 22 November 1900)

Showing early musical talent and vocal ability, Sullivan became a chorister of the Chapel Royal and continued to develop so promisingly that he became the first recipient of a Mendelssohn scholarship which took him to the Royal Academy of Music in 1857, and on to Leipzig Conservatory. He had a great success there and in London with music to The Tempest (1861), followed by a highly praised cantata Kenilworth (1864) and his 'Irish' Symphony in 1866. Seemingly set to become the shining light of English academic music, and patronized by royalty, he remained narrowly Victorian in his outlook and his 'serious' works, including an opera Ivanhoe (1891), are now only revived as an interesting sidelight to his lighter endeavours. Here, with the help of

a superb librettist, W.S. Gilbert (1836-1911), he produced a series of British operettas that (in spite of their narrowly English-speaking appeal) are the equal of anything in the genre. Starting with Thespis (1871), these really took off with Trial by Jury (1875), followed by HMS Pinafore (1878); The Pirates of Penzance (1879); Patience (1881); Iolanthe (1882); Princess Ida (1884); The Mikado (1885); Ruddigore (1887); The Yeomen of the Guard (1888); and The Gondoliers (1889). Others, less successful followed, while Sullivan suffered the happy misery of being torn between commercial success and the more serious endeavours urged upon him by his Queen and others. P.G.

KAROL **SZYMANOWSKI**

(b. Tymoshóvska, 6 October 1882; d. Lausanne, 29 March 1937)

The son of wealthy Polish landowners, Szymanowski inherited their love of music and in the early years of the century supported an organization, 'Young Poland In Music', where his early works made his name known. His musical outlook was widened by extensive travels in Europe and North Africa, and the three symphonies he wrote between 1907 and 1916 reveal a love of large-scale, voluptuous sound, obviously influenced by Richard Strauss but also tinged by more astringent, experimental elements. The political upheavals following the First World War affected him badly. His family home was destroyed and for the first time he knew financial uncertainty. Always an introverted, fastidious character, he tried to settle in many places but seemed to lack a secure sense of direction, and his health was affected by heavy smoking and drinking. Szymanowski's final years were spent in further European tours, although his nominal home was in Poland, where his reputation steadily grew. His major works are all written in the style of late-Romantic expressionism with rich scoring and exotic harmonies. Notable are his opera King Roger (1924), two violin concertos, and a choral Stabat Mater (1926). He died of tuberculosis in a Swiss sanatorium.   P.J.

ABOVE: Karlheinz Stockhausen, the perpetually avant-garde composer, photographed by Gert Schütz in 1972.

ABOVE: Sir Arthur Sullivan, the wayward composer of the Savoy operettas, photographed in London in 1884, the year of the first performance of Princess Ida.

LEFT: 'Too Early' by James Tissot (1836-1902), an oil-painting which pictures the society life of Victorian England with which Sullivan would have been familiar.

DMITRY
Shostakovich

(b. St. Petersburg, 12 September 1906; d. Moscow, 9 August 1975)

Towards the end of his life Shostakovich said: 'The Revolution, I am convinced, is what made me a composer. I was very young in 1917, but my first childish compositions were dedicated to the Revolution and inspired by it.' He remained a true Soviet composer, devoted to socialist ideals, despite two savage attacks by the regime in 1936 and 1948, which branded his music as 'formalistic' and full of 'petty-bourgeois sensationalism'. Although he suffered great personal anguish, he managed to preserve his integrity as a composer. 'By studying my music,' he declared diplomatically, 'you will find the whole truth about me as a man and as an artist.'

In Soviet terms, the Shostakovich family background in St. Petersburg was certainly petty bourgeois. Both his parents were accomplished musicians, and young Dmitry so clearly inherited their talents that Glazunov helped him to enter the prestigious St. Petersburg Conservatoire, where he showed great promise as a concert pianist. However, he resolved to concentrate on composing music 'that would serve the Soviet people'. When his diploma composition – the First Symphony – was first performed in 1926 he was recognized almost overnight as a front-rank composer.

From then on works flowed from his pen, and the musical world eagerly awaited each new composition. Success seemed assured,

RIGHT: A photograph of Shostakovich taken in 1940 when he was back in favour politically and won the Stalin Prize Award for his Piano Quintet.

BELOW: A portrait of Shostakovich painted by I. A. Serebrianyi (1907-1979) which now hangs in the Tretjakov Gallery in Moscow.

but Shostakovich belonged to the first generation of musicians educated under the Soviet system, which rewarded talent only when it conformed. When Stalin stormed out after hearing the first Act of Lady Macbeth of the Mtsensk District and 'Pravda' followed up with the first of its vicious attacks, Shostakovich retired from the public platform and turned instead to writing music for the cinema – no doubt drawing on his earlier experience as a cinema pianist 'providing musical accompaniment to the human emotions on the screen.'

By 1940 he was sufficiently back in favour to be awarded the Stalin Prize for his Piano Quintet, and after the war he was one of the Soviet delegates at Peace Congresses in New York, Vienna and Warsaw. He then became a deputy member of the Supreme Soviet, was made a People's Artist of the USSR in 1954 and was awarded the Order of Lenin in 1956.

By the time Stalin died in 1953 Shostakovich was a world figure, laden with foreign honours and degrees, and well beyond political reach. During the period of 'cultural thaw' he produced some of his finest works, including the Tenth Symphony, in which his style is more evidently inward-looking and pessimistic, and The Execution of Stepan Razin to a text by the Ukrainian poet Yevgeni Yevtushenko.

When, at the age of twenty, Shostakovich had his First Symphony performed, first in Leningrad (as St. Petersburg was then known) and then in Moscow, he sprang fully armed into the symphonic arena to win world-wide acclaim. This is a work of epic proportions in which many distinctive features of Shostakovich's composing style are already present. Furthermore, it contains music of overwhelming emotional intensity and power, and shows a mastery of form, technical invention and an astonishing command of the orchestra. Yet despite a determination 'to make his music serve the needs of the Russian people', this seminal work does not fall within the traditions of the Russian national school, but owes much to late Romantics such as Mahler, and to Berg and Hindemith.

Such universality, and the fact that his music is full of humour, parody and savage wit, perhaps made it inevitable that Shostakovich would at some stage come under fire from a repressive totalitarian regime. When the first crisis came in 1936, he withdrew to safer ground by composing patriotic cantatas and returning to an earlier interest – cinema music. He wrote over 30 film scores, but this huge output is little known outside Russia as the films are rarely seen in the West. One of the few exceptions is the music he composed for *The Gadfly*, in which his gift for pastiche is delightfully revealed.

Shostakovich patched up his first quarrel with the authorities with the publication, in 1937, of the Fifth Symphony, which carries the subtitle *A Soviet Artist's Reply to Just Criticism*. When he came under heavy fire for the second time, in 1948, he cannot have been unaware of the danger of his position. But he refused to allow political blackmail to prevail, and it is now clear that he determined to navigate a hazardous course between the force of his inspiration and the cruel pressures exercised by an ignorant tyranny.

Apart from the fifteen monumental symphonies and the same number of string quartets, Shostakovich wrote six concertos for various instruments and many works for chorus and orchestra, unaccompanied chorus and solo voices. Add

to this vast output his film music, incidental music, arrangements and important piano pieces, such as 24 Preludes and Fugues, and it is easy to understand why he is now regarded by many people as the greatest composer of the 20th century. As each year passes, that judgement appears to be increasingly well-founded and beyond challenge. R.H.

ABOVE: 'The Year 1943', a painting by Pjotr Ossowski (b. 1925) completed in 1969. It reflects the grim background to Shostakovich's work of the early 1940's. His Seventh Symphony was dedicated to the city of Leningrad which suffered prolonged siege by German forces between 1941-4.

JEAN Sibelius

(b. Hämeenlinna, 8 December 1865; d. Järvenpää, 20 September 1957)

RIGHT: *Sibelius in later life in his home in Järvenpää. For the last 30 years of his life, Sibelius wrote no major new works.*

*T*he son of a country doctor, Sibelius was christened Johan Julius Christian and later took his French-sounding name of Jean from an uncle who had also adopted it. None of these names are Finnish, and in fact his family were Swedish-speaking and it was not until manhood that he became fluent in Finnish. Since his father died when he was two, his mother and grandmother took charge of his upbringing. He started to learn the piano at the age of nine, and five years later he began a serious study of the violin. He had already tried his hand at composition at ten with a short piece for violin and cello called Water Drops, and as a teenager who enjoyed playing trios with his pianist sister and cellist brother he also composed pieces for them to perform.

Although this boy was something of a dreamer, he clearly had intellectual potential and his family intended him for a legal career. He studied law at Helsinki University for a year from 1885, but at the same time learned the violin and musical theory at the music conservatory there. It soon became clear that the pull of music was too strong and his family agreed that he should become a composition pupil of Martin Wegelius (1846-1906), the conservatory's director. He still also aspired to be a violin virtuoso, playing concertos and chamber music, but gradually came to realize that he had begun too late to reach his goal, though as late as 1891 he auditioned, without success, for a place in the Vienna Philharmonic Orchestra.

Thus composition overtook the violin as his principal interest, and after graduating in 1889 he went abroad to study, first in Berlin and then in Vienna, where his teachers were Karl Goldmark and Robert Fuchs (he also had a letter of introduction to Brahms, but Brahms refused to meet him). He already knew and loved the Finnish national epic called the Kalevala, and hearing the Kalevala-inspired Aino Symphony by his older compatriot Robert Kajanus (1856-1933) gave him the impetus in 1891 to write a big orchestral work based on Finnish legend, the choral-orchestral 'symphonic poem' Kullervo which is in fact a five-movement symphony lasting 80 minutes.

Kullervo was at once recognized as a landmark in the emergence of Finnish art music. At a time when his country was under Russian rule, it also linked Sibelius with the rising tide of nationalism, as did his marriage to Aino Järnefelt (the daughter of a

BELOW: 'The Funeral Journey of a Child' by the Finn Albert Edelfelt (1854-1905), a celebrated painter of Finnish country life. Sibelius' compositions championed the native music of his countrymen.

Finnish-speaking, nationalist family) and, later, his stirring tone poem Finlandia. From now on he was regarded (and probably saw himself) as a musical champion of his people, and he continued to draw upon Finnish legend for a series of major orchestral works from En saga in 1892 to Tapiola in 1926.

Though not every new work was well received, Sibelius was from now on Finland's leading composer, a position emphasized by the government's grant to him when he was 32 of an annuity of 3,000 Finnish Marks that was later increased to 5,000 marks. Yet this was not enough to free him from financial concerns, and over the next two decades he was often heavily in debt, partly because of his taste for high society and travel abroad. To make ends meet, he taught composition at the Helsinki Conservatory from 1892 until 1901, and was disappointed in 1897 when he sought the directorship of Helsinki University's Music School, but was passed over in favour of his friend Kajanus – who, however, was a supporter and fine conductor of his music.

Since his youth, Sibelius had been a heavy drinker and cigar smoker, but in 1908 his doctors discovered throat cancer and the price of his recovery was two operations and the renunciation of these habits. In fact he still had half a century to live, and his fame, above all as a symphonist, now spread widely. He frequently travelled abroad to conduct his music, receiving an honorary doctorate at Yale University in 1914 and making several visits to

Britain, where he was much admired. But after completing his Seventh Symphony in 1924 and the tone poem Tapiola in the following year, when he was sixty, he virtually retired and gave the world no more major works (although he worked on an Eighth Symphony, no score appeared). No one really knows why, but his innate self-doubt may have held him back, and he was now free of financial constraints to work since a government award on his sixtieth birthday gave him 150,000 marks and an increased pension. Henceforth, this family man with five daughters and fifteen grandchildren lived quietly with his wife in the country home at Järvenpää which they had owned since 1904. Yet he remained a world figure who was visited by his President on his eighty-fifth birthday and received cigars from Churchill on his ninetieth. He continued to take an interest in music, admiring Bartók and, in the 1940s, speaking warmly of Britten's opera Peter Grimes. His death was peaceful, following a stroke.

ABOVE: The young, more romantic Sibelius, aged 29, an aquatint by Akseli Gallen-Kallela (1865-1931) who was a friend of the composer, and a pioneer of Finnish nationalist art. He produced a series of paintings that illustrated the Kalevala epic, which also inspired Sibelius.

Chronology

Though Sibelius composed in many forms from piano pieces to opera (an early one-acter called *The Maiden in the Tower*), he owes his reputation to his orchestral works, which may be divided into the categories of programmatic pieces and the seven symphonies which stand like pillars in the edifice of 20th-century music. Like Brahms thirty years previously, he had supporters who elected him as a conservative champion, resisting what they saw as the onslaughts on musical tradition led by Stravinsky and Schoenberg. But he too was an innovator, though less obviously so. Above all, he brought a new way of thought to symphonic writing in which the fully fledged themes of classical times, that had still served for Bruckner and Brahms, were replaced by briefer motifs which could form and reform, coalesce or break up, and yet together build a strong, living musical structure.

An early example of the Sibelius method occurs in the first movement of his Second Symphony. At first, its ideas seem placed piecemeal and almost casually before the listener, and it is only as the music progresses that one realizes the powerful musical logic that holds all together: it is as if a number of little streams emerge in turn and then join to form a deep and purposeful river. The composer himself talked of his methods in 1907 in a conversation with Mahler which he later recounted to a friend: while Mahler thought that a symphony 'must embrace everything', his own belief was that there should be 'a severity of style and the profound logic that creates an inner connection between all the ideas'. Perhaps because of this, there is an increasing compression in the sequence of his symphonies: for example, the Fifth was originally in the conventional four movements, but he then amalgamated the first movement and scherzo into one bigger movement which, in its course, gathers an unstoppable momentum. His last symphony, the Seventh, is in a single movement lasting something over twenty minutes that has

BELOW: *'Potsdam Place' in Berlin, painted by Otto Antoine (1865-1951) in 1889. Sibelius travelled to Berlin in 1889 to study there with Albert Becker, who was a strict teacher.*

ABOVE: *Sibelius outside his house in Järvenpää near Helsinki where he lived a secluded life for over 50 years in the company of his wife. He named the house 'Ainola' after her. He is buried here.*

been called (by Professor Gerald Abraham) 'one vast development'. Another Sibelius scholar, Robert Layton, suggests that his later symphonic thinking 'is so thoroughly non-episodic that it defies the usual textbook analysis'. Having reached this point in symphonic construction, he could perhaps go no further in the same direction and this may partly explain his subsequent silence. Similarly, *Tapiola*, which grows from a single motif, was also his last tone poem.

Given Sibelius's stated intention of 'severity of style' (but perhaps 'economy of style' is a better translation), it is something of a paradox that the three symphonies mentioned above end in a mood of grandeur and triumph. But elsewhere among them there is sometimes a laconic quality that is at first disconcerting. Many listeners are puzzled by the sudden ending, in what sounds like a wrong key, of the second movement of the Sixth Symphony. This is in the conventional four movements, but lacks a slow one and is strangely cool in language; the composer said that in this work he was offering 'pure spring water' instead of the exotic cocktails devised by this contempories. He also said of his grim and granitic Fourth Symphony, a work written in the shadow of his serious illness, that it described his reflections 'on problems of life and death'. Harmonically more daring than the others, it remains his most challenging symphony but has its own dark beauty.

Alongside these works, Sibelius was always capable of writing music that was expansive and melodious. The First Symphony is a romantic utterance owing much to Borodin and Tchaikovsky, not least in the slow second movement, and although the Third has only three movements and a certain briskness of style, it is warm and invigorating. His dramatic sense, fully evident in the symphonies, is also to be felt in his tone poems such as *The Oceanides* and *Tapiola* (a depiction of the forest spirit Tapiola), and he composed incidental music for various plays including Shakespeare's *The Tempest*. His score for Arvid Järnfelt's play *Kuolema* (1903) included what was to become his most popular piece, *Valse triste*, which he must have regretted selling outright to a publisher since he earned no royalties from its countless performances.

With its lilting melodic charm, *Valse triste* reminds us that despite the austerity of some of his work, Sibelius was always capable of writing light and tuneful music. His orchestral *Karelia* suite falls into this category, as does the patriotic *Fin-landia* and many of his shorter piano pieces. Similarly, his Violin Concerto abounds in good tunes as well as extrovert virtuosity, though even here, from the quiet opening, we are aware of the cool and fundamentally northern nature of his genius. With his creed that 'classicism is the way of the future' he probably stands as a lonely figure in music, yet his example of creative independence remains a powerful one.

C.H.

AXEL GALLÉN.
1892

LEFT: *'Lake in the Wilds', a Finnish scene by Akseli Gallen-Kallela, painted in 1892. Sibelius responded profoundly to the natural world around him – he even compared the development of a symphony to the flow of a river.*

BEDŘICH
Smetana

(b. Litomyšl, Bohemia, 2 March 1824; d. Prague, 12 May 1884)

*T*he father of Czech music, although born in Bohemia, never spoke Czech fluently, and was actually christened Fridrich. At that time, Czech culture was overlaid by German, and it was Smetana's destiny to give voice to the Czech part of the wave of nationalistic feeling which swept over Europe in the middle of the 19th century. Unluckily for him, although the hour produced the man it did nothing to provide for him, and his life was a series of struggles and personal tragedies.

Smetana's father was a brewer, who sired twenty children by three wives. Smetana was the first boy and the centre of his father's ambition. He did not take to brewing, but his musical promise was equally welcome to his father, and he mastered the violin by five, the piano at six and produced his first composition at eight.

After a poorly-paid teaching job, he was appointed as resident piano teacher to Count Leopold Thun, and could then afford composition lessons. The next few years saw a number of false starts: an abortive career as a concert pianist, involvement in the 1848 revolution, a failed school of music, and engagement as piano partner to the deposed Emperor Ferdinand. Somehow he found enough resources to get married in 1849, but things did not improve. The first of what was to prove a series of domestic tragedies came with the death of three of his four daughters in 1854-6, although this did inspire his first wholly successful composition, the Piano Trio in G minor. He went to Gothenburg as conductor and teacher, and although he was successful there, his ill luck continued with the death of his wife from tuberculosis in 1859. He quickly remarried, and returned to Prague in 1862.

Nationalism was now at its height, and he attempted to express it musically, although always wary of the suspicions of the Austrian authorities. He finally broke into the new field of opera with The Brandenburgers in Bohemia in 1866. Although this was no masterpiece, and the music was not discernibly Czech, the subject matter was enough to make it popular. When it was quickly followed by The Bartered Bride, with its infectious Czech

dances, his triumph was for the moment complete. Smetana was appointed principal conductor of the Provisional Theatre in 1866 and kept the job until 1874, but things were not plain sailing. Two patriotic operas, Dalibor and Libuse were opposed because Dalibor was 'too Wagnerian' for the nationalists, and Libuse was too nationalistic for the authorities. Worst of all, in 1874 came the first symptoms of the distressing form of syphilis-related deafness, which was later to destroy his reason.

In 1876 in his First String Quartet (From My Life) he depicted his reaction to this devastating blow, and although he was to produce several more operas and the famous orchestral cycle Ma Vlast (My Country), his administrative career was quickly ended by his competitors. By 1883 he was barely able to compose, and in 1884 he was confined to an asylum where he soon died.

Smetana wrote distinguished works in most musical forms, although he is best known outside Czechoslovakia for his operas and the orchestral cycle *Ma Vlast*. Throughout his life he wrote piano music, and much of this repays attention, most notably the *Dreams* and *Czech Dances* which he wrote at the end of his life. In his native land, his numerous works for chorus are popular, but do not 'travel well', like much of his output. This is in some ways unexpected, for Smetana's music is not especially Czech in harmony or melody. He adopted Czech dance rhythms, but his musical heritage stemmed from Germany and Austria – most obviously Mendelssohn and Schumann. A strong musical personality, we now think of him as typically Czech, but this is largely because of the school to which he gave rise – especially Dvořák, who combines Smetana's influence with a more clearly Bohemian melodic profile.

Smetana's orchestral music consists of the early *Triumph* Symphony, the three symphonic poems from 1859-1861 *Richard III*, *Wallenstein's Camp* and *Hakon Jarl*, a Festival Overture, the cycle *Ma Vlast* and the final *Carnival in Prague* from his last year. Of these, only *Ma Vlast* is fully characteristic, and it is a masterpiece of national music. Depicting scenes and events in Czech history and legend, it captures the national spirit in a unique way, and despite some weak episodes in one or two of the six parts, it maintains a constant flow of inspiring melody.

The chamber music consists of the two string quartets, the piano trio and the violin and piano piece *From my homeland*. All show Smetana at his best, but the First String Quartet has especial poignancy in the depiction of the onset of deafness by a terrible high-pitched continuous note. The operas are a mixed bunch. *The Bartered Bride* needs no recommendation as a captivating rustic comedy. The solemn national operas probably mean more to Czechs. Worth investigation are two other comedies – *The Two Widows* (1873) and *The Kiss* (1875). How remarkable that a life so full of miseries and frustrations as Smetana's should be best remembered by his most unclouded and positive works!   P.L.

LEFT: 'A Country Wedding in Lower Austria' by Ferdinand Waldmüller (1793-1865). The scene is reminiscent of The Bartered Bride, one of the brightest and most vivacious operas in the comic repertoire.

THE Strauss Family

Johann Strauss I (b. Vienna, 14 March, 1804;
   d. Vienna, 25 September 1849)
Johann Strauss II (b. Vienna, 25 October 1825;
   d. Vienna, 3 June 1899)
Josef Strauss (b. Vienna, 22 August 1827;
   d. Vienna, 21 July 1870)
Eduard Strauss (b. Vienna, 15 March 1835;
   d. Vienna, 28 December 1916)

RIGHT: Johann Strauss II, a portrait by August Eisenmenger (1830-1907) painted in 1888, when Strauss was at the height of his success in Vienna.

*I*t is inevitable that the various Strausses should be looked at as a family, for not only were their careers closely linked, but they all wrote copiously and in not dissimilar styles. The small age gap between Johann I and II of 21 years also meant that father and son were nearer contemporaries than might have been expected. The dominant figure was Johann II, whose career quickly eclipsed his father's. Josef, though perhaps equally talented, was more retiring and achieved less, while Eduard devoted his time more to conducting and produced only a few distinguished works. The family as a whole bestrides the great days of Vienna from the regime of Metternich, the renowned Austrian statesman of the Napoleonic era, virtually to the First World War, and it is their music which has typified the spirit of the city for most people ever since. Uniquely popular with other composers, including Chopin, Wagner, Brahms and Schoenberg, and seemingly avoiding political cross-currents, the family presented just the image of itself that the Austro-Hungarian Empire wanted.

Johann I was himself a typical product of the Empire, with ancestry in Austria, Italy, Hungary, and Luxembourg, including a Jewish element which was to prove an embarrassment to later regimes. As a young man he played in Joseph Lanner's orchestra, which was the first to develop Austrian folk dance into the waltz, and he soon struck out for himself into running his own band and composing his own waltzes, to which he gave his own rhythmic zest. He had a turbulent marriage, producing children both by his

BELOW: 'The Hunt Ball' by Julius L. Stewart (1855-1919) painted in 1885, the sort of gathering for which the Strausses both played and wrote their bewitching melodies.

wife and by a mistress, with the result that he saw little of his legitimate children. More successful as a musician than as a husband, he became a celebrity in Vienna and throughout Europe, until he died relatively young of scarlet fever.

Johann II was initially a bank clerk, but soon yielded to the family tradition and in 1844 set up an orchestra in rivalry to his father's. His success was immediate, as he was able to develop his father's dance forms, including not only waltzes but galops, quadrilles and polkas, with richer harmonies and more ambitious structures. On his father's death in 1849 he amalgamated the two orchestras, and continued the touring tradition, also visiting the USA. In 1871, he produced the first of 17 operettas, Indigo und die vierzig Räuber, which were to include the supreme example of the genre in Die Fledermaus (1874). His married life was as complicated as his father's (he indulged in numerous affairs and flirtations), and despite continued success – he was appointed Imperial music director for balls – his depressive temperament prevented happiness.

Josef and Eduard were less prominent members of the dynasty, but still contributed a good deal. Josef was even more melancholic than his elder brother, but managed a stable home life and a career as an engineer, and took his share of the conducting responsibility. He composed less, but in his more understated style was just as distinguished. Overwork made him increasingly neurotic, and this led to his early death.

Eduard was less able as composer and conductor than his brothers, but their superior in vanity. He took over the conducting responsibility (and the title of Imperial ball director), until he wound up the family orchestra in 1901. His last years were clouded by his destruction of many family manuscripts, which may have been motivated by suppressed jealousy. Of his own compositions, nowadays only a few are performed.

LEFT: *Strauss in Heaven –
he conducts while Bach,
Beethoven, Brahms,
Bruckner, Bülow, Handel
Haydn, Gluck, Liszt,
Mozart, Schubert,
Schumann, Wagner and
Weber all waltz to his
music. This affectionate
print was made by Otto
Böhler in 1899. He called
it 'Today Strauss is
Playing!'*

Chronology

1804 *Johann I born in Vienna*
1819 *Johann I starts playing with
    Lanner*
1825 *Johann I forms own band.
    Johann II born in Vienna*
1827 *Josef born in Vienna*
1835 *Eduard born in Vienna*
1844 *Johann II forms rival
    orchestra*
1848 *Radetsky March composed
    by Johann I*
1849 *Johann I dies; orchestras
    amalgamated*
1853 *Josef begins conducting*
1863 *Johann II appointed
    Imperial ball director*
1867 *An die schönen blauen
    Donau (The Blue
    Danube) composed by
    Johann II*
1868 *G'schichten aus dem
    Wienerwald (Tales from
    the Vienna Woods) by
    Johann II*
1870 *Josef dies*
1872 *Eduard takes over as
    Imperial ball director*
1874 *Operetta Die Fledermaus
    composed by Johann II,
    first performed at Theater
    an der Wien*
1885 *Der Zigeunerbaron by
    Johann II first performed at
    Theater an der Wien*
1888 *Kaiserwalzer (Emperor
    Waltz) by Johann II*
1899 *Johann II dies*
1901 *Strauss orchestra disbanded*
1907 *Eduard burns manuscripts*
1915 *Eduard dies*

It is remarkably difficult to survey the music of the Strauss family. Although the origins of dances such as the waltz and polka in Austrian and Czech folk music are clear, it is less easy to see what elements the Strausses added – apart, of course, from their genius. The music of Johann I may now seem to us less inspired than that of Johann II or Josef, but it still shows all the distinguishing marks of the later style. Although the only piece of his which is now a household word is the famous *Radetsky March*, his waltzes and galops and polkas are still enjoyable listening, and it is very hard to discern any influence from contemporary composers, such as Beethoven or even Schubert or Hummel.

This characteristic is intensified when one comes to Johann II or Josef, or even the successful compositions of Eduard. There are many well-attested comments by such admirers as Brahms or Wagner as to their envy of Johann's ability, but he seems to have been immune to any reciprocal influence. It is also striking that there were no rivals to the Strausses at the time, and no successors, save perhaps Lehár. It may simply have been the result of some Imperial alchemy that threw up their extraordinary natural melodic and harmonic ability from their heterogeneous family origins.

The sheer scale of their oeuvre is also hard to come to terms with. Johann I in his short life wrote 250 pieces, including 150 waltzes, while the neurotic Josef managed 280 works and Eduard 300, specializing in polkas. Johann II, however, beats them all with over 450 works, adding his 17 operettas to the torrent of waltzes, polkas, marches, and quadrilles. Remarkably, the standard, especially of Johann II's and Josef's music, is very high. The operettas of course do not all reach the standard of *Die Fledermaus* or *Der Zigeunerbaron* (*The Gypsy Baron*) nor are the waltzes all up to the *Emperor* or *Tales from the Vienna Woods*, but recent comprehensive recording ventures reveal a wealth of music which is both unknown and immensely enjoyable. It is invidious to select from such a vast repertoire, but the listener should sample the lovely introductions and codas of some of Johann II's waltzes, and their amazing melodic fertility, while Josef's are notable for languishing, expressive themes. All Strausses excel in the polka, with Johann II and Eduard's quick polkas contrasting with Josef's gently swaying polkamazurkas. Such fertility of invention cannot be explained, nor should it be. It is just there to be enjoyed.   P.L.

LEFT: *Johann Strauss I, the
father of the family, a
lithograph of 1835 by Josef
Kriehuber (1800-1876).*

RICHARD

Strauss (b. Munich, 11 June 1864; d. Garmisch, 8 September 1949)

RIGHT: A portrait of Richard Strauss painted in 1918 by Max Liebermann (1847-1935), now in the National Gallery, Berlin.

'I was always fonder of composing than studying,' said Richard Strauss of his early years. He learned much about orchestration and conducting technique at the weekly rehearsals of a semi-professional orchestra conducted by his father, who was principal horn-player of the Munich Court Orchestra. His knowledge and understanding of the musical world were crucial in shaping the future career of the young composer. Curmudgeonly as he was, he was nobody's fool, and he knew the importance of making the right contacts in order to advance a career.

Before his son reached the age of 20 Strauss senior sent him to Berlin where he met many influential artists, writers and musicians, among whom was the great conductor and pianist Hans von Bülow. He invited Strauss to join him as assistant conductor at Meiningen. Within a month he became chief conductor, worked with Brahms, fell under the Wagnerian influence of Ritter, and heard his first Horn Concerto performed for the first time.

Although his reputation as a conductor and composer seemed to grow effortlessly, first in Germany and then abroad, Strauss was a prodigious worker. If success came easily to him, it did not do so undeserved. In 1894 he married the soprano Pauline de Ahna, for whom he wrote many of his songs: she proved a tempestuous, but devoted, life companion. In 1900 he met the librettist Hugo von Hoffmannsthal, with whom he created one of the most remarkable and fruitful composer/writer partnerships to have developed in the whole history of opera.

Apart from those doubts and uncertainties which afflict most creative artists from time to time, Richard Strauss led a charmed life until his seventies. After the Nazis were elected to power in 1933 they appointed him, without prior consultation, president of a state-run organization to promote German music. But Strauss later came under pressure for his collaboration with Hofmannsthal's successor, librettist Stefan Zweig, who was a Jew. The ageing composer tried to distance himself from the regime but, like most of his countrymen, suffered severe deprivation after Germany's defeat. With all their assets frozen, he and his wife were obliged to seek refuge in Switzerland during the period between 1945 and 1949.

Even after this dark period, so late in life, the gods were kind. He was eventually allowed to return to his beloved home at Garmisch, and to relish the fruits of an astonishing Indian summer of composition. Then, heavy with years, honours and renown, he died with his wife and family around him. A serene departure for the last of the great Romantics.

Chronology

Discovering Richard Strauss is one of the most rewarding and exciting musical journeys to be made, not
least because the quality of his work, as the most ardent of his
admirers will concede, is surprisingly uneven. His music can
be brash and vulgar; and yet in the same piece, a few minutes
later, in a soaring phrase for solo instrument or a beautifully
sustained *cantilena* for soprano, he can touch emotional
peaks beyond the reach of most composers.

What so distinguishes his art is his mastery of the orchestra,
both as a conductor and as a composer. He grew up in an
orchestral environment as other, less fortunate, musicians
might grow up with one instrument at their command.
Strauss thought in terms of instrumentation, attributing
almost human characteristics to each member of the orchestra. He once defined good music as that which 'expresses
most' and ignoring the controversy of his time, refused to distinguish between programme and abstract music. His genius
has room for both, as is shown in the brilliant progammatic
passages in the *Till Eulenspiegels lustige Streiche* and *Don
Quixote* and in the *Domestic* and *Alpine* symphonies.

BELOW: *'The Watzmann Mountain' by Caspar
David Friedrich (1774-1840). Strauss loved the
mountains and this might be a setting for the* Alpine
Symphony, *his great tone poem of 1915.*

ABOVE: *The cover of the solo scenes from Strauss'
Salome arranged for voice and piano, published in
1905. The drawing is by Max Tilke.*

But for all his many gifts as a composer of orchestral music,
it is to his operas and to his songs that we must turn if we are
to find the heart of Richard Strauss. The collaboration with his
librettist, the gifted and fastidious Hugo von Hoffmannsthal,
which lasted until the latter's death in 1929, is one of the
most fruitful in the whole history of opera, and produced
such masterpieces as *Salome, Elektra, Der Rosenkavalier,
Ariadne auf Naxos, Die Frau ohne Schatten* and *Arabella*. His
songs are regarded by many as the finest addition to the vocal
repertoire since the death of Schubert.

All these works, and many more, await the musical
traveller. Yes — there is much in his music that is trivial; much
that is trite. Much that is meretricious and unashamedly
manipulative. Yet there remain many works which, in
Bernard Levin's memorable phrase, go to the deepest places
in the human heart. Among these are the *Four Last Songs*,
which Richard Strauss composed during a last wonderful
burst of creativity. 'The beauty of the world and the beauty of
the female voice were uppermost in his mind to the end,'
wrote biographer Michael Kennedy. 'Has there been so conscious a farewell in music, or one so touchingly effective and
artistically so good?'   R.H.

IGOR
Stravinsky (b. Oranienbaum, 17 June 1882; d. New York, 6 April 1971)

A s a child in St. Petersburg, Stravinsky showed some moderate musical talent but nothing to suggest that he would be among the major composers of his time. His father was a singer at the St. Petersburg Opera and there was a constant stream of musical visitors and music-making in his home. He took piano lessons but, until he was 23, he studied law and only made very tentative shots at writing any music. Then, in 1900, while still a student, he met the composer Rimsky-Korsakov, and showed him some of his writings. The great composer was impressed enough to take him on as a pupil in 1903 and this private arrangement continued until Rimsky-Korsakov died in 1908. A symphony written during this time bore no resemblance to the startling new music that was to come.

While still writing in his natural Russian vein he composed, in 1908, a work called Fireworks which interested the great impresario Serge Diaghilev, who had presented a series of concerts of Russian music in Paris. In 1909 he had introduced Russian ballet to Paris and formed the Ballets Russes. In Stravinsky's Fireworks he sensed an exciting new vein of Russian music, tinged with a modern European cosmopolitanism, and Diaghilev commissioned him to write a score called The Firebird. To Stravinsky's annoyance, for he never liked his works to be loved, this turned out to be immensely and lastingly popular.

Stravinsky settled in Paris and now began to write in a vein that owed something to, but demonstrated no real affection for, jazz. For example L'Histoire du soldat (1918), written for a small orchestra and narrator, dates from this time. As he once explained: he copied his jazz from sheet music, deriving his ideas from the written page rather than from hearing the real thing. The results, as in his ragtime pieces, were curious rather than authentic.

After his early period of fashionable success in Paris, Stravinsky became very much the roving internationalist. He lived for a while in Russia, then in France and Switzerland where he spent the First World War years. Averse to the results of the 1917 Revolution in Russia, he shunned his native land until 1962. From 1920 to 1929 he lived in France, making concert tours in Europe and the USA. At the outbreak of the Second World War he finally settled in America, and started a fruitful collaboration with the Russian-born choreographer George Balanchine.

Stravinsky's first marriage was to his first cousin Katia in 1906. In the bleakest period of his life, in 1939, his elder daughter Ludmilla died of tuberculosis and three months later Katia succumbed to the same illness. He contracted the 'family' disease himself, as did his younger daughter, and had a long and painful cure. Later that year his mother died.

It was after this that he found a foreign haven in New York and launched into a spate of music-making to forget the past. In 1940 he married an artist Vera Sudeikin (née de Bosset) and settled in California. This was a much happier and more settled period of his life. In 1948 he met the young composer and conductor Robert Craft who was to become his Boswell and encourage him to publish a series of conversations and autobiographical writings. Stravinsky was a vitriolic commentator, both on his own works and those of others. Craft also led him in 1952 toward the embracing of serialism, a form of music that he had long avoided, and Stravinsky made a long study of Webern's music. In fact, the compositions of this period, filtered through the Stravinsky method, were still distinctly his own. During his last decade he industriously committed most of his major works to record under his own conductorship, thus leaving behind one of the finest libraries of composer recordings extant. His last three years were fairly barren and dogged by illness.

RIGHT: A photograph of Stravinsky taken in 1925 when he was living in Paris. His ballet Les Noces was first performed there in 1923.

Chronology

1882 Born Oranienbaum, near St. Petersburg 17 June
1901 Begins to study law at St. Petersburg University
1903 Becomes a pupil of Rimsky-Korsakov
1905 Writes his first symphony
1910 Fireworks and Scherzo fantastique heard by Diaghilev who commissions The Firebird as a result
1911 Petrushka first performed in Paris
1913 The Rite of Spring, first performance causes a riot in Paris
1916 Burlesque Rénard first performed in Paris
1917 Leaves Russia and moves around Europe. Writes The Soldier's Tale for the Ballets Russes, first performed in Lausanne in 1918
1918 Academic interest in ragtime, produces some works in that vein
1920 Settles in Paris
1922 Opera Mavra first performed at the Paris Opéra
1924 Concerto for piano and wind written
1927 His opera-cum-oratorio Oedipus Rex first performed in Paris
1928 Ballets Apollon Musagète (Washington) and Le Baiser de la fée (Paris)

BELOW: A stage design for Stravinsky's ballet Petrushka by Alexandre Benois for a Paris Opéra production of 1948. The ballet is set in a fairground in St. Petersburg's Admiralty Square.

LEFT: *Tamara Karsawina (1885-1978) portrayed by Jacques Emile Blanche (1861-1942) in her role as the Firebird in Stravinsky's ballet of the same name. It was first performed in Paris in 1910 with choreography by Fokine.*

1930 Symphony of Psalms
      written

1931 *Violin Concerto written and Duo concertante*

1934 Melodrama Perséphone
      first performed at the Paris Opéra

1938 Dumbarton Oaks
      Concerto written and performed

1939 *His wife, eldest daughter and mother all die. Stravinsky moves to the USA and starts collaborations with Balanchine*

1942 *Circus Polka written; arranged for orchestra in 1942*

1945 Ebony Concerto *written for Woody Herman*

1947 *Ballet* Orpheus *composed; first performed in New York in 1948*

1948 *Begins to write opera* The Rake's Progress *with libretto by W.H. Auden, eventually performed in Venice in 1951. Meets the writer and composer Robert Craft who arouses Stravinsky's interest in serial music*

1952 *Some serial music written*

1954 *In Memoriam Dylan Thomas for tenor, string quartet and trombones*

1958 *Writes Movements for piano and orchestra*

1965 *Writes Requiem Canticles*

1966 *Almost his last work* The Owl and the Pussycat

1969 *Increasing illness reduces his activities*

1971 *Dies in New York, 6 April*

In the wake of a strong upsurge of Russian nationalism, especially influenced by his teacher, Rimsky-Korsakov, Stravinsky quite visibly found his feet and his own style in the series of ballets that he wrote for Diaghilev. *The Firebird* (1910) hangs on to the Russian style; *Petrouchka* (1911) half makes the break; while *The Rite of Spring* (1913) sees him taking on the role of the major figure of modern music, with a work, despite the riots that attended its first performance, that became and remains one of the great masterpieces of the 20th century. With the lessons of classicism absorbed in such pastiches as *Pulcinella* (1920), the 1920s saw him developing his so-called neo-classic style with such works as the Octet (1923), the Concerto for piano and wind (1924) and the Capriccio for piano and orchestra (1929). At this period Stravinsky's music was unemotional and unexpressive.

Relaxation came in the 1930s with the Violin Concerto (1931) and the delightful *Dumbarton Oaks* Concerto (1938). In spite of his own avowed desire to seem unapproachable, the works of the '40s and '50s were increasingly warm, alive and ever creative – the Symphony in C (1940), the Symphony in three movements (1945), his earthy opera based on a series of engravings by the English artist Hogarth, *The Rake's Progress* (1951), and the ballet *Agon* (1957). Perhaps it should not be argued too strongly that Stravinsky's works always fit neatly into some creative period or other. Like any composer, masterpieces, individual and unattached, crop up all along the way. The perky *Soldier's Tale* (1918); his opera-oratorio masterpiece *Oedipus Rex* (1927); and the great *Symphony of Psalms* (1930); these are not to be categorized.

Least attractive perhaps are his 1950s excursions into serialism, or at least neo-serialism, as exemplified by the Cantata, the Septet and the *Canticum Sacrum* (1955), and many other brief and demanding experiments of the period. Exploring Stravinsky is like exploring a modern city rather than a stretch of countryside or woodland; a world of explosive activity and violent gestures; the voice of the steel girder and the traffic jam; an authentic and uncompromising evocation of 20th century life in 20th century sound, and yet an evocation achieved through traditional and approachable orchestral means.   P.G.

THOMAS **TALLIS**

(b. probably in London, 1505; d. Greenwich, 23 November 1585)

*T*he long career of Thomas Tallis spanned a century of social and religious conflicts which caused the downfall of many leading figures connected with the Court, yet he managed to survive them in apparent prosperity. Little is known of his origins, but in 1540 the dissolution of the monasteries by Henry VIII forced him to relinquish the choirmaster's post at Waltham Abbey and move to Canterbury. Three years later he was elected Gentleman of the Chapel Royal. One of his strengths seems to have been the ability to win favour with monarchs holding such conflicting views as Queen Mary and Queen Elizabeth. His church compositions reflect this skill in his easy transition from the traditional Latin liturgy to the new English Church Service as prescribed by Cranmer. The list of Tallis's choral works is long and impressive: it includes the masterly 40 part motet Spem in Alium, and the collection of Sacred Songs (Cantiones sacrae) which he and Byrd published in the year they were granted the monopoly for printing music and music paper. All the church works of Tallis are characterized by assured polyphony and strikingly original harmony, profoundly impressive in their proper ecclesiastical setting. *P.J.*

JOHN **TAVENER**

(b. London, 28 January 1944)

*B*ritish composer who studied at the Royal Academy of Music under Lennox Berkeley and worked with the Australian composer David Lumsdaine before launching out on a career that has veered between experimental academics and, latterly, a degree of popular acclaim. With some strange basic ingredients in his musical recipe, which include medieval hymnology and Indian influences, and the religious promptings of Catholicism and, latterly,

the Russian Orthodox Church, he has used the modern tools of music, serial and electronic, to produce sounds which either enchant or disenchant according to the taste of the listener. His earliest works included a Piano Concerto (1962-3) and settings of Donne and Eliot. His talents are most clearly directed in vocal works that include dramatic cantatas Cain and Abel (1965), The Whale (1966), A Celtic Requiem (1969), and fascinatingly experimental works for voices and unusual orchestral combinations that reach farthest when they achieve a simple beauty that transcends the stark bareness of the means employed. Examples are some of his later works such as Funeral Ikos (1981), Ikon of Light, a setting of Blake's The Lamb, and his recent 'hit' The Protecting Veil for cello and orchestra (1992). *P.G.*

GEORG PHILIPP **TELEMANN**

(b. Magdeburg, 14 March 1681; d. Hamburg 25 June 1767)

*T*wo factors seem to have prevented Telemann from receiving wider acclaim. Firstly, he was an almost exact contemporary of two of music's giants, Handel and Bach. Secondly, Telemann was amazingly prolific, and we naturally expect that such large numbers of works should be characterized by pleasing facility rather than profundity or originality. His catalogue lists 40 operas, 44 settings of the Passion narrative, 600 overtures, and numerous concertos, choral works and compositions for several instruments. What makes this output even more remarkable is the fact that Telemann, the son of a Lutheran clergyman, was largely self-taught in music, for at Leipzig University he had studied Languages and Science. His comparatively uneventful life was spent mainly as music director of the Protestant churches in Hamburg, but modern listeners are likely to be impressed less by his church works than by such orchestral suites as his Tafelmusik which show his talents at their most inventive and beguiling. *P.J.*

ABOVE: *Georg Philipp Telemann, prolific composer and organist; a coloured engraving by G. Lichtensteger.*

RIGHT: *'Houses by the Seine', an 1872 painting by Alfred Sisley (1839-99), depicts the sort of surroundings in which composer Ambroise Thomas lived and worked in the latter part of the 19th century.*

AMBROISE **THOMAS**

(b. Metz, 5 August 1811; d. Paris, 12 February 1896)

The precocious musical gifts of Ambroise Thomas led him naturally to the Paris Conservatoire, where he won several prizes for chamber works. Early in life, he realized that his true métier was writing for the stage, and for almost half-a-century he produced a succession of ballets and operas for fashionable Parisian audiences. But the easy triumphs of these tuneful but superficial works left no lasting satisfaction; their very titles have faded into oblivion, apart from an occasional aria or overture, e.g. Raymond. Conscious of his waning influence and the growing success of Gounod, Thomas devoted himself to composing the two operas that have best survived the passing of time: Mignon (1866) and Hamlet (1868). Both contain touching scenes and pleasing melodies of typically Gallic grace, but – as solemn critics never tire of pointing out – they are totally inadequate as musical equivalents of the literary works of Goethe and Shakespeare on which they are based. The music of Thomas is for lovers of sentiment and bygone French lyricism, not for the analytical gaze of critics.   P.J.

VIRGIL **THOMSON**

(b. Kansas City, 25 November 1896; d. New York, 30 September 1989)

Thomson was born in Kansas City, and showed early promise as a pianist. After the First World War, he went to Harvard and on a scholarship to Paris, where he studied with Nadia Boulanger (1887-1979). During his lengthy Paris stays, he met Satie and Gertrude Stein, who were crucial to his development, and also other French composers. In 1928 he produced his first opera to a Stein libretto, Four Saints in Three Acts. He also wrote a series of Portraits for various instruments in the same simplistic semi-popular style. Even before his return to New York in 1940, he showed signs of a psychological return to his roots in two distinguished film scores to The Plow that Broke the Plains (1936) and The River (1937). These showed a more tuneful, nationalist style based on hymn-tune harmony, but still deriving from his simple French works. His first two symphonies (1928 and 1931) had already anticipated this approach which Copland also adopted. In New York, he became for some years the music critic of the Herald-Tribune, and also produced his second Stein opera The Mother of Us All (1947), and the fine score for the film Louisiana Story. His final opera, Lord Byron, was unfinished. Thomson's music divides into accessible, ultra-American music (the film scores) and more prestigious, but less satisfying, Satie-esque music (the Portraits and the operas).   P.L.

EDUARD **TUBIN**

(b. Kallaste, 18 June 1905; d. Stockholm, 17 November 1982)

Tubin was an Estonian composer, born near Lake Peipus, whose music was little known until the Estonian conductor Neeme Järvi made a comprehensive series of recordings in the 1980s. It soon appeared that this was no mere pious commemoration, as the music proved to be full of melodic interest and variety. It recalls Sibelius at times, but to emphasize the resemblance is to exaggerate it. Estonia and Finland are closely related but distinct, and the same might be said of the two composers. Another discernible influence on Tubin is Prokofiev. He studied in the Estonian town of Tartu, and conducted an orchestra there until 1944, when he was forced by the war to emigrate to Sweden, where he spent the remainder of his life. As a conductor he favoured Stravinsky, Bartok and Kodály, but none of these much influenced the composing which was his main concern. Of his ten symphonies, composed at regular intervals throughout his life, the most popular is No. 2 (The Legendary) (1937), but perhaps the most distinguished is No. 8 (1966). He also wrote two operas, two violin concertos, three violin sonatas, a piano sonata and the Requiem for Fallen Soldiers (1979).   P.L.

HEITOR **VILLA-LOBOS**

(b. Rio de Janeiro, 5 March 1887; d. Rio de Janeiro, 17 November 1959)

A larger than life figure well suited to his huge and exotic country, Villa-Lobos created Brazilian music virtually single-handed. He was largely self-taught save for a few lessons from his father and a smattering of harmony, and acquired his experience like so many in the school of the cafés. Concerts gave him a taste for late-romantic composers such as Strauss, and he encountered Milhaud, who introduced him to modern French music. Trips to Europe in the 1920s consolidated these tastes, and he returned to Brazil in 1930 to spend the rest of his life there teaching and composing on a lavish scale. His music is Brazilian chiefly in colour and rhythm, and does not use folk material. Encounters with neo-classicism in France led to his series of nine Bachianas Brasileiras (1930-1944), which apply Bach's forms to modern Brazilian material. He also introduced the so-called popular form of the Chôros, of which he wrote 14 between 1920 and 1929 for different combinations of voices and instruments, depicting various aspects of Brazil. From the rest of his huge output, his two sets of guitar pieces, 12 Etudes (1928) and 15 Préludes, are well-liked, and the four orchestral suites entitled The Discovery of Brazil are also worth investigation.   P.L.

ABOVE: Ambroise Thomas, composer of Mignon and other fashionable operas, photographed by Nadar in 1866.

ABOVE: Heitor Villa-Lobos, Brazil's most important composer, photographed with a typically flamboyant cigar between his lips.

PETER ILYICH
Tchaikovsky (b. Votinsk, 7 May 1840; d. St. Petersburg, 6 November 1893)

In the prosperous Tchaikovsky household there was, of course, a piano, at which young Peter Ilyich spent 'far too much' of his time, and a remarkable instrument called an orchestrion, which mechanically reproduced the sounds of an orchestra. To this device, Tchaikovsky said, he owed his 'passionate worship' of Mozart (at a time when that composer's music was far less revered than it is today), and his 'first musical impressions'.

His father was a senior mining manager whose job took him to various parts of Russia. As the family moved from place to place Peter, a nervous and sensitive child, suffered deeply the pangs of separation. But at the age of 14 his whole world collapsed when his mother died suddenly from cholera. In later life he could never bring himself to talk about this catastrophe although he was usually so open about his inner feelings.

At the School of Jurisprudence in St. Petersburg his course in-cluded some music lessons, and by the time he had joined the Ministry of Justice as a junior clerk, at the age of 19, his sights were set on music as a career. He continued to study part-time, but when he was passed over for promotion in 1863 he resigned government service and promptly enrolled at the St. Petersburg Conservatoire. Here he attracted the attention of its director, Anton Rubinstein, who urged his brother, Niko-lay, to take on the budding young composer as a tutor of harmony at the newly-opened Conservatoire in Moscow.

After an uncertain start, he embarked upon his first symphony and an opera, The Voye-voda. There was talk of marriage with a French singer, Désirée Artôt. Her mother disapproved, as did the Rubinsteins, but Artôt unexpectedly settled matters herself by marrying a Spanish baritone. In 1868, on a return visit to St. Petersburg, Tchaikovsky was welcomed by the 'New School' of young composers, although he was never completely in

RIGHT: *A photograph of Tchaikovsky taken in 1890, the year that his opera* The Queen of Spades *was first produced in St. Petersburg.*

ABOVE: *Madame von Meck, Tchaikovsky's pen-friend and patron. They corresponded regularly but never met. The friendship ended in 1890, when Madame von Meck informed Tchaikovsky that she could no longer afford to pay him an annuity.*

sympathy with their more nationalistic views.

Exhausted after five years' composing, teaching and writing reviews, he went to Vichy in the summer of 1876 to recover his health. The following year, in Moscow, he married a student, Antonina Milyukova, 'with whom I am not in the least in love', with entirely predictable and disastrous results. A few weeks later he fled to St. Petersburg in a state of total collapse: his doctors ordered him to go abroad again as soon as possible.

By now another woman had entered his life – a well-to-do widow, Madame Nadezhda von Meck, who delicately persuaded Tchaikovsky to accept an annuity so that he could devote all his time to composing. They never met face to face, but frequently exchanged long letters during their thirteen years' friendship.

BELOW: 'Morning in the Village', a scene painted by Andrej Andrejevitsch Popov (1832-96), a Russian artist almost exactly contemporary with Tchaikovsky. The composer would have been familiar with countryside scenes like this.

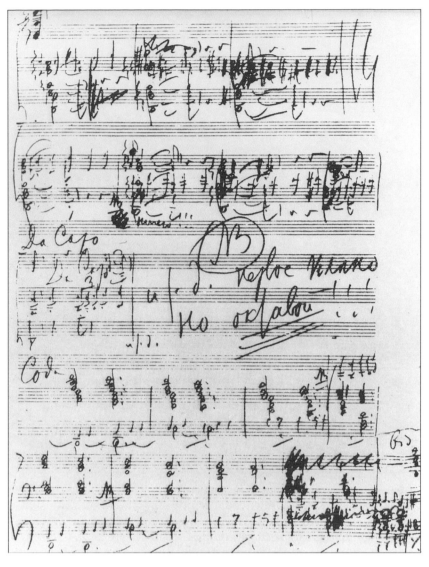

ABOVE: Part of the score of Tchaikovsky's 6th Symphony 'Pathétique', a sketch of bars 88-96 and 152-163 in the composer's own hand.

While abroad Tchaikovsky completed his Fourth Symphony, dedicated to his benefactress, and some lyrical scenes from Eugene Onegin. On returning to Moscow he resigned his professorship and then headed south again, this time to Florence, where so many artists before and since have found relaxation and inspiration under the warm Italian sun.

By 1880 his reputation was well established inside Russia, but the success of his Serenade for Strings and the triumphant debut of the First Piano Concerto in New York, brought him international fame and renown. He gained new strength, broadened his circle of friends, received many invitations to conduct abroad and was honoured in many countries. Most of his major, mature works date from this fruitful period which might have gone on much longer had not Fate, that great Russian obsession, intervened in November 1893.

Was it death by cholera, as we were told for so many years? Or was it suicide after a 'trial' by his peers, following a complaint to the Tsar's office about a homosexual relationship? 'We may never know the truth,' writes critic Rodney Milnes, 'beyond the eternal truth that the death of a man, whether by his own hand or not, only just the right side of fifty and at the height of his powers, was a cruel and tragic waste.'

Chronology

1840 Born 7 May at Votinsk, in central Russia

1848 Family moves to Moscow and then to St. Petersburg, where he is sent to boarding school. Early signs of 'abnormal sensitivity' and beginnings of serious nervous trouble

1850 Joins School of Jurisprudence at St. Petersburg

1854 Overwhelmed by mother's death from cholera. First compositions

1859 Appointed clerk at the Ministry of Justice

1861 Visits Germany, England, Belgium and France

1863 Leaves Ministry: studies composition under Anton Rubinstein

1865 Appointed professor of harmony by Nikolay Rubinstein at the new Moscow Conservatoire

1866 Arrives in Moscow. Nervous breakdown after completing First Symphony (Winter Daydreams)

onderful themes, brilliantly orchestrated, make the music of Tchaikovsky the most accessible of all the great masters. Even people who claim to have no knowledge of the classics at all will have, whether they realize it or not, one or two of his incomparable tunes firmly lodged in their musical memory – tunes used as background music, in TV commercials, or arranged in a variety of ways for the popular market. For as Leonard Bernstein once said, 'Tchaikovsky is one of the most inspired melodists on earth'.

But it is not just the tunes that captivate us, it is the way he puts them across. Was it the time spent during his infant years listening to the mechanical orchestrion that enabled him in his maturity to use the rich orchestral palette to such stunning effect? Of course we shall never know the answer to that question, but in a letter to Nadezhda von Meck, written in 1878, he said: 'I never compose in the abstract ... The musical thought never appears otherwise than in a suitable external form. In this way I invent the musical idea and the instrumentation simultaneously.'

To this natural and spontaneous lyricism must be added excitement and drama, for much of Tchaikovsky's music is as turbulent and as dramatic as the life he led. You have only to listen to the passionate climaxes in his Fantasy Overture *Romeo and Juliet*, or the sombre and sinister opening of the Sixth Symphony [*Pathétique*] to gain an insight into the soul of arguably the greatest of all the romantic composers.

But when you do so, have a care, because he wrote some of his happiest music when he was at the end of his emotional

BELOW: *'Unexpected', a painting by Ilya Repin (1844-1930) showing the return of a political exile from Siberia. Repin was a contemporary of Tchaikovsky, and studied in St. Petersburg.*

ABOVE: *Tchaikovsky with his wife Antonina (née Milyukova); a photograph taken in 1877, the year of their marriage. Tchaikovsky possibly saw marriage as a way to escape from his homosexual leanings, but the relationship collapsed within weeks.*

tether and on the brink of suicide and, conversely, some of his most doom-laden music during the more tranquil and contented periods of his life. The minds of composers, even the most romantic of them like Tchaikovsky, Schubert, Chopin and Schumann, do not always work in an expected way: genius can rarely be easily accounted for.

There is also no clear line of development in Tchaikovsky's music of the kind we can see in Beethoven, for example, or in Brahms. Such was the remarkable consistency of melodic invention and of style through his entire output that he might well have written the *Nutcracker* Suite, with all its technical brilliance, at the outset of his career instead of during 1892, a year before his death.

However, it was precisely because Tchaikovsky's musical ideas came to him so completely formed, like flowers in full bloom, that he found it difficult to compose symphonies, where so much depends upon thematic development as well as upon structure and form. Aware of this deficiency he once confessed that 'an experienced eye can detect the thread in my seams, and I can do nothing about it.' His pupil Taneiev complained that the Fourth Symphony was like 'a symphonic poem to which the composer has slapped on three more movements and called it a symphony'.

But how much weight should we give to such critical analysis? Is it not more than enough that the last three symphonies, to which must be added the less well-known *Manfred* Symphony, are among the most effective and dramatic compositions in the whole of the orchestral repertoire? They are all works of genius – a distinctively Russian genius – and we do not need a guidebook in hand to respond to their emotional intensity and power.

To many people outside Russia it comes as a surprise that in his own country Tchaikovsky is regarded primarily as an operatic composer. In the West we see him, apart from *Eugene Onegin* and *Queen of Spades*, as a composer of symphonies, ballets and, of course, the Serenade for Strings, the *1812 Overture*, the First Piano Concerto and the concerto for violin. But these and other orchestral works, together with the fantasy overtures, represent only a small fraction of his total output. He was highly critical of his work and destroyed many of his own manuscripts. Nevertheless, there survive ten operas, three major ballet suites and other incidental music, seven symphonies, a large amount of church, choral and chamber music, together with countless songs and piano pieces. All evidence not only of creative genius, but of a prodigious creative energy as well.

So anyone coming fresh to Tchaikovsky's music is on the brink of a musical experience to last a lifetime. For although it was once fashionable to sneer at his shameless emotionalism – a composer 'with his heart too much on his sleeve' as one jaundiced critic put it – the fact is that in his music he expresses, as few other composers have been able to do, the joy and the pain, the beauty and the tragedy, the ecstasy and the anguish of the human condition. R.H.

ABOVE: *Alexander Pushkin (1799-1837), author of* The Queen of Spades *and* Eugene Onegin, *both of which inspired operas by Tchaikovsky, portrayed by Orest A. Kiprensky (1782-1836).*

1869 *Opera* The Voyevoda *first performed at the Bolshoi Theatre, Moscow. Fantasy Overture* Romeo and Juliet

1871 *First String Quartet in D major (Op. 11)*

1873 *Second Symphony (Little Russian)*

1874 *Second String Quartet in F major (Op. 22)*

1875 *First Piano Concerto first performed under Hans von Bülow in New York. Third Symphony (Polish)*

1876 *Third String Quartet (Op. 30) begun. Visits Paris, Vichy and Bayreuth where he meets Liszt. Correspondence with Madame von Meck begins.* Francesca da Rimini *and the Rococo Variations completed. Opera* Vakula the Smith *produced at St. Petersburg*

1877 *Work starts on the Fourth Symphony and Eugene Onegin.* Swan Lake *opens in Moscow. Disastrous marriage leads to breakdown and attempted suicide. Madame von Meck offers financial support*

1878 *The Violin Concerto (Op. 35) and Piano Sonata (Op. 37) follow visit to Italy. Resigns Moscow Conservatoire professorship*

1879 *Eugene Onegin first performed in Moscow*

1880 *Italian Capriccio, Serenade for Strings and 1812 Overture*

1883 *Mazeppa and Second Orchestral Suite*

1884 *Third Orchestral Suite*

1886 *Manfred Symphony first performed*

1887 *Maid of Orleans first performed in St. Petersburg*

1888 *First conducting tour. Meets Brahms, Dvořák and Gounod. Fifth Symphony*

1889 *Second international tour. Sleeping Beauty completed*

1890 *Queen of Spades first performed in St. Petersburg; Souvenir de Florence. End of relationship with Madame von Meck*

1891 *Successful United States tour*

1892 Nutcracker *Suite*

1893 *Sixth Symphony (Pathétique). Honorary degree from Cambridge University. On 6 November dies from cholera – or was it suicide?*

MICHAEL

Tippett (b. London, 2 January 1905)

*T*ippett was born in London and came of a conventional middle-class background, but both his origins and his upbringing were calculated to make him a man of contradictions. His father was an entrepreneur who eventually acquired a hotel in Cannes, and gave his son an intimate knowledge of France. His mother was an early supporter of the suffragette movement, and instilled into him the militant reformist strain later so important in Tippett's makeup. He was educated in Lincolnshire and soon decided he wished to be a composer. This took him to the Royal College of Music in London where he studied composition and conducting (with Adrian Boult and Malcolm Sargent), and later, on his own initiative, he took lessons in counterpoint. At the same time he was reading widely and idiosyncratically, another important later influence.

After spending some time as a schoolmaster, he settled in Surrey and survived on various musical bits and pieces as a conductor and jobbing composer. Activities in the poorer parts of the country encouraged a left-wing philosophy which never left him. A late developer as a composer, he destroyed various 'juvenile' works from this period, and effectively emerged as a composer with his First String Quartet in 1935. From this time he developed quickly, and his early maturity came with the Concerto for double string orchestra of 1939, and the oratorio A Child of Our Time, a topical work about racial persecution in which the composer's personal libertarian convictions coincided with the mood of the country.

The Second World War had just begun, and the now well-known Tippett was appointed director of Morley College. He remained there until 1951, playing an important part in English

musical life and especially the revival of earlier English music. Tippett's conscientious objection to the war led to his imprisonment for two months, but his career was unaffected, and by 1952 he was able to resign and devote himself to composition, with the aid of some income from BBC broadcasting. From here on his life became effectively synonymous with his music.

His first opera, The Midsummer Marriage, also dating from 1952, was the culmination of his earlier 'lyrical' style, and it set the pattern for his operas by setting to music his own erudite, often obscure, mystical libretto. This was followed by the Corelli variations for orchestra, his First Symphony and his piano concerto. He was knighted in 1966, and soon after came a substantial change of style with the opera King Priam – a tough, austere work on the subject of free will, introducing what became known as his 'disjunct' period. Such formidable works as the Concerto for Orchestra and the choral Vision of St. Augustine were in the same style. In the next opera, The Knot Garden (1969), he successfully combined his two musical styles, though unfortunately the libretto, dealing with the problems of human relationships, was yet more obscure and eccentric. In this work, and the succeeding Third and Fourth Symphonies, he introduced a controversial practice of quoting other music from diverse sources.

1977 brought the next opera, The Ice Break, a futuristic piece carrying Tippett's eclecticism even further, and this was followed by the ambitious choral work The Mask of Time and the Triple Concerto. Since then he has continued to compose piano and chamber music, and another opera, New Year (1989).

Although Tippett's music clearly evolves strikingly in the 55 years from his first mature work to the present, there is still a remarkable consistency of individual character. From the first he was possessed of a form of ecstatic lyricism, accentuated by the adoption from both past and present sources of surging, syncopated rhythms. The early Concerto for double string orchestra and String Quartet No.2 both show this, and also his gift of extended melody, which is distinctively English yet untouched by folk song. Another form of the same quality is found in *A Child of Our Time*, where the use of Negro spirituals as the counterpart of Bach chorales provides at once an emotional counterpoise to the more jagged narration and a contrasted form of rhythmic impulse. This work also introduced for the first time Tippett's passionate concern for justice in society, and with *The Midsummer Marriage* the same musical resources are used in the investigation of the human psyche – it is rather like a combination of *The Magic Flute* with Jung's theories.

From now on, Tippett's restless concern with 'life, the uni-

ABOVE: 'Among London Searchlights', a view of London during the Second World War painted by C.R.W. Nevinson (1899-1946). Tippett registered as a conscientious objector at the start of the war, but was actually imprisoned for two months for contravening the registration conditions.

verse and everything' progressively invades his music, and especially his opera libretti. A musical style already indebted to Stravinsky, Hindemith, the English madrigalists and jazz is at the disposal of a similarly over-informed intellect. The result is music of ever-increasing intricacy and abundance, where the wood progressively disappears into the trees. Despite his four symphonies, piano concerto, triple concerto, four string quartets, four piano sonatas, five operas and much besides, it seems likely that Tippett will be better remembered for the joyous spontaneity and emotional warmth of his earlier works, than for his later utterances.   P.L.

RALPH
Vaughan Williams
(b. Down Ampney, 12 October 1872; d. London, 25 August 1958)

*B*ig, burly and unmistakably English, Ralph Vaughan Williams 'looked like a farmer . . . on his way to judge the shorthorns at an agricultural fair.' Rather forbidding in appearance, with a gruff manner concealing an inner shyness, he came from a cultured, upper middle-class family related to the Darwins and the Wedgwoods.

He began to compose overtures when he was only six, revealing his musical talents at a very early age. At Charterhouse, at the age of fifteen, he wrote a trio for the school concert. During his time at the Royal College of Music, where he was a pupil of Parry and Stanford, he discovered the glories of the English choral tradition. Although he was 'repelled' by the 19th century German style in music (what he called the 'Beethoven idiom'), he went to Germany to study with Max Bruch, and then to France 'to acquire a little French polish' under Maurice Ravel.

But it was from English 16th century music and, above all, by studying English folk songs that he found his own voice, and works such as On Wenlock Edge, *the* Sea Symphony *and the* Fantasia on a Theme of Thomas Tallis *established him as a distinctively English composer.*

RIGHT: *Ralph Vaughan Williams photographed by Erich Auerbach in 1958, the final year of the composer's life.*

When war came in 1914, Vaughan Williams was 42 – too old for active service. Nevertheless, he enlisted as a medical orderly and served in France and at Salonika. Commissioned in 1916 in the Royal Garrison Artillery, he spent the last year of the war more suitably employed as Director of Music of the 1st Army of the British Expeditionary Force.

Honours and senior appointments in the music world followed on his return to civilian life, and he settled down to a busy routine of teaching, conducting the Bach Choir and numerous festival choirs, and composing symphonies, operas, concertos, instrumental and chamber music, choral works, songs, as well as eleven film music scores. Yet he still found time to encourage and advise many young musicians, and to write on musical and other matters in a lively and often controversial manner.

As his first composition (later withdrawn) was published when he was 19 and his last work, Symphony No.9, was first performed when he was 86, his creative career spanned 67 years – or an incredible 80 years if you count those precocious overtures. Few men have more clearly deserved the Order of Merit, awarded to him in 1935.

ABOVE: *'Cottage in a Cornfield' by John Constable (1776-1837). This is the sort of countryside that Vaughan Williams loved and which he portrayed in works such as A Pastoral Symphony.*

'Every composer,' Vaughan Williams once wrote, 'cannot expect to have a worldwide message, but he may reasonably expect to have a message for his own people.' So modest an assessment is characteristic of the man. We can see now, more than thirty years after his death, that his genius outgrew the bonds of the nationalism in which it was rooted to make him a truly international figure, one of the most powerful and original voices of the 20th century.

There are many points of entry to his music, especially among the earlier works written while he was still deeply immersed in the study of Tudor polyphony and the English folk-song tradition. One of the most familiar is his delightful song 'Linden Lea' which is not, as many people imagine, an arrangement of a traditional tune but an entirely original setting of a text by William Barnes. The overture and witty incidental music to the *The Wasps* is a well-known orchestral piece, as is his later arrangement of *Greensleeves*, first heard in 1929 when the four-act opera *Sir John in Love*, based on Shakespeare's *The Merry Wives of Windsor*, was produced at the Royal College of Music.

Dates of composition, as Vaughan Williams himself explained, can be misleading because often the work 'spread over years'. But there is no doubt about the significance of 1910, the year of his *Fantasia on a Theme of Thomas Tallis*, the work which uses wonderful antiphonal effects, as did the Tudor composer himself, and in which Vaughan Williams found his own true idiom and style. Four years later came a romance for violin and orchestra on a poem by George Meredith, *The Lark Ascending* – a most beautiful evocation of the English countryside.

Perhaps the greatest single contribution made by Vaughan Williams to the development (some would say liberation) of English music, is to be found in his symphonic music – the nine symphonies from the *Sea Symphony* (1906-09) to the Ninth Symphony, written in the late 1950s. They are noble works, conceived on a grand scale, in which the melodic strands are clear in every detail and the highly imaginative dramatic effects achieved with startling originality. According to critic Frank Howes, the art of Vaughan Williams 'being rooted in tradition, has had the strength to be progressive . . . His music, though so personal it can be recognized in the space of a few bars, has arisen out of the community and the spirit of the time to which he belongs.'   R.H.

BELOW: 'The Coast near Folkestone' by J.M.W. Turner (1775-1851), an evocative image that suggests the composer's Sea Symphony. *This large-scale work, the first of Vaughan Williams' symphonies, took him several years to complete.*

GIUSEPPE

Verdi (b. Le Roncole, 10 October 1813; d. Milan, 27 January 1901)

RIGHT: Giuseppe Verdi, a photograph by Calzolari taken in 1870, when the composer was working on the score of Aida.

Giuseppe Verdi was born at Le Roncole, a small village near Busseto in the Duchy of Parma. His parents were of peasant stock: his father, a smallholder, ran a modest general store, which also served as the local tavern. Ill-educated as he was, he soon recognized an outstanding musical talent in his young son and consulted Antonio Barezzi, a Busseto merchant, known for his generosity and musical enthusiasms.

With the help of the cathedral organist, Ferdinando Provesi, he assumed responsibility for young Verdi, who flourished in his new environment. By the age of 16 he had started to deputize for Provesi; had a number of compositions performed; and had become a member of the Barezzi household where he was amorously attracted by their eldest daughter Margherita.

BELOW: A set design for Act 2 of Aida for a production staged at the Staatsoper, Munich in 1937. This is the work of Ludwig Sievert (1887-1966).

Two years later, Barezzi sent him to Milan only to find he was already too old to enter the Conservatorio. However, he became a private student of the chief conductor of La Scala, Vincenzo Lavigna, with whom he worked for three crucial years. On his return to Busseto in 1834 he failed to obtain the now-vacant post of cathedral organist. Instead, he took a local teaching job, which brought in just enough salary to allow him to marry Margherita Barezzi in 1836.

His sights were now set on the theatre. In 1839 he moved to Milan where his first opera, Oberto, was successfully staged at La Scala later that year, partly with the support of a talented young singer, Giuseppina Strepponi. Verdi was offered a contract by La Scala's manager, Bartolomeo Merelli.

Success seemed within his grasp, but domestic tragedies overtook him. He had already lost an infant daughter in 1838, and now his small son, Icilio, also died, to be followed by his devoted Margherita in 1840. Distraught with grief, Verdi threw himself into the production of his second opera, Un Giorno di regno, which received so hostile a reception that it had to be withdrawn after the first performance.

Merelli allowed Verdi some time to recover, and then suggested a new opera, Nabucco. It was an inspired choice of libretto, for the delivery of the Jews from slavery exactly matched the mood of the Risorgimento, the revolutionary movement then sweeping Italy. Verdi rose to the occasion with a score that established him overnight as a national figure.

He was lured from semi-retirement to compose Aida, a spectacular opera celebrating the opening of the Suez Canal, and in 1872 the death of his hero, Manzoni, inspired his great Requiem. In his 74th year, in collaboration with Boito, he turned his attention again to Shakespeare and produced another masterpiece, Otello. Astonishingly, six years later, there came an even greater work, Falstaff.

Verdi was now deeply involved in two charitable projects – a hospital he had endowed near Busseto, and a home near Milan for retired musicians, the Casa di Riposo. In 1897 Giuseppina died, bringing to an end a partnership that had endured for more than fifty years. Verdi himself survived until January 1901. At his funeral, 200,000 people stood in the streets of Milan to watch the cortège pass by, while the slaves' chorus from Nabucco 'Va, pensiero' was sung by a massed choir with the orchestra of La Scala conducted by a young Arturo Toscanini.

ABOVE: A painting of Vittorio Emanuele II (1820-78) by Dugoni. An admirer of Verdi, he was the first king of the united Italy between 1861 and 1878, and played an important role in establishing Italian nationalism.

There followed 'the years in the galleys', during which Verdi wrote at the rate of one opera a year – some huge successes, others complete failures. Bursts of intense creative activity were followed by periods of enforced rest. Invitations flooded in from abroad: he went to London for a production of I Masnadieri at the Haymarket Theatre, with the Swedish soprano Jenny Lind in the leading role, and to Paris, where he met his admirer Giuseppina Strepponi once more.

For ten years they defied convention by living together, but were eventually quietly married in 1859. Cavour persuaded Verdi to stand for election in the first parliament of the Kingdom of Italy, but he spent more and more of his time with Giuseppina at their Sant'Agata estate, which he ran as a model farm.

BELOW: Verdi's second wife, the singer Giuseppina Strepponi (1815-97) with a piano score of Nabucco. She and Verdi lived together for ten years before their marriage in 1859 despite the scandal that this caused at the time. After her death, Verdi suffered agonies of loneliness.

BELOW: *A famous pastel drawing of 1886 by Giovanni Boldini (1842-1931). This shows Verdi approaching the height of his fame, the year before the triumph of* Otello.

The twenty-six operas composed by Verdi, like a triumphal arch, link the *bel canto* tradition of Donizetti and Rossini with the dramatic realism of the modern operatic stage. His 'true artistic career' began with his third attempt, *Nabucco*, in which he broke with tradition by using a larger orchestra and chorus to achieve broader, more forceful dramatic effects. He refused to allow singers to indulge virtuosity in empty display; in his music he held clearly the separate threads of the drama and conveyed the emotional stress of each character at every twist of the plot.

The music of *Nabucco* anticipates these hallmarks of his mature style in many ways. There is another foretaste of things to come in the same opera – the well-known slaves' chorus 'Va, pensiero'. This music stopped the hard-bitten La Scala stage hands and carpenters in their tracks at its first rehearsal. Bravo, Maestro! they cried, as well they might, for the longing of the Jewish exiles for home echoed the Italian longing for freedom from Austrian domination. The tune became a symbol of the resistance, and Verdi was hailed not only as a great musician but also as a champion of an independent Italy. After *Nabucco* an acronym was everywhere to be seen – Vittorio Emanuele Re d'Italia (Victor Emmanuel, King of Italy).

Verdi followed up his success with *I Lombardi* in 1843, and *Ernani* the following year, which established his reputation abroad. *Macbeth*, in which he moved closer to the idea of music drama, marked a new stage in his development as a composer. He was too good a showman and too commercial

in his outlook to run the risk of alienating his audiences. 'In the theatre the public will stand for anything except boredom,' he once declared, and so he chose libretti more for their melodramatic content than literary merit, and made sure that in each of his operas there were arias and choruses that could be whistled by errand boys the day after. So conscious was he of the importance of this aspect of his popular appeal, and so fearful of plagiarism, that he withheld 'La donna è mobile' until the last vocal rehearsal of *Rigoletto*, and made the tenor and orchestra swear that they would not reveal the melody to anyone outside the theatre before the opening night.

With *Rigoletto*, *Il Trovatore* and *La Traviata*, the 'years in the galley' came to an end, and he looked towards Paris and the French grand opera tradition as a future source of inspiration and wealth. For he was now so successful that he could dictate his own terms. His first commission for the Paris Opéra was *Les Vêpres siciliennes*, a conventional love story set against the background of the 1281 uprising in Sicily. *Simon Boccanegra*, in which the Doge of Genoa recovers a long-lost daughter but is poisoned by his enemy, Fiesco, was

radically revised for a later production in Milan. With *Un Ballo in maschera*, which deals with regicide, Verdi ran into one of his frequent confrontations with the political censors, who insisted that the victim should be a Count, not a King, and that the location of the action be transferred from Sweden to Boston! His next production, *La Forza del destino*, contains much fine music, but has one of the most improbable of all operatic plots – which is saying a great deal.

Five years later *Don Carlos* was produced in Paris. In many ways it is a more striking and original work than its successor, *Aida*, which Verdi was commissioned to write for the celebrations that followed the opening of the Suez Canal. The first two acts are commonplace, but with the Nile scene the music changes gear, and from that point onwards the work is a masterpiece.

The scale of Verdi's achievement on the opera stage of the world is such that it is easy to overlook other music he composed for voices and orchestra. Of these, the famous Requiem dedicated to the memory of the Italian novelist Manzoni is the outstanding example, but the late *Four Sacred Pieces* must not be forgotten. There is also a string quartet,

ABOVE: 'I Vespri Siciliani', *a painting by F. Hayez. Verdi wrote an opera on this theme – Les Vêpres siciliennes – which deals with French occupation of Sicily in the 13th century.*

written in 1873, and a number of songs which appeared at various dates between 1838 and 1869.

Aida was to have been Verdi's farewell to opera but Ricordi, his publisher, persuaded him to come out of retirement with a brilliant libretto by Boito, based on Shakespeare's *Othello*. The simplified version of the plot is in many ways more dramatic than the original and inspired Verdi to compose his finest tragic opera. First performed in Milan in 1887, *Otello* would stand at the pinnacle of his achievement were it not that six years later, at the age of 80, he produced his crowning masterpiece, *Falstaff*. This is a wonderful opera full of subtle, fast-moving wit and humour, and ideas which tumble out one after the other in never-ending melodic invention. *Bravo, maestro!* indeed. *Bravissimo!*

R.H.

ANTONIO
Vivaldi (b. Venice, 4 March 1678; d. Vienna, 28 July 1741)

Vivaldi was born in Venice, the son of a barber turned violinist in the St. Mark's orchestra. He was taught the violin by his father and trained for the priesthood, though his enthusiasm for this is debatable. He was not ordained until 1703, and soon gave up saying Mass – allegedly because of a chronic chest complaint – though he was always to be known as 'Il Prete Rosso' (the red priest) on account of his red hair. He was enthusiastic about music, and obtained a position as violin teacher at the Ospedale della Pietà, a large orphanage noted for the standard of its music. He was to be associated with the Pietà for most of his life, with resident positions alternating with periods of travel, but even when travelling he continued to compose music for it. He helped to turn its orchestra into one of the most accomplished musical ensembles in Europe at that period.

His first successful work was his Op. 1, a group of trio sonatas in 1705, and his reputation was made in 1711 with the set of concertos known as L'Estro armonico (Harmonious Inspiration). In 1713 he produced his first opera, Ottone in Villa, and for the next twelve years he toured Italy producing operas and working for the imperial commander in Mantua, the Landgrave of Hesse-Darmstadt. Although he was now well-known, his reputation always stood higher in France, Germany and Holland than in Italy, where he was periodically in trouble with the Church from his failure to say Mass and his habit of travelling with female pupils who were thought to be his mistresses.

He continued to compose at a remarkable rate – allegedly faster than a copyist could produce the parts – in many forms, but especially operas and concertos and chamber music, together with sacred works for the Pietà. He spent several periods in Venice while working at the Pietà, and was admired and sought out by many composers and notables from abroad. Bach adapted and praised his concertos, and the Emperor Charles VI valued his opinion and lavished honours upon him. Eventually his absenteeism led to his final dismissal from the Pietà, and he went to Vienna, probably to seek his fortune with the Emperor. Unluckily for him, the Emperor had just died, and Vivaldi soon followed him, the victim of a gastric infection. Despite a prosperous life and a healthy regard for money, he had run out of resources and was buried in a pauper's grave.

RIGHT: A portrait thought to be of Vivaldi by an unknown artist; some historians dispute the identity of the subject, however.

BELOW: 'Festival on the Piazzetta', Venice, painted by Gabriele Bella, a contemporary of Vivaldi. Such a scene would certainly have been familiar to Vivaldi, a native son of Venice.

For many years, Vivaldi's music was largely forgotten, apart from the works adapted by Bach, but in the mid-20th century the discovery of a large number of manuscripts combined with the revival of interest in the baroque period to produce a Vivaldi renaissance. The advent of the long-playing record gave a final push, and Vivaldi's music is probably better-known today than it has ever been.

Vivaldi's works, like Haydn's for example, are so plentiful that they are almost impossible to assess, and it is tempting, though false, to believe that such quantity must be inimical to quality. He claimed to have written 94 operas (though only about 20 are now extant, and 'only' 50 have been accounted for), and he certainly wrote 550 concertos. The old joke that he wrote the same concerto 550 times is of course a calumny, even if to modern ears baroque music can have a certain sameness when heard in bulk. His variety is in fact remarkable. Of the 550 concertos, 350 are for solo instrument and orchestra (230 for violin), but the remainder are for all sorts of combinations of instruments, including 40 double concertos, 30 for multiple soloists, and some for orchestra alone. His solo instruments include bassoon, cello, oboe and flute as well as violin, and he was capable of using strange combinations such as viola d'amore and lute. He single-handedly developed the concerto into a form which remained largely unchanged for 200 years, and his resource of orchestration is exceptional.

The four concertos known as *I Quattro stagioni* (*The Four Seasons*) are part of a set of twelve entitled *Il Cimento dell'armonia e dell'inventione* written in 1723, and although their popularity is deserved, they are far from exceptional among Vivaldi's works in this style. His operas are less well-known, though increasingly highly regarded. Much of his church music is enjoyable, including the famous *Gloria* and the oratorio *Juditha triumphans*. As well as his orchestral music for public performance, he was an equally prolific composer of chamber music, writing for example 40 violin sonatas and nine cello sonatas.

Vivaldi is to be distinguished from other industrious baroque composers by his vitality, melodic invention and originality. Apart from the innovations for which he was responsible in form and orchestration, he also produced many early examples of programme music, of which *The Four Seasons* is only the best-known example. The set of concertos called *La Stravaganza* and the three concertos entitled *La Tempesta di mare* bear witness to the fact that he was well aware of the nature of his music. In contrast to many later nicknames appended to classical works, all Vivaldi's titles were his own.

Although Vivaldi cannot lay claim to the profundity of Bach or the melodic distinction of Handel, he remains Italy's most distinguished baroque composer, and as his vast output is brought to light, so his reputation grows.   P.L.

Chronology

1678 Born in Venice
1703 Ordained priest. Maestro di violino at Ospedale della Pietà
1705 Trio sonatas Op.1
1709 Violin sonatas Op.2
1711 L'Estro armonico concertos
1712 La Stravaganza concertos
1713 Opera Ottone in Villa first performed at Vicenza
1716 Oratorio Juditha triumphans
1718-20 Works for Landgrave in Mantua
1723-5 Produces operas in Rome
1725 Il Cimento dell'armonia et dell'inventione concertos
1727 La Cetra concertos
1728 Meets Emperor Charles VI
1735 Opera Griselda first performed in Venice
1737 Forbidden to enter Ferrara for moral reasons
1738 Directs festival in Amsterdam
1740 Leaves for Vienna
1741 Dies in Vienna

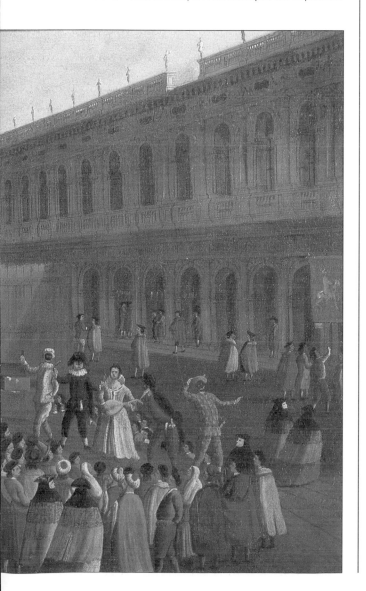

RICHARD

Wagner (b. Leipzig, 22 May 1813; d. Venice, 13 February 1883)

*I*t has been argued that Wagner's father was not the actuary Friedrich Wagner, who died six months after his birth, but the actor, poet and painter Ludwig Geyer, whom his mother married nine months after being widowed. The composer himself seems to have thought so at one time, but later he said, 'I do not believe it'. Nevertheless, he was close to his stepfather until Geyer's death in 1821, and his early childhood was spent in a theatrical home in Dresden, where he also learned to revere Weber, the father of German romantic opera, describing him as 'my true begetter, arousing in me a passion for music'. At the Dresden Kreuzschule, he also developed an interest in history.

After his family returned to Leipzig in 1828, Wagner became absorbed in artists such as Shakespeare, Goethe and Beethoven, whose symphonies finally decided him on a musical career. He neglected his school studies, tried to teach himself composition with the aid of textbooks, and managed to get an orchestral Overture in B flat major performed in Leipzig in December 1830. In the following February he entered Leipzig University as a music student, taking lessons also in composition from Christian Weinlig and in harmony from Christian Müller, both men being prominent musicians in the city. Within the same year, 1831, he published a piano sonata and in November 1832 he had his Symphony in C major performed at the Prague Conservatory. Two months later it was given at the Leipzig Gewandhaus.

RIGHT: A portrait of Richard Wagner painted in the 1870's by Franz von Lenbach (1836-1904). It is now in the Wagner Museum in Bayreuth.

BELOW: Wagner with his wife Cosima, the daughter of Liszt, photographed in Vienna, 9 May 1872, by Fritz Luckhardt. Cosima left her husband, Hans von Bülow, for Wagner.

But his interest still centred on music for the stage, and when in Prague in 1832, he wrote a libretto for an opera called Die Hochzeit. Although he never completed its music, he moved on more confidently to his next, Die Feen. Having obtained a post as a chorus master at the opera house in Würzburg, he completed this in January 1834 and sent it to the Leipzig Opera, who rejected it. However, he was undaunted, and accused the Leipzig director that he had failed to appreciate his approach. In the meantime, his work at Würzburg involved him in the production of many newish operas, and after becoming music director of an opera company at Magdeburg in 1834 he began a third one of his own, a two-act comedy based on Shakespeare's Measure for Measure. Das Liebesverbot was completed by early 1836 and performed (though only once) in Magdeburg in March.

In 1835, Wagner became engaged to the actress Minna Planer, and they were married in November in Königsberg, where he was soon to take up another operatic directorship after the Magdeburg impresario went bankrupt. She already had an illegitimate daughter, and the marriage had its troubles, partly financial and partly because of his doubts of her fidelity. In 1837 she left him temporarily for a wealthy businessman. But despite what he called 'the miseries' of his private life, Wagner soon started work on his next opera, Rienzi, a big, tragic work set in 14th-century Rome. He now directed the opera at Riga, conducted symphony concerts there, and effected a reconciliation with his wife. But when his contract ended in March 1839 he found himself unable to settle outstanding debts and the couple fled to Prussia and there boarded a ship bound for London. Eventually they reached France, where Wagner met the opera composer Meyerbeer and received his promise of an introduction to the Paris Opéra. However, no commission materialized, and during the two and a half years he spent in Paris he had to undertake menial musical work. Things became so bad that he spent some weeks in a debtors' prison.

Nevertheless these years of quasi-exile were not without profit. Wagner's sea journey was to inspire Die fliegende Holländer, composed in 1841, and a German friend in Paris introduced him to the stories of Tannhäuser and Lohengrin which were to serve for further operas in the 1840s. In April 1842 he returned to Dresden, where Rienzi and Die fliegende Holländer received their first performances in the Court Theatre. He was appointed Kapellmeister to the Saxon Court in 1843. Yet in 1849 he had to leave Dresden hastily for Switzerland after his involvement with a revolutionary movement caused the government to issue a warrant for his arrest.

Wagner now counted Franz Liszt among his supporters, and Liszt conducted Lohengrin at Weimar in 1850 and encouraged the creation of his magnum opus, the cycle of four 'music dramas' together called Der Ring des Nibelungen, which was already occupying his mind. He first wrote their librettos, and then started composing in 1853. He finally completed this mighty tetralogy in 1874, and the first complete performance was to take place in 1876 in a Bayreuth theatre that had been built for his music.

In the meantime, much had happened. Wagner's operas were increasingly performed in major European cities, and he travelled extensively. Yet he continued to have money troubles and his private life was complicated. The other women in his life included Mathilde Wesendonck, who inspired some songs and his opera Tristan und Isolde, and after separating from Minna he lived

with, and eventually married, Liszt's daughter Cosima, who left her husband for him. But on the career side things went better, and in 1864 he at last found the benefactor he needed when the young King Ludwig II of Bavaria, a passionate admirer of his work, summoned him to Munich, paid off his debts, gave him an annuity and provided him with a generous commission to complete The Ring.

Though Wagner made enemies in the Munich court and the King eventually had to ask him to leave, Ludwig continued his friendship and financial aid, and it was in Switzerland in 1867 that the composer completed his genial German comedy Die Meistersinger von Nürnberg. In the early 1870s, aided by King Ludwig,

Wagner designed and built the Bayreuth Festival Theatre, and the composer toured Germany to find the right singers for The Ring. Eventually the whole immense project was completed, and the première of the operatic tetralogy in 1876 was an event whose importance was recognized by the whole musical world. Wagner's next (and last) opera, started in 1876 and first produced at Bayreuth in July 1882, was Parsifal, a semi-Christian story. Shortly after the première, he took Cosima and their children to Venice, where he conducted his youthful Symphony in C major on Christmas Eve and talked of composing more symphonies. Seven weeks later he died of a heart attack while working at his desk.

Chronology

BELOW: *The Festspielhaus at Bayreuth, built 1872-6 to a design by Gottfried Semper and Otto Brückwald to house the Wagner operas. The first Ring cycle was performed here in 1876.*

Together with Beethoven, Wagner is the most important and influential German composer of the 19th century. Throughout his life, he greatly admired his predecessor, and it was Beethoven's Ninth Symphony that he chose to conduct in 1872 at the ceremony of laying the foundation stone of the Bayreuth Festival Theatre. He thought of his 'music dramas' as in some way continuing and fulfilling Beethoven's work, and one of their most important features is that they are constructed almost symphonically, avoiding the self-contained numbers of classical opera and instead using themes which pervade a whole work, or in the case of *The Ring* a whole cycle lasting some sixteen hours.

These themes are more properly called motifs, since most are too short to be regarded as fully-fledged melodies in the classical sense. But that in turn makes them all the more susceptible to the kind of development which was largely Wagner's invention. Indeed we may say that the drama enacted on stage in one of his operas is exactly paralleled by what occurs in the music itself, with the 'leitmotifs' corresponding to persons or even ideas. Yet this artist whose background was as much theatrical as musical did not wish to make the orchestra more important than the singers and stage action; indeed, he once remarked that the instrumental parts of Beethoven's Ninth Symphony represented 'music crying out for redemption by poetry'.

In fact, Wagner's ideal was what he called a *Gesamt-kunstwerk*, literally a 'union of the arts' such as he imagined was the chief feature of the ancient Greek theatre with its blend of text, both spoken and sung, dance and sheer spectacle. We know much about his thinking since besides his operas and other music he produced a large number of essays. Some of these are enlightening, though others are heavily obscure in a Germanic way and commentators find it hard to excuse an occasional unpleasantness, as in the pamphlet called '*Jewishness in Music*' which he published anonymously in 1850. But is is inevitable that a genius like Wagner must have strong views, and perhaps we should not be surprised that he was dismissive about Italian opera ('a trollop') and declared that much French opera suggested 'a coquette with a cold smile'.

Unlike his Italian contemporary Verdi, whose work he appreciated, Wagner had no time for operatic institutions and those impresarios and middle men whose motives were principally commercial. No 19th century composer was more passionately devoted to 'art for art's sake', and he demanded unquestioning, total loyalty from all his supporters, which for the most part they gave willingly. After his many years of struggle, he was finally rewarded and saw himself recognized as the great German composer of his time.

Wagner wrote other music besides his music dramas, but he was above all a master of opera, and not least its form and instrumentation. His harmony can be plain (and one thinks here of *Die Meistersinger*), but often it is subtle and ambiguous, particularly where the emotional tension is high: thus the Prelude to *Tristan und Isolde* uses chromatic harmony to convey intense feeling. Debussy admired the orchestration of *Parsifal* for what he called its 'unique incalculable beauty . . . that colour that seems lit from behind', and his own *Pelléas et Mélisande* owes much to *Tristan* in its mysterious story of forbidden love. Yet Debussy, and Stravinsky after him, reacted against Wagner's forcefulness, such as Holst called 'good old Wagnerian bawling', and against the dreams and

legends of Romanticism itself, for Wotan and Brünnhilde are not human characters and even Siegfried and Isolde are hardly people that we can identify with – though that is less true of Walther and Hans Sachs in *Die Meistersinger*.

Thus although Wagner wrote of 'The art of the future' (the title of an essay he wrote in 1849), he had few direct imitators, and the operas based on British and Celtic legend by Rutland Boughton (1878-1960) and Joseph Holbrooke (1878-1958) failed. Yet the extent of his influence on music was enormous. In their different ways, Richard Strauss and Mahler owe much to him, and no opera composer of the 20th

ABOVE: *A dramatic portrayal by Franz Stassen of Alberich stealing the Rhinegold from the Rhine maidens in the first scene of* Das Rheingold. *This lithograph was made in 1914.*

century has been unaware of his work even if negatively, as in the case of Britten when writing *Peter Grimes* in 1944, who declared, 'I decided to reject the Wagnerian theory of "permanent melody" for the classical practice of separate numbers'. C.H.

WILLIAM
Walton (b. Oldham, 29 March 1902; d. Foro d'Ischia, 8 March 1983)

RIGHT: William Walton, a photographic self-portrait by the composer taken in 1959 when he was living on the island of Ischia.

Walton's father was a teacher and musician in the rather drab Lancashire town where he was born, and his mother was also musical, but soon after becoming a chorister at Christ Church, Oxford, at the age of ten, he seems to have done all he could to throw off his un-sophisticated North-country roots and become a more urban and even cosmopolitan person. He began to compose when he was twelve, writing choral music, songs and organ pieces, and when his voice broke, the Dean of Christ Church, Thomas Strong, who had followed his development, persuaded his father to let his talented son go on to become an undergraduate at Oxford University, which he did at the unusually early age of sixteen. However, despite success in music itself, he left Oxford two years later, in 1920, on proving unable to pass a compulsory general examination called Responsions.

He did not, however, return to Oldham. Instead he went to live at the London home of an Oxford friend, Sacheverell Sitwell, a literary person five years his senior, whose wealthy and cultivated background was altogether different from his own, and whose brother Osbert and sister Edith were also writers. For the next ten years, his principal base was their house in Chelsea, and it was for Edith Sitwell's virtuoso English poems that he composed the music that brought him fame. This work was Façade, an 'entertainment' for speaker and small instrumental ensemble that was first per-

formed in the Sitwells' home in January 1922 and then caused a stir when it was heard at the Aeolian Hall. At around the same time Walton had also composed a powerful Piano Quartet (dedicated to Thomas Strong) and a String Quartet that was performed at the 1923 Festival of the International Society for Contemporary Music in Salzburg and praised by the composer Alban Berg. But later he was to withdraw the latter work, remarking that it was 'full of undigested Bartók and Schoenberg': this is an early example of the acute sense of self-criticism that was to remain with him, although the Quartet has been revived in recent times and proves to deserve a place in his canon of works even if some of his strictures are justified. He did not suppress the Piano Quartet, but revised it before it appeared in 1924 as his first published work.

After Façade, Walton went on to write a series of orchestral works in the 1920s and 1930s that established his reputation, including the overture Portsmouth Point, the Sinfonia Concertante for piano and orchestra, the Viola Concerto (a finer concerto than the one for keyboard), the oratorio Belshazzar's Feast with its Biblical story as retold by Osbert Sitwell, the First Symphony, and finally the Violin Concerto composed for Jascha Heifetz in 1939 and completed three months before the outbreak of the Second World War. He had also by now written incidental music for films, which, he said, 'gave me a lot more fluency', and this skill

Chronology

1902 *William Turner Walton, born Oldham, 29 March*

1913 *Enters Christ Church Choir School, Oxford*

1916 *A Litany for unaccompanied choir*

1918 *Becomes an Oxford University undergraduate*

1919 *Piano Quartet*

1920 *Leaves Oxford without a degree and makes his home with the Sitwell family in London*

1922 *Façade performed in London; completes String Quartet*

1923 *String Quartet performed at ISCM Festival, Salzburg (later withdrawn). Becomes interested in jazz and makes some dance band arrangements*

1925 *Portsmouth Point*

1927 *Sinfonia Concertante for piano and orchestra*

1929 *Viola Concerto performed, with the violist-composer Paul Hindemith as soloist*

1931 *Belshazzar's Feast*

1934 *First three movements of First Symphony completed, performed in December*

RIGHT: 'Belshazzar's Feast', a painting of 1630 by Rembrandt (1606-69). Walton's oratorio on this theme is one of his most powerful and best known choral works.

came to its finest fruition in the magnificent scores that he wrote between 1944-55 for Laurence Olivier's Shakespeare films Henry V, Hamlet and Richard III.

After his marriage in 1948 to Susana Gil, an Argentinian lady of charm and intelligence, Walton moved with his wife to the Italian island of Ischia, near Naples, and thenceforth lived there peacefully in a house whose large and beautiful garden was her special province, welcoming many visitors from the musical and social worlds including Laurence Olivier and the young British pianist John Ogdon. He continued to compose, and works of these later years include the opera Troilus and Cressida, a Cello Concerto and a Second Symphony. In 1951 he was knighted by the Queen and in 1968 was awarded the Order of Merit. But he had never been prolific, and was further inhibited by his awareness of the changes in musical fashion that took place as he himself grew older, writing sadly in 1963 to Benjamin Britten that he failed to understand ('old age maybe') a now 'chaotic and barren musical world', although he valued Britten's own work. His last orchestral work, in 1969, was a set of improvisations based on a theme by this fellow composer, and latterly he also composed some sacred choral pieces. In his last years, his health failed progressively and he died following a stroke.

Walton was for many years regarded as the principal British composer of the generation between Vaughan Williams and Britten. But in the last two decades or so, this position was challenged and arguably won by Michael Tippett, not least because Walton's chief achievements belong to the early part of his life while Tippett's best work began when he was around fifty. Of the two men, Walton was much the more conservative and, like Rachmaninov, lived to observe his work becoming unfashionable, at least with the critical cognoscenti and some other arbiters of musical taste. However, the public's affection for it remained and non-British conductors, such as Georg Szell and André Previn, supported his music by performance, while commissions for new music came from such bodies as the Cleveland Orchestra (for the Partita), the New York Philharmonic Orchestra (for the *Capriccio burlesco*) and the San Francisco Symphony Orchestra (for the *Improvisations on an Impromptu by Benjamin Britten*).

'Walton's best work was done by the time of *Troilus and Cressida*', writes the musician and scholar Christopher Palmer, although he is a strong admirer of the composer who has done much to bring about performances and recordings of his music, including the complete *Henry V* film score. At his best, it offers qualities of power, excitement and epic magnificence as well as a rich, sensuous romanticism strongly tinged with melancholy. There is a Stravinskian nervous vigour and wit in the brilliantly rhythmical overtures *Portsmouth Point* and *Scapino*, as well as the sharp-edged scherzo of the Violin Concerto, and on the other hand an Elgarian breadth and pomp in other pieces such as the coronation march *Crown Imperial*. Walton may have found difficulty in reconciling these powerful forces in his personality, and it is significant that he had problems in composing the nobly triumphant finale to his wonderfully angry and abrasive First Symphony. His orchestral scoring tends to be heavy, but it also has brilliance and is to be heard at its most inventive in *Belshazzar's Feast*. This splendidly forceful and pagan-sounding oratorio shows that the same is true of his vocal and choral writing. As for his opera *Troilus and Cressida*, its limited success at its performances in the 1950s (and in a revival in 1976 with Janet Baker in the title role, rewritten for mezzo) was mainly due to its seeming old-fashioned and conventional, and it could still be that an imaginative new production would win it friends.   C.H.

PETER WARLOCK (PHILIP HESELTINE)

(b. London, 30 October 1894; d. London, 17 December 1930)

One of the most gifted songwriters of that interwar generation that did so much to rediscover the sources and nature of English song, Heseltine found most of his initial musical education at Eton 1908-10. A profound influence on his subsequent work was a meeting with Delius in 1910, adding a flavour which combined with his natural sensitivity and romanticism and his love of Elizabethan music to produce the unique quality of his songs. It was perhaps the Elizabethan side of his tastes, the wenching and carousing element, that led him to publish his music entirely under the pseudonym of Peter Warlock. During the First World War he was a conscientious objector and lived in Ireland, returning to London in 1920 to live by musical journalism, editing, composing and promoting the music of Delius. Of a depressive nature, he committed suicide in 1930. His most substantial vocal work was a song cycle The Curlew to words by W.B. Yeats, which emphasised his melancholy side; but there is a wider variety of approach in his many songs than his scholarly interests might suggest. Most accessible is his string orchestral realization of the Elizabethan dance style in the Capriol Suite; while a neglected item worth discovering is his tender Serenade written for the sixtieth birthday of Delius.   P.G.

THOMAS WEELKES

(b. Elsted, Sussex?, c. 1575; d. London, 30 November 1623)

Until the revival of English music in the early 1900s, many composers of the stature of Thomas Weelkes had been denied their due recognition. The situation was changed by the attainments of Elgar and the delvings of the nationalist school led by Vaughan Williams and others, and the researches and writings

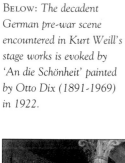

ABOVE: Kurt Weill, best-known for Die Dreigroschenoper, is seen in a photograph (later hand-coloured) taken in Berlin in 1930 by Suse Byk.

BELOW: The decadent German pre-war scene encountered in Kurt Weill's stage works is evoked by 'An die Schönheit' painted by Otto Dix (1891-1969) in 1922.

of scholars such as E.H. Fellowes. Now Weelkes is recognized as one of the great madrigal composers of Tudor times and his church music has taken its rightful place in the Anglican repertoire. Even now little is known about his early days. He was organist at Winchester College 1600-2, became a Bachelor of Music at Oxford in 1602 and spent the rest of his life as organist at Chichester Cathedral. He wrote some forty anthems but much of his church music has not survived. He contributed a fine madrigal for six voices to The Triumphes of Oriana (1601-3) which was compiled by his friend Thomas Morley (1557-1603). There is much remarkable music, some of it very advanced for its time and full of vivid characterization of the text, to be found in Fellowes' 'The English Madrigal School' (Vols. 9-13)(1921), and a fair representation of his work has been recorded in recent years.   P.G.

KURT WEILL

(b. Dessau, 2 March 1900; d. New York, 3 April 1950)

After private study in Dessau and at the Berlin Hochschule during the First World War period, Weill moved into the operatic world as coach and conductor. By 1921 he was in Berlin, studying with Busoni and writing orchestral works, such as his two symphonies (1921 and 1923) and his Violin Concerto (1924), but these now appear merely interesting and unremarkable beside the highly individual theatre music that came to fruition in the songspiel Mahagonny (1927) which was later remodelled into the full-length opera The Rise and Fall of the City of Mahagonny in 1929. Even more remarkable, and destined for undiminishing popularity, was his modern version of The Beggar's Opera, Die Dreigroschenoper (1929), typified by its haunting hit number 'Mack the Knife'. Weill's songs were inimitably performed by his wife Lotte Lenya, with whom he fled the oppressions of the Nazi regime to settle in the USA from 1935. The satirical bite and dark flavours were never quite repeated in the stage works he wrote in America, but these were intriguing and dramatically successful works by any other standards, and contained songs that have found their way into the standard theatre repertoire.   P.G.

JAROMIR WEINBERGER

(b. Prague, 8 January 1896; d. St. Petersburg, Florida, 8 August 1967)

Czech composer who studied at the Prague Conservatory and later in Leipzig with Max Reger. He taught for a year in the USA, returning to Czechoslovakia to teach music in Bratislava, later in Prague and Vienna. He lived mainly in Prague until 1937, then went to the USA in 1939 and settled in the town of St. Petersburg in Florida. He had achieved a sudden and remarkable fame with his opera Svanda Dudak (Schwanda the Bagpiper) which was first heard at the National Theatre in Prague on 27 April 1927. In the popular, danceful, Bohemian style it repeated its success in Germany and the rest of Europe and was produced at the Metropolitan Opera in New York in 1931. Lasting fame accrued from the oft-played Polka and Fugue which became a popular orchestral item. Other operas were to follow 1932-7, including a light opera A Bed of Roses, put on in Prague in 1932, and he wrote various orchestral works including the Lincoln Symphony (1941) and Czech Rhapsody the same year; but the only other work to achieve any popularity was his variations and fugue on Under the Spreading Chestnut Tree written in 1939. Schwanda lives on, but its creator, finding little other success, committed suicide by a drug overdose in 1967.   P.G.

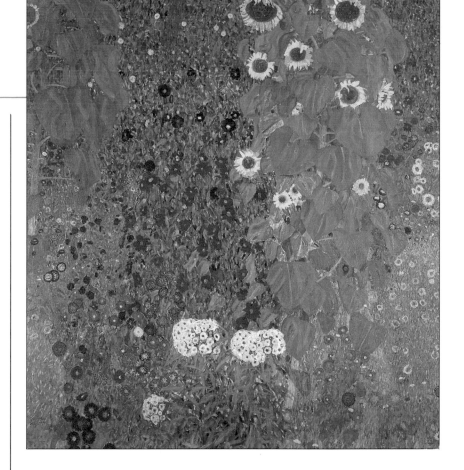

SAMUEL **WESLEY**

(b. Bristol, 24 February 1766; d. London, 11 October 1837)

*E*ngland long showed a tendency, right into the 20th century, to admire foreign composers and musicians, while neglecting many native talents that were every bit as deserving. Such a case was Samuel Wesley, brother of the organist Charles Wesley (1757-1834) and nephew of the founder of Methodism, John Wesley (1703-1791). He studied with his brother and began writing music when he was 11. He was to be described by Dr. William Boyce, with whom he studied, as 'the English Mozart'. He was also a prodigy of the organ and came to be regarded as the finest performer and improviser of his time. At the age of 21 he suffered brain damage as a result of a fall and this made him thereafter somewhat unpredictable in behaviour. He was forced into a marriage of convenience and left his wife and three children after two years. He veered between composing, playing and teaching, with a period in a debtors' prison, but, in spite of all this, became renowned for his championship and editorship of Bach's music. Under the influence of the symphonies of J.C. Bach and Karl Abel, and subsequently of Haydn, who visited London twice in his lifetime, he wrote a series of well-constructed and likeable symphonies, of which five have survived in full score. They stand comparison with all but the best Haydn symphonies. He wrote his last symphony in 1802, composed 11 organ concertos and many other works; and continued his activities as a performer until just before his death in 1837. P.G.

HENRYK **WIENIAWSKI**

(b. Lublin, 10 July 1835; d. Moscow, 31 March 1880)

*H*is mother was a pianist and she took her son, in spite of advice to the contrary, to enter the Paris Conservatoire in 1843. Her faith in his talent was rewarded when he won the first violin prize and graduated when he was still only 11, an unprecedented achievement. He played his first concert in Paris in January 1848 and in St. Petersburg in March. He returned to the Paris Conservatoire for further study in 1849 and again won the first prize in 1850. After this, with his brother as accompanist, he toured Russia in 1851-3 and visited London in 1859. In 1860 he was official violinist to the Czar, taught in St. Petersburg, played in a famous string quartet and toured the USA with Anton Rubinstein in 1872. In 1874 he succeeded Vieuxtemps as Professor of Violin in Brussels. From 1877 he began to suffer from a heart condition which killed him in 1880 at the age of 44. He was considered to be one of the greatest violinists of the 19th century; and added to his reputation by writing a masterful Violin Concerto in D minor in the Hungarian manner, still much played, a Legend for violin and orchestra, and numerous other highly regarded works of a virtuoso nature. P.G.

ERMANNO **WOLF-FERRARI**

(b. Venice, 12 January 1876; d. Venice, 21 January 1948)

*P*art German and part Italian, Wolf-Ferrari was born in Venice, but trained largely in Munich where he was taught by Joseph Rheinberger (1839-1901). Despite this German grounding, and the inevitable Wagnerian influences of the time, his music seems to owe only a certain classical elegance to Germany; his operas are otherwise predominantly Italian in style, and most have Italian subjects. Between 1895 and 1939, he divided his time between teaching in Germany and Venice, and in 1939 took over at the Salzburg Mozarteum. He composed 12 operas during his life, but as his style became unfashionable during the 1930s, he began composing orchestral music, though with no great success. He made his name with his second opera, based on a Goldoni comedy, Le Donne curiose in 1903. This light, classical piece proved successful, and its two better-known successors, I Quattro rusteghi (1906) and Il Segreto di Susanna (1909) are in similar style, with delightful orchestral interludes, which are generally the best-known and most charming parts of his operas. He then surprised his audience with the lurid, melodramatic I Gioielli della Madonna (1911) (also popular for its intermezzi) before reverting to his well-tried formula for further compositions. P.L.

ALEXANDER VON **ZEMLINSKY**

(b. Vienna, 14 October 1871; d. Larchmont, New York, 15 March 1942)

A leading figure in early 20th-century Austrian music as teacher, conductor and composer, Zemlinsky was caught between trends in history and in music. He passed his final years as an exile in the USA, and by then he was also a musical exile, fitting into none of the established schools of the time. He was born in Vienna, and during his formative years there he met Brahms, Schoenberg and Mahler. All three influenced him, but his music most resembled Mahler's with Schoenbergian overtones. As a conductor he occupied leading positions in opera houses in Vienna, Prague and Berlin, but he took every opportunity to promote the music of the Second Viennese School (without composing in their style). In 1933 he was forced by the political situation to leave Berlin successively for Vienna, Prague and the USA. His most successful music, written in the period of 1910-1925, expresses the individual's isolation and anguish in those times, especially in the middle two of his four string quartets (1914 and 1923), and the Lyrische Symphonie on poems of Tagore (1923). He also wrote three (early) symphonies, eight operas – most notably Eine florentinische Tragödie (1916) and Der Zwerg (1921) – and numerous songs. His later music tended towards neoclassicism, and although always well-written lacked the same emotional power. P.L.

ABOVE: 'Garden With Sunflowers' by Gustav Klimt (1862-1918) painted 1905-6. It is an example of the Viennese school of the early 20th century and of the culture that nurtured Zemlinsky.

ABOVE: Ermanno Wolf-Ferrari, an undated photograph probably taken around 1905 when his comic operas were achieving success.

CARL MARIA VON

Weber
(b. Eutin, ?18 November 1786; d. London, 5 June 1826)

The exact date of Weber's birth is uncertain, but he was baptized at his local church on 20 November. At the time, his father Franz Anton was musical director to the Prince-Bishop of Lübeck, but soon afterwards he formed a travelling theatre company with his wife, a singer and actress. Thus the boy formed a passionate interest in the arts, and although he was not strong (he limped slightly) and his education was patchy, it soon became clear that he had exceptional musical talent. He studied with Michael Haydn, the brother of the celebrated composer, wrote his first singspiel (comic opera to German words) at eleven and quickly went on to write others, one of which, called The Forest Maiden, *was performed in Freiberg (Saxony) in November 1800, just after his fourteenth birthday. Early in 1803 his opera* Peter Schmoll and his Neighbours *was given at Augsburg, and he went on to Vienna for further study with the Abbé Vogler. Then, at the precocious age of seventeen, he was appointed court conductor to the city of Breslau, arriving there in June 1804.*

At Breslau's opera house, Weber lost no time in making changes in the repertoire, increasing rehearsal time and dismissing some older singers. Not surprisingly, he met opposition. A curious accident – drinking engraving acid that he mistook for wine – laid him low for two months and his reforms were undone. Resigning in protest, he soon found other work, first at the ducal court of Württemberg (a period which had its ups and downs and ended in 1810 with his temporary arrest for debt), and also established his reputation as a concert pianist.

Finally in 1813, he took up a new post as the director of the Prague Opera, and threw himself enthusiastically into recruiting new artists and improving standards; but at this time he also began to suffer from the tuberculosis which was eventually to kill him. He also embarked on two stormy love affairs, the first with Therese Brunetti and the second with the singer Caroline Brandt, whom he eventually married in Prague on 4 November 1817.

By then he had already left his Prague post and moved on in January 1817 to a similar position at Dresden, where, encouraged by the royal equerry Count Vitzhum, he set about making a centre for German opera. Besides such works as Mozart's operas and Beethoven's *Fidelio* he also staged Spohr's *Jessonda* and, in time, his own *Der Freischütz* and *Euryanthe*. He also added to his catalogue of instrumental pieces, writing in 1819, his 'rondo brillant' for piano solo entitled *Invitation to the Dance*.

In 1823, Weber travelled to Austria for the première of *Euryanthe* on 25 October (he also visited Beethoven), but the opera had only a moderate success. Returning to Dresden, he realized that his health was steadily deteriorating, for his limp was worse and he had a persistent cough. A course of spa treatment the following summer did little good, and when his doctor told him that he must expect a short life, he began putting his affairs in order.

It was with his family's future in mind that he now agreed to write a new opera for Covent Garden in London. This was *Oberon*, with a fanciful libretto that worried him, although he set about composing in 1825. In the face of his wife's anxiety, he left for London early in the following February and reached the city on 4 March. Although increasingly ill during cold and foggy weather, he conducted the successful première of his new opera on 12 April. He arranged to leave London on 6 June, but was found dead in his room on the 5th. His body was buried in London, but in 1844 it was returned to Dresden, where Wagner gave a funeral oration.

RIGHT: *A portrait of Carl Maria von Weber painted by Caroline Bardua (1781-1864). It probably dates from around the time that Weber was composing* Der Freischütz.

BELOW: *Weber's birthplace in Eutin, an engraving of 1850. Weber was born into a musical family; his uncle, Fridolin, was the father of the Weber sisters, one of whom, Constanze, married Mozart.*

Chronology

1786 *Born Eutin, ?18 November*

1798 *Studies with Michael Haydn. Composes Six Fughettas (piano) and first Singspiel (now lost)*

1800 *Das Waldmädchen given at Freiberg*

1803 *Peter Schmoll und seine Nachbarn first performed at Augsburg. Studies with Vogler in Vienna*

1804 *Court conductor at Breslau*

1806-10 *Conducts at Carlsruhe and elsewhere for Duke of Württemberg. Also becomes known as a concert pianist*

1807 *Two symphonies composed for court orchestra*

1811 *At Darmstadt. Concert tour as pianist. Clarinet Concertino and two clarinet concertos composed for Heinrich Baermann. Abu Hassan first given at Munich, June*

More than any other composer, Weber was the founder of German romantic opera, and, as such, the chief forerunner of Wagner, as that composer readily admitted. He was also a major figure in the development of romanticism itself. In this sense, the most Germanic of his mature operas is *Der Freischütz*, for it is set not among the conventional gods, heroes or nobles of most older operas but in an ordinary village where the young forester Max fails in a shooting competition and is persuaded to help the evil Caspar to cast magic bullets with the aid of a demon. The blend of homeliness and supernatural in this tale is extremely powerful. So is the music itself, not least the famous Wolf's Glen scene of the moulding of the bullets, set in a forest with a waterfall, mountain background and storm, where horns, drums and eerie diminished seventh chords all contribute to the sinister atmosphere. Indeed, Weber's skill as a writer for orchestra is one of his greatest assets, and the delicate opening of the Overture to *Oberon* has been likened to a window magically opening on to the enchanted delights of fairyland. No less a master of the orchestra than Debussy went out of his way to praise this famous passage, adding that 'Weber was a master of every known means of conveying the fantastic in music [by] orchestral chemistry'. Weber's other admirers included Schumann and Liszt.

Besides operas and other stage music such as incidental music to several plays, Weber wrote a large number of works in many genre. There are numerous choral works, mostly

ABOVE: *A scene from* Der Freischütz *depicting Caspar and Max in the Wolf's Glen. This is No. 2 of 'Scenes from Der Freischütz', a set of engravings issued in 1830 in Nürnberg.*

secular but including a few that are sacred (there are three settings of the Mass), and many solo songs. There are also two symphonies and concertos for piano, clarinet (two for each of these instruments) and bassoon.

The piano was, of course, Weber's own instrument, and besides his concertos there are also four sonatas and other pieces of which the *Invitation to the Dance* is much the best known, not least because in an orchestral form it is the music for the ballet *Le Spectre de la rose*. Otherwise, this keyboard music, which once seemed central to the piano repertoire, seems during the present century to have lost its hold on performers and the public. This may be partly because of the difficulty of the composer's individual writing for the instrument, reflecting music that he wrote for himself to play. He had a very large hand as well as much dexterity, and was once described as able to draw unusual sounds from the piano, sometimes of 'an almost vocal quality'.

During his short life, Weber also demonstrated other talents. As a writer, he constantly declared his support for a new kind of German opera and, generally, what he perceived to be 'the progressive in art'. C.H.

1813 Becomes director of Prague Opera. Various love affairs and meets future wife, Caroline Brandt

1817 Director at Dresden, sets about creating centre for German opera. Marriage, 4 November

1818 Begins Der Freischütz

1819 Invitation to the Dance (piano)

1821 Konzertstück for piano and orchestra. Der Freischütz first performed in Berlin

1823 Opera Euryanthe first performed in Vienna; also visits Beethoven

1824 Deteriorating health, spa treatment in summer unsuccessful, accepts London (Covent Garden) commission for Oberon

1825 Works on Oberon; second spa treatment in July

1826 Arrives in London in March; conducts Oberon première at Covent Garden; found dead in his room on 5 June

ANTON VON Webern

(b. Vienna, 3 December 1883; d. Mittersill, 15 September 1945)

As the 'von' in his name indicates (though he dropped it later), this Austrian composer came of an aristocratic family, possessing an estate in Carinthia, although his father earned his living as a mining engineer. The Webern family moved in 1894 to Klagenfurt, where Anton attended the Gymnasium, a good quality grammar school. There he learned the violin and cello as well as developing a lifelong interest in Mahler's music, which he studied in piano transcriptions. When he was seventeen he began to compose songs, and when he left school in the following year, his father rewarded him with a trip to the Bayreuth Festival to see Wagner's operas. Karl von Webern was now appointed to a government post in Vienna and, with some reluctance, agreed that his son should read music at Vienna University and aim for a doctorate. There, from 1902 until taking his D. Phil. degree in 1906, the future composer sang in the university choir, studied the usual academic areas of musicology, harmony and counterpoint, and wrote a doctoral thesis on the music of the Flemish renaissance composer Heinrich Isaac (c. 1450-1517).

But he also looked for teaching that might prove more fruitful for his composition, and in 1904, aged twenty, he approached the composer Hans Pfitzner (1869-1949) in Berlin. However, Pfitzner's disdain for Mahler upset him, and he returned to Vienna, where, in the autumn of the same year, he went with some of his songs to Arnold Schoenberg, who then took him on as a pupil. This powerful and magnetic musician was only nine years Webern's senior, but he was an inspired though dominating teacher and the younger man came fully under his spell. Later he was to write a tribute to this mentor who helped him to find his own

musical personality and acquire the compositional techniques to express it. From this period of some four years date several pieces including a sonata movement for piano, a string quartet and his Five Songs to poems by Richard Dehmel, but the work that he regarded as his graduation piece, ending this apprenticeship in 1908, was the Passacaglia for orchestra that he designated as his Op. 1.

Though lacking serious training as a conductor, Webern spent the next twelve years or so as the uneasy holder of various conducting posts in provincial cities of the German-speaking world, principally performing operettas and other light music for which his talents were somewhat unsuited. He married his cousin Wilhelmine Mörtl in 1910, and their first child, Amalie, was born in the following spring; later they had a son and two more daughters, so that he needed to work to support a largish family. However, his fortunes improved after he returned to Vienna in 1918 and settled close to Schoenberg in the suburb of Mödling, near the famous Vienna woods.

In 1921, Universal Edition began to publish his work, and his conducting of the Vienna Workers' Symphony Concerts and Chorus gave him precious opportunities to perform his own music. In 1927 he took on a conducting post for the Austrian Radio which he held until 1938, losing it after the German Anschluss (annexation of Austria). During the war years, he and his family remained in Mödling, except when he travelled to Switzerland in 1943 for the première in Winterthur of his Variations for orchestra, Op. 30. In the final weeks of the war, he and his wife were visiting their daughters near Salzburg when he was caught up in an army arrest and mistakenly shot dead by an American soldier.

Like Schoenberg, Webern frequently saw his music ridiculed, as when the critic of the *New York Times*, Olin Downes, declared in 1929 that his recently completed Symphony, Op.21, was 'one of those whispering, clucking, picking little pieces which Webern composes when he whittles away at small and futile ideas, until he has achieved the perfect fruition of futility and written precisely nothing . . . The yells of laughter that came from all over the hall nearly drowned the sounds of Webern's whimpering orchestra'. Another critic who attended the same concert wrote in a similar vein, ending, 'At least the work had von Webern's cardinal merit of brevity'.

Yet a decade after this composer's death, young composers revered him as a prophet of the musical future superior even to Schoenberg, and Pierre Boulez summed up their admiration by calling him, and more specifically his later works such as the Symphony and the orchestral Variations. 'THE threshold'. They learned most, perhaps, from what has been called Webern's 'concentration on minutiae' and his foreshadowing of styles 'in which each note was separately composed'. For these musicians of Boulez's generation, coming to terms with Webern's highly individual music may have presented few if any problems. But the fact remains that after fifty years his work, though much respected, has not become popular in the way that other challenging music of his time – such as the major works of Stravinsky and Bartók – has done.

To enjoy Webern, and above all to appreciate his art, it helps to understand the kind of music that he aimed to create. Although a lifelong follower of Schoenberg's serial methods,

ABOVE: *A sample of the work of Webern as seen in a manuscript score. The precision of the musical notation is very evident; it was characteristic of Webern's musical personality.*

and arguably more faithful to them than Schoenberg himself, he was far from being a mere intellectual speculator or theoretician. From childhood, when he and his cousin Ernst took mountain walks and collected plants and minerals, he adored Nature and books of pressed flowers remained among his most cherished possessions. He declared that 'no essential difference prevails between the products of nature and those of art', and sought for a musical equivalent to the forms of natural objects like flowers and crystals, writing beside a manuscript musical sketch in 1928 of 'snow and ice, crystal clear air, cosy, warm, sphere of the high pastures – coolness of the first spring'.

Looked at in this light, Webern is fundamentally a Romantic, as his much richer early music (up to the String Trio of 1927) shows; indeed, his Piano Quintet is somewhat Brahmsian. But as always with art, the 'proof of the pudding'

ABOVE: 'Park Near Lu', a 1938 painting by Paul Klee (1879-1940) which shares the same sparse qualities and a delight in the symmetry evident in nature that Webern's music expresses.

lies in his music rather than the thought that lay behind it. We can perhaps agree with the critic who called Webern's Concerto for Nine Instruments (1934) 'a twentieth-century Brandenburg [Concerto]', and the composer's own linking of his Second Cantata (1943) to 'a Renaissance mass' if we think of these works principally as his use of 'structural models from the past'. But no persuasion convinces us of a musical resemblance between his mature idiom and the works of Bach or other earlier musicians, and he must be approached in his own individual terms.   C.H.

HUGO Wolf

(b. Windischgraz, Styria, 13 March 1860; d. Vienna, 22 February 1903)

RIGHT: Hugo Wolf, a portrait by Ludwig Nauer. It shows Wolf at about the time of his creative peak, before his final illness took hold.

olf's birthplace, now called Slovenj Gradec, lied to the north-east of the Slovenian capital Ljubljana, but although his mother was partly of Slovene origin, his father was German. Philipp Wolf owned a leathermaking business, but he was also musical, had taught himself to play several instruments, and gave his son his first piano and violin lessons. From 1865 to 1869 the boy attended a local school and his piano teacher there, Sebastian Weixler, also gave him theory lessons. At eight he was deeply impressed on seeing his first opera (Donizetti's Belisario) and at around this time Philipp Wolf formed a five-piece household ensemble in which the future composer played second violin. Unfortunately, this gifted boy also had a difficult temperament, which may have been exacerbated by the misfortune that occurred in 1867 when his father's business was destroyed in a fire, reducing the prosperous household to a poorer one. In September 1870 he entered a secondary school at Graz, but although his musical talent was noticed, he was expelled after only a term with a report reading 'entirely unsatisfactory'. He then spent two years at a church school, where he played the violin and organ at services and began to compose, but again he disappointed in school work.

Wolf was now fifteen, and showing a passion for music that was matched by a contempt for all other study, and it was agreed that he should go to Vienna to lodge with an aunt and attend the Vienna Conservatory. He developed an enthusiasm for Wagner's music and managed to meet the great composer when he visited the city in November. His studies included the piano with Wilhelm Schenner and composition with Robert Fuchs and later Franz Krenn, and he also made friends with his fellow student Gustav Mahler. But even here, he again clashed with authority, in the person of the Conservatory's director.

In November 1877, aged seventeen, Wolf was back in Vienna with a view to earning his living as a private teacher, but although he acquired some pupils he showed little patience with them or aptitude for teaching. In 1878, his composer friend Adalbert von Goldschmidt took him to a brothel and here he probably caught the disease, syphilis, which caused his eventual insanity and death. However, he formed an attachment at this time to a woman called Vally Franck, and later he acquired a lover, Frau Melanie Köchert. For several years he struggled along, unsuccessful and unfulfilled, and although Goldschmidt got him a conducting post at Salzburg in 1881, he soon quarrelled with his superiors and returned to Vienna. Uncertainties also plagued his composing (he began and

Chronology

1860 Hugo Filipp Jakob Wolf born Windischgraz, 13 March

1865 At local primary school, taught piano and theory by Weixler

1870 Goes to secondary school in Graz, September

1871 Leaves with poor report; enters Benedictine school of St. Paul

1873 Leaves St. Paul to enter school at Marburg (Maribor)

1875 Composes first songs; incomplete Violin Concerto; incomplete Piano Sonata; set of piano Variations, Op. 2. Again leaves school after poor work; enters Vienna Conservatory, September; meets Wagner and receives encouragement, November

1876 Die Stimme des Kindes for voices and piano. At Conservatory, studies with Schenner (piano), Fuchs and Krenn; makes friends with Mahler

1877 Expelled from Conservatory. Works on opera (fragments only) called König Alboin. Returns to Vienna in November

RIGHT: 'Spring', a painting by Jean François Millet (1814–75) which shows the sort of scene that inspired Wolf, as, for example, in his setting of Mörike's poem 'In Spring'.

then abandoned no less than three symphonies in 1876-9) in all fields except that of song, for he had already composed many Lieder. But even here he was hurt when he showed some songs to Brahms in 1879 and was advised to take lessons in counterpoint.

In May 1887, Wolf's father died, and he regretted that 'for him my music never sounded'. Yet almost at once his fortunes improved when a publisher took twelve of his songs later in the year: his mood changed to one of buoyancy and he entered a creative period in which he himself hardly dared believe. In February 1888 he borrowed a house near the Vienna woods and in three months produced over forty settings of Mörike's poems; more songs soon followed to words by Eichendorff and Goethe, and by November 1890 this period had yielded over a hundred and seventy songs.

Apart from songs, the 1890s also saw the composition of Wolf's Italian Serenade and the opera Der Corregidor, which was staged at Mannheim in 1896. He was now as happy as at any time in his life, although he still had depression and once told a friend. 'I could as soon start speaking Chinese as compose anything'. But in September 1897 his mind began to give way and he was taken to a Viennese private asylum. A remission occurred, and he was released in January 1898, but in October, while staying with the family of Melanie Köchert, he attempted suicide and entered another asylum where he died on 22 February 1903. Melanie remained a steadfast friend who visited him in these years; three years after his death she threw herself from a fourth floor window of her home in Vienna.

LEFT: 'Heine and his Wife' painted by Ernst Kietz (1815-92). Heinrich Heine's poetry, with its lyrical simplicity, was much favoured by songwriters like Wolf.

The scholar Eric Sams has pointed out that Wolf dedicated all his songs to Melanie, as 'the one who understood him and his music best of all'. More than with most composers, his work was inseparable from his personality. When in his most exalted state, in the immensely rich period of 1888 to 1890, he was probably not strictly of sound mind as doctors today might define it, and he wrote, 'this state of inspiration is more a delicious torment to me than an unalloyed pleasure . . . Am I called, or perhaps even chosen?'. After he was medically declared insane, he still tried to write music, including another opera called *Manuel Venegas* of which he completed a few scenes, but produced nothing worthy to stand beside his other work.

Compared with Schubert's songs, with Schumann's and even those of Brahms, which are often in a strophic form in which each stanza of a poem has the same music, Wolf's are commonly more through-composed, with new music to fresh words as they progress. Before him, most German songs have shapely melodies designed for repetition, although there are occasional examples of something different, such as Schubert's sombre Heine setting 'Der Doppelgänger'. But Wolf frequently adopts freer methods which are often dramatic in a way reminding us of opera, and not least Wagner's operas. Indeed, in his own time, Wolf was called 'the Wagner of song'. But the keenness of his psychological insight, which was evident as much in the choice of poems as in his treatment of them, gives his songs a quality of concentration that is unlike anything in Wagner or in his fellow songwriters, with the exception of Mahler, with whom he has more in common than with any other composer. However, Mahler's liking for the epic and grandiose (shared, of course, by Wagner, and German in nature rather than Austrian) has little place in Wolf's make-up, and in this connection we remember his symphonies attempted and abandoned. Though the *Italian Serenade* is a successful piece, Wolf was first and foremost a songwriter. At his best, he is the most sophisticated master of the German art song or Lied, and singers and pianists performing his music need sensitivity as well as artistic rapport.   C.H.

1878 Earns some living from teaching during the next few years. Acquires ultimately fatal form of syphilis. In love with Vally Franck; composes many songs

1879 Meets Melanie Köchert, later his mistress and faithful friend

1881 Teaching Frau Köchert, and their friendship deepens

1882 Writes in his diary of a 'terrible moral hangover'

1883 Meets Liszt, who advises composition of larger works

1884-7 Music critic of 'Wiener Salonblatt'

1885 Symphonic poem Penthesilea completed

1887 Publishing firm of Wetzler accepts twelve of Wolf's songs

1888 Exceptional creative period begins. First public performance of a Wolf song, March; Ferdinand Jäger and Wolf perform together for the first time, with success, 15 December

1890 Completes Spanisches Liederbuch (44 songs)

1891 Completes Italianisches Liederbuch, Vol. 1 (22 songs)

1892 Recital of his music in Berlin, 3 March

1895 Opera Der Corregidor completed

1896 Italianisches Liederbuch, Vol. 2 (24 songs); Der Corregidor produced at Mannheim, June

1897 Wolf's sanity begins to fail, suffers delusions in September; enters private asylum of Dr. Wilhelm Svetlin

1898 Remission and release, but final collapse in October and enters Lower Austrian Provincial Asylum in Vienna

1903 Dies, 22 February, and is buried in Vienna Central Cemetery near Beethoven and Schubert

Recommended recordings

Note: All the recordings in this list are issued on Compact Disc. Items marked with an asterisk (*) are particularly recommended as outstanding recordings. A dagger mark (†) indicates that the music by another composer with which the entry is coupled is itself also a recommendation. Items marked ‡ may not be currently available in the U.S.A., but should be obtainable by mail order.

Albeniz *(page 6)*
- Guitar music (*Cantos de España,* etc) – J. Bream – RCA RCD14378
- Piano music (*Suite española,* etc) – A. de Larrocha – Decca 417 887

Albinoni *(page 7)*
- Adagio (Baroque concert) – I Musici – Philips 410 606
- Concerti a cinque, Op. 5 – I Musici – Philips 422 251

Arne *(page 7)*
- Keyboard concertos 1-6 – Williams/Cantilena – Chandos CHAN8604/5
- Vocal music – Kirkby/etc/Goodman – Hyperion CDA 66237

Arnold *(page 7)*
- Symphonies 2 and 5, etc – Groves – Angel CDM7 63368
- Symphony 6 / *John Field* Fantasy / etc – Handley – Conifer CDCF224
- *English, Cornish and Scottish dances*/etc – Arnold – Lyrita SRCD201

Arriaga *(page 12)*
- ‡ Symphony in D / Overture – Arambari – GME GME225
- String quartets 1-3 – Chilingirian Qt – CRD CRD33123 (2)

Bach, C. P. E. *(page 12)*
- Double concertos – Koopman / Mathot – Erato 2292 45306
- Hamburg sinfonias – Pinnock – DG 415 300

Bach, J. C. *(page 12)*
- ‡ Symphonies – Montgomery – Classics for Pleasure CD-CFP4550
- Quintets – English Concert – DG 423 385

Bach, J. S. *(pages 8-11)*
- *Brandenburg* concertos 1-6 – Marriner – Philips 400 076/7
- Harpsichord concertos – Leppard/etc – Philips 422 497/426 084/426 488
- Violin concertos/etc – Grumiaux/etc/De Waart – Philips 420 700
- Orchestral suites – Koopman – DHM 7864-2-RC (2)
- Unaccompanied cello suites – Schiff – Angel CDS7 47471 (2)
- Organ music – Hurford – Decca 417 711
- Cantatas – Ansermet – Decca 433 175
- Mass in B Minor – Gardiner – DG 415 514 (2)
- *St. John Passion* – Gardiner – DG 419 324 (2)
- *St. Matthew Passion* – Münchinger – Decca 414 057 (3)

Balakirev *(page 12)*
- Symphony 1 / *Tamara* – Beecham – Angel CDM7 63375

Barber *(page 13)*
- Adagio/Essays/*School for Scandal* – Slatkin – Angel CDC7 49463

Bartók *(pages 14-15)*
- Concerto for Orchestra / 4 Orchestral Pieces – Boulez – DG 437 826
- Piano concertos 1-3 – Kocsis / Fischer – Philips 416 831 (3)
- Violin concerto / [Berg] – Chung / Solti – Decca 425 015 †
- String quartets 1-6 – Emerson Qt – DG 423 657 (2)
- *Bluebeard's Castle* – Fischer – Sony MK44523

Bax *(page 13)*
- *The Garden of Fand*/etc – Thomson – Chandos CHAN8307
- Symphony 4 / *Tintagel* – Thomson – Chandos CHAN8312

Beethoven *(pages 16-19)*
- Symphonies 1-9 – Harnoncourt – Teldec 2292 46452 (5) [also separately]
- Piano concertos 1-5 – Perahia/Haitink – Sony M3K44575 (3)
- Violin concerto / Romances – Perlman/Barenboim – Angel CDC7 49567
- Piano trios 1-3, 5-7, 9-10 – Du Pré/Barenboim/Zukerman – Angel CDMC 63124 (3)
- ‡ Piano trio 7 'Archduke'/[Schubert] – Beaux Arts – Philips 438 308 †
- String quartets 1-16 – Vegh Qt – Valois V4400 (8)
- Piano sonatas 1-32 – Kempf – DG 429 306 (9)
- * *Fidelio* – Klemperer – Angel CDMB 69324 (2)
- *Missa solemnis* – Gardiner – Archiv 429 779 (2)

Bellini *(pages 20-21)*
- *Norma* – Sutherland / Bonynge – Decca 425 488 (3)
- *La Sonnambula* – Sutherland / Bonynge – Decca 417 424 (3)

Berg *(pages 22-23)*
- Violin concerto / [Bartók] – Chung / Solti – Decca 425 015 †
- *Lulu* – Stratas / Boulez – DG 415 489 (3)
- *Wozzeck* – Waechter / Dohnányi – Decca 417 348 (2)

Berkeley *(page 13)*
- Serenade / Divertimento / etc – Berkeley – Lyrita SRCD226
- Piano music – Headington – Kingdom KCLCD2012

Berlioz *(pages 24-25)*
- Overtures – Davis – Philips 416 430
- *Symphonie fantastique* – Davis – Philips 411 425
- *La Damnation de Faust* – Davis – Philips 416 395 (2)
- *Roméo et Juliette/Symphonie funèbre et triomphale* – Dutoit – Decca 417 302 (2)
- * *Les Nuits d'été* / Songs – Gardiner – Erato 22920 45517
- * *Les Troyens* – Davis – Philips 416 432 (4)
- Requiem – Bernstein – Sony MZK47526 (2)

Bernstein *(page 28)*
- *Candide* – Bernstein – DG 429 734 (2)
- *Chichester Psalms* / Symphonies 1-3 – Bernstein – Sony SM3K47162 (3)

Berwald *(page 28)*
- Symphonies 1-4 – Järvi – DG 415 502 (2)

Bizet *(pages 26-27)*
- * Symphony in C / *L'Arlésienne* – Beecham – Angel CDC7 47794
- *Carmen* – Baltsa / Karajan – DG 410 088 (3)
- ‡ *La jolie fille de Perth* – suite – / *L'Arlésienne* – suites / etc – Munch / Ansermet – Decca 421 632

Bliss *(page 28)*
- *Colour* symphony / *Checkmate* – Handley – Chandos CHAN8503
- String quartets 1 and 2 – Delmé Qt – Hyperion CDA66178

Bloch *(page 28)*
- *Schelomo* / [Bruch] – Harnoy / Mackerras – RCA RD60757

Boccherini *(page 29)*
- String quintets – Berlin Philharmonic Ensemble – Denon CO2199

Borodin *(pages 30-31)*
- Symphony 2 / *In the Steppes of Central Asia* – Tjeknavorian – RCA 60535-2-RV
- String Quartets 1 and 2 – Borodin Qt – Angel CDC7 47795
- *Prince Igor* – Ghiaurov / Tchakarov – Sony S3K44878 (3)

Boyce *(page 29)*
- Symphonies 1-8 – Thomas – CRD CRD3356

Brahms *(pages 32-35)*
- Symphonies 1-4 – Wand – RCA 60085-RG (3)
- Piano concertos / Fantasias – Gilels/Jochum – DG 419 158 (2)
- Violin concerto / [Beethoven] – Heifetz / Reiner – RCA RCD1 5402
- Violin and cello concerto – Stern/Ma/Abbado – Sony MK42387
- Hungarian dances 1-21 – Masur – Philips 411 426
- Clarinet quintet/trio – King/Gabrieli Qt – Hyperion CDA66107
- String sextets 1 and 2 – Raphael Ensemble – Hyperion CDA66276
- Violin sonatas 1-3 – Suk/Katchen – Decca 421 092
- Piano music, Ops.116-9/etc – Kovacevich – Philips 411 137 / 420 750 (6)
- Vier ernste Gesänge / Lieder – Hotter/Moore – Angel CDH7 63198
- German Requiem – Klemperer – Angel CDC7 47238

Brian *(page 29)*
- Symphony 1 'Gothic' – Lenárd – Marco Polo 8 223280/1 (2)

Bridge *(page 42)*
- Suite/Summer/There is a willow/[*Bantock/Butterworth*] – Del Mar – Chandos CHAN8373

Britten *(pages 36-37)*
- Bridge variations / [*Butterworth*] – Marriner – Philips 421 391
- *Les Illuminations* / Serenade – Pears/Tuckwell/Britten – Decca 417 153
- ‡ *The Golden Vanity* / *Noye's Fludde* – Del Mar – Decca 425 161
- *St. Nicholas* / *Hymn to St. Cecilia* – Best – Hyperion CDA66333
- * *War Requiem* – Britten – Decca 414 383 (2)
- *Albert Herring* – Britten – Decca 421 849 (2)
- *Billy Budd* / songs – Britten – Decca 417 428 (3)
- *A Midsummer Night's Dream* – Britten – Decca 425 663 (2)
- * ‡*Paul Bunyan* – Brunelle – Virgin VCD7 90710 (2)
- * *Peter Grimes* – Britten – Decca 414 577 (2)

Bruch *(pages 38-39)*
- Violin concerto 1 / *Scottish Fantasy* – Lin / Slatkin – Sony MK42315
- *Kol Nidrei* / [*Lalo; Saint Saëns*] – Haimovitz / Levine – DG 427 323

Bruckner *(pages 40-41)*
- Symphonies 1-9 – Karajan – DG 429 648 (9)
- Symphony 4 – Jochum – DG 427 200
- Symphony 8 – Karajan – DG 427 611
- Symphony 9 – Walter – Sony MYK44825
- Masses / Motets – Jochum – DG 423 127 (4)

Busoni *(page 42)*
- Piano concerto – Donohoe / Elder – Angel CDC7 49996
- *Doktor Faust* – Leitner – DG 427 413 (3)

Butterworth *(page 42)*
- *Banks of green willow* / *Shropshire Lad* /etc – Marriner – Decca 421 391

Byrd *(page 42)*
- ‡ Great Service – Cleobury – Angel CDC7 47771
- Masses – Willcocks – Decca 433 675 (2)

Canteloube *(page 43)*
- * ‡*Songs of the Auvergne* – Davrath – Vanguard OVC 8001/2 (2)

Carter *(page 43)*
- Piano concerto / Variations – Oppens/Gielen – New World NWCD347

Castelnuovo-Tedesco *(page 43)*
- ‡ Guitar concerto / [*Concert*] – Yepes / Navarro – DG 413 156

Chabrier *(page 50)*
- Orchestral works – Paray – Philips 434 303
- * *L'Etoile* – Gardiner – Angel CDC7 47889 (2)

Charpentier *(page 50)*
- *Le Malade imaginaire* – Minkowski – Erato 2292 45002
- ‡ Midnight Mass / Te Deum – Willcocks / Ledger – EMI CDM7 63135
- * *Medée* – Christie – Harmonia Mundi – HMC901139/41 (3)

Chausson *(page 50)*
- Poème / [*Sarasate*/etc] – Perlman / Mehta – DG 423 063
- Symphony in B Flat etc – Serebrier – Chandos CHAN8369

Cherubini *(page 50)*
- String Quartets 1-8 – Melos Qt – DG 429 185 (3) (nas)
- *Medea* – Gardelli – Hungaroton HCD11904/5

Chopin *(pages 44-45)*
- Piano concertos 1 and 2 – Zimerman/Giulini – DG 415 970
- Ballades 1-4 – Rubinstein – RCA RCD1 7156
- Etudes – Ashkenazy – Decca 414 127
- Mazurkas – Rubinstein – RCA 5614-2-RC (2)
- * Nocturnes 1-19 – Rubinstein – RCA 5613-2-RC (2)
- Piano sonatas 2 and 3 – Perahia – Sony MK37280
- Polonaises – Rubinstein – RCA 5615-2-RC
- 24 Preludes / Impromptus – Ashkenazy – Decca 417 476
- Waltzes 1-19 – Ashkenazy – Decca 414 600

Cimarosa *(page 51)*
- *Il Maestro di Capella* / [*Telemann*] – Pál – Hungaroton HCD12573

Clementi *(page 51)*
- Symphonies – D'Avalos – ASV CDDCA802 (B flat and D flat); 803 – 1 and 3; 804 – 2 and 4
- Piano sonatas – Van Immerseel – Accent ACC67911

Copland *(pages 46-47)*
- *Appalachian Spring* (original)/*Billy the Kid*/etc – Copland – Sony MK42431
- Clarinet Concerto / etc – Goodman/Copland – Sony MK42227
- Symphony 3 / *Quiet City* – Bernstein – DG 419 170
- *The Tender Land* – Brunelle – Virgin VCD791113 (2)

Corelli *(page 51)*
- Concerti grossi 1-12 – Pinnock – DG 423 626 (2)

Couperin *(pages 48-49)*
- *L'Apothéose de Corelli*/*L'Apothéose de Lully* – Gardiner – Erato 2292 45011
- Concerts royaux – Trio Sonnerie – ASV CDGAU101
- Harpsichord suites – Gilbert – Harmonia Mundi HMA190351/3 4/6 7/8 9/10

Debussy *(pages 52-53)*
- *Images* / *Iberia* – Reiner – RCA 60179-RG
- *Jeux* /*La Mer* /*Prélude à l'après-midi d'une faune* – Baudo – Angel CDM62012
- String quartet in G minor / [*Ravel*] – Italian Qt – Philips 420 894
- Piano music – Vasary – DG 429 517
- Préludes – Gieseking – Angel (M)CDCC 61004
- *Pelléas et Mélisande* – Karajan – Angel CDS7 49350 (3)

Delibes *(page 60)*
- *Coppélia* / *Sylvia* – suites – Ormandy – Sony SBK46550
- ‡ *Lakmé* – Bonynge – Decca 425 485 (2)

Delius *(pages 54-55)*
- * Orchestral works – Beecham – Angel CDS7 47509 (2)
- ‡ Cello concerto / Double concerto – Mackerras/etc – EMI CD-EMX2185
- *Florida* suite / *North Country Sketches* – Handley – Chandos CHAN8413
- String quartet / [*Elgar*] – Brodsky Qt – ASV CDDCA526
- Vocal music – Fenby – Unicorn DKPCD9008 & DKPCD9009

Dohnányi *(page 60)*
- *Variations on a Nursery Theme* / [*Tchaikovsky*] – Schiff / Solti – Decca 417 294

Donizetti *(pages 56-57)*
- *Anna Bolena* – Bonynge – Decca 421 096 (3)
- *Don Pasquale* – Muti – Angel CDCB 47068 (2)
- *L'Elisir d'amore* – Bonynge – Decca 414 461 (2)
- * *La Fille du régiment* – Bonynge – Decca 414 520 (2)
- *Lucia di Lammermoor* – Bonynge – Decca 410 193 (2)
- *Maria Stuarda* – Bonynge – Decca 425 410 (2)

Dukas *(page 60)*
- *The Sorcerer's Apprentice* / *La Péri* / [*Chabrier*] – Tortelier – Chandos CHAN8852

Duparc *(page 60)*
- *Mélodies* – Walker / Allen / Vignoles – Hyperion CDA66323

Dvořák *(pages 58-59)*
- * Cello concerto / [*Tchaikovsky*] – Rostropovich/Karajan – DG 413 819 †
- Violin concerto/ [*Suk*] – Suk/Ancerl – Supraphon 110601
- Serenades – Schneider – ASV CDCOE801
- Slavonic dances – Kubelik – DG 419 056
- Symphonies 1-9 – Järvi – Chandos CHAN9008/13 (6)
- Piano quartets – Domus – Hyperion CDA66287
- * ‡Piano quintet / [*Franck*] – Curzon/VPO – Decca 421 153 †
- *Rusalka* – Neumann – Supraphon 10 3641-2 (3)

Elgar *(pages 62-65)*
- * Cello concerto / *Sea Pictures* – Du Pré/Baker/Barbirolli – Angel CDC7 47329
- Violin concerto – Chung / Solti – Decca 421 388
- Elegy / Introduction and allegro / etc – Marriner – Decca 421 384
- * ‡ *Falstaff* / *Enigma* Variations – Barbirolli – Angel CDM7 69185
- Symphonies 1 and 2 / etc – Boult – Angel CMS7 63099 (3)
- ‡ Piano quintet / String quartet – Chilingirian Qt – Angel CDC7 47661
- *The Dream of Gerontius* – Hickox – Chandos CHAN8641 / 2
- *The Kingdom* – Hickox – Chandos CHAN8788/9
- Partsongs – Hunt – Hyperion CDA66272/2
- *The Starlight Express* (exc)/ etc – Mackerras – Argo 433 214
- NB: Elgar's own recordings of many of his works are also available and (in spite of their age) should be sampled

Falla *(pages 66-67)*
- *El Amor brujo* /*The Three-Cornered Hat* – Dutoit – Decca 410 008
- *Nights in the Gardens of Spain* /etc – Larrocha/De Burgos – Decca 433 908 (2)
- *La Vida breve* – De Burgos – Angel CDM7 69590

Fauré *(pages 68-69)*
- ‡ *Masques et bergamasques* / *Pelléas et Mélisande* / etc – Plasson – Angel CDC7 47938/9 (2)
- Piano quartets – Domus – Hyperion CDA66166
- Violin sonatas – Grumiaux / Crossley – Philips 426 384
- Piano music – Rogé – Decca 425 606
- Vocal music – Baker / Parsons – Hyperion CDA66320
- Requiem / etc – Rutter – Collegium COLCD109

Field *(page 61)*
- Nocturnes – O'Rourke – Chandos CHAN8719/20

Finzi *(page 61)*
- Clarinet concerto / *Dies Natalis* / *Farewell to arms* – Hickox – Virgin VC 790718
- Hardy Songs – Hill/Varcoe/Benson – Hyperion CDA6616 / 2
- *Let Us Garlands Bring* (orch)/[*English Songs*] – Hickox – Chandos CHAN8743

Franck *(pages 70-71)*
- Symphonic variations / Symphony in D / etc – Plasson – Angel CDC7 63889
- ‡ Piano quintet / [*Dvořák*]- Curzon / VPO Qt – Decca 421 153 †
- Violin sonata / [*Debussy/Ravel*] – Mintz / Bronfman – DG 415 683

Gershwin *(pages 72-73)*
- *An American in Paris* / *Rhapsody in Blue* – Thomas – Sony MK42240
- * *Girl Crazy* – Mauceri – Nonesuch 7559-79250
- * *Porgy and Bess* – Maazel – Decca 414 559 (3)

Glass *(page 61)*
- Dance pieces / etc – Riesman – Sony MK44765
- *Einstein on the Beach* – Riesman – Sony M4K38875 (4)

Glazunov *(page 74)*
- Violin concerto / *The Seasons* – Shumsky – Chandos CHAN8596

Glinka *(page 74)*
- *Ruslan and Ludmilla* / [*Prokofiev*] – Reiner – RCA 60176-RG

Gluck *(page 74)*
- ‡ Opera arias – Baker/Leppard – Philips 422 950

Goldmark *(page 74)*
- *Rustic Wedding* / *Sakuntala* – Butt – ASV CDDCA791

Górecki *(page 75)*
- Symphony 3 – Zinman – Elektra Nonesuch 7559 79282

Gottschalk *(page 75)*
- Piano music – Martin – Hyperion CDA66459

Gounod *(pages 76-77)*
- *Faust* – Davis – Philips 420 164 (3)
- *Messe solenelle* – Prêtre – Angel CDC7 47094

Granados *(page 75)*
- Guitar music – Bream – RCA RCD14378
- *Danzas españolas* – Larrocha – Decca 433 923 (2)
- *Goyescas* – Larrocha – Decca 433 920 (2)

Grieg *(pages 78-79)*
- Piano concerto / [*Schumann*] – Perahia / Davis – Sony MK44899
- *Holberg* suite / etc – Marriner – Philips 412 727
- *Peer Gynt* – Dreier – Unicorn UKCD2003/4
- Lyric pieces – Gilels – DG 419 749
- Songs – Von Otter / Forsberg – DG 437 521

Handel *(pages 80-83)*
- * ‡*Love in Bath* / suites / etc – Beecham – Angel CDM7 63374
- 12 Concerti grossi Op. 6 – Brown – Philips 410 048 (3)
- *Royal Fireworks* / Anthems – King – Hyperion CDA66350
- *Water Music* – Malcolm – ASV CDDCA520
- *Acis and Galatea* / Cantata – King – Hyperion CDA66361/2
- * *L'Allegro, il Penseroso ed il Moderato* – Gardiner – Erato 2292 45377
- *Joshua* – King – Hyperion CDA66461/2 (2)
- *Messiah* – Parrott – Angel CDS7 49801 (2) [modern version]
- *Messiah* – Davis – Philips 420 865 (2) [traditional version]
- * *Solomon* – Gardiner – Philips 412 612 (2)

Harty *(page 90)*
- *Irish* Symphony / Comedy Overture – Thomson – Chandos CHAN83414

Haydn *(pages 84-87)*
- Cello concertos – Schiff/Marriner – Philips 420 923
- Symphonies 93-104 – Davis – Philips 432 286 (4)
- Symphonies 93-104 – Beecham – Angel CMS7 64066 (2) / 64389 (2)

‡ String quartets 17, 63 and 76 – Italian Qt – Philips 426 097
String quartets 50-56/etc – Kodaly Qt – Naxos 8.550346
Piano trios 24-27 – Beaux Arts Trio – Philips 422 831
The Creation – Marriner – Philips 416 449 (2)
Nelson Mass (No. 11) / *Te Deum* – Pinnock – DG 423 097
The Seasons – Marriner – Philips 411 428 (2)

Hindemith *(page 90)*
Mathis der Maler / etc – Blomstedt – Decca 421 523

Holst *(pages 88-89)*
‡ *Egdon Heath* / *Brook Green* / *The Perfect Fool* / etc – Bedford/Previn – Angel CDC7 49784
The Planets – Dutoit – Decca 417 553
The Hymn of Jesus / [*Elgar*] – Boult – Decca 421 381 (2)
Savitri / *Dream City* – Hickox – Hyperion CDA66099

Honegger *(page 90)*
Symphonies 2 and 3 – Karajan – DG 423 242

Howells *(page 90)*
Hymnus Paradisi / [*Concert*] – Handley – Hyperion 66488

Hummel *(page 91)*
Piano concertos, Op.85 and 89 – Hough/Thomson – Chandos CHAN8507
Trumpet concerto / [*Haydn/Hertel/Stamitz*] – Hardenberger/Marriner – Philips 420 203

Humperdinck *(page 91)*
Hänsel und Gretel – Pritchard – Sony M2K 35898 (2)

Ireland *(page 91)*
Piano concerto / *Legend* / *Mai-Dun* – Parkin/Thomson – Chandos CHAN8461

Ives *(pages 92-93)*
Symphony 2 / *Central Park in the Dark* / etc – Bernstein – DG 429 220
Symphony 3 / Orchestral Set 2 – Thomas – Sony MK37823
Songs – Alexander / Crone – Etcetera KTC1020
Three Places in New England / etc – Hanson – Mercury 432 755

Janáček *(pages 94-95)*
Sinfonietta / *Taras Bulba* – Mackerras – Decca 430 727
Piano music – Firkusny – RCA 60147-RC
The Cunning Little Vixen – Mackerras – Decca 417 129 (2)
* *Jenůfa* – Mackerras – Decca 414 483 (2)
Glagolitic Mass / Sinfonietta – Kempe – Decca 425 624

Khachaturian *(page 100)*
Piano concerto/ *Gayaneh* / *Masquerade* Suites – Orbelian/Järvi – Chandos 8542

Kodály *(page 100)*
Háry János suite / *Dances of Galanta* / [*Bartók*] – Schwarz – Delos DE3083

Lalo *(page 100)*
Symphonie espagnole / [*Saint-Saëns*] – Perlman / Barenboim – DG 429 977
Cello concerto / [*Saint-Saëns*] – Ma / Maazel – Sony MK35848

Lambert *(page 100)*
The Rio Grande / etc – Lloyd-Jones – Hyperion CDA66565

Leoncavallo *(pages 96-97)*
I Pagliacci / [*Mascagni*] – Karajan – DG 419 257 (3) †

Liszt *(pages 98-99)*
* Piano concertos 1 and 2 – Richter / Kondrashin – Philips 412 006
Faust Symphony – Beecham – Angel CM7 63371
Totentanz / Fantasia / etc – Bolet / Fischer – Decca 430 726
Piano music – Bolet – Decca 410 257
Etudes – Arrau – Philips 416 458
Hungarian Rhapsodies – Szidon – DG 423 925 (2)
Piano sonata / etc – Pletnev – Olympia OCD172

Lloyd *(page 101)*
Symphonies 2 and 9 – Albany TROY055

Lully *(page 101)*
Le Bourgeois gentilhomme/[*Campra*] – Leonhardt – Harmonia Mundi 77059-RG (2)

Lutoslawski *(page 101)*
‡ Concerto for Orchestra / [*Bartók*] – Dohnányi – Decca 425 694

MacDowell *(page 112)*
Piano concertos 1 and 2 – Amato / Freeman – Olympia OCD353

Mahler *(pages 112-113)*
Symphonies 1 and 2 – Walter – Sony M2YK45674 (2)
Symphony 4 / Lieder – Szell – Sony SBK46535
Symphony 5 – Barbirolli – Angel CDM7 69186
Symphony 8 – Tennstedt – Angel CDS7 47625 (2)
Symphony 9 / *Kindertotenlieder* – Haitink – Philips 416 466 (2)
Das Lied von der Erde – Klemperer – Angel CDC7 47231
Song cycles – Baker/Barbirolli – Angel CDC7 47793

Martin *(page 112)*
Le Vin herbé – Desarzens – Jacklin Disco JD581/2
Requiem – Martinů – Jacklin Disco JD631

Martinů *(page 112)*
Symphonies 2 and 6 – Thomson – Chandos CHAN8916
Nonet / [*Spohr*] – Berlin Ensemble – DG 427 640 †

Mascagni *(pages 104-105)*
Cavalleria rusticana / [*Leoncavallo*] – Karajan – DG 419 257 (3) †

Massenet *(pages 106-107)*
Cendrillon – Rudel – Sony M2K 35194 (2)
Chérubin – Steinberg – RCA 09026 60593 (2)
Don Quichotte / Scenes – Kord – Decca 430 636 (2)
Le Roi de Lahore – Bonynge – Decca 433 851 (2)
Werther – Davis – Philips 416 654 (2)

Maxwell Davies *(page 112)*
Violin concerto – Stern / Previn – Sony MK42449
An Orkney Wedding / etc – Maxwell Davies – Unicorn DKPCD9070
The Martyrdom of St. Magnus – Rafferty – Unicorn DKPCD9100

Mendelssohn *(pages 108-109)*
Piano concertos 1 and 2 / etc – Perahia / Marriner – Sony MK42401
Violin concerto / [*Tchaikovsky*] – Chung / Dutoit – Decca 410 011 †
Overtures – Flor – RCA 7905-RC
Symphonies 1-5 / etc – Abbado – DG 415 353 (4)
Octet / String quintet 2 – Academy of St. Martin's – Philips 420 400
Piano music – Perahia – Sony MK37838
Songs without words – Schiff – Decca 421 119
A Midsummer Night's Dream – Flor – RCA 7764-RC
Elijah – Hickox – Chandos CHAN8774/5 (2)

Menotti *(page 113)*
‡ *Amahl and the Night Visitors* – Syrus – That's Entertainment CDTER1124

Messiaen *(pages 110-111)*
Turangalîla Symphony / *Quartet for the end of time* – Rattle/Kontarsky – Angel CDS7 47463 (2)
Catalogue d'oiseaux – Hill – Unicorn DKPCD9062/9075 (2)
La Nativité du Seigneur / *Le Banquet celeste* – Bate – Unicorn DKPCD9005

Meyerbeer *(page 113)*
Les Huguenots – Sutherland/Bonynge – Decca 430 549-2DM4 (4)

Milhaud *(pages 114-115)*
Le Carnaval d'Aix / *Le Boeuf sur le toit* / etc – Corp – Hyperion CDA66594
Suite provençale / etc – Järvi – Chandos CHAN9072
La Création du monde / [*Ibert*] – Tortelier – Chandos CHAN9023

Monteverdi *(pages 116-117)*
Solo vocal music – Kirkby/etc – Hyperion CDA66021
Madrigals from Books 7 and 8 – Christie – Harmonia Mundi HMC901068
* ‡*Selva morale e spirituale* – Parrott – Angel CDS7 49876
Vespro della Beata Vergine – Parrott – Angel CDCB 47078 (2)
L'Incoronazione di Poppea – Hickox – Virgin VCT90775 (3)
Orfeo – Gardiner – DG 419 250 (2)

Mozart *(pages 118-121)*
* Horn concertos 1-4 – Brain/Karajan – Angel CDH7 61013
* ‡Clarinet concerto / Flute and harp concerto – Brymer/Beecham – Angel CDZ7 67007
Piano concertos – Perahia/ECO – Sony SK12K 46441 (12)
Violin concertos – Suk / Brown – Decca 433 170 (2)
Serenade for 13 Wind Instruments – ASV CDCOE804
Symphonies 21-41 – Marriner – Philips 422 502 (6)
* ‡ Symphony 25, 29 and Serenade – Britten – Decca 430 495
Clarinet quintet / Clarinet concerto – King / etc – Hyperion CDA66199
String quintets 1-6 – Juilliard Qt – Sony M3YK 45827 (3)
String quartets 14-19 'Haydn' – Chilingirian Qt – CRD CRD3362/3/4 (3)
Masses K257/8/9/etc – Neumann – Angel CDC7 54037
Requiem – Schreier – Philips 411 420
* *Così fan tutte* – Karajan (1954) – Angel CDHC 69635 (3)
* *Le Nozze di Figaro* – Ostman – L'Oiseau-Lyre 421 333 (3)
Der Zauberflöte – Klemperer – Angel CDHB 69631 (2)

Mussorgsky *(pages 122-123)*
Pictures at an Exhibition (orch. and pno) – Ashkenazy – Decca 414 386
Pictures at an Exhibition (pno)/[*Tchaikovsky*] – Pletnev – Virgin VC7 91169
Boris Godunov – Fedoseyev – Philips 412 281 (3)
Complete songs – Christoff – Angel CHS7 63025 (3)

Nicolai *(page 113)*
* *The Merry Wives of Windsor* – Overture – Kleiber – Sony SK48376

Nielsen *(pages 124-125)*
Little Suite / Symphony 1 – Salonen – Sony SK42321
Symphony 2 (*The Four Temperaments*) / *Helios* – Salonen – Sony SK44934
Symphony 3 (*Espansiva*) / Symphony 5 – Thomson – Chandos CHAN9067
Symphony 4 (*Inextinguishable*) / Symphony 6 – Thomson – Chandos CHAN9047
Maskarade – Frandsen – Unicorn DKPCD9073/4 (2)
Violin concerto / [*Sibelius*] – Lin/Salonen – Sony MK44548 †
Springtime in Funen / [*Fynks Forar*] – Segerstam – Chandos CHAN8853

Offenbach *(pages 126-127)*
Overtures – Karajan – DG 400 044
* *Les Contes d'Hoffmann* – Bonynge – Decca 427 363 (2)
* ‡*Le Papillon* (ballet) / [*Tchaikovsky*] – Bonynge – Decca 425 450
Gaîté Parisienne [*Gounod*] – Dutoit – Decca 430 718
* *La Périchole* – Lombard – Erato 2292 45686 (2)

Orff *(page 128)*
Carmina Burana – Blomstedt – Decca 430 509

Paganini *(pages 130-131)*
Violin concerto 1 / [*Sarasate*] – Perlman / Foster – Angel CDC7 47101
Violin concerto 1 and 2 – Ashkenasi / Esser – DG 423 270
Violin concerto 6 / etc – Accardo / Dutoit – DG 423 717
24 Caprices – Perlman – Angel CDC747171

Palestrina *(page 128)*
Litaniae de Beata Vergine Maria / etc – Willcocks – Decca 421 147

Parry *(page 128)*
Blest pair of sirens / *I was glad* / etc – Hill – Argo 430 836
Symphonies 1-5/ Symphonic variations – Bamert – Chandos CHAN120/2

Penderecki *(page 128)*
St. Luke Passion – Penderecki – Argo 430 328

Pergolesi *(page 129)*
La Serva padrona – Németh – Hungaroton HCD12846

Piston *(page 129)*
Symphony 4 – Schwarz – Delos DE3106

Ponchielli *(page 129)*
La Gioconda – Bartoletti – Decca 414 399 (3)

Poulenc *(pages 132-133)*
‡ *Les Biches* / Piano concerto / *Gloria* – Ortiz / Frémaux – Angel CDM7 69644
Piano music – Rogé – Decca 417 438
La Voix humaine – Serebrier – Chandos CHAN8331
Songs – Lott/Johnson – Hyperion CDA66147

Prokofiev *(pages 134-135)*
Cinderella – Ashkenazy – Decca 410 162 (2)
Piano concertos 1-5 – Ashkenazy/Previn – Decca 425 570 (2)
Violin concertos 1 and 2 – Mintz / Abbado – DG 410 524
‡ *Lieutenant Kijé* / *The Love of Three Oranges* – Mata – RCA RD85168
Peter and the Wolf/ [*Saint-Saëns*] – Gielgud/Stamp – Virgin VC7 90786
Romeo and Juliet – exc – Dutoit – Decca 430 279
Symphonies 1 and 5 – Dutoit – Decca 421 813
Alexander Nevsky / Lt Kijé – Abbado – DG 419 603

Puccini *(pages 136-137)*
* *La Bohème* – Beecham – Angel (mono) CDCB 47235 (2)
* *La Fanciulla del West* – Capuana – Decca 421 595 (2)
Gianni Schicchi – Patanè – Eurodisc 7751-RC
Madama Butterfly – Karajan – Decca 417 577 (3)
Tosca – Karajan – Decca 421 670 (2)
Turandot – Mehta – Decca 414 274 (2)

Purcell *(pages 138-139)*
Come ye sons of art / *Funeral music* – Gardiner – Erato 2292 45123
Ode on Saint Cecilia's Day / etc – Gardiner – Erato 2292 45187
Songs and Airs – Kirkby/Hogwood – Oiseau-Lyre 417 123
Songs and Dialogues – Kirkby/Rooley – Hyperion CDA66056
Dido and Aeneas – Leppard – Philips 416 299
The Fairy Queen – Gardiner – DG 419 221 (2)
King Arthur – Gardiner – Erato 2292 45211 (2)

Rakhmaninov *(pages 140-141)*
Piano concertos 1-4 – Wild/Horenstein – Chandos CHAN8521/2
Piano concerto 2 / *Rhapsody on a theme of Paganini* – Ashkenazy / Previn – Decca 417 702
Piano concerto 4 / [*Ravel*] – Michelangeli / Gracis – Angel CDC7 49326 †
‡ Symphonies 1-3 – Ashkenazy – Decca 421 065 (3)
24 Preludes / Piano sonata 2 – Shelley – Hyperion CDA66081/2 (2)
The Bells / *Three Russian Songs* – Ashkenazy – Decca 414 455

Rameau *(page 144)*
Anacréon – Christie – Harmonia Mundi HMC90190

Ravel *(pages 142-143)*
Orchestral music – Abbado – DG 429 768 (3)
Piano concerto in G / [*Rakhmaninov*] – Michelangeli / Gracis – Angel CDC7 49326 †
‡ Piano concerto in G / Piano concerto for left hand – Rogé/Dutoit – Decca 410 230
Daphnis et Chloé – Munch – RCA 60469-RG
Rapsodie espagnole / *Alborada del gracioso* / *Pavane* / *Valses* / etc – Reiner – RCA 60179-RG
‡ Introduction and allegro for harp / [*various*] – Ellis/Melos – Decca 421 154
Piano music – Crossley – CRD CRD3383/4
L'Enfant et les sortilèges – Maazel – DG 423 718

Respighi *(page 144)*
Fountains of Rome / *Pines of Rome* / *The Birds* – Marriner – Philips 432 133
Botticelli Triptych / *Lauda* / etc – Hickox – Collins COLL1349

Rimsky-Korsakov *(pages 146-147)*
Sheherezade / [*Borodin*] – Beecham – Angel CDC7 47717
Capriccio espagnole / Symphony 1-3 / etc – Järvi – DG423 604 (2)
Orchestral opera extracts – Järvi – Chandos CHAN8327/9 (3)

Rodrigo *(page 144)*
Concierto de Aranjuez / etc. – Romero/Marriner – Philips 432 581 (3)

Rossini *(pages 148-149)*
La Boutique fantasque / [*Chopin*] – Bonynge – Decca 430 723
‡ String sonatas – Marriner – Decca 430 563 (2)
Overtures – Reiner – RCA 60387-RG
Petite messe solennelle – Corboz – Erato 2292 45321 (2)
Stabat Mater – Hickox – Chandos CHAN8780
* *Il Barbiere di Siviglia* – Marriner – Philips 411 058 (3)
La Cenerentola – Marriner – Philips 420 468 (2)
* *Le Comte Ory* – Gardiner – Philips 422 406 (2)
Guillaume Tell – Chailly – Decca 417 154 (4)
L'Italiana in Algeri – Abbado – DG 427 331 (2)
* *Il Viaggio a Reims* – Abbado – DG 415 498 (2)

Rubbra *(page 144)*
Symphonies 3 and 4 – Del Mar – Lyrita SRCD202

Saint-Saëns *(pages 150-151)*
Le Carnaval des animaux / [*Prokofiev/Mozart*] – Stamp – Virgin VC7 90786
Piano concertos 1-5 – Rogé / Dutoit – Decca 417 351 (2)
‡ Violin concerto 1 / [*Lalo*] – Chung / Dutoit – Decca 436 483
Violin concerto 3 / [*Mendelssohn*] – Lin/Thomas – Sony MK39007
Symphony 3 / [*Poulenc*] – Munch – RCA 85750-RC
Samson et Dalila – Barenboim – DG 413 297 (2)

Satie *(page 144)*
Piano music – Queffélec – Virgin VC7 90754

Scarlatti *(page 145)*
Keyboard sonatas – Verlet – Philips 422 496

Schnittke *(page 145)*
Concerti grossi / etc – Chailly – Decca 430 698

Schoenberg *(pages 152-153)*
Variations for orchestra / *Verklärte Nacht* – Karajan – DG 415 326
Gurrelieder – Ozawa – Philips 412 511
Erwartung / [*Berg*] – Dohnányi – Decca 417 348 (2)
Choral music – Boulez – Sony S2K44571 (2)
Moses und Aron – Solti – Decca 414 264 (2)

Schubert *(pages 154-157)*
Symphonies 1-9/etc – Marriner – Philips 412 176 (6)
‡ Symphonies 3 and 5 – Beecham – Angel CDM7 69750
Symphony 8 / [*Schumann*] – Sinopoli – DG 427 818
Symphony 9 – Mackerras – Virgin VC7 90708
Octet – ASMF – Chandos CHAN8585
Trout quintet – Schiff / Hagen – Decca 411 975
String quintet – Lindsay/etc – ASV CDDCA537
‡ Piano Trio 1 in B flat / [*Beethoven*] – Beaux Arts – Philips 438 308 †
String quartets 12 and 14 – Lindsay Qt – ASV CDDCA560
Piano sonatas 16 and 18 – Lupu – Decca 417 640
Piano sonata 21 / etc – Curzon – Decca 417 642
Impromptus – Perahia – Sony MK37291
Lieder (20 Volumes) – various/Johnson – Hyperion CDJ33001-20 (more to come)

Schumann *(pages 158-159)*
Cello concerto / [*Dvořák*] – Harrell/Marriner – Decca 430 742
Piano concerto / [*Grieg*] – Kovacevich/Davis – Philips 412 923 †
Symphonies 1-4 – Karajan – DG 429 672 (2)
Fantasia / *Kreisleriana* – Rubinstein – RCA 86258-RC
Kinderszenen / Sonata 1 / etc – Ashkenazy – Decca 421 290
Dichterliebe / *Liederkreis* – Fischer-Dieskau/Eschenbach – DG 415 190

Schütz *(page 160)*
Christmas oratorio / [*Praetorius*] – Parrott – Angel CDC7 47633

Scriabin *(page 160)*
Poem of ecstasy / *Prometheus* / *Poem of fire* / Piano concerto – Ashkenazy/ Maazel – Decca 417 252

Shostakovich *(pages 162-163)*
Cello concertos 1 and 2 – Schiff/M. Shostakovich – Philips 412 526
‡ Piano concertos 1 and 2 / etc – Alexeev/Jones/Maksymiuk – CFP CD-CFP4547
Violin concertos 1 and 2 – Mordkovitch/Järvi – Chandos CHAN8820
Symphonies 1 and 9 – Haitink – Decca 414 677
Symphonies 2 and 3 / *Age of Gold* – Haitink – Decca 421 131
Symphony 5 / *Fragments* – Ashkenazy – Decca 421 120
Symphony 10 – Karajan (1966) – DG 429 716
Symphony 15 / etc – Haitink – Decca 417 581
Piano quintet / Piano trio 2 – Beaux Arts/etc – Philips 432 079
String quartets 3, 8 and 13 – Fitzwilliam Qt – Decca 421 475
Lady Macbeth of Mtsensk – Rostropovich – Angel CDCB 49955 (2)

Sibelius *(pages 164-167)*
Violin concerto / [*Nielsen*] – Lin / Salonen – Sony MK44548 †

Finlandia / Karelia / Tempest /etc – Beecham – Angel CDM7 63397
4 Legends – Järvi – BIS CD294
Symphonies 1-7 – Ashkenazy – Decca 425 028/430 737 (4)
Tapiola / Finlandia / Swan of Tuonela / etc – Karajan – DG 413 755
Songs – Hynninen / Haggander / Panula – BIS CD270
The Maiden in the Tower / Karelia – Järvi – BIS CD250
Smetana (pages 168-169)
Ma Vlast – Kubelik – DG 429 183
String quartet 1 / [Dvořák] – Guarneri Qt – Philips 420 803
The Bartered Bride – Kosler – Supraphon 10 3511 (3)
Spohr (page 160)
Nonet / Octet – Nash Ensemble – CRD CRD3354 or
Nonet / [Martinů] – Berlin Ensemble DG 427 640 †
Stanford (page 160)
Clarinet concerto / [Finzi] – King / Francis – Hyperion CDA66001 †
Irish Symphony / Irish Rhapsody – Handley – Chandos CHAN8545
Stockhausen (page 160)
Donnerstag aus Licht – Stockhausen – DG 423 379 (4)
Strauss, J. (pages 170-171)
‡ *Waltzes, polkas, etc* – Boskovsky – Decca 425 425-9 (5)
New Year Concert 1989 – Kleiber – Sony MK45938 (2)
New Year Concert 1992 / [Nicolai] – Kleiber – Sony SK48376 †
Die Fledermaus – Karajan – Angel (mono) C4B 69531 (2) or
Die Fledermaus – Kleiber – DG 415 646 (2)
Strauss, R. (pages 172-173)
Also sprach Zarathustra / Don Juan – Karajan – DG 410 959
‡ *Le Bourgeois gentilhomme / Don Quixote* – Beecham – Angel (mono) CDH7 63106
Horn concertos 1 and 2 – Tuckwell/Ashkenazy – Decca 430 730
Death and Transfiguration / Don Juan / Till Eulenspiegels lustige Streiche – Abbado – DG 429 492
Metamorphosen / etc – Karajan – DG 410 892
* *Four Last Songs / etc* – Schwarzkopf / Szell – Angel CDC7 47276
Ariadne auf Naxos – Karajan – Angel CDMB 69296 (2)
Capriccio – Sawallisch – Angel (mono) CDS7 49014 (2)
Elektra – Solti – Decca 417 345 (2)
* ‡ *Die Frau ohne Schatten* – Solti – Decca 436 243 (3)
* *Der Rosenkavalier* – Karajan – Angel CDS7 49354 (3)
Salome – Solti – Decca 414 414 (2)
Stravinsky (pages 174-175)
The Firebird / Fireworks / etc – Dutoit – Decca 414 409
Petrushka / Chant du Rossignol / etc – Dutoit – Decca 417 619
* *The Rite of Spring / Petrushka / Symphony in C / Symphony in 3 Movements / Symphony of Psalms* – Stravinsky – Sony 22K46290 (22)
The Soldier's Tale – Lee / Friend – Nimbus NI5063
‡ *String concerto in D / Danses concertantes / Dumbarton Oaks* – Davis – Decca 425 622
The Rake's Progress – Chailly – Decca 411 644 (2)
Sullivan (page 161)
* *The Mikado* – Mackerras – Telarc CD80284
* *The Pirates of Penzance* – Mackerras – Telarc CD8080353
Szymanowski (page 161)
Symphonies 2 and 3 – Dorati – Decca 425 625

Tallis (page 176)
Spem in alium / Sancte Deus / etc – Phillips – Gimell CDGIM006
Tavener (page 176)
Funeral Ikos / Ikon of Light / etc – Phillips – Gimmell CDGIM005

Tchaikovsky (pages 178-181)
Capriccio italien / Francesca da Rimini / Romeo and Juliet / etc – Ashkenazy – Decca 421 715
Piano concerto 1 / [Chopin] – Ashkenazy/Maazel – Decca 417 750
Piano concertos 2 and 3 – Lowenthal / Commisiona – Arabesque Z6583
Violin concerto / [Mendelssohn] – Chung / Dutoit – Decca 410 011 †
1812 Overture / Hamlet / The Tempest – DePriest – Delos CD3801
Nutcracker / Sleeping Beauty / Swan Lake – suites – Rostropovich – DG 429 097
Serenade for strings / [Dvořák] – Karajan – DG 400 038
Symphonies 1-6 /Manfred/etc – Jansons – Chandos CHAN8672/8 (7 discs for the price of 5; also available separately)
Eugene Onegin – Solti – Decca 417 413 (2)
Telemann (page 176)
Tafelmusik / Viola concerto / etc – Edinger – Naxos 8.550156
Thomas (page 177)
Mignon – Overture / [concert] – Ozawa – DG 423 698
Thomson (page 177)
Acadian Songs and Dances / etc – Corp – Hyperion CDA66576
Tippett (pages 182-183)
Concerto for double string orchestra / etc – Tippett – Virgin VC7 9070
Symphonies 1-4 / etc – Solti – Decca 425 646 (3)
A Child of Our Time – Davis – Philips 420 075
The Mask of Time – Davis – Angel CDS7 47707 (2)
King Priam – Atherton – Decca 414 241 (2)
Tubin (page 177)
Symphonies 2 and 6 – Järvi – BIS CD304; *4 and 9* – Järvi – BIS CD227

Vaughan Williams (pages 184-185)
Greensleeves fantasia / Tallis fantasia / The Lark Ascending / [Elgar] – Warren-Green – Virgin VC790819
Symphony 1 'Sea Symphony' – Haitink – Angel CDC7 49911
Symphony 2 'London' / Symphony 8 – Barbirolli – Angel CDM7 64197
Symphony 3 'Pastoral' / Symphony 5 – Boult (1953) – Decca 430 060
Symphony 6 / Symphony 9 – Previn – RCA GD90508
‡ *Symphony 7 'Antartica'/Serenade to Music* – Handley – Angel CD-EMX2173
Job – Haitink – Angel CDC7 47516
‡ *The Wasps / etc* – Handley – Angel CD-EMX9508
Verdi (pages 186-189)
Requiem / Choruses – Shaw – Telarc CD80152 (2)
Aida – Karajan – Angel CDMC 69300 (3)
Un Ballo in maschera – Solti – Decca 410 210 (2)
Don Carlos – Giulini – Angel CDCC 47701 (3)
Falstaff – Giulini – DG 410 503 (2)
La Forza del destino – Levine – RCA RCD31864 (3)
Macbeth – Sinopoli – Philips 412 133 (3)
Nabucco – Gardelli – Decca 417 407 (2)
Otello – Levine – RCA RCD22951 (2)
Rigoletto – Bonynge – Decca 414 269 (2)
Simon Boccanegra – Abbado – DG 415 692 (2)
La Traviata – Bonynge – Decca 430 491 (2)
Il Trovatore – Mehta – RCA 6194-2-RC (2)
Villa-Lobos (page 177)
Bachianas brasileiras 1, 2, 5, 6 – Los Angeles/Villa-Lobos – Angel CDH7 61015
Bachianas brasileiras 1 and 5 / [Bach] – Gomez – Hyperion CDA66257
Vivaldi (pages 190-191)
L'Estro armonico – Hogwood – L'Oiseau-Lyre 414 554 (2)

The Four Seasons / Violin concertos – Accardo – Philips 422 065
La Cetra – Hogwood – L'Oiseau-Lyre 421 366 (2)

Wagner (pages 192-195)
Siegfried Idyll / Preludes – Walter – Sony MPK45701
Der fliegende Holländer – Nelsson – Philips 416 300 (2)
Götterdämmerung – Solti – Decca 414 115 (4)+
Lohengrin – Solti – Decca 421 053 (4)
Die Meistersinger von Nürnberg – Jochum – DG 415 278 (4)
Parsifal – Karajan – DG 413 347 (4)
Das Rheingold – Solti – Decca 414 101 (3)+
Siegfried – Solti – Decca 414 110 (4)+
Tannhäuser – Solti – Decca 414 581 (3)
Tristan und Isolde – Karajan – Angel CDMD 69319 (4)
Die Walküre – Solti – 414 105 (4)+
+ *(Ring complete)* – Solti – Decca 414 100 (15)
Walton (pages 196-197)
Façade / etc / [Arnold] – Sitwell/Collins – Decca 425 661 (mono)
Viola and Violin concertos – Kennedy/Previn – Angel CDC7 49628
Symphonies 1 and 2 – Ashkenazy – Decca 433 703
Belshazzar's Feast / Coronation Te Deum – Solti – Decca 425 154
Warlock (page 198)
Capriol Suite / [English Music] – Marriner – Decca 421 391
Songs – Luxon / Willson – Chandos CHAN8643
Choral works / [Finzi] – Spicer – Chandos CHAN9182
Weber (pages 200-201)
Clarinet concertino / [Crusell] / etc – Johnson/Groves – ASV CDDCA559
Clarinet concerto / [Crusell/Debussy/etc] – Johnson/Tortelier – ASV CDDCA585
Clarinet quintet / [Beethoven] – Ancient Music Ensemble – L'Oiseau Lyre 433 044
Overtures – Goodman – Nimbus N15154
Oberon – Kubelik – DG 419 038 (2)
Der Freischütz – Kleiber – DG 425 432 (2)
Webern (pages 202-203)
5 Movements / 6 Pieces / etc – Karajan – DG 423 254
Chamber Music – Italian Qt – Philips 420 796
Weelkes (page 198)
Hosanna to the Son of David / etc – Neary – ASV CDQS6036
Weill (page 198)
Die Dreigroschenoper – Bruckner-Ruggerberg (1958) – Sony MK42637
Weinberger (page 198)
Schwanda the Bagpiper – Wallberg – CBS CD79344 (2) (deleted, due back)
Wesley (page 199)
Symphonies 3, 4, 5 and 6 – Wetton – Unicorn DKP9098
Wieniawski (page 199)
Violin concerto 2 / [Tchaikovsky] – Bell/Ashkenazy – Decca 421 716
Wolf (pages 204-205)
Lieder / [Mahler] – Von Otter/Gothoni – DG 423 666
Goethe Lieder – Fischer-Dieskau/Barenboim – DG 415 192
Mörike Lieder / Goethe Lieder – Lott / Parsons – Chandos CHAN8726
Spanisches Liederbuch – Schwarzkopf/Fischer-Dieskau/Moore – DG 423 934 (2)
Wolf-Ferrari (page 199)
* *Overtures/Intermezzi/etc* – Marriner – Angel CDC7 54585

Zemlinsky (page 199)
Symphony 2 / Psalm – Chailly – Decca 421 644
Der Geburtstag der Infantin – Albrecht – Schwann CD11626

Picture credits

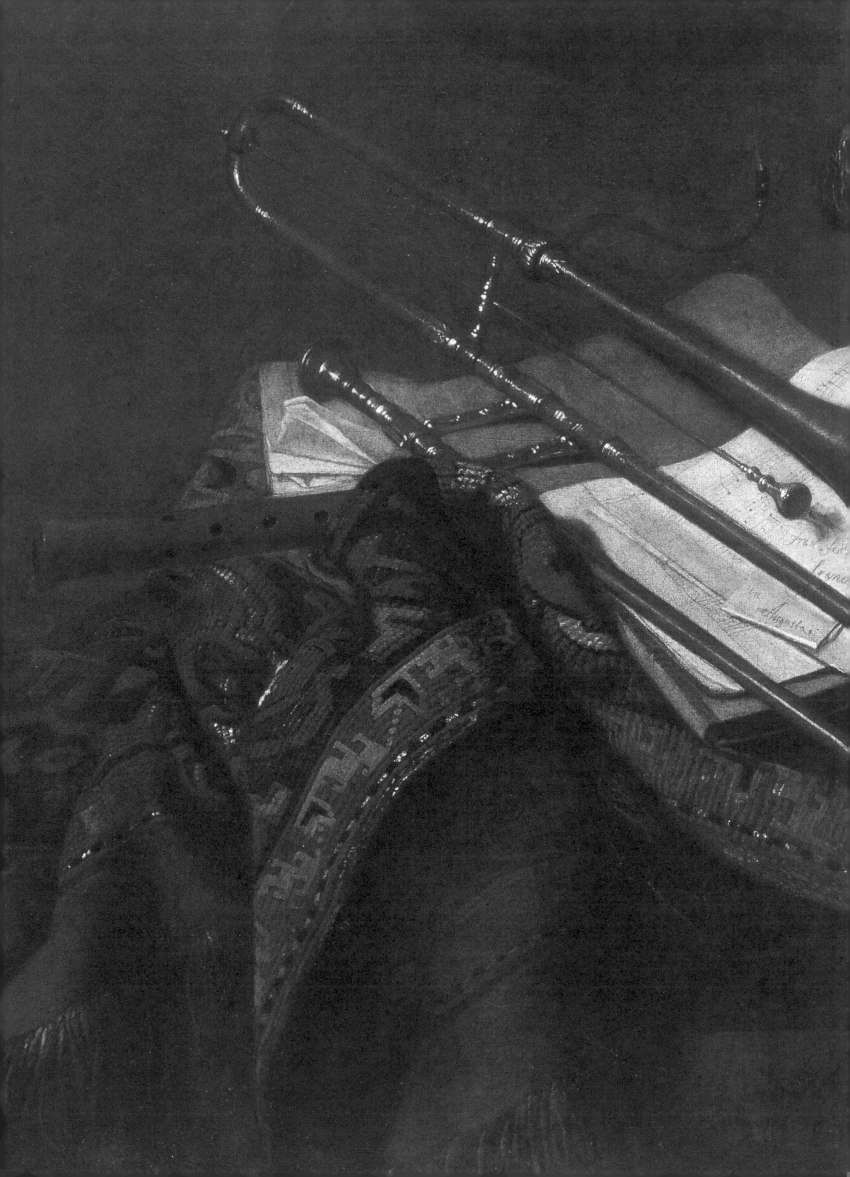